Philosophy & Psychoanalysis Book Series
Jon Mills
Series Editor

Philosophy & Psychoanalysis is dedicated to current developments and cutting-edge research in the philosophical sciences, phenomenology, hermeneutics, existentialism, logic, semiotics, cultural studies, social criticism, and the humanities that engage and enrich psychoanalytic thought through philosophical rigor. With the philosophical turn in psychoanalysis comes a new era of theoretical research that revisits past paradigms while invigorating new approaches to theoretical, historical, contemporary, and applied psychoanalysis. No subject or discipline is immune from psychoanalytic reflection within a philosophical context including psychology, sociology, anthropology, politics, the arts, religion, science, culture, physics, and the nature of morality. Philosophical approaches to psychoanalysis may stimulate new areas of knowledge that have conceptual and applied value beyond the consulting room reflective of greater society at large. In the spirit of pluralism, *Philosophy & Psychoanalysis* is open to any theoretical school in philosophy and psychoanalysis that offers novel, scholarly, and important insights in the way we come to understand our world.

Titles in this series:

Psychology as Ethics: Reading Jung with Kant, Nietzsche and Aristotle
Giovanni Colacicchi

Shame, Temporality and Social Change: Ominous Transitions
Edited by Ladson Hinton and Hessel Willemsen

Psychoanalysis, Catastrophe & Social Action
Robin McCoy Brooks

Metaphysical Dualism, Subjective Idealism, and Existential Loneliness: Matter and Mind
Ben Lazare Mijuskovic

For a full list of titles in this series, please visit
www.routledge.com/Philosophy-and-Psychoanalysis/book-series/PHILPSY

Metaphysical Dualism, Subjective Idealism, and Existential Loneliness

Since the ages of the Old Testament, the Homeric myths, the tragedies of Sophocles and the ensuing theological speculations of the Christian millennium, the theme of loneliness has dominated and haunted the Western world. In this wide-ranging book, philosopher Ben Lazare Mijuskovic returns us to our rich philosophical past on the nature of consciousness, lived experience, and the pining for a meaningful existence that contemporary social science has displaced in its tendency toward material reduction.

Engaging key metaphysical discussions on causality, space, time, subjectivity, the mind body problem, personal identity, freedom, religion, and transcendence in ancient, scholastic, modern, and contemporary philosophy, he highlights the phenomenology of loneliness that lies at the very core of being human. In challenging psychoanalytic and neuroscientific paradigms, Mijuskovic argues that isolative existence and self-consciousness is not so much of a problem of unconscious conflict or the need for psychopharmacology as it is the loss of a sense of personal intimacy.

The issue of the criteria of "personal identity" in relation to loneliness has long engaged and consumed the interest of theologians, ethicists, philosophers, novelists, and psychologists. This book will be of great interest to academics and students of the humanities, and all those with an interest in the philosophy of loneliness.

Ben Lazare Mijuskovic, PhD (Philosophy), MA (Literature), is a retired professor of philosophy and humanities at California State University at Dominguez Hills, Humanities Department. He is a licensed clinical social worker (LCSW) and is a retired Los Angeles County Department of Mental Health therapist.

Metaphysical Dualism, Subjective Idealism, and Existential Loneliness

Matter and Mind

Ben Lazare Mijuskovic

LONDON AND NEW YORK

First published 2022
by Routledge
2 Park Square, Milton Park, Abingdon, Oxon OX14 4RN

and by Routledge
605 Third Avenue, New York, NY 10158

Routledge is an imprint of the Taylor & Francis Group, an informa business

© 2022 Ben Lazare Mijuskovic

The right of Ben Lazare Mijuskovic to be identified as author of this work has been
asserted by him in accordance with sections 77 and 78 of the Copyright, Designs
and Patents Act 1988.

All rights reserved. No part of this book may be reprinted or reproduced or utilised
in any form or by any electronic, mechanical, or other means, now known or
hereafter invented, including photocopying and recording, or in any information
storage or retrieval system, without permission in writing from the publishers.

Trademark notice: Product or corporate names may be trademarks or registered trademarks,
and are used only for identification and explanation without intent to infringe.

British Library Cataloguing-in-Publication Data
A catalogue record for this book is available from the British Library

Library of Congress Cataloging-in-Publication Data
A catalog record has been requested for this book

ISBN: 978-0-367-74116-7 (hbk)
ISBN: 978-0-367-74127-3 (pbk)
ISBN: 978-1-003-15613-0 (ebk)

DOI: 10.4324/9781003156130

Typeset in Times New Roman
by Newgen Publishing UK

To my father, a debt that is sadly far too late to ever repay

Contents

	Introduction	1
1	The Achilles of rationalist arguments: the simplicity, unity, and identity of thought and soul from the Cambridge Platonists to Kant—a study in the history of an argument	6
2	Consciousness, spontaneity, and synthetic *a priori* relations	21
3	Kant and Schopenhauer on reality	60
4	Kant and Hegel on the quality-quantity distinction	74
5	The science of determinism and the consciousness of freedom	100
6	Descartes's bridge to the external world: the piece of wax	123
7	Locke and Leibniz on personal identity	151
8	Shaftesbury and Hume on personal identity	171
9	Hume on space (and time)	194
10	Kant's two premises in the transcendental deductions	211
11	Brentano's intentionality of consciousness	222

viii   Contents

12 The science of matter and the philosophy of mind   236

13 Loneliness: an interdisciplinary approach   253

14 Loneliness and the dynamics of narcissism   288

15 The limits of self-knowledge   301

16 The dynamics of intimacy and empathy   317

Index   322

Introduction

The goal of the present study is to survey the kaleidoscopic history of Western theories of consciousness and conclude on the inevitability of existential loneliness. The book defends the metaphysical immateriality of human consciousness along with its epistemic activity, while insisting on three inherent forces within the mind: (a) its spontaneity; (b) the reflexive nature of self-consciousness; and (c) its transcendent intentionality. It opposes the principle of causal psychological determinism endorsed by the sciences of psychoanalysis; cognitive behavioral therapy; and the current neurosciences and biosciences. It opposes Freud's principle of libidinal sexual energy as the determinant source of human affect and behavior; the stimulus>response paradigm of cognitive behavioral psychology; and the neuroscientific metaphor of the brain as a programmed computer. Instead, I wish to propose that the primary universal motivational drive in human beings is two-fold: to avoid loneliness and to secure intimacy with other members of our species. I offer a comprehensive systems-approach grounded in (a) metaphysical dualism; (b) subjective idealism; and (c) its culmination in man's solitary existential condition. My guiding *premises* are that both active immaterial minds and a material world exist; that each self epistemically fashions reality for its self alone; and therefore that each of us uniquely transpires throughout life alone. We do, however, manage to forge strong sustaining alliances along the way that makes the voyage of life worthwhile and meaningful.

What follows is an attempt to offer an interdisciplinary and comprehensive approach to the historical and conceptual relationship between consciousness and loneliness. In pursuit of this goal, I am guided by a

DOI: 10.4324/9781003156130-1

2 Introduction

far-reaching dichotomy initially suggested by Plato's prescient allusion to the metaphysical exchange between the Gods and the Giants, the Idealists and the Materialists, in his dialogue, the *Sophist*.

STRANGER. What we shall see is something like a Battle of Gods and Giants going on between them over their quarrel about reality.

THEAETETUS. How so?

STRANGER. One party is trying to drag everything down to earth out of heaven and the unseen, literally grasping rocks and trees in their hands; for they hold upon every rock and stone and strenuously affirm that real existence only belongs to touch. They define reality as the same thing as body, and as soon as the opposite party asserts that anything without a body is real, they are utterly contemptuous and will not listen to another word.

THEAETETUS. The people you describe are certainly a formidable crew. I have met quite a number of them before now.

STRANGER. Yes, and accordingly their adversaries are very wary in defending their position somewhere in the heights of the unseen, maintaining with all their force that true reality consists in certain intelligible and bodiless [immaterial] Forms. In the clash of argument, they shatter and pulverize those bodies, which their opponents wield, and what those others allege to be true reality they call, not real being, but a sort of moving process of becoming [i.e. physical change]. On this issue an interminable battle is always going on between the two camps.

(*Sophist*, 245E-246E)[1]

The history of philosophy confirms this foresight and prophetic utterance as it pits Plato against Democritus; Plotinus against Epicurus; Augustine and Aquinas against Skeptics and Atheists; Ficino against Valla; Boehme against Bacon; Descartes against Hobbes; Leibniz against Locke; Kant against Hume; Hegel against Marx; Husserl against Russell; and Sartre against Ryle. Historically, in the more contemporary terminology of "-isms," the clashing arguments begin and continue uninterruptedly between two warring camps: the advocates for dualism, rationalism, idealism, epistemic spontaneity, ethical freedom, phenomenology, and existentialism against the proponents of materialism, mechanism, determinism, empiricism, phenomenalism, behaviorism, and the current neurosciences.

But the nucleus and pivotal center of the controversy, however, rests on a single issue: Can senseless matter *alone* think? I wish to contend that human consciousness—although it is "contingently" dependent on matter—is not reducible to, identical with, or caused by matter and motion alone; and although consciousness *spontaneously* "emanates" or "arises"—evolves is not the right word—from material conditions, it does not follow that the terms "brain" and "mind" are interchangeable. Two quite different entities, realities, i.e. substances populate the world: quantitative aggregations of matter and qualitative acts of consciousness. There are other forms of idealist philosophies, including Hinduism, Judaism, Christianity, Islam, Buddhism, mysticism, spiritualism, and others I suppose, all seeking in their own fashion to escape loneliness. Nevertheless, my own commitment is basically circumscribed by the narrower ranges of Western idealism and existentialism. What I find unacceptably restrictive, and indeed false, is to reduce reality to space, matter, and motion alone.

Accordingly, I intend to pursue the controversy between these opposing theoretical dichotomies—materialism against idealism— by recruiting a "comparison and contrast" methodology. There are two forces "at play," so to speak, involved in the issues surrounding loneliness: both cognitive as well as motivational factors and both must be accounted for. In pursuing this "back and forth" method, I intend to revisit and reconceptualize a variety of my earlier themes, which I believe will show a basic unity and continuity in how my own reflections on these critical issues have deepened, but not widened, over half a century. I believe I have strengthened my earlier reflections and interpretations as I now seek to buttress the original themes. To offer a metaphor, the original articles serve as seeds from which the roots, trunk, and branches have proliferated. The richer secondary sources consulted offer a deeper perspective and a wider vision of the works they interpret. It was a time before the current internecine "publish or perish" dictates of professional self-survival ruled. They predate our current period of over specialization and fragmentation along with the infatuation that "the newest interpretations are the truest;" that it is sufficient to pick a narrow question and show its linguistic and

4 Introduction

analytic inadequacies. This contemporary attitude is sadly coupled with the misapprehension prevalent in our own time as philosophy seeks to mimic America's technological infatuation with the most recent gadgets, cell phones, computers, cars, and fads, while armed with the conviction that whatever is new is better than what existed before. The impressive "advances" of the hard sciences, especially behaviorism, cognitive psychology, and the current neurosciences, do not, in my estimation, always promise the keenest insight and the surest understanding into human consciousness nor into the more complex dynamics of loneliness.

In effect, what follows is a battle between brains and minds; science and values; behavior and consciousness; determinism and spontaneity; physical stimuli and mental insight; quantitative factors and qualitative aspects; relativism and absolutism; the Is and the Ought; and so on. But in the end, I hope to show, as Max Weber argues in "Science as a Vocation," that science is not only unable but indeed constitutionally unfit to "explain" the *reality* of ethical (and aesthetic) *values* as well as to "account" for the ultimate *meaning* of individual human existence.[2] These values and goals will be represented as "tertiary qualities," in opposition to the primary ones of matter and motion; the secondary ones of sensations and feelings; and the tertiary judgments of qualitative values.

Primary "qualities" essentially involve *quantitative factors, which operate causally.* And they reduce to matter *plus* motion. They fall within the domain of what William James calls the "hard sciences," within the province of objective experimentations and the application of descriptive tools, e.g., mathematics and statistics. Secondary qualities, however, vary from person to person; they are subjective in their guises of sensations and feelings; they float and flee as mere appearances; and they remain *essentially* unsharable, personal, and intimate. My sensations and emotions are my own and not yours. *But* tertiary qualities deal with human *values.* For example, *evaluative* judgments can be applied to a spectrum of *qualitative* intellectual, aesthetic, and/or ethical values ranging from ignorance to wisdom; from ugliness to beauty; or from evil to goodness. Humans are the only species able to create personal and subjective values—judgments and principles—as guides for each of us to live our separate lives. No other creature in the animal kingdom exists with the capacity to create and be guided by the values each of us chooses to fashion. *Existentially* each *psyche*, soul, self, mind, person, or ego is completely free to choose different values throughout their lives—to opt between shadings from misery to happiness, cowardice to courage, egoism to altruism, faith to science and their reverses.

The problem with science is that it reduces tertiary qualities to the subjective qualities of pleasure and pain, and the primary and secondary qualities, sensations and feelings, to the quantitative factors of material motions in the brain. But clearly there are differences between (a) physically *bumping* into a chair; (b) the sensation of *seeing* a red chair; and (c) the *qualitative act of evaluating* and *judging* the chair as a beautiful American piece of Victorian antique furniture circa 1875 made by Herter Brothers. We share the possession of objective primary and secondary subjective qualities with higher order animals, but each human being *intentionally* creates and decides what the *meaning* of their life will be *at that special moment in time.*

Notes

1 *Plato's Theory of Knowledge: The* Theaetetus *and the* Sophist *of Plato*, translated with a running commentary by F. M. Cornford (London: Routledge & Kegan Paul, 1964), 228–232.

2 Weber, Max, *The Vocation Lectures: "Science as a Vocation" and "Politics as a Vocation,"* translated by Rodney Livingstone (Cambridge: Hackett, 1994). According to Weber, both science and "politics," actually ethics, are unable to address questions of moral value because their first principles are incompatible. Science addresses facts and ethics deals with values, with the Humean and Kantian distinction between the Is and the Ought.

Chapter 1

The Achilles of rationalist arguments

The simplicity, unity, and identity of thought and soul from the Cambridge Platonists to Kant—a study in the history of an argument

Prior to Plato, ancient Greek atomism, advocated by Leucippus and Democritus, reduces all reality to matter *plus* motion, with physical atoms and compound objects moving between the voids of empty space. Importantly, *the atoms are conceived as qualitatively equal; they are essentially homogeneous.* Their only differences are measured in terms of their compounded quantities. Analogously, for our current neurosciences, the neurons are not qualitatively distinguished and human cognition now—as well as before—is reduced and explained by the causal interactions occurring between the quantitative motions of sensory matter striking human bodily organs and then transmitted to the brain.

By contrast, Plato posits a metaphysical dualism based on a conceptual distinction between immaterial and active souls and thoughts playing against the backdrop of the ever-changing movements of matter, thus anticipating the critical difference between *qualitative* thought and *quantitative* matter (*Republic*, Divided Line). Essentially then, Plato's *Phaedo*, by inducting both the soul's (a) immaterial essence, its simplicity and indivisibility, when combined with (b) its activity serves as a basis for one of his several proofs for immortality. The entire issue centers on establishing the conception of the soul to be a distinct substance, an independent reality existing apart from everything else, to be a stand-alone substance (*Phaedo,* 78B). Plato, of course, conceives death as an escape from man's bodily nature, his physical element. Death is merely the dissolution of man's bodily compound, which releases the soul from its physical imprisonment thus allowing it (presumably) to flee unencumbered toward an ethereal or spiritual realm of immaterial, eternal, and unchanging Forms.[1] These *a priori*

DOI: 10.4324/9781003156130-2

conceptual distinctions characterize the rational soul as constituted by (a) an immaterial essence, which is coupled with (b) an awareness of its own reflexive activity of thinking, with *self*-consciousness, metaphorically a *circular* activity, as well as an awareness of its own *temporal* mode of thinking *during* which the cognitive subject conceives its self as the source of its own thoughts and (c) *forms judgments concerning conceptual objects, events, or values.*

SOCRATES: And do you accept my description of the [temporal] process of thinking.

THEAETETUS: And How do you describe it?

SOCRATES: As a discourse that the mind carries on [reflexively] with its self about any subject [i.e., issue] it is considering. You must take this explanation ... I have a notion that when the mind is thinking, it is simply talking to itself, asking questions and answering them and saying Yes or No. When it reaches a decision—which may come slowly or in a sudden rush—when doubt is over and the two voices affirm the same thing, then *we call that 'judgment.'* So I should describe thinking as a [mediate and inferential] discourse, and *judgment* as a [decisional] statement pronounced, not aloud to someone else, but silently to one's self (*Theaetetus,* 189E; italics mine).

Notice the dual relation between (a) the self and (b) its "subject," i.e., its *conceptual* object or issue. Again:

SOCRATES: And next, what of thinking and judgment and appearance. Is it not now clear that all these things occur in our minds both as false and true?

THEAETETUS: How so?

SOCRATES: You will see more easily if you begin by letting me give you an account of their nature and how each differs from the others.

THEAETETUS: Well let me have it.

SOCRATES: Well thinking and discourse are the same thing, except what we call thinking is, precisely, the inward dialogue carried on by the mind with itself without spoken sound (*Sophist,* 263E).

In Plato, this in turn leads to a metaphysical triad of conceptual distinctions between (a) an independent and external realm of material

8 The Achilles of rationalist arguments

moving objects; (b) immaterial active judgmental souls; and (c) an independent realm of eternal unchanging Universals, Forms, Ideas, or Archetypes serving as the ultimate constituents of Reality. For Plato and Plotinus, man exhibits a dual nature. Human bodily sensations involve *passive* responses to the Heraclitean flux of ever-changing physical movements of objects and events. But the *active* soul is capable of constantly seeking for an immersion, a sharing, an entrance—a *participation*—into and within a higher and purer realm of reality, an epistemic penetration, a cognitive admission into a transcendent realm of values. For Plato, the *psyche* innately seeks to reach toward a higher *qualitative* sphere of cognitive states, a non-sensory unification, into a reality that is "akin" to the soul's own inherent makeup of immaterial conscious states. While human thought is active, the Platonic Forms are unchanging; but both human souls and the Forms are immaterial. Thus, the soul is able to pursue its entry into this higher realm because human consciousness shares an affinity, a likeness to the eternal Forms. This is only possible because both are conceived as immaterial, pure, without parts. For Plato, this *constitutes* a necessary condition, a prerequisite for like (the soul) knowing Like (the Forms).

> When in seeking knowledge the soul uses the senses, the soul is presented with things that change and is confused; when it seeks truth all by itself, it contemplates what is invariable, and suffers no confusion, which suggests that it has an [immaterial] affinity with it. Hence for two reasons we may say that the soul is probably more akin to the invariable than to that which [is compound and] changes and hence [by implication] the soul is likely to be incomposite, i.e. simple [immaterial, spatially unextended, and partless] and therefore immortal.
>
> (*Phaedo*, 79E)

As we shall see, this ability of the soul to make *judgments* and pursue values and ideals, but not necessarily transcendent ones, dovetails with the individual subject's thinking processes to formulate and pursue values for its self alone. The values are immanent—as opposed to transcendent—to consciousness.

Further, according to Plato, the individual eternal Forms, the cardinal Ideas of Justice, Temperance, Courage, and Wisdom, can each be singly penetrated, i.e., "defined" by rational thought, by the soul's intellectual intuitive powers, but together, *qua judgments*, they can also epistemically *constitute, form*—not cause—comprehensive synthetic *a priori* systems of internally coherent judgments as unified by a single principle. In short, my contention is that Plato is an early exponent of the coherence theory of truth. Plato's unifying principle of the Good is similar to Kant's ideal *regulative* principle of the Unconditioned, an ideal of systematic unity (*Critique*, A 323-B 379). According to Kemp Smith, "Kant is the real founder of the coherence theory of truth."[2] In addition, we shall see a connection between Plato's *Republic* and Hegel's *Lectures on the History of Philosophy* and the *Science of Logic.* I bring this up early because I believe Freud's psychoanalytic system is a unified coherence theory grounded in a single principle—libidinal energy. And I wish to propose a corresponding theory based on the twin principles of the fear of loneliness and the desire to secure intimacy. This is my primary goal in all that follows. By contrast, neuroscience reduces all human behavior and thinking to *discrete* neuronal cells and electrical synapses.

Whereas Leucippus and Democritus are metaphysical materialists and Plato is a dualist, Aristotle appears to be of two minds. According to Aristotle, a substance is defined as an entity that can exist independently of all other entities; it is an individual existent, a particular thing, a unity of matter and form. The only exception is the Unmoved mover, which is "pure" form, i.e., immaterial activity alone. By contrast, predicates attributed to human substances are generally called accidents or properties, which can vary in terms of age, health, race, etc. (Aristotle, *Categories*, Chapter 5). On this account, Aristotle can be classified as a *metaphysical dualist,* since on the one hand (a) he identifies the human mind as a *passive* wax tablet upon which sensations and experiences *physically* write (*De Anima*, 430a; cf. 407a); and, on the other hand (b) he claims that human thoughts, like the Unmoved Mover's thoughts, are both immaterial and active, i.e., reflexive (*Metaphysics*, 1075a; cf. 1073a).

Roughly speaking, Aristotelian science is based on the *quantitative* accumulation of factual, contingent, particulars grounded in a relational correspondence to an external reality, which can be captured by language. By contrast, Platonic knowledge is grounded in *qualitative* hierarchical structures of lower to higher orders of coherence and comprehension.

10 The Achilles of rationalist arguments

During the extended period of the millennial Christian age, the Age of Faith, Catholicism is essentially dependent on the precepts of Tertullian, "I believe because it is absurd," pertaining to the incarnation of Christ, Augustine's conviction, "I believe so that I may understand," and followed by Anselm's intuitive faith in the ontological "argument" for the existence of God.

In 1974, I began to historically and conceptually trace the simplicity premise and argument from Plato's *Phaedo* into the Hellenistic period, as it migrates toward the philosophy of Plotinus and proliferates into five different modes or aspects of self-conscious activity: (a) the soul's immaterial substantiality; (b) its self-conscious unity; (c) its continuous temporal identity; (d) its inherent ideality; and (e) its immortality.[3]

But not until the Italian Renaissance and the translations, commentaries, and the revival of the Platonic dialogues of Marsilio Ficino (1438–1499), in his *Theologia Platonica de Immortalitate Animarum* and *Opera Omnia*, is the simplicity argument for immortality resurrected, along with its expanding Neoplatonic themes, as the soul becomes the ontological center between dark matter and the Plotinian One. Later in competition with Ficino, Faustus Socinus (1539–1604) proposes the doctrine of the soul's *natural* and *simultaneous* death as *both* the soul *and* the body expire. Nevertheless, he stipulates a selective resurrection of the soul for those who had truly adhered to the teachings of Christ. Historically, these Socinian tenets were later explicitly promulgated in the Calvinist doctrines of Augustinian predestinarianism, while stipulating the provision that only the "elect," only those souls signified as truly virtuous, would be saved by the "grace of God." In frustration, Pope Leo the Tenth admonished all thinkers, who would attempt to prove the soul's immortality through reason, rather than grounding it in faith, to desist and stop pursuing their fruitless speculations.

But soon after, the simplicity premise and its quintet of arguments and conclusions are closely followed and asserted by others, including Descartes, Malebranche, Cudworth, the British Platonists, and Leibniz. In Leibniz, it serves as the ultimate linchpin for his metaphysical, epistemological, and ethical idealism, until its five recruitments are collectively addressed and criticized by Kant in his two editions of the Paralogisms tendered in 1781 (four Paralogisms) and 1782 (a single Paralogism).

In the seventeenth century, however, the battle lines between materialism and idealism are once more redrawn and the simplicity proof resurfaces in Descartes (Synopsis), as well as in the strongly Neoplatonic thought of the Cambridge Platonists and in Leibniz. By contrast, the materialism of Hobbes serves as an opposing force to metaphysical immaterialism. Thus, the simplicity principle functions as an underived assumption, which stealthily moves among various inferences and mediate processes of thought, eventually culminating in the set of five conclusions mentioned above. I have mapped the incidence and force of these demonstrations from its ancient roots into its modern and even contemporary expressions (even as late as Brentano). But unless one gains an insight and an understanding into the depth and breadth of these foundational possibilities, its various inferences, and its conclusions, one will be at a disadvantage to appreciate the historical and conceptual Battle between the Idealists and the Materialists, Plato's Gods and Giants.

Kant in the first edition of the *Critique of Pure Reason* (1781), in the section titled the Paralogisms (i.e., fallacies) of pure "dogmatic" reason (1781), criticizes the four *a priori* rationalist proofs as metaphysical illusions and six years later the remaining argument for immortality meets the same fate in the second edition (1787). In the Dialectic, the simplicity premise had clearly attained its distinct formulations and Kant sought to demonstrate their metaphysical and rationalist inadequacies, while curiously the fifth argument, dealing with the original immortality, singly remained to be dispatched in the second edition of 1787. Thus, the fifth demonstration, on immortality, was postponed—and we shall see why—until the second edition as the sole Paralogism. This puzzling delay and neglect will be addressed in a later chapter.

There is an important epistemic distinction between the immediate acts of intuition, e.g., Descartes's cogito, as opposed to the *mediate* relational acts of connection when applied between two (or more) conceptions, judgments, and/or inferences. This distinction will prominently come into play throughout the text as we now turn our attention to the first edition First Paralogism titled *Of Substantiality*.

12 The Achilles of rationalist arguments

> That, the representation of which is the *absolute subject* of our judgments and cannot therefore be employed as determination of another thing, is substance.[4]

Expressed in this manner, it follows that the soul is *monadically* alone and separate.

> First Paralogism: Of Substantiality. I, as a thinking being, am the *absolute subject* of all my possible judgments, and this representation of myself cannot therefore be employed as a predicate of any other thing [i.e., another subject]. Therefore I, as thinking being (soul), am *substance* (A 348).

For Kant, all *self*-consciousness is judgmental. I, as substance, actively *predicate* judgments from within my self. Basically, this amounts to Descartes's solipsistic position, *intuitively*, in the statement "I think," the soul's existence is immediately known. But for Kant, it is a mediate judgment, the "I think," *and* my predications concerning my self, my judgments all belong to me *as an absolute substance.* My thoughts and judgments cannot be predicated as belonging to another being. I am self-aware that my judgments and assertions are my own—and not someone else's. Because of its immaterial essence, the soul is defined in terms of *quality* and not as a material quantity (cf. A 344=B 402).

The Second Paralogism seeks to establish the "unity of consciousness."

> Second Paralogism: Of Simplicity (i.e., Unity). "That, the *action* of which can never be regarded as the concurrence of several [material] things acting is *simple.* Now the soul, or the thinking 'I,' is such a being. Therefore, etc." (A 351, italic mine).

Essentially, this represents Leibniz's monadic, reflexive "unity of self-consciousness" principle. That the soul's nature or essence is not only to think but that its *action*, its power resides in its ability to reflexively, self-consciously, and *synthetically, relationally bind, unify* all my thoughts into a unity because of its utter simplicity; what is simple must be a unity; therefore it is cognitively constituted as a unity of consciousness; it possesses the capacity to actively *synthesize, unify all my thoughts within a unique monadic consciousness.* Note well the reference to "things" *means* material things, physical objects. Differently put, senseless matter *alone* cannot think.

Third, it confirms the soul's epistemic *continuity, its temporal identity*—and by implication its ethical and "personal identity," which, although not stated, is required for moral responsibility as well. To judge a subject as morally accountable, it must be the *identical* self that committed the act.

> Third Paralogism: Of Personality. "That which is conscious of the numerical identity of its self at different times is in so far a *person* [i.e., a moral substance]. Now the soul is conscious, etc. Therefore, it is a person" (A 361).

Again, this is Leibniz once more. Since the soul is a self-enclosed unit, this constitutes the necessary and sufficient criterion in establishing a *continuous, temporal* personal, i.e., moral self-identity.

Fourthly, and most critically, it establishes the metaphysical and epistemological status of the soul as confined within its own epistemic boundaries as consisting of—and leading to—a complete *subjective and qualitative idealism.* All immaterial acts, states, and contents of the mind can only *appear as ideal, as mental representations, as immaterial entities* that are not situated in space—although they are "situated" in time—because they solely exist within, to, or for an individual, substantial, subjective mind. Since the soul is both immaterial and active, it follows that whatever immediately, directly "appears" to or within its "span" of consciousness must be *ideal* despite any illusory *appearances* of spatial extension.

But, as we shall see, the Fourth Paralogism exhibits a disconcerting similarity to Kant's *transcendental* thesis regarding his Copernican Revolution, in which noumenal reality is compelled to conform to the internal acts, categories, principles, judgments, and structures of phenomenal consciousness (*Critique*, B xvi).

> Fourth Paralogism: Of Ideality. "That, the existence of which can only be *inferred* as a [material and external] cause of given perceptions, has merely a doubtful [i.e., Cartesian] existence. Now all external [phenomenal] appearances are of such a nature that

14 The Achilles of rationalist arguments

> their existence is not immediately perceived [therefore it is inferential], and that we can only [mediately] infer them as the [external] cause of given perceptions [to the mind]. Therefore the existence of all objects of the outer senses is doubtful. This uncertainty I entitle the [immaterial] ideality of outer appearances, and the doctrine of this ideality is called *idealism* (A 367).

Descartes's First Meditation shows that because of the intuitional *immediacy* of consciousness, it only allows him to *doubt* the existence of an external world; he is restricted; he cannot *know* it. But basically, this is Leibniz again. *Because* his Monads are absolutely self-enclosed and self-contained, *it necessarily follows* that all acts and contents of self-consciousness can only occur *within* the confines of the monadic substance. *The Fourth Paralogism is the basis for all idealisms, both subjective (Descartes, Leibniz, Kant, Fichte, Royce) as well as objective (Hegel, Schopenhauer?).* The Paralogism not only subscribes to this idealist metaphysical principle but it is the impregnating source for all idealisms. Kant's Copernican "solution" to the problematic relation between phenomenal appearances and noumenal reality is its epistemic endorsement. For if we contend that the *only* conceivable instrument, i.e., *means* of contact open to us as human beings, that we possess in our efforts to reach or contact an independently existing material world, is restricted to our subjective *mental* sphere of awareness, that we are confined within our own mind, then it becomes not only problematic but inconceivable how we can either *know* or *interact* with "something" beyond or transcendent to our self; it is impossible and self-contradictory. On these idealist terms, the mind— in principle—becomes unable either (a) to cognitively know or (b) to physically interact with an external world or other selves because it is trapped within its own "veil of perception," its own "way of ideas." As Berkeley rhetorically inquires, "What can be like an idea but another idea." "Resemblances" can only occur between entities that share a common ideal origin and therefore they can only exist *within the mind alone.*

> The view that consciousness (or, in general the mind) and its physical basis (or, in general the body) seem so essentially different from one another that they must have distinct existences is based

on a deep-rooted idea in the history of philosophy. This idea and its variants were constitutive arguments for the independence of mind and body throughout early modern philosophy of the seventeenth and eighteenth centuries, perhaps most notably in the work of Descartes [and Leibniz]. The essential and complete nature of the mind seems to consist solely in thinking, and, as such it must be unextended, simple (with no parts), essentially different from the body and therefore immaterial. This was Descartes's idea in a nutshell, ultimately drawing a strong ontological conclusion (regarding the distinctness of mind and body) from a starting point constituted by epistemic considerations (regarding the distinctness of their appearances). As Ben Mijuskovic observes (1974, Chapter 5), in this type of argumentation, "the sword that severs the Gordian knot is the principle that what is conceptually distinct is ontologically separable and therefore independent" (page 123). Mijuskovic, in locating this form of reasoning in its historical context, also notes the presence of the converse of its inference: "If one begins with the notion implicit or explicit, that thoughts and minds are simple, unextended, indivisible, then it seems to be an inevitable step before thinkers connect the principle of an unextended, immaterial soul with the impossibility of any knowledge of an extended material, external world and consequently the relation between them" (page 121). That is, this time an epistemological conclusion regarding an epistemic gap (between mind and body) is reached from a starting point constituted by ontological considerations (regarding the distinctness of their natures).[5]

Because the *psyche*, soul, cogito, monad, self, mind, or ego is monadically self-enclosed, it *necessarily* follows that all its epistemic images, ideas, conceptions, representations, and thoughts, and inferences are all reciprocally self-enclosed. If ideas and thoughts are immaterial and alone present to consciousness, it becomes problematic how a disembodied soul can conceivably *know* and/or *interact* with either a spatially extended material world or other selves.

It is important to underscore the context in which the first four Paralogisms appear (absent the fifth on immortality, which will follow six years later). Despite Kant's rejection of their noumenal origins and

16 The Achilles of rationalist arguments

heritage, all four are specifically intended and designed to challenge the materialist metaphysical principle that "senseless matter alone can think." It is in this larger context of its continuing historical and conceptual role that we must follow Plato's insight regarding his comments about the Battle between the Giants and the Gods.

Welcome confirmation of my interpretations comes in the form of scholarly acknowledgements of my early studies.

> A work that touches on the same issues [concerning materialism] is Ben Lazare Mijuskovic's *The Achilles of Rationalist Arguments: The Simplicity, Unity, and Identity of Thought and Soul from the Cambridge Platonists to Kant* (Nijhoff, 1974). Mijuskovic recognizes the central role played by Cudworth's formulation of the doctrines in the eighteenth-century about the soul, the person, and the nature of thought.[6]

And:

> In the following discussion on the relationship between immaterial substances and personal identity, I am indebted to two studies. Ben Lazare Mijuskovic's *The Achilles of Rationalist Arguments* and John Yolton's *Thinking Matter.* Mijuskovic shows how the argument about immaterial substances and the grounding of personal identity developed independently in England prior to Descartes as a reaction to the perceived threat of the rise of Epicurean and newer forms of materialism. Mijuskovic details the intense sensitivity of orthodox thinkers to the threat of materialism posed by immaterial substance and documents their defenses against the threat.[7]

Again:

> In and after the seventeenth century, consciousness figured in a central role in at least four fairly distinct themes: personal identity, immortality of the soul, epistemic certainty, and the transcendental conditions of experience in Ben Mijuskovic's discussion in *The Achilles of Rationalist Arguments* (1974), which touches on all four thematics.[8]

Further:

> What remains surprising, however, is that so little work has been done before on the Achilles argument. Ben Lazare Mijuskovic's pioneering work was the first in modern times to draw attention to the importance of the argument, but aside from the work he has done, there is little else in print.[9]

And lastly:

> Few of the commentators saw a continuity in what we are here calling 'internalization,' from Cudworth to Kant, with the exception of Ben Lazare Mijuskovic in *The Achilles of Rationalist Arguments: The Simplicity, Unity, and Identity of Thought and Soul from the Cambridge Platonists to Kant*.[10]

Although Kant critically discounts all four arguments as illicit metaphysical illusions and "dogmatic," rationalist fallacies, the second and the fourth Paralogisms, *Of Simplicity* (i.e., unity) and *Of Ideality* paradoxically enough manage to find positive applications in the Analytic in the guise of the transcendental unity of apperception and his Copernican Revolution, as he argues that the noumenal realm must "conform" to the innate pre-existing *a priori* synthetic structures of the mind. Prior to Kant, all these insoluble dualist difficulties regarding the interactions between body and soul, or matter and mind were unsuccessfully addressed by Descartes's assurance that God is not a deceiver; Malebranche's occasionalist doctrine that it is God who coordinates my thought of moving my arm with its physical result; Leibniz's divine pre-established harmony during which God synchronizes a universe of distinct Monads *appearing* to synchronically interact with each other; and Berkeley's conviction that "we see all things in God," that we perceive "all the furniture of heaven and earth," and "all the laws of nature" through the mind of God.

In 1787, half a dozen years after his first edition, Kant quite surprisingly, in the *Critique's* second edition, the B edition, completely excises the first edition *four* Paralogisms of 1781, writes a totally new *single* Paralogism as he pens an insipid criticism of Moses Mendelssohn's proof for the immortality of the soul in the B edition. Although

18 The Achilles of rationalist arguments

the immortality demonstration is conspicuously absent in the first A edition, it is now oddly the sole proof in the second edition as he criticizes Moses Mendelssohn's defense of the immortality of the soul based on its immaterial simplicity (*Phaedo*, 1767). Now, according to Kant, its *qualitative* simplicity, although spatially dimensionless, can still be gradually diminished into non-existence by "elanguescence," by vanishing *degrees* in its quality, by a diminution until it reaches zero (B 413–415). This possibility is problematic. If the qualitative simplicity of the soul is truly unextended, there is nothing left to diminish. Only quantities can be reduced. Either it exists or it does not: it cannot "faintly" exist.

Equally baffling is Kant's excision of the first edition transcendental Deduction, the very heart of the *Critique*, and its complete rewriting.

The cause of all these bewildering and drastic adjustments, I believe, is forced by the fact that in the first edition Second Paralogism, *Of Simplicity—with its proof for the unity of consciousness—*it prominently brings into high relief a direct conflict, indeed a contradiction, between his positive exposition in support of his argument for the transcendental unity of apperception in the second edition Deduction at B 131–132, versus his compromising version of the soul's simplicity, i.e., its unity of consciousness in the first edition Second Paralogism, *Of Simplicity* at A 351–352. The obvious contradiction is highlighted by comparing Kant's *positive* account of the reflexive unity of consciousness in the Analytic, at B 131–132, versus his *negative* criticism and the deletion of his earlier account of the Second Paralogism in A 352. *In short, in the A Paralogism, he destroys the "unity of consciousness," and in the B Analytic, he asserts it!* In a later chapter, I shall revisit this inconsistency more fully because what is at issue is the ultimate premise of the Analytic.

Conclusion

In earlier writings, I began with the universal premise that "All human beings are lonely" and then moved on to a theory of consciousness. In the present study, I rather start with consciousness and then try to show *why* and *how* loneliness is inevitable because of the activities and structures of human consciousness. In what follows, I intend to argue my case based on *a priori* synthetic acts and structures

The Achilles of rationalist arguments 19

permeating human consciousness; epistemic spontaneity; dynamic activity; the reflexivity of self-consciousness in conjunction with transcendent intentionality; the assurance that the self both knows and interacts with a material world; the establishment of an irretrievable, subterranean, creative subconscious below Leibniz's and Freud's mnemonic unconscious; that consciousness is qualitative whereas matter is quantitative; that freedom rules over determinism; that immanent time-consciousness is primary, while scientific time is secondary; that loneliness is intrinsically narcissistic and highly vulnerable to feelings of hostility, anxiety, depression, rejection, envy, guilt, shame, and much more; and that its only possible remedy for loneliness depends on mutual intimacy, which can only be gained through and along a reciprocating path of shared empathy.

Notes

1 *Plato's Phaedo*, translated by R. S. Bluck, with a running commentary (Indianapolis: Bobbs-Merrill, 1955), 73 ff. *Dynamis* is both the corresponding "power" to affect change as well as to be affected by it; cf. the *Sophist*, 247E. For Plato, consciousness is intrinsically *active*, as opposed to the *passive* model of sensation promoted by materialism. According to the materialist paradigm of Leucippus, Democritus and later Epicurus and Lucretius, the natural motions attributed to the solid atoms physically *cause* sensations as they strike human organs. The atoms are qualitatively homogeneous and as they "fall" (in the absence of gravity) throughout an infinite void, they form compound bodies. By anticipation, we remark that the neurons of neuroscience are equally homogeneous. Accordingly, their permutations can only be quantitative, whereas human consciousness in essence is qualitatively heterogeneous.
2 Kemp Smith, Norman, *A Commentary to Kant's 'Critique of Pure Reason'* (New York: Humanities Press, 1962), xxxviii, 36. Kemp Smith also suggests that Kant's concept of the Unconditioned has its roots in Plato's unifying notion of the Idea of the Good, 416–417, 433–434.
3 Plotinus, *The Enneads*, translated by Stephen MacKenna (New York: Pantheon, 1969), IV, 7, 6; cf. 7, 3; cf. Ben Mijuskovic, *The Achilles of Rationalist Arguments: The Simplicity, Unity, and Identity of Thought and Soul from the Cambridge Platonists to Kant: A Study in the History of an Argument* (The Hague: Martinus Nijhoff, 1974); consult Chapters I, "Introduction to the Argument Prior to the 17th and 18th Centuries," 1–18; II, "The Immortality of the Soul in the 17th and 18th Centuries," 19–57; III, "The Unity of Consciousness in the 17th-18th Centuries," 58–92; IV,

20 The Achilles of rationalist arguments

"Personal Identity in the 17th and 18th Centuries," 93–118; and V, "The Simplicity Argument and Its Role in the History of Idealism," 119–142; cf. also Ben Mijuskovic, "The Argument from Simplicity: A Study in the History of an Idea and Consciousness," *Philotheos*, Vol. 9 (2009), 228–252.

4 Kant, Immanuel, *Critique of Pure Reason* (New York: Humanities Press, 1962), A 348–349; cf. *The Achilles of Rationalist Psychology*, edited by Thomas Lennon and Robert Stainton (Springer, 2008), based on my *Achilles* but unfortunately the discussion is solely restricted to Kant's Second Paralogism "unity of consciousness" principle, while leaving the remaining four proofs unattended.

5 *The Nature of Consciousness: Philosophical Debates*, edited by Ned Block, Owen Flanigan, Guven Gezeldere (Cambridge, MA: MIT Press, 2007), 10–11.

6 Yolton, John, *Thinking Matter: Materialism in Eighteenth-Britain* (Minneapolis: University of Minnesota Press, 1983), xiii; and cf. John Yolton's book review of the *Achilles* in *Philosophical Books*, 16:2 (1975), 17–19.

7 Todd, Dennis, *Imagining Monsters: Miscreations of the Self in Eighteenth-Century England*, Chicago: University of Chicago Press, 1995), 304; and Raymond Martin and John Baresi, *The Rise and Fall of the Soul and Self: An Intellectual History of Personal Identity* (New York: Columbia University Press, 1995), 6. Cf. Patricia Easton, "The Cartesian Doctor, Francois Bayle" (1622–1709) on Psychosomatic Explanation," *Studies in the History and Philosophy of Biological and Biomedical Sciences*, Volume 2 (2011), "For an excellent discussion of the tradition that views Descartes as the father of rational psychology, see Ben Mijuskovic (1974)," 203.

8 *Consciousness: From Perception to Reflection in the History of Consciousness*, edited by Sara Heinamaa, Vili Lahteenmaki, & Paula Remes (New York: Springer, 2007), 7.

9 *The Achilles of Rationalist Psychology*, edited by Thomas Lennon and Robert Stainton (Springer, 2008), 2. Unfortunately, although crediting me, the anthology completely disregards my discussion of the other four applications of the simplicity premise and only addresses the unity of consciousness.

10 Wolfe, Charles T., discusses the *Achilles* at some considerable depth: "Elements for a Materialist Theory of the Self," No. 3, published December 4, 2015; the text is both in English and French: htpps://archives-ouverte.fr/hal-01238149. Cf. William James, who alludes to the Second Paralogism in his *Principles of Psychology* (New York: Dover, 1950), I, 160–161) and to the Third Paralogism, respectively, in "The Stream of Thought" during his pre-neutral monism period (I, 224 ff., 274, 338–340).

Chapter 2

Consciousness, spontaneity, and synthetic *a priori* relations

In the first chapter, I sought to distinguish human consciousness in opposition to the external world of physical objects, events, and other selves on the ground that the former is immaterial and active, while by contrast the latter is materially and spatially extended as well as often presumed as "inert," which directly leads to the epistemic principle that "matter *alone* cannot think." In this chapter, I wish to explore the intrinsic nature of this mental activity by distinguishing its *constitutive* acts and features within consciousness: (a) the *immediacy* of sensations and feelings; (b) the *act of spontaneity;* and (c) the consequent qualitative *mediacy*, i.e. the *relational* aspect of thought, which results in conceptual meanings, relations, and above all judgments. Constitutive (a) acts and (b) its unification of the sensory elements, are both internal and subjective elements within consciousness and they are to be distinguished from an external realm of material objects and events. Based on these distinctions, I intend to defend metaphysical dualism. And further, I would add that Aristotle, in his *Physics* and *Metaphysics*, Locke in his *Essay*, Hume in his *Treatise*, as well as Sartre in *The Transcendence of the Ego* and *Being and Nothingness*, together collectively defend metaphysical dualism as they propose various arguments in its behalf.

Untold eons and eternities ago, all matter was inanimate, "lifeless." None of the ancient Greeks, not the Pre-Socratics, Plato, Aristotle, Manicheans, Epicureans, or Stoics believed in creation "out of nothing," *ex nihilo.* "Out of nothing, nothing comes" (Epicurus). The Epicureans did, however, assume an element of chance as the atoms moved through empty space and during certain undetermined moments of flux, they were said to be vulnerable to "swerves" in

DOI: 10.4324/9781003156130-3

22 Consciousness, spontaneity, and *a priori* relations

their paths, thus producing novel events. But all this was upstaged by Augustine's declaration that God created Time and Space instantaneously, the heavens and the earth, the entire material universe, and subsequently each individual soul "out of nothing" in time. But presumably it was only the human soul that he endowed with a "freedom of the will," a *liberium arbitrium.* Along with free will, He provided humans with the "power of faith," the ability to paradoxically believe a contradiction.

In any event, it seems that *"In the beginning..."* all matter was inanimate, devoid of both sensation and animation and inexplicably living matter came to *be*; and then plant, animal, and human life followed suit; and then spontaneous consciousness; and then, in higher order animals and humans self-consciousness came to *be.* Who knows what might happen should the Stoic and Nietzschean notion of the "eternal recurrence" reoccur, if the whole universe begins anew once more?

Philosophers define a proposition or a judgment as a *meaningful* statement that is either true or false. It is either (a) a *reflexive* statement about its self, it is self-referential, e.g., Descartes's cogito; or (b) an *intentional* (often purposive) statement about a state of affairs that points beyond the self, e.g., "The Sun is shining." Following Hume, propositions concerning "matters of fact" are contingently or *factually* true or false; they are *a posteriori* or empirically grounded. Importantly, the opposite assertion—its contradictory—is always *conceivably* possible; it can be imaginatively entertained. For example, the proposition "The world is flat" is imaginable but it is not true. These propositions are classified as synthetic, ampliative, additive in the sense that they relate two distinct and separable concepts—subject and predicate(s)—to each other, e.g., "There are mountains on the other side of the moon" (A. J. Ayer). Thus, empirical judgments are mediate, relational. They can only be confirmed or verified by factual experiences.

By contrast, judgments concerning "relations of ideas" are *a priori* or analytically related; they exhibit both (a) *universality*: they are *always* and *everywhere* true in any conceivable universe, e.g., the law of identity, $A=A$; and (b) they are *necessary*; the opposite assertion implies either a logical or a metaphysical contradiction, e.g., "Matter is unextended." They are categorized as analytic because the predicate concept is intrinsically contained within, or equivalent to, the subject concept. Examples of "true" or valid—as opposed to factual—propositions are 2+3=5; or "All bachelors are unmarried males." They are always "valid" or "true by definition" and experience is irrelevant to their truth, falsity, or validity. In short, they are tautologies; both sides of the equation exhibit or entail identical meanings.

Now as it turns out, there is a limited group of philosophers, who subscribe to the possibility that there are judgments that are *both* synthetic *and a priori* and consequently tell us something true about experience independently of and/or logically prior to experience. Together Plato, Kant, Fichte, Husserl, Royce, Peirce, and Sartre—and perhaps others—form their number, although to be sure their individual implementations of this relation are significantly different.

Philosophically the first instance alluding to this important possibility of an *absolutely pure relation*—as opposed to a contingent, sensory, empirical, or a psychological "association of ideas"—appears in Plato's discussion of a synthetic *a priori* relation in his dialogue, the *Meno*, when he conceptualizes a unifying connection between two distinct meanings, actually *Forms*, citing the connection between Virtue and Knowledge, as analogous to the relation unifying the *meanings* of color (*chroma*) and extension (*schema*). The universal meaning of color is defined as a sensory *intensive*, i.e. unextended *quality*. By contrast, the meaning of space is defined as an *extensive*, i.e. extended *quantity*. But although they are conceptually distinct, they are always universally and necessarily, i.e. *a priori* unified, bound together. They form a synthetic *a priori* unity. It is inconceivable to experience a color without extension or an extension without *some* color. Thus, the following synthetic *a priori* proposition: "All colors are extended."

> Socrates: Well now, let's try to tell you what shape is. See if you accept this definition. Let us define it as the only thing which *always* [universally and necessarily] accompanies color ... I should be content if your definition of virtue [and knowledge] were on similar lines.
>
> (*Meno*, 75b-c)[1]

A colorless extension is a contradiction in terms. This third relational possibility establishes the validity of meaningful synthetic *a priori* judgments. The mind is somehow able, in some inexplicable fashion,

24 Consciousness, spontaneity, and *a priori* relations

to *spontaneously create relations* from within its self, through its own internal resources. In such cases, *meaningful* cognitive relations are neither empirical nor rational alone but rather both at once. For empiricists, by contrast, all relations are contingently, *passively given by the imagination*—not actively thought—by the psychological principle of the "association of ideas," by the sensations themselves simply appearing repetitiously together. Basically, the connection is imagined rather than intrinsically synthetically *a priori* "constituted."

The absolute divide *within* consciousness between the "categories" of Quality and Quantity—color and extension—raises the question whether they rule equally; or one is primary and the other secondary; and whether the first is substantial and the second dependent. These twin distinctions promise to be critical issues as far as insights into the *activity* of consciousness is concerned. For subjective and objective idealists, the relation between the two categories is the result of a *pure act*, an *uncaused* creation attributed to the activity of the mind; it is generated *spontaneously*. The mind produces both the distinction and the relation, while the external world passively provides the sensations.

In Plato, the relational *act* of synthesizing, unifying, or binding the conceptual *meaning* of "color" with the conceptual *meaning* of "shape" provides us with an important insight into the relation between the dual essences of Knowledge and Virtue: "Virtue is Knowledge (of the Good)," i.e. *acting* virtuously is only conceivable if one *already innately* possesses knowledge of the Good. Virtue is ethical and Knowledge is epistemic. When the two *distinct* meanings are unified, they *constitute*—not cause—a doubling insight into Reality. By contrast, the empirical sciences instead seek to collect their facts one brick at a time. *But* only if synthetic *a priori* relations are possible is the formulation of a *system* possible. All else is merely a contingent aggregation of material compounds and facts.

Plato is an early exponent of the coherence theory of truth. The Divided Line in the *Republic* is completely dependent on the possibility of synthetic *a priori* relations. The system, as a unified whole, is ideally self-contained. It is so for Plato and later for both Kant and Hegel; and it is self-validating in the sense that its "truths" are judged in terms of internal and graduated lower and higher relations leading to more comprehensive and coherent unities.

By contrast, in the correspondence theory of truth, empiricism seeks to "match" our subjective sensations with an external reality, either by contingent associations of reflective—but not reflexive—representations i.e. resemblances with the external objects or events it sees; not unlike the external relation between a mirror (the mind) and its reflection of the objects it sees/thinks. Aristotle's empirical organization of knowledge is predicated on collecting—as opposed to unifying—factual particulars and by distinguishing various enclosed epistemic fields and boundaries, each with its own guiding principle, e.g., physics, logic, rhetoric, metaphysics, psychology, etc. For example, the principle of productive knowledge guides us in collecting facts about making useful or beautiful things; practical knowledge consists in knowing how to act virtuously in particular circumstances; and metaphysics consists in seeking purely theoretical knowledge for its own sake. The Aristotelian sciences are self-separating and so are its confirming factual data. It consists in the accumulation of separate facts and then testing their correspondence with an external reality. For Aristotle, language essentially reflects reality.

Psychoanalysis is a good example of an internally self-contained Platonic system. And as such, it has served as a powerful, liberating, and therapeutic enterprise. But my issue concerns its deterministic foundation, its inflexible causal principle connecting the patient's psychic traumas with his neurotic symptoms. That is why I wish to replace it with a subjective idealist and existential approach. I wish to replace Freud's principle of libidinal energy with the fear of loneliness and the desire to secure intimacy; and his determinism with spontaneity by establishing the formation of a comprehensive and coherent system of synthetic *a priori* relations in regard to the interrelated disciplines of loneliness and intimacy.

The spontaneity of consciousness

Plato attributes two critical "aspects or "modes" to consciousness: (a) the immaterial nature of the mind along with (b) its inherent activity of transcending the passive features of our *immediate* sensory inputs, our sensations, while (c) displaying the ability to connect concepts to each other thereby resulting in synthetic *a priori* judgments, inferences and ultimately ending in a *conditionally* coherent "rational" system.

26 Consciousness, spontaneity, and *a priori* relations

I say "conditional" because there are many choices in the selection of foundational "first principles" as well as for the ensuing creation of different systems, e.g., scientific, ethical, aesthetic, etc. Various systems are always imaginable, possible, and conceivable. But every system must always begin with a defining "first principle" and include two "elements": *contents*, i.e. sensations as well as relational *acts* unifying the conceptual elements. And when these twin factors are combined and secured, the resulting system can be structured coherently and comprehensively.

All *scientific* endeavors presuppose causality, determinism, and the ability to predict events and behaviors. Freud's first principle is that dynamic libidinal *sexual*—and aggressive—energy can account for all the primary motivational endeavors of mankind, from sadism to sublimation. The phrase "can account" means that it can be deterministically structured within a causal and predictable relational system. But my issue with psychoanalysis is twofold. First, that sexual disorders comprise a fairly limited set of dysfunctions, whereas the motivation to avoid loneliness and secure intimacy is universal. I regard sexuality as a means among many others to reduce loneliness. And I assume the spontaneity of consciousness over determinism.

But it all begins by gaining insight and understanding into how synthetic *a priori* relations are connected to human loneliness and intimacy, and thus our task is to determine precisely *how* the acts of relating and unifying the contents are set in "motion"; how does it all begin; how is the nexus between (a) *passive* sensations and feelings unified within reflexive self-consciousness and transcendent intentionality? What *creates* the *relation* between the *acts* within consciousness and its *contents*? The answer is the *epistemic* spontaneity of consciousness—as opposed to the *ethical* freedom of the will.

In the Platonic dialogue, *Ion*, the poetic *interpretations*, the *meanings* attributed to Homer's two epics, the *Iliad* and the *Odyssey*, are performed by the rhapsode, Ion, and they are described as "creative inspirations." As Benjamin Jowett declares, "Genius is often said to be unconscious, or spontaneous; a gift of nature: 'that genius is akin to madness' is a popular aphorism of modern times." Whether the *Ion* is a product of Plato's hand, or that of a disciple, Plato's dialogue strongly *suggests* a spontaneous, an emotional, an inspirational "trigger" as it animates the rhapsode's mimetic affective *acts*, as he interprets Homer's epics

(Benjamin Jowett's translation of Plato's *Ion*). Two millenniums later, this same insight is echoed by Schopenhauer: "It is often remarked that genius and madness have a side where they touch and even pass over into each other, and even poetic inspiration has been called a form of madness," virtually an origination arising from subconscious sources.[2] Schopenhauer greatly admired artistic genius, readily relating it to his irrational Will, and especially as exemplified in the *creation* of works of art (*WWR,* II, 75, 291–292, 376, 409). But the salient point is that already in the Greek myths, dramas, and tragedies, there are strong indications of the interplay between the spontaneous acts of aesthetic creation and their various interpretations by the rhapsodes. There is an innate artistic talent in depicting subhuman forces as they spawn the richness of the dark Greek myths of Sophocles. It is the same spontaneity, which two thousand years later, Nietzsche appreciated in the turbulence of Dionysian art. For psychological determinists, however, the distinction between affective and cognitive states of consciousness disappears because everything is reduced to the causal nexus as it eliminates the quantity-quality difference.

In his *Metaphysics*, Aristotle draws an epistemic distinction between potentiality (*dynamis*), actuality (*energeia*), and completion (*entelecheia*), as *internal* forces, responsible for initiating novel changes within consciousness, as indefinable powers within the human substance in creating, in fashioning events beyond the self.[3] Later Leibniz and Hegel will draw heavily on the above triad of forces as they become internalized within self-consciousness. And in the *Nicomachean Ethics*, Aristotle makes it clear that virtue is grounded in the potentiality to voluntarily *choose* the mean between vice and virtue (*Ethics*, 1107a).

The concept of spontaneity is transformed into the freedom of the will in Christianity. It is presented as intervening within religious and ethical contexts during the reigning millennial age of Medieval Christian theology. For the Greeks, man is essentially a "rational animal." But for Augustine, man is specifically blessed with freedom of the will, *liberium arbitrium*, the ability to obey or disobey God, the capacity to choose good from evil; to choose between faith or skepticism. Man's "free will" is set apart from his cognitive faculties. Spontaneity in this context is represented as an underived and untethered source for committing acts of ethical freedom and in general choosing salvation over damnation. As a faculty, the will is distinct from the intellect

28 Consciousness, spontaneity, and *a priori* relations

and consequently from our "rational" modes of thought. An applicable dictionary definition of "spontaneity" describes it as "arising from internal *qualities* without external causes." Qualities, in this context, are essentially immaterial creations, whereas external causes are materially determined and inflexible. Spontaneity and causality are opposites and so are freedom and determinism.

For the earlier pagan Greek thinkers, the faculties of "free will" and "faith" are inconceivable. So is the concept of creation *ex nihilo.* In Plato's Divided Line passage, there is *belief*, which specifically applies to the realm of sensory appearances but there is nothing even remotely similar to the concepts of Christian "free will" or "faith" (*Republic*, VI, 509). In the development of Christianity, there are at least four different, but closely related acts of spontaneity exemplified in Christian thought. First, there is God's absolute power in creating both the universe and each human soul *ex nihilo* in time, which for the ancient Greeks is simply a metaphysical impossibility, a contradiction in terms, an inconceivability since "Nothing comes from nothing."

Second, spontaneity appears through God's endowment of "freedom of the will" to man, so that he can choose between good and evil. For both Augustine and later Descartes, the faculties of the intellect and the will are distinct, separate; there is *both* the intellect *and* the will, and they can operate alone or conjointly (Descartes's Fourth Meditation). I can cognitively consider a judgment and either affirm, deny, or avoid it. What follows for Christian theism is that God's divine act of spontaneity, in creating the universe, is analogously transferred from God to man as the freedom to create either evil or goodness by his ethical choices. Man, by *choosing* the *quality* of goodness, creates a Good World, a Good Substance.

For example, the dual dynamics of choice become significant in Augustine's concentration on the "Problem of Evil," as well as later in Thomas Aquinas' "Five Ways To Prove the Existence of God," when he scholastically *begins* by dramatically positing the atheistic antithesis in proving God's *inexistence* because of all the evil prevalent in the world. "If, therefore, God existed, there would be no evil discoverable; but there is evil in the world. Therefore, God does not exist." Call it spontaneity or "free will," but the theological question is first and foremost whether there i*s* evil in the world; and *if* there is, what is its source: God, man, or both?

By way of example, this critical theological issue unfolds in Camus's novel, *The Plague*, as he narrates the story of a small town in Algiers, when the townspeople are unexpectedly visited by a deadly plague. Commentators have viewed it as symbolizing the Nazi occupation of Vichy France during the Second World War. As the disease progresses, Father Paneloux, an Augustinian priest, offers a sermon warning the people that although he does not intellectually comprehend *why* this tragedy has descended upon them, still he speculates that in the eyes of God the populace must have deserved this visitation for something they have done, some collective sin. God's reason is transcendent, infinite, and thus beyond human reason, whereas man's knowledge is finite and limited and therefore we cannot understand God's divine purposes; we will never know "the ways of God toward man" (John Milton, Alexander Pope).

As the plague advances with increasing ferocity, one of the protagonists, Rieux, a doctor, tries to develop an antidote for the plague, which is tested on an "innocent" ten-year-old boy with the disastrous consequences of prolonging the child's pain and suffering and ending in his agonized death. (Of course, for Augustine, no one is innocent because of Original Sin.) But in his second sermon, as the plague continues to ravage the town, Paneloux lectures his audience:

> My brethren, I don't know what you have done but know that the time has now come either to will what God has willed or not to will it; either to love God or to hate him, whether or not we understand Him.[4]

Third, the role of spontaneity in Christian thought offers the only possible solution to the paradox of faith, which asserts the identity of God with Christ; not only is God omnipotent, omniscient, and omnibenevolent but, in the same moment, He is identical to and with the forlorn, suffering human figure on the Cross (Tertullian). And yet, what an incredible symbol of man's poignant loneliness without God! We recall Christ's words on the cross: "My God, My God, why hast you forsaken me" (Matthew, 27:46, Mark, 15:34). In this context, the "relation," the *identification* of God *as* Christ, is only conceivable through an act of *theistic* spontaneity.

30 Consciousness, spontaneity, and *a priori* relations

Fourth, consider God's bestowal of the "gift of grace" to mankind as it exemplifies neither forethought nor afterthought; it is a unique spontaneous act in itself; it is an act of pure forgiveness independently of the issue whether it is deserved or not (the Catholic confessional; the Calvinist doctrine of the "elect"), which is to be emulated by man in so far as he is capable of providing moral comfort to his fellows. *But my point is simply this: Christianity without these four acts of theistic spontaneity, i.e. free will is inconceivable.*

My interest in Plato's *Ion*, Aristotle's *dynamis-energeia-entelecheia* distinction, and Camus's *The Plague* derives from reflecting that within the context of the "History of Ideas" discipline, there is, from the very beginnings of Western thought, a continuous acknowledgment of *both* an affective *and* a cognitive role played by spontaneity as a primary dynamic. Without spontaneity, aesthetic expressions, ethical commandments, and scientific revolutions would be inconceivable (Thomas Kuhn, *The Structure of Scientific Revolutions*). Facts do not determine theories, rather theories make the "facts" meaningful. Facts without functioning within a coherent context are meaningless. *But it is human spontaneity that creates values, the spectrum of values from beauty to ugliness, goodness to evil, and intelligence to stupidity. What distinguishes man from all other creatures is his capacity to create valuative principles, which are critically geared to guiding his feelings, thoughts, and conduct.*

In sum, I suggest that it is the act of spontaneity that binds together aesthetic expressions, Aristotelian choices, Christian free will, and the selection of scientific principles.

Descartes's spontaneity

Descartes belonged to the Augustinian Oratory and he affirmed the common Catholic separation, the distinction between the intellectual and the willing faculties. In Meditation III, he states:

> Whereupon, regarding myself more closely, and considering what are my errors, I answer that they depend on a combination of two causes, to wit, on the faculty of knowledge [the active intellect] that rests in me, and on the power of choice or [ethical] free will—that is to say, of the understanding and at the same time of the will. For

Consciousness, spontaneity, and *a priori* relations   31

by the understanding alone I neither assert nor deny anything but apprehend the ideas of things as to which I form a judgment [by willing its affirmation or denial].[5]

According to Descartes, there are two separate operations in consciousness: we can either reflexively contemplate an issue and never determine whether we affirm it as true or deny it as false; or we can spontaneously invoke the will and affirm or deny it. It thus follows that spontaneity can actively function in two radically different contexts: ethical and epistemic (and theistic). *Qualitatively* these are quite different acts because the contexts, the purposes they serve are distinct.

In Georges Poulet's *Studies in Human Time*, he offers the following interpretation regarding Descartes's three dreams, which occurred in 1619 (over two decades before the publication of the *Meditations*), a time during which he committed himself to his singular religious mission to seek the truth at all costs. In pursuing Poulet's theme, I wish to connect (a) the *qualitative* meaning and purpose of Descartes's religious mission; (b) the purely spontaneous nature of his critical acts; with (c) his overwhelming sense of loneliness and his anxiety of being abandoned by God. (See Augustine's prayer in Chapter Five of the *Confessions*.)

> To the physical instability, easy enough to comprehend, there corresponds a moral instability very much more difficult to lay hold of. Descartes' mind was *fixed*. He had a goal. He devoted all his efforts to reaching it. But from the very fixation of the mind, from the concentration of energy which operates it, there emanates [Plotinus?] certain eddies of thought which travel consciously in opposite directions. In the first place, single in its aim, his inquiry was double in its method; "to distinguish the true from the false" is within oneself, two distinct operations, the first of which is suffused with enthusiasm [i.e. spontaneity?]; but the second with suffering … Thus to physical exile and material solitude are added moral exile and solitude.[6]

In Descartes's three dreams,

> he discovers that he is an unhappy being, like a man who walks alone in utter darkness, through that first stage of human life,

32 Consciousness, spontaneity, and *a priori* relations

> which exists subterraneously within us, exposed to subterranean—[i.e. *sub*conscious]—regions of the soul as he has become acquainted with the anguish of one who has lost his way.
>
> (page 56)

A prey to the lonely religious terror of the times, the insecurity of his own mortal existence, and the fear about continuing to the next stage of immortality, he is anxious about his identity and continuity. "It does not follow that I must still exist afterward if I am not created anew at each moment by some cause [namely God]" (ibid.)

Metaphysically, God not only creates and sustains the entire universe as a whole but each unique soul separately as well; He continually *re-creates, conserves* them at each instant of time. Further, as Poulet relates, what alone can give Descartes hope is that eventually "from the first act toward God, to Whom one is turned spontaneously by a 'first thought'; an act of freedom, an act essentially voluntary," will he be able to receive the assurance of his continuing existence. "This act he will later identify and define as the reflexive intuition of the cogito: I think=I exist" (page 58). It is a sense of security that can only be secured and guaranteed by God's continual intervention and conservation. In the dream, however, God appears to him unexpectedly: "The spontaneous act by which he turns toward God does not as yet possess *pure* spontaneity" (page 59). Consequently, he realizes precisely what it is that he must further accomplish in order to persevere in his mission, in his desperate yearning for both truth and immortality.

> Truth is attained only by a pure, spontaneous act, which can only be achieved by a pure act excluding any constraints or mediating thoughts [i.e. by an intuition]. In this manner the idea of God—and later the cogito—appears to Descartes in a genuine spontaneous act.
>
> (page 60)

In addition, Poulet proceeds by characterizing this concept of spontaneity as an "instantaneous transmutation," a "naked instant," which "is complete as a point without duration" (page 63; Bergson?); "spontaneity is what is veritably present [i.e. immediately]," and it is "absolutely instantaneous," an "*activitas instantanea*" (page 64). Clearly for

Descartes, this pure act is immaterial, unmediated, and intuitional. It is not only "pure," i.e. immaterial but also a continually repetitious beginning. As such, it qualifies as an absolute *agency* in various contexts; (a) metaphysically in the pure spontaneous intuitional discovery of God, more specifically in Descartes's version of St. Anselm's ontological intuition of God's existence in Meditation V; (b) in the implementation of freedom of the will in moral situations; (c) in the declarative cogito: "I think=I am" (Second Meditation); and (d) in epistemic judgments and decisions regarding yea or nay, truth or falsity (Fourth Meditation).

Both St. Anselm and Descartes are advocates for the intuitional version of the ontological "argument" for the existence of God, which *directly, intuitively, spontaneously* asserts—rather than demonstratively proves—the being of God. It is an *intuition, not an inference*: God exists; He alone is *necessary* Being; He cannot not exist. Unlike both (a) the cosmological and (b) the teleological arguments for God's existence, which inferentially move from God as the *cause* (a) of the world and (b) its purpose, the ontological argument is intuitive—and so is the cogito. What better twin reassurances for God's existence and his own immortality! God exists; I exist; and God is beneficent; He will not deceive me; He has not given me a faculty, reason, which is inherently deceptive.

As we examine these passages, we begin to discover how spontaneity functions in theological, ethical, and epistemic crises. The mortal nature of human existence permeates the intense loneliness of Descartes, which can only be quelled by the assurance that *both* the spontaneous, i.e. intuitive assurance of God's existence is true *and* (b) the cogito's certitude of his own existence are fundamentally one and the same in their indubitable power of self-affirmation. Anything less, grounded in the mediacy of thought, is open to doubt. He must first be sure of God—and his goodness—*before* he is sure of his own existence. Religious certainty must be first, otherwise the cosmic terror of his soul's eternal loneliness will engulf him. But both certainties are equally spontaneous. In addition, faith, as opposed to reason, of course, is spontaneous. That is the heritage of Christianity. And Descartes is careful to insist that our knowledge of God is antecedent to his own existence, otherwise he is vulnerable to the charge that he created God and therefore liable to the charge of atheism.

Leibniz's monadic spontaneity

Metaphysically, Leibniz is an extreme, subjective idealist, as opposed to Descartes, who is a dualist. Although Leibniz does not *specifically* invoke synthetic *a priori* relations, it is his version of *spontaneity* that sparks its positive exploitation later in the idealist principles of Kant, Fichte, Schopenhauer, Husserl, and later in the Gallic version of Sartre. In Leibniz, the conceptual roots of spontaneity are clearly related to the twin Christian declarations of (a) God's creation of the world "out of nothing," *ex nihilo* and (b) the ethical doctrine of free will, as it continues to be recruited to account for the existence of sin and moral evil in mankind (Leibniz's *Theodicy*). But in Leibniz's theory, the emphasis on spontaneity is explicitly pressed into service as an *epistemic*—as opposed to a *theological* and/or an *ethical*—principle. Leibniz's form of subjective idealism maintains that only immaterial, active souls exist, namely God and human souls. Since the material external world does not exist, it follows that all activity must be generated by and contained within the soul. Spontaneity then becomes the soul's *sui generis*, *causa sui* activity, which is required in order to allow for his spiritual Monads to act completely from *within* the confines of their monadic existence, since each spiritual substance is metaphysically, unconditionally, and absolutely self-enclosed and above all "windowless." All monadic activity must not only arise from *within* the self, but it must also remain confined *inside*, *within* consciousness. This is the most explicit formulation of subjective idealism in Western philosophy. According to Leibniz, as opposed to Locke, the mind *always* thinks at some level. Locke believes that as matter can exist without motion, so the mind can exist without thought, e.g., in dreamless sleep and swoons. But for Leibniz, there are unconscious thoughts, *petit perceptions*, as well as reflexive self-conscious thoughts. And *if* the external world does not exist, *then* it necessarily follows that the activity of the soul can only occur spontaneously, from within its self. It cannot—in principle—be caused by external forces, since they simply do not exist. Further, the unity of self-consciousness, its ability to form conceptual *synthetic and presumably a priori relations*, can only occur in so far as it is dependent on its own spontaneous acts. And since only minds exist, then obviously these relational unities must arise *a priori*. As Professor Latta comments: *Freedom is Spontaneity + Intelligence.*

The intelligence alluded to is originally Aristotelean and directly constituted by his triadic distinctions of *dynamis* (possibility), *energeia* (actuality), and *entelecheia* (completion).

> Accordingly, Leibniz, following Aristotle, regards freedom as consisting essentially in *spontaneity* and intelligence. But intelligence is not to be interpreted merely as the abstract understanding of pure self-consciousness [per Descartes]: it includes every degree [as well as differing levels] of perception or representation. There is thus an infinite variety of degrees in freedom ... And as all Monads alike have *spontaneity* (for they unfold the whole of their life from within themselves), the degree of freedom belonging to any Monad depends on its degree of intelligence, that is to say, on the degree of clearness and distinctness of its perceptions. Similarly, in human beings, an action is free in proportion to the clearness and distinctness of the reasons which determinate it (italics mine).[7]

Precisely because (a) each soul Monad is a perfectly *sealed*, i.e. a self-contained, self-sufficient, self-conscious *substance*, internally consisting of (b) different levels of consciousness and numerous perceptions and relations that are (c) necessary and universal, i.e. *a priori*, as well as (d) informative, i.e. synthetic and (e) constitutive of the unity of self-consciousness; and *unless* (f) these epistemic conditions are met, then (g) human reflexion cannot exist. These implications will play out in Kant's own recruitment of spontaneity and we will see how critical all this is to his transcendental argument.

Similarly, for Aristotle, the "internal" *agency* of spontaneity can *only* arise from *within the Unmoved Mover*. Spontaneity is already embedded in Aristotle's self-generating twin conceptions of *dynamis* and *energeia*, as exemplified in the absolute self-containment of reflexive, self-conscious thought firmly ensconced within Aristotle's Unmoved Mover. By analogical argumentation, man's active consciousness is identical to that of the Unmoved Mover.

> Since, then, thought and the [conceptual] object of thought are not different in the case of things that have not matter, the divine thought and its [conceptual] object will be the same, i.e. the thinking will be one with the [conceptual] object of its thought. A

36 Consciousness, spontaneity, and *a priori* relations

further question is left—whether the object of the divine thought is composite [i.e. material and sensory]; for if it were, thought would change in passing from part to part of the whole. We answer that everything which has not matter is indivisible [i.e. simple, partless, immaterial]—as human thought, or rather the thought of composite [physical] beings, is in a certain period of time ... so throughout eternity is the thought which has *its self* for its [conceptual] object.

(*Meta,* 1074b-1075a; cf. 1072b)

Since "thought and the [conceptual] object of its thought" are *qualitatively* identical, i.e. immaterial, it follows that their unity directly derives from their shared immaterialist premise as well. The divine thought is eternal, i.e. non-temporal. In man, of course, his mortal nature compels him to live within and through immanent time-sequences, as well as through seemingly *external* empirical changes. Nevertheless, this critical passage in Aristotle functions as one of the most significant of all the principles in Western thought and it continually grounds metaphysical dualism (Aristotle), subjective idealism (Leibniz, Kant, Fichte, Schopenhauer?), and objective idealism (Hegel). The reflexive, conceptual thoughts referred to above, it should be noted, are immaterial *qualities* and in no sense should be taken to represent sensory *quantities.* Because Leibniz's paradigm of consciousness is *dynamic,* it follows that it is self-expressed through temporal manifestations. By contrast, the thought of the Unmoved is not in time; it is pure reflexivity. Metaphysically, for Aristotle, the Unmoved Mover—without Itself moving—moves everything else; it functions as a centering and guiding *"object of desire,"* as a "final cause" for man, and as it indirectly moves all fifty-five of the heavenly spheres in their perfectly circular orbits as well as everything below the ever-changing sublunar realm. This Aristotelian conception relates directly to man's *intentional* desire to attain a *final* purpose in the contemplation of God. But as we shall later document, it is also the incipient source for the intentionality of consciousness principle heralded by Brentano's scholastic theologians.

In *Hegel's Lectures on the History of Philosophy*, in his discussion of Aristotle's *Metaphysics*, he states:

Consciousness, spontaneity, and *a priori* relations   37

There are two leading forms, which Aristotle characterizes as that of potentiality (*dynamis*) and that of actuality (*energeia*) … free activity has its end in itself … All that is contains matter, it is true, all change demands a [physical] substratum to be effected by it; but because matter itself is only potentiality, and it is not actuality—which belongs to form—matter cannot truly exist without the activity of form (*Meta.*, VIII, 1, 2). With Aristotle, *dynamis* does not therefore mean force but rather capacity, which is not even undetermined possibility; *energeia* is, on the other hand, pure *spontaneity*.

(Hegel, *Lectures,* II, 138–139)

Hegel never denies the existence of a material universe. He only denies that it can be *known* without a mind. As a helpful hint to the reader, whenever Hegel discusses a philosopher, it worth looking at the corresponding article in his *Lectures*.

Energeia, spontaneity is the activity of potentiality (*dynamis*) realized. Just as in Aristotle's version of god, just so in Hegel's conception of human consciousness, both potentiality and actuality are spontaneously determinative. The analogy consists in the following. The Unmoved Mover is pure self-consciousness; nothing enters from without or leaves from within. And although all nature desires to be self-sufficient, the Unmoved Mover desires nothing. Its activity therefore must act spontaneously, from within. Man's self-consciousness, like the Unmoved Mover's, is reflexive and during certain moments of pure contemplative activity, it is self-generative. The relation between the active soul and its knowledge, between the subject and the conceptual object, the knower and the known, all occur within consciousness; and the relation between spontaneity and knowledge is essentially a synthetic *a priori* one. Since there is nothing coming in from without, from external sources, then everything must originate from within—and in Leibniz's case remain contained and confined subjectively within the mind. And, when we consider Aristotle's Unmoved Mover, as comparable to human thought, which is—during special human moments of consciousness—absolutely self-contained and self-sufficient, then the only activity that can conceivably *arise* in human consciousness must be spontaneously generated and arise *from within*—and for Leibniz

38 Consciousness, spontaneity, and *a priori* relations

remain there. Leibniz is arguing by extension; each Monad, each soul, each monadic consciousness consists of a spontaneously constituted sphere, a center, a circle of self-conscious activity. External causes are not only irrelevant and unnecessary; they cannot be conceptualized because the external world simply does not exist.

I am not, of course, suggesting Leibniz is right about the solitary existence of Monadic substances. Unlike Leibniz, I am arguing for metaphysical dualism. Essentially, then, Leibniz's version of subjective idealism proceeds by analogizing Aristotle's description of the *acts* and the *contents*, i.e. the conceptual "objects" in the thought of the Unmoved Mover, as applicable as well to human self-consciousness. Both Aristotle's God and Leibniz's Monads are absolutely self-contained. Since nothing possessed by the mind can enter from without and nothing can escape from within, it *necessarily* follows that all activity must "arise" or "emanate" (Plotinus?) from within, i.e. spontaneously. This is the grounding assumption of *all* subjective and objective idealisms, whether Leibnizian, Kantian, Fichtean, Hegelian, or Roycean.

For Leibniz, sensory perceptions are confused conceptions, which nevertheless allow for ideal and epistemic *relational* constructions. But freedom is secured when intelligence and reason are unencumbered and free, "determined" from within and not from without; when the soul acts independently of confused perceptions; then the soul is free as it formulates its own laws and self-consciously follows what it has created. As we shall see, both Rousseau and Kant will agree; man is only free when he self-consciously formulates the law and then obeys his own (presumably) rational law (Kant's principle of autonomy).

Kant's transcendental spontaneity

In the *Critique of Pure Reason*, Kant establishes an intrinsic constitutive connection between (1) spontaneous acts and its consequents (2a) synthetic a *priori* relational categories; (2b) the formation of immanent time-consciousness (*Critique*, A 99–104); and (2c) reflexive self-consciousness, more technically the transcendental unity of apperception, as distinguished from empirical perception (B 131–132), thus accounting for both the constitutive acts required for ordinary consciousness as well as Newtonian science. These "aspects" or "modes" of consciousness are only made possible because Kant's transcendental categories are anchored in acts of pure, i.e. non-empirical spontaneity. The following mentions of "spontaneity" are in the Analytic and the two Deductions, except for the last, which occurs in the Third Antinomy, in his Dialectic and discussion concerning noumenal freedom, where he clearly identifies spontaneity with man's free will.

In his commentary on Kant's ethics, Lewis White Beck uses the terms spontaneity and freedom interchangeably and throughout the text where clearly it functions as a noumenal "postulation." But, in the German text, "duty" replaces spontaneity. That is because the *Critique of Practical Reason*, unlike its predecessor, the *Critique of Pure Reason*, is transcendentally grounded, while the second *Critique* in effect exploits the "impure" Stoic notion of man's *sense of duty* to mankind in general. Meanwhile as late as 1790, in Kant's aesthetic treatise, he declares the following: "Now, if in the [aesthetic] judgment of taste, the imagination must be considered in its freedom, it is in the first place not regarded as reproductive [i.e. phenomenal] as it is subject to the laws of [empirical] association, but as productive and spontaneous," i.e. creative (*Critique of Judgment*, Section 22). So interestingly, spontaneity rules in the first and third *Critiques* but is absent in the second where it is replaced by the empirical *postulation* of Stoic "duty" and transcendent "free will."[8]

Accordingly, the important question arises whether the epistemic status of spontaneity is transcendental or noumenal. And the answer is that it is an immediate, creative, productive *transcendental* act, whereas the categories by contrast are mediate and relational. The categories, although relational, are not acts; they are pure "logical" forms. Thus, Kant credits spontaneity as the ultimate *triggering* agent or principle, which serves in creating—not causing—synthetic *a priori* relations. By contrast, empirical causes and their effects merely *appear* phenomenally, representationally as "objective," i.e., intersubjective experiences conditioning the cognitive possibility of achieving empirical "scientific facts."

In Josiah Royce's *The World and the Individual*, Lecture I, he confirms this Kantian thesis when he states, "Intelligent ideas [i.e. the categories] then, belong, so to speak, to the motor [i.e. active] side of your life rather than to the merely sensory. This is what Kant meant by the spontaneity of the understanding."[9]

40 Consciousness, spontaneity, and *a priori* relations

Although Kant would reject Plato's sensuously based example of color and extension as a synthetic *a priori* relation, rather seeing it as a contaminated, non-formal, impure, and therefore a merely contingent "association of empirical ideas," insufficient in providing any insight into the truly constitutive acts of consciousness, nevertheless, as we shall see, both Husserl and Sartre, from very different biases and perspectives —phenomenological and existential—will also cite Plato's color-extension example.

Fichte's absolute spontaneity

In Fichte's *Science of Knowledge*, he states, "we shall not merely argue here, but will cite the words of Kant himself." At B 132 he says: "But this representation ('I think') is an act of *spontaneity,* that is, it cannot be regarded as belonging to sensibility" (page 49). Consequently, while crediting Leibniz (pages 82–83), Fichte announces the following:

> The self's own positing of its self is thus its own pure activity. The *self posits its self,* and by virtue of this mere self-assertion it *exists;* and conversely, the self *exists* and *posits* its own existence by virtue of merely existing (sic). It is at once the agent and the product of its action; the active, and what the activity brings about; action and deed are one and the same, and hence the 'I am' expresses an Act, and the only one possible.[10]

The term spontaneity is invoked some twenty times throughout the text. Further, spontaneity is directly and intimately related to synthetic acts: "it is *determinant* insofar as it posits its self, through absolute spontaneity, in a determinate sphere among all those contained in the absolute totality of its realities" (page 135). Basically, Fichte's Ego is endowed with the ability, the power to *synthetically* create not only its self, but also a realm of "non-ego" objects, to thetically posit the *appearance* of an external world, as well as the presence of separate other-than-self-egos in order to operate ethically ("negation is determination," Spinoza). Explicitly following Kant,

> The thing is nothing else but *the totality of these relations united by the imagination,* and that all these relations together constitute

the thing; the object is surely the original synthesis of all these concepts.

(page 23; cf., 48, 111–113 and passim)

Indeed, in *The Vocation of Man*, in Book II, Fichte maintains that spontaneity can also generate the *appearance* of spatial extension by the relational ordering of the *minima sensibilia*—which includes the *minima visibilia* of sight and the *minima tangibilia* of touch. In short, the spontaneity of consciousness creates, produces, constitutes the entire panoramic *appearance* of space and time from simple, immaterial, unextended points and their ordering.

> This act of the mind is called thought; a word which I have hitherto employed; and it is said that thought takes place with spontaneity, in opposition to sensation, which is mere receptivity.[11]

And:

> I see clearly that I really perceive only my own state and not the object; that I neither see, feel, nor hear this object; but that, on the contrary, precisely there where the object should be, all sense, feeling and so forth comes to an end. Sensations, as *affections of my self,* have no extension whatever.

(page 50)

Again, these assertions can only be made if one assumes the validity of the simplicity premise and its epistemic force in the conceptual history of subjective idealism.

Hegel's *qualitative* spontaneity

One of Western philosophy's great divides within consciousness lies between its qualitative intensities versus its quantitative extensities. This distinction explicitly begins in Kant's first *Critique,* in his "table" of transcendental principles or judgments, when he prominently places the Axioms of Intuition as constitutive *extensive quantitative* magnitudes, as *spatial* "expanses" of objective units of measurement, and therefore as the essential elements for the formulation of

42 Consciousness, spontaneity, and *a priori* relations

Newtonian space (Kant, *CPR,* A 162=B 202 ff.), while, by contrast, he situates the Anticipations of Perception, as varying *intensive qualitative* "degrees" of subjective sensations, to a *relative*—but essential—secondary role (Kant, A 166=B 207 ff.). Both are, of course, required but the first applies to the realm of "science"" and the latter to the sphere personal "subjectivity." But as we shall see more fully in Chapter 4, Hegel will reverse their priority by favoring the *qualitative* aspects of Consciousness over the *quantitative* dimensions of Measurement, i.e. the empirical sciences. The reason for this is that Kant's interest in consciousness favors starting with a mature ego and the *quantitative aspects of Newtonian science*, whereas Hegel elects for a developmental, i.e. an "organic," dialectical beginning with the *qualitative modes consciousness* beginning with Sense-Certainty in the *Phenomenology* (1807) and the category of Being in the *Science of Logic* (1812–1816, 1931), while also appealing to spontaneous acts within consciousness. But the point is that this is not merely a distinction between the categories of Quality and Quantity *but a ranking*! The categories of quality will generate, develop the categories of "empirical science."

> This [active] movement of Mind, which in its [immaterial] simplicity gives itself its determinateness and hence self-identity, and which is thus the immanent self-development of the Notion—this movement is the Absolute Method of knowledge and at the same time the immanent soul of the Content of Knowledge.—It is I maintain, along this path of self-construction alone that Philosophy can become objective and demonstrated science.—It is after this fashion that I have tried to present consciousness in the *Phenomenology of Spirit.* Consciousness is Spirit as [determinate] knowing, which is concrete and engrossed in externality; but the *schema of movement* of this concrete knowing (like the development of all physical and intellectual life) depends entirely on the nature of the pure [conceptual] essentialities which make up the content of Logic [i.e. the *Science of Logic*]. Consciousness as manifested Spirit, which develops frees itself from its immediacy and external [sensory] concretions, becomes Pure Knowing, which takes as an object of its knowing those pure essentialities as they are in and for themselves. They are pure thought, Spirit thinking its own essence. Their *spontaneous* movement is their spiritual life: by

this movement [of thought] philosophy constitutes itself; and philosophy is just the exhibition of this movement (italic mine).[12]

For Hegel, human consciousness embarks on its voyage in search of knowledge with an inherent spontaneous movement; it is a continuous philosophical journey through manifold tributaries but always toward the same destination: the absolute Being of Consciousness. The sojourner restlessly seeks a port that ultimately can never be attained. But it is the spontaneous movement of Spirit that initiates the Odyssey. Its ultimate goal is to reach the superstructure of absolute knowledge and it all begins with the *Quality* of Being: "Quality therefore is immediate determinateness and, as such, is prior and must constitute the beginning" (page 92).

> Let space be one, and let time be one, and let consciousness be one; say how does one of these three Ones, purely and in itself, engender multiplicity? Each is one and no other; an indifference, a self-identity of space, time, and consciousness can be asserted; for these nouns [i.e. categories] still slumber in the infinite naught of the indeterminate [in the Parmenidian nothingness of consciousness], whence each and every determinate has yet to issue. What introduces finitude in these three infinities? What renders Space and Time, *a priori,* pregnant with Number and Measure and changes them into pure multiplicity; what causes pure *spontaneity* (the Ego) to oscillate?
>
> (*Logic*, I, 108)

In opposition to Kant, Hegel criticizes him for "presupposing" the categories, whereas by beginning with Sense-Certainty in the *Phenomenology*, Hegel has successfully executed a circular "presuppositional beginning," which will ultimately return to Itself as absolute Spirit (*Logic*, II, 484–485). All idealisms spontaneously *constitute* their formative relations and subprinciples *from within*; they are *not caused* by material conditions and/or the external motions of sensory matter resulting in physical sensations. This is Leibniz's intellectual heritage. All must be accounted for within self-consciousness (Kant) or Being/Consciousness (Hegel). But both Kant's transcendental

44 Consciousness, spontaneity, and *a priori* relations

synthetic *a priori* categories and Hegel's dialectical synthetic ones are created by the generative *acts of spontaneity.*

Schopenhauer's (spontaneous) irrational Will

The overriding principle in Schopenhauer's metaphysics and psychology is that there are insurmountable limits to man's self-knowledge. Following Kant, Schopenhauer posits the representational intuitions of space and time but reduces Kant's dozen categories of mediate relations to the sole category of an inflexible causality. Instead of his predecessor's "formal" categories, he confines the phenomenal world within the boundaries of the causal relation alone and a commitment to *both* a physical *and* a psychological determinism. He does not use the term spontaneity. However, his version of Kantian spontaneity is expressed through his treatment of a noumenal, subterranean irrational Will, which is in principle both (a) unpredictable and (b) inaccessible to human penetration. In describing subjective consciousness, he declares "the *will* is therefore the thing-in-itself proper." Schopenhauer's *subconscious* Will is absolutely indeterministic—as opposed to Freud's deterministic unconscious. It is like a magic lantern, a kaleidoscopic device that distorts all that it sees, feels, and erroneously thinks it knows.

> Just as a magic lantern shows many different pictures, but it is only one and the same flame that makes them all visible, so in all the many different phenomena which together fill the world or supplant one another in *successive* [phenomenal] events, it is only the *one will* that appears, and everything is its visibility, its objectivity; it remains unmoved in the midst of this change. It alone is the thing-in-itself; every object is phenomenon, to speak Kant's language of appearance.
>
> (*WWR*, I, 153)[13]

Again, the Will-in-Itself is blind, purposeless, irrational, and thus absolutely unknowable.

> [T]he will dispenses entirely with an ultimate aim or object. It always strives because striving is its ultimate nature to which no

Consciousness, spontaneity, and *a priori* relations 45

ultimate goal can put an end. Such striving is therefore incapable of final satisfaction; it can only be checked by hindrance but in itself it goes on forever. We saw this in the simplest of all natural phenomena, namely gravity, which does not cease to strive and press toward an *extensionless* central point, whose attainment would be the annihilation of itself and of matter; it would not cease even if the whole world were already rolled into a ball.

(*WWR*, I, 308; italic mine)

This passage demonstrates Schopenhauer's idealist metaphysical commitment to the simplicity premise and argument. Once more:

The world is my representation: this is a truth valid with reference to every living and knowing being, although man alone can bring it into self-conscious, abstract consciousness (first sentence of his magnus opus).

Even the natural forces of Newtonian gravity are subsumed and swallowed within the suctioning power of the immaterial metaphysical Will. For Schopenhauer, both man and the universe are through and through expressed by Will alone; but man can only *feel* the striving; he can never know it. All that man can know about his deeper self, if he is honest, is his own narcissistic egoism. This "egoism is in actuality the [spontaneous] starting-point of all conflict."

Therefore, everyone wants everything for himself, wants to possess, or at least control, everything, and would like to destroy whatever opposes him ... This disposition is *egoism,* which is essential to everything in nature. But it is precisely through egoism that the will's inner conflict with itself attains to such a fearful revelation ... Hence for him his own inner being and its preservation come before all others taken together. Everyone looks on his own death as the end of the world, whereas he hears about the death of his acquaintances as a matter of comparative indifference.

(*WWR*, 331–334; cf. 351–352)

This psychological starting point is the inheritor of Spinoza's *conatus* and the origin of Nietzsche's "will to power" principle. In punctuating this

46 Consciousness, spontaneity, and *a priori* relations

universal premise of self-centered egoism, he cites La Rochefoucauld's *maximes* and Hobbes' *bellum omnium contra omnes*, "a war of all against all," as examples of "an egoism peculiar to all." It follows, as Hobbes declares, that all human "life is solitary, poor, nasty, brutish and short" (*Leviathan*, Chapter 13). Schopenhauer's egoism will subsequently be transformed into Freud's narcissism. But the overall result of all this narcissistic egoism is obvious. For Schopenhauer human life is steeped in both painful *physical* miseries as well as in a pronounced susceptibility to gratuitous, i.e. malicious *moral* evil (*WWR*, I, 81).

> Hence, we are all innocent to begin with and this merely means that neither we nor others know the evil of our own nature. This only appears in the motives and only in the course of time do the motives appear in knowledge. Ultimately, we become acquainted with ourselves as quite different from what *a priori* we considered ourselves to be; and then we are alarmed at ourselves.
>
> (*WWR*, I, 296; cf. I, 325)

Schopenhauer's *noumenal* Will is intrinsically unknowable; it is rooted in *subconscious* acts; even adequate self-knowledge is a permanently closed door. By contrast, although Freud's *empirical* Id is *humanly* instinctual, yet it remains in principle psychologically accessible; human aggressions and lusts are psychologically "explainable" in human terms. Between Schopenhauer's subconscious and Freud's unconscious, there exists an insurmountable qualitative chasm. Both are *phenomenal* determinists, but *beneath, subterraneously*, Schopenhauer is a metaphysical indeterminist.

Schopenhauer, of course, is an atheist but he cites Augustine throughout his two volumes, and we recall that for the Saint man is innately evil, born in Original Sin (*WWR,* I, 405 ff). Positively citing Voltaire's comedic *Candide*, while criticizing Leibniz's misplaced optimism, Schopenhauer announces:

> But against the palpably sophistical proofs of Leibniz that this is the best of all possible worlds, we may even oppose seriously and honestly the proof that it is the *worst* of all possible worlds. For possible means not what we may picture in our imagination, but what can actually exist and last. Now this world is arranged as it

had to be if it were to be capable of continuing with great difficulty to exist; if it were a little worse, it would no longer be capable of continuing to exist. Consequently, since a worse world could not continue to exist, it is impossible; and thus, this world itself is the worst of all possible worlds.

(*WWR*, II, 583)

Schopenhauer preferred Kant's first edition of the *Critique*. In the Preface, Kant distinguishes two very different approaches to consciousness. First, in offering an "objective," formal treatment, which he will systematically unfold in the course of the Aesthetic and the Analytic. But he also hints that there is also a "hypothetical" underlying, hidden *subconscious* force below human awareness, which is hidden from any self-conscious access; a much deeper power that is responsible for "how the faculty of thought itself is possible?" (*Critique*, A xvii). Schopenhauer, who prefers the first edition over the second—perhaps because of this "hypothetical" hint—grasped this pregnant suggestion and ran with it. His evaluative conviction concerning man's evil led him to posit a dark, unknowable, inaccessible, and irretrievable irrational Will as the ultimate source of consciousness and indeed of all "realities," noumenal as well as phenomenal, intimate as well as scientific. In this fashion, the Will acts spontaneously, unpredictably in all the affairs of men. In effect, then, Schopenhauer exploits the principle of spontaneity as a metaphysical irrational Will, while simultaneously positing it as the hidden source for all the evils of human nature, both collectively and individually. Schopenhauer's entire metaphysical stance in regard to human evil can only work if the irrational Will is grounded in the *qualitative* features of an inaccessible human *subconscious*, as opposed to the crude and superficial *quantitative* natural and psychological motions prevalent in the human brain. Throughout the text, the brain is frequently cited. However,

Every explanation leading back to such a relation to which no Why can be further demanded, stops at an accepted *qualitas occulta;* but this is also the character of every force of nature. Every explanation of natural science must ultimately stop at such *qualitas occulta,* and thus at something wholly obscure.

(*WWR,* I, 180; cf. 122, 125)

48 Consciousness, spontaneity, and *a priori* relations

Several comments are in order. It is important to highlight the differences between Kant and Schopenhauer, while anticipating Freud. Kant's "hypothetical" subconscious would be epistemic, but unlikely transcendental and probably not accessible even indirectly. Schopenhauer's, however, is subconscious and in principle forever unknowable, irretrievable, while Freud's unconscious (like Leibniz's) is in principle accessible through recaptured memories, free association, and the interpretation of dreams.

Philosophers frequently distinguish physical pain from moral evil, both natural suffering and moral sin. For Schopenhauer, man and the world are gorged with both. In 1755, there was an earthquake on Saint Souls' Day in Lisbon that wiped out pretty much the entire city of 50,000 inhabitants and the question naturally arose how could an all-beneficent God allow this tragedy? For Schopenhauer both are not only possible but inevitable; together they are the result of an underlying reality, the noumenal Will.

But the metaphysical problem is that Schopenhauer *inconsistently* wishes to claim both that (a) man is evil, the inexplicable, "indirect result" of a noumenal irrational Will, *and* he also wants to defend (b) psychological determinism as an empirical science. *But if* man is psychological determined, *then* he cannot be responsible for the evil. *If* the irrational Will is the source of all human "evil," and human pain and suffering, *then* it is simply a natural phenomenon devoid of any ethical implications. In a chapter by Wayne Sheeks, these conflicting themes are highlighted.

> 1. The intellect cannot know the Will as the thing-in-itself by the usual way of acquiring knowledge. 2. The intellect can know the Will as the thing-in-itself. 3. The intellect is the servant of the Will. 4. The intellect can function free from service to the will. 5. The intellect can quiet and stifle the Will.[14]

Obviously, Schopenhauer can't have it both ways. *Either* man is evil by choice *or* he is determined by natural causes, but he *cannot* be both.

I am reminded of Joseph Conrad, who was influenced by Schopenhauer and who authored *Heart of Darkness*. There the dark and hidden motivations permeate the heart of man.

Husserl's phenomenological spontaneity

Edmund Husserl cites the validity of synthetic *a priori* meanings and relations, including not only its occurrences in "pure" synthetic *a priori* judgments, but also in instances of "material," i.e. sensuous, empirical judgments as well in order to support his stance that *both* pure *and* material synthetic *a priori* relations can be derived from their common fount through spontaneous acts of consciousness.

> It is then to this world, the world in which I find myself and which is also my world-about-me [i.e. my lived-world [*Lebenswelt*], that the complex forms of my manifold and shifting *spontaneities* of consciousness stand [synthetically] related: observing in the interests of research in the bringing of meaning into the conceptual form through description; comparing and distinguishing, collecting and counting, presupposing and inferring, the theorizing activity of consciousness. Related to it likewise are the diverse acts and states of sentiment and *disapproval,* joy and sorrow, desire and aversion, hope and fear, decision and action. All these together are sheer *acts* of the Ego, in which I become acquainted with the world as *immediately* [i.e. intuitively, eidetically] given me, through *spontaneous* tendencies to turn towards it and to grasp it, are included in the one Cartesian expression: Cogito.[15]

Not only is the wide variety of types of judgments lumped together but also their *qualitative* differences: "disapproval," for instance, is a *valuative* meaning. That is precisely the sort of *evaluative* judgment that the neurosciences reduce to merely subjective feelings. *But valuative and qualitative judgments are peculiar to man alone; essentially they define what it means to be a human being.*

For Husserl, in opposition to Kant, these spontaneous synthetic *a priori* meanings and relations can be either *material* and *sensory*, as well as *conceptual* and *formal*, with both open to eidetic insights and phenomenological descriptions.

> Among the most important challenges to Kant's interpretation of the synthetic *a priori* has been that issuing from the camp of Husserl and the phenomenologists. Their case is especially interesting

because, unlike the empiricists, who deny the occurrence of synthetic *a priori* judgments altogether, they contend that Kant has unduly *restricted* the range of such judgments. Far from applying only to the relatively narrow field which he granted them, there is an enormous range over which such judgments are possible; only because Kant misunderstood the nature of the synthetic *a priori* did he fail to grasp this. This was the conviction of Husserl himself, and it was endorsed by many of his disciples and collaborators, especially among the earlier phenomenologists.[16]

Further:

What Husserl is holding for is a necessity [and universality; the two marks of the *a priori*], which is based upon insight into essential connections between the *content* of subject and predicate. In this sense, the insight into necessity far from being a formal condition for the experience of objects, is rendered possible *through* experience of certain objects. He is, therefore, simply rejecting the Kantian view that universality and necessity cannot be founded on experience. When one judges, for example, that "Everything colored is extended," "Every tone has pitch," or "Nothing that is red is green," he is not uttering an analytic statement, and yet he is uttering a necessary [and universal] truth.

(ibid., 343)

Bergson's durational spontaneity

In his classic study, *Time and Free Will*, Bergson invokes the act of spontaneity frequently in order to fuse, to meld, to compress qualitative differences into an absolutely unextended and instantaneous temporal *duration*, into moments of pure freedom.[17] According to Bergson, consciousness displays a twofold distinction between extended quantities and unextended qualities. The extended dimensionalities of space versus the pure immanence of time-consciousness are absolute antitheses. For science, objective time is measured by the movement of objects through empty space, not dissimilar to the ancient Greek conceptions of the void and atomism. Additionally, quantitative factors both define and determine the causal chains ubiquitously

Consciousness, spontaneity, and *a priori* relations   51

manifest in the realm of science. But for Bergson, qualities permeate both human self-consciousness and freedom. They invade and inhabit the entire sphere of the "whole person." Pure freedom—duration—is intuitively, immediately "grasped," *apprehended*, as opposed to scientifically *comprehended.* The empirical and analytic disciplines, along with the abstractions of the understanding, are mediately disconnected from consciousness and the throbbing vibrancy of life.

> Regarded from this point of view, the idea of spontaneity is indisputably simpler than that of [material gravitational] inertia, since the second can be understood and defined only by means of the first, while the first is self-sufficient. For each of us has the immediate knowledge of his free spontaneity, without the notion of [gravitational] inertia having anything to do with this knowledge.
>
> (*TFW,* pages 141–142; cf. 217)

And he concludes that:

> It is now time to add that the relation of inner causality [i.e. spontaneity] is purely dynamic, and has no analogy with the relation of two external [physical] phenomena which cause one on the other ... Freedom is the concrete [immediacy of the] self to the act, which it performs. This relation is indefinable just because we *are* free. For we can analyze a thing, but not a process; we can break up extensity, but not duration. Or, if we persist in analyzing it, we unconsciously transform the process into a thing and duration into extensity. By the very fact of breaking up concrete [i.e. heterogeneous qualitative] time, we set out its moments in homogeneous space; in place of the doing we put the already done; and as we have begun by stereotyping the activity of the self, we see spontaneity settle down into inertia and freedom into necessity.
>
> (*WWR*, page 220)

Scientific space and time are quantitatively homogeneous, while duration is heterogeneous, each temporal moment unique unto itself. The past is gone while the future is not yet. Only the present exists on the precipice of sheer becoming and human *decisions; free choices* can only be consummated in pure duration.

52 Consciousness, spontaneity, and *a priori* relations

Sartre's existential spontaneity

In the *Transcendence of the Ego*, Sartre distinguishes his version of spontaneity from that of Brentano and Husserl both of whom posit an ego.

> His contention is precisely that there is no ego "in" or "behind" consciousness. There is only an ego *for* consciousness. The ego is "out there," in the world, an object among other objects. The question may now be asked: by whom or by what shall the *contents* of consciousness be fashioned into intended objects for consciousness, since this duty was performed in the phenomenology of Husserl by the transcendental ego? And the answer given by Sartre is that nothing shall constitute the contents of consciousness into intended objects, for the important reason that *consciousness has no contents.* All content is on the side of the object. Consciousness contains neither a transcendental ego nor anything else. It is simply spontaneity, a sheer activity transcending toward objects.[18]

In Descartes, the cogito is a pure contentless act; at other times, it appears to serve as a translucent medium in which objects simply appear in the manner of Sartre. And yet, Sartre requires "something" to perform the duties of epistemic unification.

> But if it is in the nature of the ego to be a dubitable [i.e. non-existent] object, it does not follow that the ego is a *hypothetical.* In fact, the ego is the spontaneous transcendent unification of our states and our actions (page 76; cf. 79, 80, 96–98). Indeed, the *me* [as object] can do nothing to this spontaneity, for *will is an object which constitutes itself for and by spontaneity* (page 99).

But the epistemic status of these detached objects floating around in an impersonal field of consciousness are no better than Hume's flux of impressions and bundle theory of the "self." Spontaneity, by definition, belongs to an active self, otherwise his paradigm of randomness is no better than the model offered by quantum mechanics.

Having denied all semblance of substantiality to the ego, nevertheless, half a dozen years later, Sartre attributes to spontaneity the ultimate power of unification, for it is exactly this spontaneity that

Consciousness, spontaneity, and *a priori* relations   53

is responsible for the *a priori* synthetic unification of Being and Consciousness, for the in-itself and the for itself, for *l'etre et le neant.*

> If the in-itself and the for-itself are two modalities of *being,* is there not a hiatus at the very core of being? And is its comprehension not severed into two incommunicable parts by the very fact that its extension is constituted by two radically heterogeneous classes? What is there in common between the being which is what it is, and the being which is what it is not, and which is not what it is [i.e. Spinoza and Hegel's "determination is negation"]? What can help us here, however, is the conclusion of our preceding inquiry. We have just shown in fact that the in-itself and the for-itself are not juxtaposed. Quite the contrary, the for-itself without the in-itself could not exist anymore than a color could exist without a form [i.e. extension] or a sound without pitch and without timbre [Plato's *Meno.*]. A consciousness which would be consciousness *of* nothing [i.e. the for-itself] would be an absolute nothing. But if consciousness is bound to the in-itself by an *internal* [synthetic] relation, doesn't this mean it is articulated with the in-itself so as to constitute a totality [i.e. an *a priori* synthetic unity], which would be given the name *being* or reality? Doubtless the for-itself is a nihilation but, as a nihilation it *is;* and it is an *a priori* unity with the in-itself.[19]

Although Kant would reject Plato's synthetic *a priori* example of the relation between color and shape, it is asserted by both Husserl and Sartre.

But this last description is fatally flawed and unpersuasive as Marjorie Grene has indicated for the reason she offers.

> It is precisely here, in founding philosophy on this immediate non-cognitive *cogito* that Sartre has floundered. He has cut off the bridge from thinker to thought [from self to object] and has insulated the empty self against any impact, except through negativity, from or on the world.[20]

As we shall see, this is precisely the error Descartes will avoid by invoking the mediacy of judgment in a later chapter. But once more, without a substantial self, loneliness is a meaningless concept.

54 Consciousness, spontaneity, and *a priori* relations

We can thus conclude that within a "history of ideas" context, both spontaneous and synthetic *a priori* relations and judgments have assumed an enormously significant role in Cartesian metaphysical dualism; in Leibnizian, Kantian, and Fichtean subjective idealism; in Hegelian objective idealism; in Husserlian phenomenology; in Bergsonian intuitional *duration*; as well as in Sartrean existentialism.

Lawrences' affective spontaneity

We began the chapter with a discussion of Plato's *Ion*. But not only does spontaneity assume a critical role in epistemic and ontological domains, it also functions as a pivotal agent in affective contexts as well. Although we can conceptually distinguish cognitive and emotional spontaneities, of course, they operate in unison or tandem. Spontaneity and creativity obviously assume a critical role in all the major cognitive areas of human endeavors and enterprises—including the intellectual; the scientific; the religious; the ethical; and the aesthetic—but also as well as in our affective acts and decisions (Bergson). Spontaneity isn't restricted solely to cognitive contexts alone. It also extends to our emotional situations as well. Consider, for example, its eruption in D. H. Lawrence's *Women in Love* as human passion finds its powerful expression within a synthetic *a priori* relation between volition and sensuality as it arises from a deeply subconscious source.

> "Spontaneity!" he cried. You and your spontaneity! You the most deliberate thing that ever existed and crawled. You'd be verily deliberately spontaneous—that's you. Because you want to have everything in your own volition, your deliberate voluntary consciousness. You want it all in that loathsome little skull of yours that ought to be cracked like a nut. For you'll be the same till it is cracked, like an insect in its skin. If one cracked your skull perhaps one might get a spontaneous woman out of you with real sensuality.[21]

This passage phenomenologically describes the act of spontaneity as it binds volition and passion; their intrinsic synthetic tension and interplay; and their temporal unification. Spontaneity, the noumenal Will, passion, volition, and anger all betray a subconscious source.

Consciousness, spontaneity, and *a priori* relations   55

And all the while, the emptiness, the nothingness of his loneliness surrounded him on silent haunches.

> He was suspended on the edge of a void, writhing. Whatever he thought of was the abyss—whether it were friends or strangers, or work or play, it all showed him only the same bottomless void, in which his heart swung perishing. There was no escape, there was nothing to grab hold of. He must writhe on the edge of a chasm, suspended on chains of invisible physical life ... the bottomless pit of nothingness. And he could not bear it. He was frightened deeply, and coldly, frightened in his soul.
>
> (Women in Love, 330)

Amazingly enough, *The Encyclopedia of Philosophy*, throughout its eight volumes and more than 5,000 pages, only cites spontaneity once and insignificantly enough it is in connection to Alexander Bain, the famous associationist psychologist, when he discusses the spontaneity of the eyes blinking in anticipation to being subjected to a bright light.

Notes

1   *The Collected Dialogues of Plato*, edited by Edith Hamilton and Huntington Cairns (New York: Pantheon, 1966), *Meno*, 75 b-c. Cf. Paul Shorey, *What Plato Said* (Chicago: University of Chicago Press, 1558), 98; and consult Plato's *Phaedrus* for a description of the highest form of divine madness, 245 ff.
2   In the Platonic dialogue, *Ion*, the rhapsode's poetic exegetical inspirations of Homer's epics are described as animated by acts of "spontaneity" and an enthusiasm akin to a divine madness. As Benjamin Jowett declares, "The elements of a true theory of poetry are contained in the notion that the poet is inspired. Genius is often said to be unconscious, or spontaneous, or a gift of nature: that 'genius is akin to madness' is a popular aphorism of modern time." translated by Benjamin Jowett; www.gutenberg.org.files/1635/1635-h.ht.; cf. Arthur Schopenhauer, *The World as Will and Representation*, translated by E. F. J. Payne (New York: Dover, 1969), I, 190, 191–192; II, 387–389; hereafter cited as Schopenhauer, *WWR*.
3   Lloyd, G. E. R., *Aristotle: The Growth & Structure of His Thought* (Cambridge: Cambridge University Press, 1968), 175 ff.; Wheelwright, Philip, *Aristotle* (New York: Odyssey Press, 1951, passim); and Randall, J. H., *Aristotle* (New York: Columbia University Press, 1965), 129–130, 171–172.

56   Consciousness, spontaneity, and *a priori* relations

4 Mijuskovic, Ben, "The Problem of Evil in Camus's *The Plague, Sophia*," 15:1 (1976); cf. Maquet, Albert, *Albert Camus, The Invincible Summer* (New York: George Braziller, 1958), 108–109. On Camus's *engagement* in the Resistance, see page 19. Camus's Master's thesis was on Plotinus and Augustine. For Plotinus, dark matter is evil while the One is pure perfection and goodness. And it is Augustine who virtually creates the "problem of evil." Thomas Aquinas, in his "Five Proofs for the Existence of God," cites "those men who argue that because evil exists, God cannot exist" before attacking the premise. Both Camus and Sartre are atheists.

5 Descartes, Rene, *Philosophical Works of Descartes*, translated by E. S. Haldane and C. R. T. Ross (New York: Dover, 1931).

6 Poulet, Georges, *Studies in Human Time* (New York: Harper Torchbooks, 1956), 52–54.

7 *Leibniz: The Monadology and Other Philosophical Writings*, translated and Introduction by Robert Latta (Oxford University Press, 1968), 145; cf. 39; see also the *Theodicy*, translated by E. M. Huggard (New York: Bobbs-Merrill, 1966), Section 288. For Aristotle, the spontaneity arises from his conceptions of *energeia* and *dynamis* in his *Metaphysics* and confer the self-contained thought of the Unmoved Mover (*Meta.*, 1075a); Cf. Bertrand Russell, *A Critical Exposition of the Philosophy of Leibniz* (London: George Allen & Unwin, 1956), 193; and C. A. Van Peursen, *A Guide to Leibniz's Philosophy* (New York: Dutton, 1970), 69, 90, 95. Cf. G. W. F. Hegel, *Lectures on the History of Philosophy* (London: Routledge and Kegan Paul, 1968); "With Aristotle's *dynamis* does not therefore mean force but rather capacity which is not even undetermined possibility; *energeia* is, on the other hand, pure spontaneous activity" (II, 137–139); hereafter cited as Hegel, *Lectures*. According to Henri Ellenberger, "It was Leibniz who proposed the first theory of the unconscious supported by purely psychological arguments. He pointed to the small perceptions, that is, those that are under the threshold of perception even though they play a great part in our mental life," *The Discovery of the Unconscious: The History and Evolution of Dynamic Psychiatry* (New York: Basic Books, 1970), 312; on Leibniz, cf. Hegel, *Lectures*, III, 330 ff; and cf. Mijuskovic, Ben, "The Simplicity Argument and the Unconscious: Plotinus, Cudworth, Leibniz, and Kant," *Philosophy and Theology*, 20:1&2 (2008).

8 Kant, Immanuel, *Critique of Pure Reason*, translated by Norman Kemp Smith (London: MacMillan, 1929). On spontaneity, see A 97; A 50=B 74, A 51=B 75, A 68=B 93, B 130–131, B 158 note and also A 446=B 474); and cf., B 430 and the Third Antinomy. Cf. Robert Pippin, "Kant on the Spontaneity of the Mind," *Canadian Journal of Philosophy*, 17:2 (1987), 449–475; Ben Mijuskovic, *Feeling Lonesome: The Philosophy and Psychology of Loneliness* (Santa Barbara, CA: Praeger, 2015), 62–63, 99,

155–156, 158; and Corey Dyck, "Spontaneity *before* the Critical Turn: The Spontaneity of the Mind in Crucious, the Pre-Critical Kant, and Tetens," *Journal of the History of Philosophy*, 54:4 (2016), 625–648. Clearly Kant's pre-critical dependence on spontaneity suggests Leibnizian affiliations. Also, spontaneity and synthesis are credited in connecting, in creating a "genuinely new addition" (*Critique*, A 9=B 13, A10= B14). In his commentary on Kant's ethical philosophy, Beck substitutes the term "spontaneity" for Kant's intuitive *immediacy* of the "sense of duty." But remember that the *Critique of Practical Reason* is not "pure." Lewis White Beck, *A Commentary on Kant's Critique of Practical Reason* (University of Chicago Press, 1960), passim; cf. also H. J. Paton, *The Categorical Imperative: A Study in Kant's Moral Philosophy* (New York: Harper Torchbooks, 1967), 142, 144. But significantly, Kant, in the *Critique of Judgment*, translated by J. H. Bernard (New York: Hafner, 1951, originally published in 1790) states: "Now if in the judgment of [aesthetic] taste the imagination must be considered in its freedom, it is in the first place not regarded as [empirically] reproductive, as it is subject to the laws of association, but productive [i.e., creative] and spontaneous" (Section 22); cf. also Section 78 where the term *Spontaneitat* is explicitly mentioned in the German edition. Spontaneity is always connected with the free play of the productive imagination, page 259. The point being that Kant continued to positively cite spontaneity to the very end.

9 Royce, Josiah, *The World and the Individual* (New York: Dover, 1959), 22; cf. Kant, A 9=B 13, A 10=B 14.

10 Fichte, J. G., *Science of Knowledge*, translated by Peter Heath and John Lachs (New York: Appleton-Century-Crofts, 1970), 97; "However we shall not merely argue here but will cite the words of Kant himself." At B 132 he says: "But this representation (I think) is an act of *spontaneity*, that is, it cannot be regarded as belonging to sensibility," 49; see also the many references to "absolute spontaneity" (135, 150, 188, 205, 233, 256); "the productive faculty is always the imagination" (205); and "from spontaneity alone arises consciousness" (page 262). Cf. Jon Mills, *The Unconscious Abyss: Hegel's Anticipations of Psychoanalysis* (Albany, NY: SUNY Press, 2002), 137–138.

11 Fichte, J. G., *The Vocation of Man*, translated by William Smith (La Salle, IL: Open Court, 1955), 57. Spontaneity is even credited with creating the appearances of both space and time by the acts of the productive imagination as it orders the minima *sensibilia* and *visibilia*, 43, 44, 47, 50, 68–69, 81. Fichte also posits spontaneity as a synthetic *a priori* act., pages 112–113.

12 Hegel, G. W. F., *Science of Logic*, translated by W. H. Johnston and L. G. Struthers (London: George Allen & Unwin, 1951), I, 36–37; italics mine. The best discussion of the opening section of the *Science of Logic*

58 Consciousness, spontaneity, and *a priori* relations

is by the Scottish Hegelian Edward Caird, in *Hegel* (Edinburgh and London: William Blackwood and Sons, MDCCCLXXXIII), 157 ff.

13 Schopenhauer, Arthur, *The World as Will and Representation*, translated by E. F. J. Payne (New York: Dover, 1969), WWR, I, 153; cf. "the Will does not have its seat in the brain," II, 246; hereafter cited as *WWR*. On Schopenhauer's influence on the Freudian Id, see R. K. Gupta, "Freud and Schopenhauer," in *Schopenhauer: His Achievement*, edited by Michael Fox (Sussex: Harvester Press, 1980); and cf. Henri Ellenberger, op. cit., 208–209, 311–312, 513, 537, 542, for Schopenhauer's influence on dynamic psychiatry and the unconscious.

14 Sheeks, Wayne, "Schopenhauer's Solution of the Will-Intellect Problem," in *Schopenhauer: His Achievement*, edited by Michael Fox (Sussex: Harvester Press, 1980), 70–71.

15 Husserl, Edmund, *Ideas: General Introduction to Pure Phenomenology* (New York: Collier Books, 1962), translated by W. R. Boyce Gibson), Chapter 28; cf. Chapters 16 and 23.

16 Gallagher, Kenneth, "Kant and Husserl on the Synthetic A Priori," *Kant Studien*, 63:3 (1972), 341.

17 Bergson, Henri, *Time and Free Will: An Essay on the Immediate Data of Consciousness*, translated by F. L Pogson (New York: Harper & Row, 1960); cf. Ben Mijuskovic, "The Simplicity Argument and Time in Schopenhauer and Bergson," *Schopenhauer Jahrbuch* (1977); cf. Ellenberger, op. cit. 321, 354–355, for Bergson's influential interest in the unconscious.

18 Sartre, Jean-Paul, *The Transcendence of the Ego*, translated by Forest Williams and Robert Fitzpatrick (NY: Noonday Press, 1962); translator's Introduction, 21.

19 Sartre, Jean-Paul, *Being and Nothingness: An Essay on Phenomenological Ontology*, translated by Hazel Barnes (New York: Washington Square Press, 1966), Conclusion, 760–761. Although Kant would reject Plato's synthetic *a priori* example of the relation between color and shape, it is asserted by both Husserl and Sartre. But he repeatedly inducts spontaneity throughout *The Transcendence of the Ego*, which is later replaced by the term of ek-stasis as meaning "standing *beyond* one's self, as *transcendent* to one's self, i.e., the act of intentionality in *Being and Nothingness.*" Ek-stasis means temporally nihilating the in-itself in the three dimensions of past, present, and future; in reflection as the for-itself tries to adopt an external point of view on itself; and in being-for-others and discovering that it has a Self, for-the-Other, a Self which it is without ever being able to know it or getting a hold of it (translator's comments (page 772).

20 Grene, Marjorie, *Sartre* (New York: New Viewpoints, 1973), 122 ff.

21 D. H. Lawrence, *Women in Love* (New York: Viking Press, 1950), 330. Cf. Eleanor Green, "Lawrence, Schopenhauer, and the Dual Nature of the Universe," *South Atlantic Bulletin*, 42:4 (1977), 36, 84–85, 92. Again

this universal theme is anticipated by Spinoza's concept of the *conatus,* "that by which each thing endeavors to persevere in its own being"; "a desire for self-preservation is the first law of nature" (Spinoza); as well as Schopenhauer's "Will to live," and Nietzsche's "will to power." Indeed, all things, from stones to souls, struggle to preserve their being in so far as it is in their power and all sexual fantasies are intrinsically spontaneous and inexplicable.

Chapter 3

Kant and Schopenhauer on reality

What are the limits of human knowledge regarding reality and the self? Kant and Schopenhauer both posit a noumenal realm of things-in-themselves beyond any possible human experience. And Kant speculates "hypothetically" that there is a subconscious that inexplicably underlies and acts below his transcendental faculties, while Schopenhauer posits an irrational unfathomable Will as the origin for man's evil. Accordingly, the question is how can we positively prove that such realities exist? And more specifically, how can we "explain" that during the Second World War, there were unimaginable atrocities conducted in the Nazi concentration camps: The question arises can there be a sufficient "explanation" for man's inhumanity to man?

The present chapter discusses the possible *limits* of human self-knowledge. It also addresses the efficacy of the alleged "hard" sciences, and more specifically their dependence on the "law of causality," which is collectively assumed by psychoanalysis, behavioral and cognitive psychology, and the current neurosciences and biosciences. The relevant issues lead us back to Kant and Schopenhauer's discussions of spontaneity and the irrational Will, respectively, as we explore their positions regarding their differing views concerning noumenal reality. And it concludes by contrasting both their theories with Freud's principle of the unconscious.

Kant and Schopenhauer contrast appearance and reality, phenomena and noumena, while Freud basically remains a phenomenalist, a theory which contends that both "reality" and the "ego" are *constructions* of empirical sense data. This allows Freud to investigate the mnemonic "unconscious" and gain insight into consciousness by implementing the methods of free association and the interpretation of dreams. But, if ultimate reality is *absolutely* unknowable, per Kant

DOI: 10.4324/9781003156130-4

and Schopenhauer, then it is epistemically worthless. For something to *be* a difference, it must conceivably *make* a difference. Thus, the first question is whether Kant can prove there is a noumenal realm? And the second question is whether Schopenhauer can prove that an Irrational Will "influences" not only natural phenomena but human thought and behavior as well?

Although Kant and Schopenhauer posit the existence of a noumenal realm of unknowable things-in-themselves, Kant's are relegated to a *transcendent*—as opposed to a transcenden*tal*—realm, which nevertheless allows Kant to postulate the existence of God, the freedom of the will, and the immortality of the soul for ethical purposes, while Schopenhauer assumes an unknowable *originating* power of an irrational Will, well *below* human awareness and experience, as a grounding base for human evil.

Kant, who is a Pietist, states he found it "necessary to deny knowledge in order to make room for faith" (*Critique*, B xxx), and he postulates the *conceivability*, the *possibility* of God's existence, free will, and the immortality of the soul in his *Critique of Practical Reason*. Assuming these grounds allow mankind to *hope* for the possibility of a deserved happiness in the afterlife.

But Kant is a psychological determinist. In the *Prolegomena to Any Future Metaphysics*, Sections 19 and 29, Kant draws a distinction between subjective judgments of perception and objective judgments of experience, but this distinction is abandoned in the second edition *Critique*. So, the critical question is whether there is any *proof* of a noumenal reality at all? And if there is not, then the postulations by both philosophers are without meaning.

There are two issues playing out. The first concerns the spontaneity of consciousness and the second the status of metaphysical reality. And there are two passages in Kant, which could stimulate such questions. First, his discussion of a possible hidden subconscious (*Critique*, A xvi-xvii), and his description "of the power of the imagination, a blind but indispensable function of the soul, without which, we should have no knowledge whatsoever, but of which we are scarcely ever conscious" (A 78=B 103). Thus, the question forcing itself before us is twofold. First, precisely what *is* the role of Kant's *epistemic* spontaneity—as opposed to its role *qua* free will in an *ethical* context? And how is Kant's epistemic spontaneity *qualitatively* different

62 Kant and Schopenhauer on reality

from Schopenhauer's irrational Will? One difference is that Kant's appears to be transcendental, whereas Schopenhauer's is universal and subterranean: it "grounds" both natural and human phenomena. In the previous chapter, I argued that Kant's spontaneity is transcendental; it is required in creating the categories, which in turn leads to the immanence of subjective time-consciousness, as opposed to scientific, objective time, and the unity of self-consciousness. And I think that is correct. But I also speculated that it influences Schopenhauer's irrational Will and that further he assigns a moral dimension by claiming it is the ultimate source of human evil.

For Kant, whereas spontaneity can assume both an epistemic and an ethical function, by contrast, for Schopenhauer the Will alone serves as an all-encompassing metaphysical force that somehow *indirectly* "influences," not only the causal order of natural events, but also all human intentions and behaviors. The reason for this divergence between the two thinkers is that their purposes are radically different. Schopenhauer's goal is to "anchor" the irrational Will as the ultimate but hidden source for the existence of human evil. But for Kant, spontaneity, along with the mediating faculty of the imagination, together function as an *epistemic* ground. In the previous chapter, I point out that Schopenhauer cannot have it both ways: both (a) as the subterranean operational force in man's motivation in committing gratuitous acts of evil, malicious evil for its own sake; and yet still defend (b) psychological determinism in the phenomenal world. He is, of course, free to *directly* connect the irrational Will to the inherent evil in human nature (Sheeks' discussion), but it cannot be *both* metaphysically irrational *and* empirically determined.

But the second issue is different. Are there two worlds or only one? Is there a noumenal (Kant) or a "primeval" realm? (Schopenhauer)? If the latter, why doesn't Schopenhauer simply declare that the *origin* of evil is in human nature (Augustine)?

Commentators have suggested that Kant nowhere demonstrates the existence of the thing-in-itself but rather that he merely *assumes* that "beyond" the phenomenal world of appearances, there is a noumenal realm. These interpreters have fallen into two classes. The first group maintains that perhaps there is only one world, that of appearances, of subjective representations, e.g., Berkeley's immaterialism; Hume's

Kant and Schopenhauer on reality   63

phenomenalism; the subjective idealism of Leibniz, Kant, Fichte; and objective idealists, Hegel.

In response, the second party objects to Kant that despite his conclusions offered in the Aesthetic, it is still conceivable that our subjective representations are, *in the same moment*, also comprehensions of an independent reality, independent in the sense that they would still exist without human consciousness. H. J. Paton belongs to the first group of interpreters and A. O. Lovejoy defends the second party. Thus, according to Paton, Kant has shown in the Aesthetic that space and time are human forms of sensibility, but he has not shown that, as such, there must be anything else beyond their representational powers.

> Now we cannot prove that sensuous intuition is the only possible kind of intuition. But equally we cannot prove that there is any other kind of intuition. The fact that in thinking we can entertain a concept in abstraction from sensibility is quite inconclusive. It still remains an open question whether our concept [of a noumenal realty] is not the mere form of a concept, whether in abstraction from sensibility it can have any object, and indeed whether in such abstraction any possible intuition remains at all.[1]

As Paton insists, this "seems to me to leave the question open whether we must still think that there is an unknown 'something,' a 'thing-in-itself,' a reality of which we know only the appearance to us" (ibid.).

The second group of Kantian critics point out that it may be the case, for aught we know, that the forms of subjective sensibility are *also*, in the same moment, the forms of reality itself. Kant, of course, does not *believe* this to be the actual state of affairs because it would *assume* unreflectively, dogmatically a miraculous Leibnizian pre-established harmony between the soul and the external world as well as a perfect synchronicity with other presumably distinct monadic souls. But still Kant has not shown that this could *not* be the case. Accordingly, Lovejoy states:

> Why should not space or time be both an idea with which our mind is furnished *a priori* and also in the same moment a real characteristic of the objective universe of *Dinge-an-sich*? In the 'Aesthetic' Kant is certainly constantly guilty of the paralogism of translating

the proposition, "Space is the subjective form of perception of phenomena of the external senses" into the proposition "Space is *nothing but* the subjective form of the perception of the phenomena of the external senses." To assert dogmatically the existence of space on both sides of the Kantian antithesis of thought and thing[-in-itself] would perhaps be to multiply entities beyond necessity. But the proof that such a hypothesis is not necessary is not equivalent to a proof that it is false or impossible or absurd. After all of Kant's reasoning upon this subject [in the Aesthetic], one is left with a fairly open option between two perfectly conceivable hypotheses, namely: Space and Time are exclusively subjective forms; or, space and time are at once subjective forms and objective realities. The latter hypothesis is the less simple of the two, it is less in conformity with the maxim known as "Ockham's razor;" but, on the other hand, it seems more natural and more congenial to the human intellect. Consequently, though admitting the validity of every one of Kant's reasoning in the Aesthetic, a fair observer ... could hardly say more than that, at the end of that part of the discussion, the conflict between critical idealism and physical realism has issued in a draw.[2]

To be sure, Kant offers *some* arguments for a noumenal reality elsewhere in the *Critique*. He states, for example, "that though we cannot *know* these objects as 'things-in-themselves,' we must yet be in a position at least to *think* [i.e., conceive] them as 'things-in-themselves'; otherwise we should be landed in the absurd conclusion that there can be an appearance without anything [i.e., noumenal] that appears." The postulation of things-in-themselves is not self-contradictory. But, of course, this argument is too facile; it merely depends on the analytic meaning of the term "appearance" and relies on the contention that it entails the correlative term "reality." Nevertheless, the important question remains: whether there is anything intrinsically, epistemically, or "psychologically" unknowable, a noumenal reality *beyond or beneath* Kant's and/or Schopenhauer's worlds independently of our subjective representations? Is there an active unattainable human consciousness somehow "operating" below and independently of our perceptions and our reflexive and intentional thoughts?

Kant has, however, a supportive defender, with whose views I agree, A. C. Ewing.

> The Antinomies, if valid, prove that space and time cannot be regarded as real without self-contradiction, and thus confirming the *Aesthetic*. They indeed, if valid, not only corroborate but extend the argument for the subjectivity of space and time by showing not merely that we cannot justify our belief in their independent existence, but that this independent existence is impossible, since it would lead to self-contradictions. Thus they supply something of which the lack has always been felt by critics of the *Aesthetic* and provide the only proof that reality cannot possibly be spatial and temporal [at once], as opposed to proofs that we cannot know reality to be so or justify the belief that reality is so.[3]

This is a critical answer because both empiricism and the neuroscience simply assume the reality of space, time—and matter—independently of human consciousness. But if both space and time are of human origin, then the entire superstructures of the various sciences are suspect. In other words, the proof that there are things-in-themselves does not require that it can be shown that noumenal realities actually do exist, but instead it rests upon proving that both space, time, and matter lead to insuperable difficulties and internal contradictions, namely they cannot be *both* infinite and finite; eternal and temporal, and indivisible and divisible. The premise supporting this argument is that reality, whatever it is, cannot be self-contradictory. Therefore, if the paradoxical puzzle cannot be solved, it demonstrates that there *is* or *are*, "beyond" or "below," the natural and social sciences a hidden, unreachable realm of "existence(s)." And if this is the case in natural sciences, how much more likely is likely to be the situation regarding human consciousness, in our presumed *psychological* "sciences"? At the center of these issues lies the possibility of a distinguishing principle, which not only separates consciousness and science, but also demonstrates that our human knowledge *concerning the self* is limited and unobtainable.

In the early part of the eighteenth-century, a brief pamphlet appeared bearing the descriptive title of *Clavis Universalis*, the universal key to true metaphysics.[4] In this brief treatise, Collier argues on behalf of a thoroughgoing metaphysical and epistemological idealism insisting that all external reality, including space, time, and matter are self-contradictory because reason can demonstrate that the alleged spatial world is *both* finite *and* infinite in space, *both* temporal *and* eternal, and matter is *both* indivisible and compound. It follows that an independent material world cannot exist "in itself." Concepts that produce contradictory conclusions cannot *both* be true or real independently of the mind.

> There can be no doubt that Collier's "third" and "fourth" arguments anticipate Kant's first and second antinomies. Just as Kant argues that "the world is not a whole existing in itself" from the fact that it can be proved to be both finite and infinite in time and in space, so Collier argues that "an external world must be both finite and infinite" and "that which is both finite and infinite is absolutely non-existent." And as Kant argues that material substances are "nothing outside our representations" from the fact that they can be shown to be both infinitely divisible and ultimately indivisible, so Collier affirms "in like manner as before, that external matter is both finitely and infinitely divisible, and, consequently that there is no such things as external matter.
>
> (ibid., page xxiv)

Collier's idealistic theory concerning matter was formulated at nearly the same time as Berkeley's immaterialism but in apparent independence. These inherent contradictions certainly led both Collier and Berkeley to God as the only reality. And, of course, ultimately this is Kant's position as well.

Just as Collier's arguments demonstrate that the very concept of matter leads to antinomial conclusions, so do Kant's in his first two Antinomies because if we take space and time *as if* they were things-in-themselves, *then* contradictory conclusions result. One cannot assert that space, time, and matter, are *both* finite and infinite, temporal and eternal, and indivisible and compound. But if this paradox cannot be resolved, then it follows that reality—as a scientific system—cannot be conceived as a coherent unity, as a whole. It would also follow that the foundations of Newtonian science would be questionable in terms of their "reality" but not in terms of Kant's subjective phenomenal appearances.

But let us turn to Kant's own declaration concerning his conclusion on the issue.

> Thus the antinomy of pure reason in its cosmological ideas [of space and time] vanishes when it is shown that it is merely dialectical, and that it is a conflict due to an illusion which arises from our applying to appearances that exist only in our representations, and, therefore, so far as they form a series, not otherwise than a successive regress, that ideas of absolute totality which holds only as a condition of things-in-themselves. From this antinomy we can, however, obtain, not indeed dogmatic, but a critical and doctrinal advantage. It affords indirect proof of the transcendental ideality of appearances—a proof which ought to convince any who may not be satisfied by the direct proof given in the Transcendental Aesthetic [that space and time are pure intuitional forms of sensibility]. This proof would consist in the following dilemma. If the world is a whole existing it itself, it is either finite or infinite. But both alternatives are false (as shown in the proofs of the antithesis and thesis respectively). It is therefore also false that the world ... is a [unified] whole existing in itself. From this it then follows that appearances in general are nothing outside our representations—which is just what is meant by their transcendental ideality.[5]

Unlike Collier and Berkeley, who directly "jump" from the soul to God, Kant interposes (1) a mediating bridge of transcendental categories grounding (2) the empirical sciences from (3) an independent material substance. But the reader may with interest revisit Kant's Fourth Paralogism, *Of Ideality*.

Closer to our own time, these sorts of paradoxical dilemmas have led Alfred North Whitehead to the following declaration in 1926.

> The stable foundations of physics have broken up. The old foundations of scientific thought are becoming unintelligible. Time, space matter, material, ether, electricity, mechanism, organism, configuration, structure, pattern, function, all require reinterpretation. What is the sense of talking about a mechanical explanation

68 Kant and Schopenhauer on reality

when you do not know what you mean by mechanics ... If science is not to degenerate into a medley of ad hoc hypotheses, it must become philosophical and must enter upon a thorough criticism of its own foundations.[6]

This was also Husserl's concern as well as his attack on "naturalism" and "psychologism," as he promotes his phenomenological methodology grounded in eidetic, immediate, intuitive insights (*Phenomenology and the Crisis of Philosophy*, 1911).

For neuroscience, all these mysteries are resolved and put aside by a reduction to the brain's neuronal causal interactions and electrical synapses.

The significance of this critical issue centers on its possible application to our initial opening question: Is spontaneity transcendental or noumenal? *If* it is noumenal, *then* scientists can simply deny its reality just as it is open for them to deny the freedom of the will with their counter-thesis of causal determinism. However, *if* it is transcendental, *then* it can serve in initiating and structuring the Kantian relational activities of consciousness, in grounding Kantian reflexivity and Husserlian intentionality, as not only possible but actual. But *if* it is entirely subconscious, *then* it is *in principle* (a) inaccessible to reflexive cognition and its acts are (b) psychologically unpredictable. If the "self" is as paradoxical as the "external" manifestations of space, time, and matter are, then there are ineluctable limits to epistemic self-knowledge. Does any self really know what it will do in extreme or even ordinary circumstances?

In the Preface to the first edition *Critique* (1781), Kant refers to his preliminary work on the Transcendental Analytic, between the time of his *Dissertation* of 1770 until the publication of the *Critique*, and more specifically to his efforts in regard to the *Deduction of the Pure Concepts of the Understanding*, in the following terms.

They are those which have cost me the greatest labour—labour, as I hope, not unrewarded. This enquiry, which is somewhat deeply grounded, has two sides. The one refers to the objects of pure understanding, and it is intended to expound and render intelligible the objective validity of its *a priori* concepts [the twelve categories]. It is therefore essential to my purposes. The other seeks to

Kant and Schopenhauer on reality   69

investigate pure understanding itself, its possibility and the cognitive faculties upon which it rests; and so deals with it in its subjective aspect. Although this latter exposition is of great importance for my chief purpose, it does not form an essential part of it. For the chief question is always simply this:—what and how much can the understanding and reason know apart from all experience? not:— how is the faculty of thought itself possible. The latter is, as it were, the search for the cause of a given effect, and to that extent somewhat hypothetical in character (though, as I shall show elsewhere, it is not really so).

(*Critique,* A xvi–xvii)

Thus, Kant separates the possibility of engaging in a "Subjective Deduction," which is speculative, "hypothetical" from his "Objective Deduction," which is "critical," "formal," "logical," and transcendental as it functions as the ground for Newtonian science and ordinary human consciousness.

According to Kemp Smith, in the last moments before publication, in his first Preface, "written on the very eve of the *Critique's* publication," Kant suspected an even deeper subjective force underlying consciousness generating cognitive dimensions hidden below his transcendental conditions as requiring an even deeper and more primordial investigation.

Now that he has shown that the consciousness of the self and consciousness of objects mutually condition one another, and that until both are attained neither is possible, *he can no longer regard the mind as even possibly conscious of the existence whereby experience is brought about. The activities generative of consciousness have to be recognized as themselves falling outside of it…* Only the finished products of some such activities, *not the activities themselves,* can be presented to consciousness; and only by general reasoning, inferential agencies lying *outside* the conscious field, can we hope to determine them. Now Kant appears to have been unwilling to regard the 'understanding' as ever unconscious of its activities. Why he was unwilling to do so, it does not seem possible to explain … In order to develop the distinction demanded by the new Critical attitude, he had therefore to introduce a new faculty, capable of taking over the activities recognized as *non-conscious*. For this purpose, he selected the imagination, giving to it the special title, *productive* imagination. The empirical reproductive processes hitherto once recognized by psychologists are, he declares, exhaustive of the nature of the imagination. It is also capable of *transcendental* activity ... The productive imagination is viewed as rendering possible the understanding, that is, the conscious apprehension of the *a priori* as an element embedded in [Newtonian] objective experience. Such apprehension is possible because in the *preconscious* elaboration of the given manifold the productive imagination has conformed to those *a priori* principles which the understanding demands for the possibility of its exercise in conscious apprehension. Productive [spontaneous? creative?] imagination acts in the manner required to yield experiences which are capable of relation to the unity of consciousness., i.e., of being found to conform to the unity of the categories [*Critique,* A 117–118]. *Why it should act in this manner cannot be explained;* but it is nonetheless, on Critical principles, a legitimate assumption, since only in so far as it does so can [a unified] experience, which *de facto* exists, be possible in any form. As a condition *sine qua non* of actual and possible experience, the existence of such a [subconscious] faculty is, Kant argues, a legitimate inference from the results of the transcendental deduction.[7]

If such a subconscious force exists, *then* it would be "below" or at least distinguishable from the Leibnizian and Freudian mnemonic unconscious. And could it point to Schopenhauer's purely irrational Will?

Kant never followed through on his promise to show how "thought itself" is possible independently of his transcendental investigations. His transcendental method is *indirect.* It analyzes the "conditions" for the *possibility* of thought but not thought itself. I have quoted this passage at length because what is at stake in all this is the distinction between empirical causes, transcendental acts, and the possibility of occult noumenal powers. In any case, clearly Kant was speculating about a possible subconscious and not simply a mnemonic unconscious in the manner of Leibniz and later Freud.

Up to this point, I have concentrated on Kant's speculations regarding the natural sciences and the self and have only peripherally mentioned

Schopenhauer's references to the evil in man. I believe Schopenhauer's conception of the irrational Will was directly influenced by Kant's speculations concerning the possibility of an underlying *epistemic* Subjective Deduction and that he recruited it when he formulated his own conception of an *ethical* evil Will. Kant's scientific limitations clearly inclined Schopenhauer to plunge deeper into consciousness and invoke his own conceptions of ultimate *qualitas occulta* so liberally sprinkled throughout his two volumes. And if we cannot plumb the depths of our physical world, what are our chances of insight and understanding into the more profound mysteries into *why* human beings act, feel, think, and behave the way they do? If all causes are intrinsically occult, then human self-knowledge will remain at an incredible disadvantage.

Schopenhauer sought to exploit Kant's two pillars of (a) an active spontaneity as well as (b) his references to an undeveloped subconscious force as the foundations for his own philosophical system. His phenomenal self is self-conscious but in the same moment absolutely oblivious to "our" underlying realities. Kant is concerned how we *know*. Schopenhauer is concerned *why* we act, the *motivational* aspects of our conduct, and his conclusion is that such knowledge is ultimately inaccessible; we are complete strangers to our selves, the underlying instinctual dark forces are cognitively irretrievable, subconscious, subterranean. Long before Freud, Schopenhauer recognized the force of sexual instincts and drives. But the critical difference between Kant and Schopenhauer is that Kant is concerned with cognitive, epistemic acts and contents constituting Newtonian science, while Schopenhauer is concerned with the origin of man's evil, as later exhibited in Freud's *Civilization and Its Discontents*, *Beyond the Pleasure Principle*, and *The Ego and the Id*, as he connects narcissism and sadism.[8]

Both Kant and Schopenhauer are physical and psychological determinists. The problem with Kant's determinism is that an act of ethical "free will" cannot under any circumstances—in principle—be observed in the phenomenal realm, not even a flicker! By the same token, neither can Schopenhauer's manifestations of an irrational Will betray a ripple on the relatively placid waters of consciousness. Schopenhauer's insistence that the Will's subterranean forces underlie natural phenomena as well seem to be simply a deference to Kant's

72 Kant and Schopenhauer on reality

noumenal realm, but his corresponding declaration that it somehow "applies" in accounting for man's predilection to foster evil seems problematic when he inconsistently argues that human actions are phenomenally determined. Rather the sad truth seems to be that the irrational Will is within human nature-in-itself, *within individuals.* In any case, Schopenhauer's perspective is spontaneously *affective*— as opposed to Kant's *epistemic* recruitment—as his strong moral pessimism wins out.

Notes

1 Paton, H. J, *Kant's Metaphysics of Experience* (New York: Humanities Press, 1965), II, 445. That Kant does not "prove" the existence of a noumenal realm is an interpretation also shared by Norman Kemp Smith in *A Commentary to Kant's Critique of Pure Reason* (New York: Humanities Press (1962), 406. Other commentators have simply rejected the distinction and have transformed Kant into a phenomenalist. Indeed, Kemp Smith emphasizes the internal strain running throughout the *Critique* between interpreters championing Kant's subjective idealism versus his phenomenalism for their own purposes. Cf. A. J. Ayer, *Language, Truth, and Logic* (New York: Dover, 1946), 34; P. F. Strawson: *The Bounds of Sense* (London: Methuen, 1960), 41–42; and Jonathan Bennett *Kant's Analytic* (Cambridge, 1966), 25–26. Kant's paradigm of a self-conscious substance is derived from Leibniz, who defines monads as simple, immaterial entities (*The Monadology*, Section 4; and the *Principles of Nature and Grace Founded on Reason* (Section 1 ff., 1714). Kant may not have had direct access to Leibniz's *Monadology*, but he did have access to the *New Essays Concerning Human Understanding.* According to Kant, both noumenal reality and the mind are unextended. Even sensations as pure *qualities* are *ideal* indivisible *minima sensibilia* (so Berkeley and Hume).
2 Lovejoy, A. O., *Essays Philosophical and Psychological in Honor of William James*, edited by "His Colleagues at Columbia University" (Longmans, Green, 1908), 281–282).
3 Ewing, A. C., *A Commentary to Kant's Critique of Pure Reason* (University of Chicago Press, 1967), 208–209.
4 Collier, Arthur, *Clavis Universalis; or, a new inquiry after the truth. Being a demonstration of the non-existence, or the impossibility of an external world*, edited by E. Bowman (Chicago: Open Court; 1909); originally published in London, 1713). Collier's study appeared along with Berkeley's *Dialogues* in a German translation by J. C. Eschenbach, under the title *Samlung der vornnehmsten Schriftsteller die Wirklichkeit ihren eigenes Korper und den Gnazen Korperwelt leugnen* (Rostock, 1756). Possibly Kant may have come across Collier's views in translation.

5 Kant, Immanuel, *Critique of Pure Reason*, translated by Norman Kemp-Smith (New York: Humanities, 1962), A 506=B 534.
6 Spiegelberg, Herbert, *The Phenomenological Movement: A Historical Introduction* (The Hague: Martinus Nijhoff, 1965), I, 178; quoted from A. N. Whitehead, *Science in the Modern World.*
7 Kemp Smith, Norman, *A Commentary to Kant's 'Critique of Pure Reason,'* (New York: Humanities Press, 1962), "The Later Stages of the Subjective Deduction," 263–265; cf. 273–274.
8 Schopenhauer, Arthur, *The World as Will and Representation*, translated by E. F. J. Payne (New York: Dover, 1969), I, 328–329, II, 237, 351, 452, 510 ff., 531 ff.; cf., R. K. Gupta, "Freud and Schopenhauer," in *Schopenhauer: His Achievement* (Sussex: Harvester Press, 1980); and Christopher Young and Andrew Brook, "Schopenhauer and Freud," http://http-server.carlton.ca/-abrook/SCHOPENY.hum

Chapter 4

Kant and Hegel on the quality-quantity distinction

The harbingers of the Scientific Revolution are Galileo, representing science, Descartes representing rationalism, and Locke representing empiricism. Science is based on (1) primary quantitative predicates: all matter is extended; sometimes motion is cited (but nature may be at rest, Aristotle, Descartes); solidity (but air and water recede when pushed, Henry More); divisibility; inertness (but gravity and electricity may be active); measurement; and above all causality leading to predictability. The attributes of material substances are objective and can be shared intersubjectively. Objects and events exist independently of human consciousness. (2) By contrast, secondary qualities are qualitatively, intimately subjective; they vary from person to person, e g. sensations and feelings; they are dependent upon human consciousness and more specifically on perception; they cannot be directly shared with an other consciousness. And (3), by contrast, tertiary qualities are qualitatively evaluative; all human beings throughout the entirety of their lives continuously engage in value judgments. Only human beings create, express, and intentionally pursue values. Man is the only creature who conceives of values. And only human beings can change their values at will.

Let me start by distinguishing three varieties of academic discipline. Intellectual History, for example, studies the politics, science, literature, and culture of a particular period, and it is interdisciplinary. By contrast, the History of Philosophy chronologically studies individual thinkers sequentially, for example the rationalism of Descartes, Spinoza, and Leibniz against the empiricism of Locke, Berkeley, and Hume in that order. But the History of Ideas studies special self-contained Ideas. For example, in A. O. Lovejoy's *The Great Chain of Being*, it is the continuity of the concept of Being that is traced throughout the ages and it is also interdisciplinary. It is now with this

DOI: 10.4324/9781003156130-5

Kant and Hegel on the quality-quantity distinction   75

latter emphasis in mind that I wish to violate chronology and present Hegel's *solution* to the Cartesian "problem of dualism" in this chapter, while I only later *introduce* the dynamics of the problem in Chapter 6 when I discuss Descartes. I assume this editorial liberty because the relation of Kant to Hegel highlights the crisis while the historical connection between Descartes and Hegel is much more tenuous. The reader is free, of course, to reverse their reading of the chapters. In any case, they are closely connected.

According to neuroscience, neurons are homogeneous; there is no distinction between quantitative and qualitative neurons. But for both dualism and idealism this difference is crucial in understanding human consciousness. Although both Kant and Hegel distinguish the categories of Quantity and Quality, Kant puts Quantity first and Hegel reverses the order. That is because Kant's emphasis is on defending Newtonian science and he *separates* the categories of Quantity and Quality, while Hegel *dialectically creates, generates, develops, and fashions the subservient secondary categories of quantities inherent in Science from within the primary qualitative categories of Self-Consciousness*. In the *Science of Logic*, Quality will seamlessly evolve into the quantitative modes of empirical science and measurement.

But I caution in advance that qualitative distinctions are irrelevant to the neuroscientific paradigm of the brain as they are reduced to the secondary, subjective qualities of sensations and feelings.

The claim that material objects can exist *independently* of any considerations concerning human consciousness is in principle untestable. How could one prove it? What sense is it to claim that the planet Mercury will continue to revolve around the sun if there were no human life in the universe? How could one confirm it?

In what follows, we will see why and how Kant and Hegel seek to negotiate between the quantitative predications supporting science and the quite different qualitative features and aspects prevalent within subjective and objective modes of reflexive consciousness.

The empirical sciences are predicated on the assumption that the world is regulated by external, physical *cause-and-effect* sequences. By contrast, dualists and idealists summon *constitutive* sensory contents, spontaneous acts, and the mediate structures of thought as substantially distinct and independent from an opposing material realm. This leads to the dualisms of mind and matter, soul and body. But a second critical divide distinguishes physical quantities from mental qualities. Philosophers separate primary quantities (generally matter and motion) from secondary qualities (sensations and feelings) but neglect to recognize the existence of tertiary qualities. It is more accurate to distinguish three elemental constituents, three different kinds of existents in consciousness: (a) primary *quantities*, accompanied by the essential predications of material extension; (b) secondary, subjective *qualities* related to the five senses and the feelings of pain and pleasure, joy and sorrow; and (c) tertiary qualities, which span a spectrum of *value judgments* regarding intelligence, beauty, goodness, cowardice, bravery, etc. Empiricists, however, reduce this third set of *judgments of quality* to the secondary ones of feelings of pleasure and pain. But if we fail to distinguish a tertiary set of judgmental *qualities* as significantly special, *as guiding determinants for human conduct*, we will be unable to understand why and how Hegel begins the *Phenomenology of Spirit* with the subjective category of Quality, with Sense-Certainty and ends with Absolute Knowing.[1] And in the *Science of Logic* he begins with the objective category of abstract Quality and ends with the values of the True and the Good.[2] Only if the beginning and the end are qualitatively compatible can Hegel achieve his desired presuppositionless beginning. While Hegel criticizes Kant's synthetic *a priori* categories as static and lifeless, Hegel's are "organically" dialectical and developmental.

We recall Plato's conflict between the Giants and the Gods, the Materialists and the Idealists, as it signals his radical distinctions between the quantitative features of matter, motion, and change, Heraclitus' flux, between the sensory world and the intellectual realm, and between lower and higher unifications of qualitative judgments of value as outlined in the *Republic's* Divided Line passage. Two thousand years later, Max Weber offers his admonition that the empirical sciences are constitutionally incapable of generating ethical values and I would add other values as well, including intellectual, aesthetic, etc. Science and Values are opposites, indeed often adversaries. Facts and Values dwell in separate universes.

To understand Hegel's idealism as a system, one must begin with the *Science of Logic* (1812–1816, 1831). Hegel initially planned to begin with the *Logic* before the *Phenomenology* (1807) and he was still working on the *Logic* when he died, still revising it, thereby underscoring his commitment to its importance above the more popular and earlier *Phenomenology.*

The *Phenomenology* begins with the *qualitative* modes and attitudes of subjective consciousness—with the categories of Sense-Certainty, Perception, Understanding, and the Lordship and Bondage conflict as they further develop toward fuller incorporative stages of Self-Consciousness concluding in Absolute Knowing. Correspondingly, the *Logic* begins with the abstract *qualitative* values of Speculative and Metaphysical Being. To his own query, "With what must science begin," Hegel's answer is with "Quality before Quantity," thus anticipating what he regards as the Newtonian limitations, abdications, and bankruptcies of the empirical sciences.

To advance beyond Hegel's more abstract expressions, I have found it helpful to read the *Logic* in partnership with his *Lectures on the History of Philosophy*, lectures which he revised nine times between 1805 and 1830.

The present chapter emphasizes the category of Quality in Hegel as he formulates it in the opening sections of his *Science of Logic*. For Hegel, the great divide in philosophy between soul and body cannot be successfully consummated without drawing upon the critical distinction and interplay between Quality and Quantity in consciousness as it contrasts with Kant's transcendental support for Newton's empirical science, while Hegel's commitment lies in an all-encompassing allegiance to an unswerving *speculative* idealism, as he rejects Kant's dualism between phenomenal science and noumenal reality.

There are two ways to begin a discussion concerning consciousness and reality. One can start with the natural world, with the material quantities populating our universe, which, according to Newtonian science, are mechanically regulated by the law of gravity and can be readily translated into the precise language of mathematical formulas originally instituted by God in Newton's case. During the advent of the Scientific Revolution, and especially for rationalist thinkers, God is credited as having formulated the laws of nature in accordance with the language of mathematics. That is why Kant, in the Aesthetic, begins with intuitional cognitions, with the "pure forms of sensibility," which readily translate into the *quantitative* measurements of space and time. Time especially presents problems for Kant; it both serves

78   Kant and Hegel on the quality-quantity distinction

as (a) an *a priori* pure form of sensibility, a *form* of intuition in the Aesthetic and yet (b) in the first edition Deduction, time-consciousness is the "product"—not cause—of a complex threefold synthetic *a priori* activity (A 97–104). Nevertheless, the intuitions serve as the initial building blocks for his transcendental establishment of an empirical, i.e., phenomenal science. In opposition to Kant's formal, mathematical intuitions of space, as we have already indicated, Hegel commences the *Phenomenology* with the *qualitative* immediacy of human consciousness, with the category of subjective Sense-Certainty.

Both Hume and Kant are convinced that the necessary establishment for Newtonian science must begin with a plausible philosophical account of the "objective" nature of space and time. In Hume's *Treatise of Human Nature*, astoundingly enough, he starts with the "*ideas of space and time*"—thereby violating his epistemic principle of always beginning with simple, i.e., unextended impressions. And Kant, in the Aesthetic, begins with a presupposed pure matrix, a schema of intuitional forms, which provide for the possible placement, structuring, organizing, and ordering for sensory quantitative measurements. The essence, the purpose of the physical sciences is above all to achieve causal predictions accompanied by exact, i.e., measurable outcomes, to structure mathematical laws *for quantitative predictions*. By contrast, Hegel starts with the most rudimentary *qualities* of consciousness, with an amorphous, indeterminate mass of *sensory* qualities in the *Phenomenology*. And in the *Science of Logic*, he initiates his system of *Logic*, his "science," with the most abstract concept of Being. These divergent directions between Kant and Hegel are grounded in the Quantity–Quality distinction.

Of course, for Kant and Hegel, both quantity and quality are constitutive categories of consciousness. But for Kant, following Aristotle's "clue," they are peremptorily *posited*, while in Hegel's case they need to be dialectically developed as Quality conceptually "evolves" into Quantity and both are subsumed by the qualitative objectivity of the Absolute Idea at end of the *Science of Logic*.

Kant begins with Newtonian science. His Table of Categories initiates a sharp conceptual distinction between the objective categories of Quantity (measurement) in contrast to the subjective ones of Quality (perception) (A 80=B 106), as he draws a strict separation between the principles of the Axioms of Intuition in contradistinction to the Anticipations of Perception.[3]

The principle of the Axioms is: "All intuitions are *extensive* [quantitative] magnitudes" and "Appearances, in their formal aspect, contain an intuition in space and time, which conditions them, one and all *a priori*" (A edition). And when he turns to the principle of the pure understanding, he states: "All appearances are, in their intuition, extensive magnitudes" (note added in B edition). This means that they are susceptible to mathematical, scientific, and objective measurements and in their "Appearances contain an intuition of space and time, which conditions them, one and all, *a priori.*" This characterization is also universally applicable to the *representations* of both "matter" and "motion," in short, the empirical sciences.

By contrast, the principle of the Anticipations of Perception is: "In all appearances, the real is the object of [human] sensation [i.e., perception] and exhibits *intensive* magnitude, that is [a non-mathematical] degree." Mental sensations are unextended. And further: The principle, which anticipates, all perceptions is as follows: "In all appearances, sensation and the *real,* as corresponding to the object, has an *intensive magnitude*, that is, a degree." While space and time are "extended" and hence mathematically measurable and objective, i.e., intersubjective, conceptually shared, by contrast sensations, *qua qualities,* are unextended, simple, and intensive—as opposed to extensive—and therefore purely subjective qualities. *Subjective* perceptions do not exhibit spatial characteristics. Colors, for example, are intensive qualities and not extensive quantities. And why? Because for idealism, the mind as an immaterial substance is unextended. Thus, spatial extension is epistemically merely an *appearance* within the mind.

In Kant's "critical"—as opposed to Hegel's "speculative"— philosophy, the Axioms essentially represent the undergirding for the empirical sciences, while the Anticipations (presumably) represent varying subjective sensory appearances, individual phenomenal perceptions in human subjects. Against Kant's Critical philosophy, however, Hegel's Speculative philosophy stands in direct opposition with its challenging qualitative metaphysical underpinnings. In this context, it is important once again to realize that for Hegel, "science" itself is metaphysical—and it will continue to be so in a fundamentally idealist respect.

80   Kant and Hegel on the quality-quantity distinction

In the *Phenomenology*, Hegel begins with the qualitative *immediacy* of consciousness, of "thises" and "nows," a burgeoning but internally restricted "sphere" of Sense-Certainty; similar to William James' illustration of infant consciousness as it "spontaneously lapses into the indiscriminating state of consciousness" amid "its pristine unity," the infant's "buzzing, blooming confusion" (William James, *Principles of Psychology*, Dover, 1950, I, 488). It is also comparable to Freud's description of infant consciousness as a boundless "oceanic feeling" (*Civilization and Its Discontents*, Part I).

> Mind is, therefore, in its every act only apprehending itself, and the aim of all genuine science [i.e., his *Science of Logic*] is just this; that mind shall recognize itself in everything in heaven and on earth. An out-and-out other simply does not exist for mind.
>
> (Philosophy of Mind, Section 377)

By "idealizing" Nature, by processing it through the activity of thought, however, Hegel distinguishes *within* Consciousness the category of Quality, describing it as *intensive*, *simple*, and *unextended*, and by opposing it to Quantity, which is both spatially *extensive* and hence mathematically "measurable." Quantity represents an objective, scientific, and inter-subjective "reality." Further, for Hegel, Quality is primary and original, while Quantity is secondary and derivative. But the critical issue for all forms or versions of idealism—as opposed to materialism—is that the activity of consciousness can only arise or emanate from *within* consciousness—it cannot be caused or instituted from the outside. The lifeless sensory contents of materialism are merely externally given. An illuminating passage appears in Hegel's *Logic*, when he contrasts the qualitative all-encompassing monistic Substance of Spinoza with the solitary subjectivism of the Leibnizian Monad (*Logic*, II, 167–172), as he seeks to dialectically, synthetically elevate, sublate both into a higher unity, indeed an *absolute* unity. As Hegel points out in his discussion, the term "emanation" has "Oriental," i.e., Egyptian and Plotinian connotations suggestive of a *temporal, emanative* "overflowing," whereas the *act* of spontaneity is essentially immediate, non-flowing (*Lectures*, II, 415). It sets thought in "motion," in "becoming" and it is opposed to gravitational motions, which serve as a symbolic passkey to Newtonian science.

Thus, Quality is the emanative starting point of the *Phenomenology of Spirit.*

> When I say 'quality,' I am saying simple determinateness; it is by quality that one existence is distinguished from another, or it *is* an existence; it is for itself; or it subsists through this [immaterial] simple oneness with itself. But it is thereby a thought. Comprehended in this is the fact that Being is Thought.
>
> (Preface to the *Phenomenology*, Section 54)

Hegel's concept of evolution is epistemic and societal. By contrast, Darwin's principle of the evolution of animal species followed three decades later.

That Consciousness and Being are identical, of course, is the hallmark of objective or absolute idealism. Hegel seeks to phenomenologically *describe*—rather than explain—*how* consciousness generates itself from "inside," from within the self, as it progressively leads to the formation of systems of ontological and epistemological categories; richer and more complex circles within larger circles. In this fashion, he transforms Kant's synthetic *a priori* categories by criticizing them as presupposed, assumed without proof, as static, non-developmental, and therefore dogmatically "superimposed" on a non-existent noumenal realm, while promoting his own dialectical version of synthetic unities. "Cognition is to be a progress or a development of distinctions … but Kant spared himself the trouble of demonstrating this veritably synthetic progress—the self-producing Notion" (*Logic*, II, 430–431). "Synthetic Cognition endeavors to form a Notion of what is, that is to seize the multiplicity of determinations in their unity" (II, 435).

> Consciousness, as manifested Spirit, which as it develops frees itself from its immediacy and external concretions, becomes Pure Knowing, which takes as an object of its knowing those pure essentialities as they are in and for themselves. They are pure thought. Spirit thinking its own essence. Their *spontaneous* [developmental] movement is their spiritual life: by this movement philosophy constitutes itself; and philosophy is just the exhibition of this movement.
>
> (*Logic*, I, 37; cf. 92, italic mine, and 108)

82 Kant and Hegel on the quality-quantity distinction

"Quality therefore is immediate determinateness and as such is prior and must constitute the beginning." It creatively, *sui generis* posits itself. It is the nature of the mind to be intrinsically self-assertive, i.e., spontaneous.

Epistemically there are only three philosophical paths forward: skepticism (nothing is true; all is appearance); empiricism (sensations are contingently associated and result in psychological *beliefs*); and rationalism (concepts are intrinsically synthetically related and thus produce coherent systems of knowledge). One of Hegel's primary watchwords is that "the rational is real and the real is rational," but obviously the relation between Consciousness and Being is more than a mere identity, a tautology, A=A. Consciousness and Being are two poles that are *a priori* synthetically related by the dialectical movements of thought.

Hegel studiously distances himself from Kant by characterizing his dialectical categories as developmental, while Kant's are criticized as rigidly frozen and formally vacuous. But I would still insist that for both the source of the *dynamism*—whether transcendental or dialectical—derives spontaneously from within the mind. This is the legacy of Leibniz and it heralds the absolute loneliness of the psyche, soul, mind, self, or ego.

Hegel accordingly begins the *Science of Logic* with the category of Quality by proclaiming that "Being indeterminate immediacy is Nothing" and yet that "Nothing *is* (or does exist)." For Hegel, every category pregnantly promises a continuous synthesizing mode of consciousness, a promise of things to come, of "becomings." Qualitative Being generates dialectical fruitions from within its own sphere of consciousness and internal resources. From this basic premise, Hegel concludes that "Pure Being and Nothing are, then, the Same" (*Logic*, I, 94–95). As William Wallace remarks in his article on Hegel in the *Encyclopedia Britannica* (1953 edition), "the proposition that Being and its contradictory, not-Being or Nothing, *mean* the same proved to be to most people a stumbling-block at the very door of the [Hegelian] system." For Hegel, the opening sections of the *Science of Logic* are dedicated to promoting the categories of Quality as the primary elements of Reality. And they strategically appear long *before* Quantity will be introduced as the method for the scientific measurement of "external" Being.

It has been traditional to interpret Hegel's meaning in these opening passages of the *Logic* as suggesting the following. Being is a word; as a mere concept, devoid of determinacy and empty of meaning, it is just an *empty* meaningless word. In this sense Being is nothing—but a word. On the other hand, Nothing is also a word, and as such it is *something*, a word—just as Being is a word. In a sense, then, Being and Nothing are the same; and since they are the same, they are interchangeable.

As a beginning, it has been criticized by subsequent philosophers as an attempt to generate existence from pure non-sensuous thought, to create a world of objects from a world of empty concepts and ideas. It is this view of Hegel which has caricatured him as the "armchair philosopher *par excellence*," as a thinker enclosed in his study, who "deduces" the external world of science and culture and religion and art through the sheer process of *his* personal thought alone. As Marx complains, Hegel begins with Consciousness rather than with the practical concerns of human Life and its economic circumstances, while he, Marx, proposes to turn Hegel upside down, on his head (*Theses on Feuerbach*). Similarly, existentialists since Kierkegaard and Nietzsche have been especially intolerant of this method of constructing reality from "whole cloth." It is as if Hegel has created a splendid and elaborate airy castle only to be forced to live outside of it in a humble hut (Kierkegaard); he has substituted a lifeless abstract system at the expense of concrete existential man.

Later philosophers, like Heidegger, have taken every available opportunity to attack the bankruptcy of the Hegelian system as ontologically sterile. One only needs to read Heidegger's *Introduction to Metaphysics* to discover a basic and general dissatisfaction with the entire Hegelian program.

> Of course, we can, seemingly with great astuteness and perspicacity, revive the old familiar argument to the effect that "being" is the most universal of concepts, that it covers anything and everything, even the nothing which also in the sense that it is thought or spoken, "is" something. Beyond the domain of this most universal concept "being," there is, in the strictest sense of the word, nothing more, on the basis of which being itself could be more closely determined. The concept of being is an ultimate. Moreover,

84 Kant and Hegel on the quality-quantity distinction

> there is a law of logic that says: the more comprehensive a concept is—and what could be more comprehensive than the concept of "being"?—the more indeterminate and empty is its content.[4]

The tendency to interpret Hegel's *Logic* as starting with a triad of mere words—Being<>Nothing<>Becoming—with empty, vacuous concepts and the abstractions of language, is symptomatic of the general reaction against "Hegelianism." Sartre begins his criticism of Hegel in terms of an opposition between "first principles." For Hegel, "essence precedes existence," while for Sartre individual "human existence precedes essence." The Individual before the System! Allegedly then, for Hegel, the abstract system is primary, while for existentialists it is the concrete individual.

> The "logic" of Hegel "moves" in its ponderous way from being and essence to actuality and existence—or, rather, from being and essence, through existence, to the higher synthesis of both in Mind (*Geist*) or Concept (*Begriff*). But ... the whole notion of starting with "pure being" and moving from it to existence is absurd. Out of pure logic, pure thought, can come no movement of any sort, for movement implies [empirical] change, time, nonbeing. Least of all can pure thought produce the movement of emergence into actuality, into the hard, resistant fact of what is forever distinct from the conveniently definable nature of what might be. The Hegelian play with essence is a pompous professorial game, great in pretensions but despicably trivial in its basic reality.[5]

William Barrett in his book, *Irrational Man*, echoes the same prejudice.

> Hegel's peculiar offence [against philosophy] lay not in following the tradition by leaving existence out of his system but rather in the way in which he tried to bring it in, having begun by excluding it. At law, I suppose, this would come under the heading of a compound felony. All his philosophical predecessors, or nearly all of them, had committed the theft, but poor Hegel was caught in the act of trying to restore the misappropriated article. The means he chose were most unfortunate; he tried to bring back existence through logic. Reason become omnipotent, would generate

existence out of itself! Even here, Hegel was not really flying in the face of tradition, as it might seem; he was only giving a more audacious expression to the over inflation of reason and its powers that had been the peculiar professional deformation of almost all earlier philosophers. This conjuring up of existence, like a rabbit out of a hat, Hegel accomplished by means of his famous dialectic … We begin, says Hegel, with the concept of Being, a pure empty concept without existence; this begets its opposite, Nothing, and out of the pair comes the mediating and reconciling concept that is the synthesis of both. This process goes on until at the proper stage of the dialectic we reach the level of Reality, which is to say Existence. The details of the derivation we need not go into here; what concerns us is the general structure of Hegel's argument, through which thought begets existence.[6]

Hegel's Science of Logic is his solution to Cartesian dualism. Hegel's never denies the existence of material substance, but he argues that empirical science is generated from the distinction between qualitative categories and *devolves* into an inferior *subdivision* of the *Logic* only to be validated as an essential contributor within the dialectical process. But whereas the narrative structure of the *Phenomenology* proceeds continuously from beginning to end, the *Logic* briefly introduces the categories of Being, Nothing, and Becoming, and then suddenly launches into a myriad of metaphysical premises and systems. So instead of dialectically progressing in his usual determinative fashion, Hegel unexpectedly overwhelms us with a compendious summary of metaphysical principles and conclusions from Parmenides' Being to a criticism of Kant's attack on the ontological argument. The reason for this abrupt change of proceeding is because he wished to be explicit about his pantheistic commitment before dying, as he unfolds the reciprocity between Being and Consciousness and the active qualitative movement of dialectical thought that the manifold categories of Quality and their involuted identification, their self-negation ("negation is determination"), and their continual self-resolving syntheses as spontaneously initiated Becoming—the temporal essence of consciousness—will be generated between Being and Nothing (*Logic*, I, 95). In Barrett's quote (above), we notice that it is initially thought that "begets" itself—and *not* "factual" existence. The categories are

86 Kant and Hegel on the quality-quantity distinction

spontaneously generated from within consciousness through its own internal resources; that is the ultimate controlling principle of idealism. Hegel's *Logic is Self*-Consciousness revealing its Self to its Self, *both* individually *and* absolutely, subjectively and objectively. Metaphysically there are only two opposing choices: science, unremitting chains of causality, uncompromising predictions, and quantitative measurements versus consciousness and qualitative realities and valuative distinctions. In what follows, it is critical to bear in mind that Hegel's extended discussion regarding the implicitude of the Substance of Quality will first concentrate on its aspects, attributes, predicates, or properties before turning to its dependent and subsequent treatment of *Quantitative* manifestations. Hegel thus initiates his work with the following declarative question: "With What Must Science [i.e., 'the *Logic*'] Begin?"

There are two possibilities: Either Newtonian science, which *assumes* absolute space, time, matter, motion, causality, universal gravity, and their quantitative manifestation; or with the gradations of qualitative Consciousness. The empirical sciences are a patchwork of distinct, disconnected separate "facts." But Hegel envisions a Platonic, comprehensive, and coherent system of interrelated and systematically graduated and ascending Truths (*Phenomenology*, Sections 798, 802). In the *Logic*, Hegel starts with defining Being, Nothing, and Becoming in three short paragraphs. Being *means* Consciousness. Being, however, is conceptually meaningless without its opposite concept: Nothing. "Negation is determination" (Spinoza, Sartre). Thus, Being spontaneously *begets* Nothing. Begets indicates a creative and temporal *movement* of thought—*both in the individual and in history.* Therefore, Becoming is the generation, the fruition of the temporal nature of human consciousness as Being dialectically *moves* to Nothing and into Becoming.

Hegel is a panentheist.[7] I began our discussion by emphasizing that Hegel's goal is to develop a *presuppositionless* philosophy, a "logical," internally consistent, and coherent system (*Logic*, II, 463, 484 ff.). That is why after his three short opening paragraphs, he launches into a compendious catalogue of historical metaphysical theories. Hegel does this because as a panentheist, he wishes to validate the multifaceted expressions that metaphysical Being has expressed from the age of Parmenides to Kant's *Critique.*

Kant and Hegel on the quality-quantity distinction 87

For Hegel, Quality is the *essence* of his *Science of Logic* but science as a rational self-understanding of its historical speculative development, the march of Consciousness toward the freedom of Spirit. Hegel's science seeks insight and understanding, not predictions. By contrast, empirical "objective" science deals with Quantity and its Measurements, the external, accidental features of Being. Consciousness, by contrast, *is* Quality. Hegel's beginning supports and reinforces my thesis that it is *only* human beings, in the entire realm of the animal kingdom, who are capable of drawing a distinction between empirical quantitative measures, e.g., extension and motion, versus (b) the tertiary qualitative aspects *of values* and making epistemic *judgments* concerning values. But again, values are not reducible to sensations and feelings or secondary quantities of feeling states. Immediate sensations and feelings are not cognitive judgments. It is valuative judgments that teleologically guide each human being—for better or for worse—in how to pursue one's life. Thus, Hegel offers a philosophical discussion of teleological theoretical speculations. In the three lengthy ensuing Observational notes (I, 95–116), Hegel highlights a dozen and more thinkers, each described with an identifying phrase or two, which can be readily matched with extensive discussions of their philosophies in his three volumes of *Lectures on the History of Philosophy*, e.g., Parmenides' conception of Being is cited (*Logic*, I, 95), and it corresponds to his fuller discussion in the *Lectures* (I, 239–240; 243–244, 252–254). In his expansive following notes, he discusses Kant and Fichte as well as many other metaphysicians, which match extended discussions throughout the three volumes of the *Lectures* corresponding to the host of the philosophers mentioned in the *Logic*. For example, the *Logic* cites the Nothingness of Buddhism and the void of Democritus (*Logic*, I, 95); the Stoic concept of reality as an "indeterminate Something," as well as Plotinus' "One," which are both amplified and further elucidated in the *Lectures* (II, 407, 410–413); he cites the "first" German philosopher, Jacob Boehme's "placing of the intellectual world within one's own mind and heart and experiencing and knowing and feeling one's own self-consciousness, all that was formerly conceived as Beyond" (Lectures, III, 191, 193), "God is and the Devil likewise" and "how the evil is present in God" (III, 194); Kant's criticism of the ontological proof for God's existence also appears in the *Logic* (I, 98–102), as it is foreshadowed by Anselm's version in the

88   Kant and Hegel on the quality-quantity distinction

Lectures (III, 62–65); Spinoza's pantheistic Substance is cited (*Logic*, I, 96) and it also appears in the *Lectures* (III, 156 ff.). Thus unless my interpretation of panentheism is accepted, it is difficult to understand why Hegel discusses Being, Nothing, and Becoming in three brief paragraphs (I, 94–95) and then immediately launches into four expansive explanatory notes, which begin by pointing out that the "simple [immaterial] idea of pure Being is first enunciated by Parmenides as the Absolute Truth" (I, 95) and concludes by attacking Kant's criticism of the ontological argument. In the Observations, Hegel compares the "abstract pantheism of the Eleatics," in all its essentials, to the "pantheism of Spinoza" (I, 96, cf. *Lectures*, III, 256–258). All this would be quite puzzling if we were to interpret the opening triad of Being<>Nothing<>Becoming as merely signifying three empty words. But even more mysterious would be Hegel's positive acceptance and defense of Anselm's ontological "proof," i.e., his intuitive certainty of God's existence and his following criticism of Kant's objection that "existence is not a predicate" (*Logic*, I, 98–102). Quite the contrary, "God's existence," his Being is the fullest of all categories. Hegel's disputation of Kant's refutation that the idea of God is distinct from his existence; and that "I can no more extract the existence of God from his essence than I can derive the actual existence of one hundred Thalers from their mere conception" is a failure. And Hegel also defends Anselm, whose "proof"—i.e., intuition—identifies essence and existence in *God and God alone* (*Logic*, I, 98–102; cf. *Lectures*, III, 62–66). Hegel, in the *Lectures*, devotes seven pages to Anselm, while Thomas' cosmological and teleological arguments are dispatched in a single page, which should offer a reliable clue to the respect in which Hegel upholds Anselm's version as it stresses the immediacy of Being and Consciousness. The intuitive nature of Being discloses the essential characteristic of the ontological argument that in God—and God alone—existence is immediately apprehended rather than mediately or discursively comprehended as they are in the cosmological and teleological proofs for His existence. In God, all his infinite attributes are identical precisely because of the perfect simplicity of His metaphysical nature.[8] Hegel's entire argumentative display is intended to show that what distinguishes human consciousness above everything else is its commitment to the *essentiality* of qualitative entities and values.

We need to remember that Hegel's official profession was to provide lectures in philosophy to university students and that these presentations could not sustain the depths of abstraction that permeate the *Science of Logic.* Accordingly, when Hegel speaks of Being in the introductory passages of the *Logic* (I, 94), he has in mind Anselm's conception, which he elaborately transforms into his own version of a pantheistic God. Hegel's Being, like Anselm's, is defined as "that Being greater than which none other can be conceived;" an infinite Being. Both Anselm and Descartes learned to amend their versions of their ontological proofs by insisting that to God and God *alone* necessary existence pertains. For Hegel, of course, although God is absolute simplicity, it is a simplicity, which is continually in the process of Becoming as it dialectically "moves" toward greater *qualitative* development and differentiation. In short, Hegel's Being is a developing immanent—not transcendent—Reality (*Logic* (I, 102; *Lectures*, III, 62–69).

But then of course, one wants to know in what sense Hegel intends that Being and Nothing are identical, if indeed Hegel means God. Again, the answer is to be found in the history of ideas. The Good, according to Plato, is non-being in the sense that it is *beyond* Being and Truth (*Republic* V, 509b; *Lectures*, II, 422; III, 63–64). By characterizing it in this manner, Plato clearly intends that the Good cannot be described in human terms, in language, discursively—and thus "nothing" can be said meaningfully of it; it is as good as "Nothing."[9] By the same token, the Stoics held that the most general concept, in terms of Being, is *Something*; and in that *meaning* it is beyond determinate existence. "The genus that which exists is general [i.e., universal] and has no term superior to it ... Certain of the Stoics regard the primary genus as even beyond that which exists ... and call it the Something."[10] Again, "the term *Something* is a more general one than that of *Reality,* for reality can be used only of incorporeal entities, while the genus Something, by contrast, includes everything." But that transcendence, that "beyondness" does not mean that Being is immune from development; Being is only the beginning of man's ongoing journey toward an ultimate Reality that he creates and fashions from his own consciousness.

With Philo of Judaea, the term *Something* takes on an even deeper significance; it implies the un-knowability and even the anonymity of

God that later was transformed into the negative theological writings of the Pseudo-Dionysious the Aeropagite (*Lectures*, III, 59, 76); and even the term "existence" is inapplicable to God. Drawing upon the Stoic distinction of *Something*, Philo declares that "Manna means Something, and that this is the most generic of all terms."[11] But what Philo means is that Manna, i.e., God, being the highest genus, has within Him no distinction of genus and species, for only that which is between the highest genus and the ultimate species has within it the distinction of genus and species, being the genus of that which is below it and the species of that which is above it. But since God is the highest genus, He has no distinction of genus and species; that is, He belongs to no class and hence we do not know *what* He is but only *that* He is. Philo is thus drawing on the Stoic teaching that the term *Something* is the most generic term of all and concludes that since God has no genus or species, we cannot know his essence, again He is unknowable. This conception of God was a landmark in the history of ideas in virtue of the explicitness of its formulation. No previous philosopher or theologian had achieved such precision in expressing the inconceivable and ineffable essence of God. Hegel, who was well versed in this historic tradition, makes it quite clear that for him Philo exemplifies the culmination of his predecessors. Accordingly Hegel begins his discussion of Philo by emphasizing the point we have just made above, namely that God's existence *can* be immediately, directly, intuitively known as a universal Quality but not *what* He *is*; His Essence but not His existence; that, however, allows for further human development.

> God cannot be discerned by the eye of the soul; the soul can only know *that* He is, and not *what* He is ... But the All is likewise, as with Parmenides, the abstract, because it is only substance, which remains empty beside that which fills it ... God himself in contrast to this, as the One, as such, is Pure Being (*to on*) only—an expression which Plato also used ... For as this Being God is only abstract existence, or only his own Notion; and it is quite true that the soul cannot perceive what this being is, since it is really only an empty abstraction. What can be perceived is that pure existence is only an abstraction and consequently a nothing, and not the true God. Of God as the One it may therefore be said that the only

thing perceived is that He does exist ... This *logos* is the innermost meaning of all Ideas.

(*Lectures*, II, 390–391)

The Greek and Jewish concept of the *logos*—the word—is the beginning of Hegel's *Science of Logic.* For Hegel, this is of course the mere beginning of philosophy. It is not knowledge of the "true God," the Absolute, for Philo's conception of God remains an empty abstraction. But in that capacity, it is not merely an empty word because it is rich in *implicit* meaning and it has a deeply speculative significance, which remains to be discovered and developed. Intellectually although the Idea of the Good may have been an abstraction, it nevertheless had great emotional significance. But in the beginning,

> it was Plato who grasped in all its truth Socrates' great principle that ultimate reality lies in consciousness, since according to him, the absolute is in thought, and all Reality is thought ... it is the thought which embraces in an absolute unity reality as well as thinking, the Notion and its reality in the movement of science as the [comprehensive] Idea of a scientific whole. While Socrates had comprehended the thought which is existent in and for itself, only as an object for self-conscious will, Plato forsook this narrow point of view and brought the merely abstract right of self-conscious thought, which Socrates had held and raised it to a principle, into the sphere of science [namely, into the realm of the *Science of Logic*].
>
> (*Lectures*, II, 1–2 ff.)

In his version of the Platonic Battle between the Gods and Giants, Hegel wishes to claim that modern philosophy begins not with Descartes, Hobbes, and Locke but with the theosophical writings of Jacob Boehme and the empiricism of Francis Bacon. And he credits Boehme with the "restlessness" of Quality as the origin of the activity of consciousness.

> "Qualation" or "Inqualation"—an expression belonging to Jacob Boehme's philosophy, a philosophy which goes deep but into a murky depth—means the movement of quality ... as it posits and

confirms itself in its negative nature (*quale*) as opposed to an other and is its own restlessness, so that it is only by means of a struggle that it produces and maintain itself.

(Logic, I, 127)

We also recall that Hegel cites the spontaneity of thought in the *Logic* (21.8, 21.83), whereas for materialism, empiricism, and the current neurosciences, of course, science begins with matter and motion and naively ends with matter and motion.

Panentheism is the beginning of the elevation of the spirit in conceiving everything in the universe to be animated by the Life of the Idea. Parmenides' Being as Quality is not simply a word; it is *Something qua Everything*! And through the ineffability of Nothingness it is the start, the movement of Heraclitus' Becoming—*the flux and start of time*. This is Hegel's foundational Panentheism.

The Good of Plato and the Unmoved Mover of Aristotle are both panentheistic "objects of desire" for the human soul, whether they are knowable in their true natures or not. What is at stake is that the *conceptual* "creation" of the world, *ex nihilo*, as viewed through the categories of the Hegelian *Logic* (I, 96–97), favors a panentheism grounded in *qualitative* distinctions beginning with Sense-Certainty in the *Phenomenology* and Being in the *Logic*. And further that dialectical synthetic *a priori movements* and *relations* within human consciousness, within thought will result in the "creation" of the world—through its immanent Becoming in an "eternal-temporal consciousness by knowing and including the world through its own reflexive activity." again, "Pure Being and pure Nothing are then the same; their truth is *not* either Being *or* Nothing, but that Being—not passes—but has already *passed* over into Nothing and Nothing into Being (*Logic*, 95) thus Becoming therefore a higher form of Being" (*Logic*, I, 95).

To reiterate, Hegel never denies the reality of a material world. In that regard, he is a traditional metaphysical dualist. There is an unfortunate misunderstanding regarding his idealism. It is epistemic not metaphysical in the manner of Berkeley. In *Hegel's Philosophy of Mind*, he announces the following.

External nature, too, like the mind, is rational, a divine representation of the Idea. But in Nature, the Idea appears in the element of asunderness, is external not only to mind but also to itself, precisely because it is external to that actual, self-existent inwardness which constitutes the essential nature of mind. This Notion of Nature which was already enunciated by the Greeks and quite familiar to them, is in complete agreement with our ordinary idea of Nature. We know that natural things are spatial and temporal, that in Nature one thing exists alongside another, that one thing follows another, in brief, in Nature all things are mutually external *ad infinitum;* further that matter, this universal basis of every existent form in Nature, not merely offers resistance to us, exists apart from our mind, but holds itself asunder against its own self, divides into concrete points, into material atoms, of which it is composed.[12]

Conclusion

I am aware that the interpretation I have offered for the beginning of the *Logic* differs markedly from the standard interpretation of that work. Thus, for instance, neither Stace,[13] Findlay,[14] Kaufman,[15] nor McTaggart,[16] adopt the line of thought which I have presented above. And yet, if one does not invoke such a position, I think it is difficult to absolve Hegel of the charges brought forward by existential critics. Consequently, I have contended that Hegel's Being cannot be understood apart from considering the qualitative issues broached in his observational remarks.

I would also argue that there are two senses of *presuppositionless* beginnings in Hegel. First in the *Phenomenology*, which starts with the immediacy of Consciousness—the indubitability of Sense-Certainty— not unlike Freud's "oceanic feeling" and secondly in the *Logic* in which Consciousness pursues its circular mission by starting with abstract Being and ending with the richness of the Absolute Idea (*Logic*, I, 82). In Being, the truth is merely implicit but in the Absolute Idea it has evolved to self-conscious fruition and a *relative* "completion," Minerva's owl. However, unless the truth were there already to begin with, in its primitive aspect, it could never attain its full fruition as anticipated in Hegel's organic metaphor of the bud, blossom, and fruit proposed in the *Phenomenology of Spirit*.

> Logic is the System of Pure Reason, as the Realm of Pure Thought. *This realm as it is, without husk in and for itself.* One may therefore express it thus: that this content shows forth *God as he is in his eternal essence before the creation of Nature and of a Finite Spirit.*

Traditional metaphysics merely conceived Being and the World, as mere abstractions, externally related, whereas their truth consists in their dynamic, organic, internal relationship. Put differently, and more concretely, and by contrast: For Hegel, as for Aristotle, God's knowledge is reflexive, self-conscious—but Aristotle's Being only knows its own thought and not the world (*Metaphysics*, 1075a), whereas Hegel's God in knowing its self knows the world.

But implicit within the category of Being is the entire richness of Western ontological metaphysics, as he informs us in his four appended Observational notes citing the philosophies of Parmenides and the Eleatics, the void of Democritus and the atomists, the flux of Herakleitos and Becoming, the Greek principle of ex *nihilo nihil fit* against Christianity's creative God, the pantheism of Spinoza, the rejection of Kant's critique of Anselm's ontological intuition. But whether Hegel begins with subjective consciousness in the *Phenomenology* or with speculative metaphysics in the *Logic*, in both instances, the category of Quality not only precedes but it also generates the scientific category of Quantity.

Finally, having completed his discussion of Quality in Section One of the *Logic*, his opening paragraph of Section Two announces that

> We have indicated the difference between Quantity and Quality. Quality is primary and immediate determinateness; quantity is such determinateness as has become indifferent to Being [i.e., reality].
>
> (II, 198)

Consciousness *is* first and foremost qualitative Being. Try to imagine the infant in his crib measuring its dimensions. Quality is incipient Spirit spontaneous and pregnant as it points to infinite fulfillments. Hegel's Qualitative Being and pantheism fits as a hand in a glove. The owl of Minerva is perched on a branch surveying what has already passed. Hegel's "science" is concentrated on insight and understanding and not predictions. By contrast, Neuroscience is Quantity, Magnitude, and Measurement and has not conceptually progressed beyond the age of Leucippus and Democritus.

> Philosophy concerns itself only with the glory of the Idea mirroring itself in the History of the World. Philosophy escapes from the weary strife of passions that agitate the surface of society into the calm regions of [Aristotelian] contemplation; that which interests it is the recognition of the process of development, which the Idea has passed through in realizing itself— i.e., the Idea of Freedom, whose reality is the consciousness of Freedom. That the History of the World, with all its changing scenes which its annals present, is this process of development and the realization of Spirit—this is the true *Theodicae,* the justification of God in History. Only *this* insight can reconcile Spirit with the History of the World.[17]

A practical application

According to Hegel, the empirical sciences are permeated by quantities and measurements. But science and quantity *alone* can never generate the qualitative judgments of *ethical* values. Hegel, more than any other philosopher, except possibly Plato, brought into prominence the contrast between science and values. Perhaps Plato's Battle between the Giants and the Gods finds its most dramatic application in ethical values. For example, in an article, I offer an exhaustive matrix of quantitative and qualitative principles, criteria, and meanings, from Relativism (the Sophists to Ayer) and Absolutism, including Rationalism (Plato to Kant); Empiricism (Aristotle to Hume); Fideism (Augustine to Kierkegaard); and Existentialism (Sartre to Tillich).[18]

Finally, for Hegel, the qualitative value of human loneliness, what loneliness *means*, is described in the section on the Unhappy Consciousness as it portrays the individual's wretched religious self-alienation from other selves as well as from the entirety of human community (*Phenomenology,* Sections 207 ff.). Hegel's descriptive juxtaposition in these passages takes the form of man's estrangement

96 Kant and Hegel on the quality-quantity distinction

from God, as well as from the Greek communal consciousness, as instantiated by the unhappiness of the Jewish religion and the monastic Christian consciousness. It serves as a paradigm of man separated from his fellow man.

> The unhappy consciousness is the fundamental theme of the *Phenomenology*. Consciousness as such is in principle always unhappy consciousness, for it has not yet reached the concrete identity of certainty and truth, and therefore it aims at something beyond itself. The happy consciousness is either a naïve consciousness, which is not yet aware of its misfortune, or a consciousness that has overcome its [lonely] duality and discovered a unity beyond separation. For this reason, we find the [universal] theme of the unhappy consciousness present in various forms throughout the *Phenomenology* ... This subjectivity must discover its own inadequacy and experience the pain of the self that fails to reach unity with itself.[19]

Oedipus' search for the self begins outwardly only to be painfully turned inwardly, Odysseus' voyage home is equally fraught with uncertainty and danger. The Socratic command to "Know thyself" is neither an easy nor a painless adventure.

Notes

1 Hegel, G. W. F., *Phenomenology of Spirit*, translated by A. V. Miller (Oxford: Clarendon Press, 1977).
2 Hegel, G. W. F., *Science of Logic*, translated by W. H. Johnston and L. G. Struthers (London: George Allen & Unwin, 1951), I, 82; II, 469 ff., 484 ff.; hereafter cited as *Logic*. Only if the qualitative beginning and its ends are identical can Hegel achieve his goal of attaining a presuppositionless circular philosophy. The coherence theory strives for truth as it seeks a complete *internal* consistency. A helpful summation in understanding the "greater" *Logic* is by consulting the "lesser" one.

> Each of the three spheres of the logical idea proves to be a systematic whole of thought-forms and a phase of the Absolute. This is the case with Being, containing the three grades of quality, quantity, and measure. Quality is, in the first place, the character identical with being; so identical, that a thing ceases to be what it is, if it loses its quality.

Kant and Hegel on the quality-quantity distinction   97

Quantity, on the contrary, is the character external to being, and does not affect being at all, *The Logic of Hegel,* translated by William Wallace, (Oxford University Press, 1959), 157.

3 Kant, Immanuel, *Critique of Pure Reason,* translated by Norman Kemp Smith (London: Macmillan, 1958), A 162=B 202 ff.

4 Heidegger, Martin, *An Introduction to Metaphysics,* translated by Ralph Manheim (New Haven, CT: Yale University Press, 1959), 40; cf. 75–76, 78–79, 93, 122, 178–180, 187 ff. Heidegger, of course, believes the very opposite to be true. Being is the fullest and most determinate concept wherein truth resides waiting to be uncovered and disclosed; *aletheia* or truth is the unconcealment of Being.

5 Grene, Marjorie, *Introduction to Existentialism* (Chicago: University of Chicago Press, 1958), xi.

6 Barrett, William, *Irrational Man: A Study in Existential Philosophy* (New York: Doubleday, 1962), 159–160. Similarly, Nietzsche complains that for Hegel that "which is last, thinnest, and emptiest is put first," as the concept of God is, through "the brain affliction of sick web-spinners" (from *The Twilight of the Idols,* translated by Walter Kaufman (New York: Viking Press, 1954), 481–482.

7 "Modern panentheism conceives of God as eternal-temporal conscious-ness knowing and including the world in his own actuality but not in his essence," Charles Hartshorne and William Reese, *Philosophers Speak of God* (University of Chicago Press, 1953), 234, 266, 269, 291, 358–359, 360; cf. Jacob Loewenberg, *Hegel's Phenomenology: Dialogues in the Life of Mind* (La Salle, IL: Open Court, 1965), 348–350; Walter Kaufman, Cf. *Hegel: A Reinterpretation, Texts, and Commentary* (New York: Doubleday, 1965), 294; Harold Henry Joachim, a Hegelian, in *The Nature of Truth* (Oxford: Clarendon Press), defends the coherence theory of truth; he is best known for his commentary on Spinoza's pantheism; G. H. R. Parkinson, "Hegel, Pantheism and Spinoza, *Journal of the History of Ideas,* 38:3 (1977); and John McTaggart and Ellis McTaggart, *A Commentary on Hegel's Logic* (New York: Russell & Russell, 1964) as the authors describe the dialectical progress from Quality to Quantity to Measure; see also *Hegel's Lectures on the History of Philosophy,* translated by E. S. Haldane and Frances Simpson (London: Routledge, 1968) discussion of Spinoza, III, 256 ff. But that Hegel is aware of this possible criticism is evident from his discussion of the objections made against Proclus, which he admires because of his insight into the dialectical method; *Lectures,* II, 435–437 and *Lectures,* III, 62–68, where Hegel once again defends Anselm's intuitional ontological "proof." In a similar fashion, both Anselm and Descartes learned to amend the first versions of their inferential onto-logical arguments—actually intuitions—by insisting that to God and God

98 Kant and Hegel on the quality-quantity distinction

alone *necessary* existence pertains, which protects the ontological intuition from Gaunilon's criticism of a "perfect island" and Kant's objection that existence is not a predicate. Finally, whereas Kant was quite explicit about his belief in the immortality of the soul, Hegel makes no such avowal.

8 Wolfson, H. A., *The Philosophy of Spinoza* (Cambridge, MA: Meridian, 1958), I, 119 ff., 154 ff. The "problem of divine attributes" is how can God be absolute simplicity and unity if He has manifold and indeed infinite attributes? It is because of his immaterial essence; the utter simplicity of his nature; He is not extended in space or time. The "problem of divine attributes" in relation to God is solved because again in God—and God alone—His absolute simplicity guarantees a perfect unity and identity; all His attributes are as one. Conceptually this will be the same *principle of simplicity* that supports the thesis of the "unity of consciousness" in man. Concepts being ideal or immaterial they can be compressively unified into a single unity. Cf.

9 Taylor, A. E., *Plato: The Man and His Works* (New York: Meridian, 1960), 231; cf. W. T. Stace, *The Philosophy of Hegel: A Systematic Exposition* (New York: Dover, 1955), "Thought is a spontaneous operation of the mind which works up the raw material of sensation into knowledge. All this, says Kant, has been universally admitted ever since the time of Plato" (page 37).

10 Von Arnim, H., *Stoicorum verterum fragmenta* (Leipzig, 1905–1924); Alexander Aphrodisias, II, 329; and Seneca, II, 332; cf. Hegel, *Logic,* 95–96.

11 Wolfson, H. A., *Philo: Foundations of Religious Philosophy in Judaism, Christianity, and Islam* (Cambridge, MA: Harvard University Press, 1962), 109 ff.; cf. Hegel, *Lectures:* "the First is the abstract, the unknown, the nameless," II, 390–394; see ibid., 95, 104. Again, God is said to be absolute simplicity in his essential nature in virtue of his immateriality. Cf. Plato, *Republic*, II, 380d; Aristotle, *Metaphysics*, XII, Ch. 9.

12 *Hegel's Philosophy of Mind*, Being Part Three of the Encyclopaedia of the Philosophical Sciences (1830), translated by William Wallace (Oxford: Clarendon Press, 1971), 9. Cf. pages 11, 14, 31, 34,111; Hegel was sympathetic to Anton Mesmer's experiments on the brain (115 ff.) and was personally concerned because both his sister Christianne and his friend Holderlin were afflicted with schizophrenia.

13 Stace, W. T., *The Philosophy of Hegel* (New York: Dover, 1955).

14 Findlay, J. N., *The Philosophy of Hegel* (Collier, 1966).

15 Kaufman, Walter, *Hegel: A Reinterpretation* (Anchor, 1966).

16 McTaggart, J. M. and McTaggart, E., *A Commentary on Hegel's Logic* (Russell, 1964); and J. McTaggart, Ellis, "Hegel's Treatment of the Categories of Quality," 504 ff., *Mind*, www.jestor.org/stable/2248570

17 Hegel, G. W. F., *The Philosophy of History*, translated by J. Sibree, 1956), 457, concluding paragraph.
18 Mijuskovic, Ben, "Ethical Principles, Criteria and the Meaning of Life," *Journal of Thought*, 40:4 (2005).
19 Hyppolite, Jean, *Genesis and Structure of Hegel's Phenomenology of Spirit*, translated by Samuel Cherniak and John Heckman ((Evanston, IL: Northwestern University Press, 1974), 190.

Chapter 5

The science of determinism and the consciousness of freedom

One of the most basic controversies between idealism and science revolves around the issue of freedom versus determinism pitting the doctrines of epistemic spontaneity, ethical free will, and reflexive self-consciousness, i.e., Kant's autonomous freedom, against the inflexible laws of physical and psychological determinism. In opposition, I wish to offer three perspectives on freedom that challenge the scientific dogma that human actions are enchained by unyielding causal laws. Determinism and value judgments are antithetical just as the principles of sociological relativism and qualitative epistemic and ethical judgments are.

In Pre-Socratic philosophy, according to Leucippus and Democritus, and later Lucretius and the Epicureans, a spatial void is posited as a primary quasi-substance in-itself devoid of physical objects or events. By contrast, both matter and motion consist of movements, collisions, and accordingly account for the infinite and continuous reconfigurations of atomic particles as they travel through the endless emptiness of space. The primary premise in classical atomism is the impossibility of *qualitative* change because the atoms are uniformly homogeneous. For Democritus, the material interactions are mechanically determined, whereas for Epicurus there are instances of chance, of random "swerves," in the moving trajectories of atoms and therefore a certain "indeterminism," including human events, which may account for a (questionable) sense of ethical freedom.

Interestingly, during the 1930s, a group of neuroscientists, including Rudolph Carnap, Moritz Schlick, Otto Neurath, and others, the Vienna Circle of philosophers, sought to apply Heisenberg's indeterminism or uncertainty principle, namely that quantum physics is in

DOI: 10.4324/9781003156130-6

principle unable to predict *both* the velocity *and* the position of sub-atomic particles (Zeno's paradox), to the brain and therefore there are theoretical limitations in predicting human behavior. At best, all we can muster are statistical probabilities. Inducted as an argument for ethical freedom, it woefully failed to account for moral responsibility, since the "agent" would be oblivious to what s/he would do next.

In the seventeenth century, however, Hobbes' reductive materialism is correspondingly deterministic as it presents an "associationist" psychological view. For Hobbes, however, an immaterial soul is a contradiction in terms; all that exists is matter plus motion. Our sensations are the result of physical objects impinging on our animal bodies. In turn, these motions *cause* sensations, ideas, and/or "phantasms," i.e., appearances (presumably via the brain, which he does not mention). Thus, all motions are generated by one body moving against another. Animal and human sensation is the result of the motion of objects moving through a spatial medium (usually air), which in turn then strikes receptive bodily, sensory organs (*De Corpore*, 25.2). The animal body resists the outward motions and pushes back as it reacts. This results in the illusion that the object is external as physical matter strikes and intrudes against the animal body. The sensations, however, are one and all appearances. The eye does not see objects; it sees colors, i.e., subjective *appearances.* Only moving bodies cause effects and every effect is the result of the causal motion of some *other* body. A physical object is a cause "not because it is a body but because it is ... so moved" (*De Corpore*, 9.3). And therefore "All changes are causally explained in terms of the motions of bodies."[1] Hobbes is also an early exponent of the psychological principle of the "association of ideas." For example, if someone utters the phrase, "thirty pieces of silver," the listener imagines the betrayal of Christ. Ideas become connected by repetition. Hobbes, however, is not strictly speaking a behaviorist because he acknowledges an "introspective" element in consciousness, an awareness of ideas as mental, non-reductive, and non-eliminable entities, which he calls phantasms, sensations, or ideas indifferently. Hobbes thus defines the imagination in terms of "decaying sensations." Nevertheless, what is being denied, of course, are self-conscious reflexions. There is only matter, motion, animal bodies, sensations, phantasms, and nothing else. This is precisely the same paradigm of

102 Determinism and the consciousness of freedom

cognitive awareness offered by behavioral psychology, the current neurosciences, and the evolutionary Darwinian biosciences.

According to our current neurosciences, the composition of *single, basically atomic neurons* in the brain become physically grouped together, they contiguously touch each other, and when they are electrically charged, they set in motion the adjoining neurons resulting in causal synapses in the brain. But synapses are not relations; they are merely electrically charged physical motions, like turning on a light bulb. Physical motions in the environment are identified as the causes resulting in sensations and feelings that are then assigned, identified with the body's behavioral responses and the brain's re-actions. Further, the effects can be traced back to the brain by an electro-encephalograph and charted and "assigned" to specific locations of brain cells as the source of the re-action. The emotion of fear is then interpreted in terms of physiological responses, a rapid heartbeat, sweating palms, etc. For the neuroscientist, the colonies of brain cells consist of identifiable cellular groupings causing behavioral re-actions and re-sponses. Both (a) the distinct external object as well as (b) the brain is situated in the external world. There is only one world—not two. But the metaphors are the same now as in Hobbes' paradigm, which harks back to the theories of Leucippus and Democritus. This same model is also readily applicable to the causal stimulus>response paradigm promoted by cognitive behavioral psychology and again both are compatible with Hobbes' seventeenth-century *explanations*—and predictions—as all three versions serve in defending physical and psychological determinism. According to Hobbes, all human endeavors are controlled by a single motivational principle: self-preservation, self-interest, or egoism.

But, during the time of Descartes, Hobbes, and Locke, Newtonian gravitational forces were not yet visible on the horizons of scientific thought. Prior to Newton, the predication of motion was not attributed to the universal law of gravity and electrical forces but rather to the weight of bodies, to a "natural fall or movement" of objects moving through space. We also recall the "scientific" acceptance of Aristotle's claim that matter's natural state consists of *both* motion *and* "rest," i.e., inertness and that ultimately it is the Unmoved Mover alone, as an "object" of desire, which causes the circular movement of the intelligible heavenly spheres, as well as all things inanimate and animate

Determinism and the consciousness of freedom   103

below the sublunar realm, as it moves everything, material and immaterial, toward a "final cause." All these metaphors are in the process of being challenged and rejected by the Scientific Revolution as the paradigm of mechanism wins the day over teleology. The issue then becomes whether any notion of *freedom* can be preserved, if all reality is reduced to causal material forces?

But embedded in Western thought, there is an argument for freedom, which asserts the reflexive activity of self-conscious thought, when our historical and conceptual scene radically shifts in the eighteenth century with Rousseau's conception of freedom.

> The doctrine of autonomy was only anticipated by Rousseau, for only Rousseau saw the essential connection between freedom and law, while others in the eighteenth century saw law only as a restriction on freedom. Though Rousseau worked out their essential connection only in politics and had his doctrine adopted there with little change by Kant, the doctrine of self-government through law by free citizens is deepened into a moral and metaphysical doctrine by Kant. With Rousseau, Kant can then say that obedience to a law that one has himself [self-consciously, rationally] prescribed is the only real freedom.[2]

In Western thought, there are two distinct conceptions of freedom: doing as you *please* or doing as you *should.* For Hobbes, and by extension the neurosciences, physical "freedom" is conceived as an unimpeded movement, freedom from external restraints. For example, a river is free if it can overflow its banks. Hobbes and the neurosciences applaud the first formulation and Rousseau and Kant champion the second, while Hegel will offer an expanded version of the latter.

Kant's first principle of moral, i.e., ethical *intentionality*, in opposition to Bentham and Mills' premise grounded in utilitarian *consequences*, is steeped in good intentions; an act is good even if the consequences fail. Kant's synthetic *a priori* formulation of the categorical imperative consists in doing as you should; doing your duty: "Always act so that the principle of your action [your subjective will] can become [an objective] universal law legislating for all rational beings in any conceivable universe" (Kant believed that there may be other rational beings elsewhere in the universe.) Contemporary commentators during his time compared this to the Stoic conception of universal ethical duties toward all mankind. Kant's version, however, is considerably more sophisticated. His moral command is constituted as a synthetic *a priori* relation unifying the subjective will to the objective moral law. Kant's third formulation advocating for human freedom then follows: "Man is free when he conceives the law and freely follows his own law"; this judgment forms Kant's principle of autonomy, i.e., self-legislation. Accordingly, this conception serves as a distinct formulation of the principle of rational freedom.

Beck also mentions "political freedom." There is a famous statement in Hegel when he observes that historically the ancient Persians believed that only one man is free; the Greeks that some are free; but the Germans that all men are free. For Hegel, it is philosophy alone that sets the collective human Spirit free. His entire philosophy can be described as the Spirit's rational unfolding of the discoveries of its own self-conscious historical realization of that freedom.

> The only Thought which Philosophy brings with it to the contemplation of History, is the simple conception of *Reason;* that Reason is the Sovereign of the World; that the history of the world, therefore, presents us with a [self-conscious] rational process.[3]

And further that:

> The History of the World is none other than the progress of the consciousness of Freedom, which history brings with the [political] fact that the Eastern nations knew that only *One* is Free; the Greek and Roman World, that *some* are Free; the German World knows that *All* are Free.
>
> (Hegel, ibid., 19)

We also saw this play out in Hegel's dialectical movement of thought generating the empirical categories of Quantity from the internal resources of its own *qualitative* distinctions.

Hegel rejects Kant's *postulation* of a noumenal principle of ethical autonomy, that man can be transcendently free, *a priori* rationally free because for Hegel the categorical imperative is fatally flawed due to its noumenal heritage. Hegel's argument for freedom is radically

Determinism and the consciousness of freedom   105

different. Freedom exists in *this* world and it is based solely on the activity of reflexive self-consciousness, as it endows the human Spirit. Hegel seeks to rationally *demonstrate*—rather than simply *assume*—human freedom as a gratuitous "postulation" in the manner of Kant. In the *Phenomenology*, in the section on the Understanding, Hegel criticizes the insufficiency of natural gravitational and electrical forces to be causally explanatory in addressing the transition from perception to empirical science. Rather Newtonian gravity symbolizes the inadequacies of the scientific method in relation to the freedom of Spirit.

Instead, Hegel's argument will draw on the principle of the unity of self-consciousness developed in Aristotle's *Metaphysics*, 1075a. The thinking self and the *conceptual* object of its activity are *both* congruently and reciprocally mental, ideal—*both* the act *and* its content(s). Consequently, they can be merged, fused, and unified because they are both immaterial, "spiritual" elements, while sharing in the dual activity of Self-Consciousness. In turn this unity and identity of the act of thinking with the content of its own thoughts, of subject and object, of knower and known is metaphorically represented for Hegel by the symbol of a circle, a unity, a beginning which returns upon itself and is self-contained, self-sufficient, and therefore free. This principle writ large symbolizes Plato's coherence theory. It is independent of all material conditions. Gravity is composed of material but *separate* parts, parts that are resistant to unification as they *exclude* each other. These separate parts mimic the flaws of the factual sciences. Scientific facts are contingently and quantitatively tacked on and separated from each other and therefore constitutionally unable to form a coherent and systematically unified system. They merely *represent*—rather than constitute—an external aggregation, a superficial collection of isolated facts and cognitions.

> The nature of Spirit may be understood by a glance at its direct opposite—*Matter*. As the essence of Matter is Gravity, so, on the other hand, we may affirm that the substance, the essence of Spirit is Freedom. All will readily assent to the doctrine that Spirit, among other properties, is also endowed with Freedom; *but philosophy teaches that all the qualities of Spirit exist only through Freedom; that all are means for attaining Freedom; that all seek and produce this and this alone.* It is a result of speculative Philosophy

106 Determinism and the consciousness of freedom

[as opposed to Kant's Critical Philosophy] that Freedom is the sole truth of Spirit. Matter possesses gravity in virtue of its tendency toward a central point. It is essentially composite, consisting of parts that exclude each other. It seeks its Unity; and therefore exhibits itself as self-destructive, as verging toward its opposite (an indivisible [simple, immaterial] point). If it could attain this, it would be Matter no longer, it would have perished. It [i.e., Spirit] strives after the realization of its Idea; for in unity it exists *ideally.* Spirit, on the contrary, may be defined as that which has its centre in itself. It has not unity outside itself but has already found it; it exists *in* and *with itself.* Matter has its centre out of itself; Spirit is *self-contained existence.* Now this is freedom exactly. For if I am dependent, my being is referred to something else which I am not; I cannot exist independently of something external. I am free, on the contrary, when my existence depends upon myself. This self-contained existence of Spirit is none other than self-consciousness—consciousness of one's own being. Two things must be distinguished in consciousness; first the fact *that I know;* secondly, *what I know.* In *self*-consciousness these are merged in one; for Spirit *knows itself.*

(Hegel, *History*, 17)

Hegel had addressed the Cartesian problem of dualism by identifying Being and Consciousness in the *Science of Logic*, as deriving from the categories of Quality (Chapter 4) and he also criticizes the empirical scientific account attempting to measure gravitational forces in terms of quantum and magnitudes, in terms of quantitative measurements (*b. Measure as a series of measure-relations, Logic*, 21.343 and 21.363).

But the italicized phrases in the passage above are critical to my thesis. Freedom is a quality; it is a value. The empirical sciences are in principle causally incapable of explaining human values. They reduce values to the subjective secondary qualities of feelings, of pain and pleasure. Similarly, Freud's psychoanalytic principle is basically hedonistic, it promotes pleasure, the diminution of anxiety rather than qualitative distinctions. But let me be clear, I am not suggesting values are or can be absolute; they cannot. They are existentially, i.e., individually subjective—and spontaneously unpredictable and free! To each his own.

Determinism and the consciousness of freedom 107

In whatever manner we define freedom, it must arise from within the mind. Gravity certainly has physical force, weight, and mass, but the power is external to the substance; it is reciprocally controlled, determined by antecedents beyond its own physical composition; it is vulnerable to larger gravitational fields and determined by more massive forces.

In an illuminating passage in the *Philosophy of Right*, Hegel provides an instructive insight into what he has in mind regarding freedom and the synthetic *a priori* relation between the "theoretical attitude" (knowing) and its "practical attitude" (willing). Once more the connections are completely in line with the simplicity premise, argument, and one of its conclusions.

> In thinking an object, I make it into thought and deprive it of its sensuous [material] aspect. I make it into something which is directly and essentially mine. Since it is in thought that I am first by myself. I do not penetrate [*a physical*] object until I understand it; it then ceases to stand over against me and I have taken from it the character of its own which it had in opposition to me ... An idea is always a generalization and generalization is an activity of thinking. To generalize means to think [to universalize meanings, concepts]. The ego is thought and so the universal. [The ego is universally present as subject in all its particular acts of cognition.] When I say 'I,' I *eo ipso* abandon all my particular characteristics, my disposition, natural endowment, knowledge, and age. The ego is quite empty, a mere point, simple [i.e., immaterial], yet active in this simplicity. The variegated canvas of the world is before me; I stand over and against it; by my theoretical attitude to it. I overcome its opposition to me and make its content my own. I am at home in the world when I know it, still more so when I have [self-consciously recreated and] understood it.[4]

The opposite of freedom is to be enchained by one's own mind. Although Hegel does not cite melancholy or loneliness as a distinct mental illness, nevertheless his descriptions of madness depicts it as a form of self-alienation, a splitting of the self against its self; "a state in which the mind is shut up within itself, has sunk into itself, whose peculiarity consists in its being no longer in immediate contact with

108   Determinism and the consciousness of freedom

actuality but in having positively separated itself from it."[5] For Hegel, there is a conceptual bridge connecting madness and reason, the subconscious and the self-conscious, the feeling soul and the rational soul, the inner sphere of dreams and the outer realm of reality.

Schopenhauer

In the case of Schopenhauer, man's "freedom" is by proxy; actually it is the irrational Will that is free but acting sub rosa, subconsciously through the unsuspecting agency of human consciousness, as it inexplicably and surreptitiously usurps and "influences"—not causes— the human propensity toward malicious evil, from motives unknown even to the "agent." Its source amounts to a noumenal spontaneity; a reality more properly *below* consciousness as opposed to Kant's transcendent *beyond*. For Schopenhauer, although man is phenomenally self-conscious, he is not free; all human thought and action are determined in *this* world. But the irrational Will, *once removed* from the realm of human experience, *indirectly* acts unknowingly *through* each of us.

Schopenhauer, who had been a medical student, marshals a list of natural causes, including gravity, electricity, animal magnetism, chemical reactions, instinctual sexual drives, and so on. He frequently refers to the brain. Basically, he is a precursor to Freud. But while citing Malebranche, Schopenhauer undermines all the empirical sciences as ultimately grounded in unknowable *qualitas occulta, qualitates occultae*, which remain inherently inexplicable while the Will forms the *universal* underlying ground for all phenomenal existence, both animate and inanimate. Whereas Hegel's freedom is rational, Schopenhauer's is radically irrational. On the surface of consciousness, everything is predictable, but below it is a seething, unfathomable turbulence.

> Malebranche is right; every natural cause is only an occasional cause. It gives only the opportunity, the occasion, for the phenomenon of that one and indivisible Will, which is the in-itself of all things, and whose graduated objectification is this whole visible world. Only the appearing, the becoming is visible, in such a place and at such a time, is brought about by the cause, and it is to that extent dependent on it, but not the whole of the phenomenon, not

its inner nature. This is the Will itself, to which the principle of sufficient reason [that a cause can always be given for something being the way it is and not another way] has no application and which is therefore groundless [i.e., causeless].[6]

These subterranean and subconscious forces underlying our surface experiences are completely unsuspected by the human "agent," who thus remains vulnerable to the delusion that man acts freely; that his decisions are explicable and predictable, that they are his own. Man believes he is free because he is aware of his desires but not their causes (Spinoza). On the relatively deceptive surface waters of human behavior, all appears placid, calm, and under control but below the surface, the powerful forces of the irrational Will, with its assortment of seething *qualitates occultae*, reign supreme (*WWR*, I, 80, 122, 125, 127, 131, 140; II, 14, 249–250; 314, 317, 334). Schopenhauer in a single stroke supplants and commandeers Kant's "*spontaneous* productive imagination" by catapulting into his own exploitation of a noumenal, radically unknowable turbulent Will as it lies hidden and seething well below any possible human accessibility.

Bergson

Henri Bergson's conception of the freedom of consciousness is grounded in the simplicity argument. Concentrating on his early work, *Time and Free Will*, he begins with the principle that consciousness is immaterial and concludes that only "the *real* and *whole* self" is able to function freely, i.e., act independently of material and mechanistic determinants. Again, in the idealist tradition, sensory and affective qualities are unextended, whereas matter is quantitatively extended.[7] Consciousness consists of immaterial *qualitative* existences, fused *qualities*, as opposed to extended sensory images, which science implements as abstractions, as singularly applicable to spatial and measurable *quantities*. "The fact is there is no point of contact between the unextended and the extended, between quality and quantity" (*TFW*, 70). But the purely subjective qualities—colors and sounds, pleasures and pains are directly, immediately present to the mind; and they are to be distinguished and contrasted to the objective and impersonal abstractions of science.

110 Determinism and the consciousness of freedom

> Considered in themselves, the deep-seated conscious states have no relation to quantity, they are pure quality; they intermingle, interpenetrate in such a way that we cannot tell whether they are one or several ...The duration which they thus create is a duration [without extension] whose moments do not constitute a numerical multiplicity.
>
> (*TFW*, 137)

Because they have no temporal extension, no past or future, they are perfectly self-contained and therefore free. Without a spatial presence, causality cannot occur. The pure qualitative data permeating consciousness are open to moments of privileged access, intuitions, and reflexive freedom; they are directly accessible as *durational* moments within the presence of an immanent time-consciousness. This distinction is only made possible in so far as we can separate the two opposed conceptions of time: (a) external, scientific, objective time, which measures the motion of objects traveling through space; the time of clocks, calendars, and birthdays, in contradistinction to the moments of pure immediacy, of qualities alone, of immaterial *qualitative* sensations and feelings. Feelings are clearly unextended; they are not in space and hence they serve and function as intimate "non-mathematizable" existences as Bergson insists. But even colors, by virtue of their purely qualitative existences, are not spatial or dimensional magnitudes but rather ideal or mental data. And why? Because—once more—the mind as the "medium" of consciousness, as its "instrument," is immaterial. By contrast, quantities are extended, material, spatial, measurable, divisible, physical, and homogeneous, i.e., each part of space is indistinguishable from all the other parts. Space in terms of its scientific interest is a mathematical abstraction. We recall Kant's conviction that space can be experienced as completely devoid of objects (presumably an empirical impossibility).

For Bergson, self-consciousness is immanent time, the reality. Qualities are intrinsically heterogeneous with each quality different from every other. But although they are different, nevertheless within the durational moment of a purely immanent temporal consciousness, the qualities become fused; they interpenetrate. But if time, according to science, is extended, and it is sequential in terms of motion, then it follows that it must be *externally* determined causally and its effects

Determinism and the consciousness of freedom 111

predictable. Only if time-consciousness is immanently, intuitively *durational, i.e., uncaused* can consciousness be free (*TFW*, 6, 31–32, 112, 213).[8]

Since qualities are perfectly unique—and must remain so—it follows they cannot be structured in a causal, objective, determinist, or scientific sequence. And when the real or whole self is immersed in intuitive or durational time, then immanent time *becomes* independent of both "its" past and "its" future; it *becomes* sheer possibility. At this juncture, at this pure instant, the whole self is decisionally "telescoped" on the immediacy of the present moment and it is both absolutely free and perfectly unencumbered. The problem of free will and determinism only arises when we erroneously try to quantify our purely mental, ideal, and qualitative inner temporal moments of consciousness by transforming them into elongated sequences. A conceptual distortion arises whenever we confuse pure durational moments, which do not occupy space, with those that are spatial. The critical distinction intrudes whenever quality opposes quantity; intuition opposes conception; inextensity opposes extensity; heterogeneity opposes homogeneity; identity opposes difference; duration opposes motion; inner opposes outer; and the simple, indivisible, and unextended opposes the manifold, divisible, and extended (*TFW,* ix, 3, 51, 70, 80–81, 87, 90). The attribution of mathematical "intensities" or "degrees" of "more" or "less," quantitative numerical measures, are futile because a feeling is what it is; you *uniquely* own it. It is abstractly unshareable. For example, try comparing your feeling of guilt with someone else's. Or your feeling of sibling rivalry *when* you were ten years and how you feel *now.* Every feeling is unique unto itself. It simply is what it is; feelings are intrinsically incomparable and unrepeatable even within your own self. When we try to compare feelings as more weak or strong, we have lost any semblance of their reality. The attempt to mathematize varying degrees in which feelings and psychic states are exhibited is a distortion produced by our conceptual and practical faculty of the understanding, which freezes reality by imposing spatial and mathematical structures upon it. Imagine trying to compare the happiness of your childhood with those of your maturity.

Bergson stands solidly in the tradition against the principle that "matter alone can think," the notion that consciousness can be mechanically and causally structured, as he expounds a theory that is

112 Determinism and the consciousness of freedom

antithetical to the principles of behavioral psychology (*TFW*, 154 ff.). He contends that during most of our lives we are guided by our habits. But there are unique moments in life when "the whole self gathers its self within its self" and then it is free from all past causal structures, as it confronts the sheer possibility of freedom looming before it (*TFW*, 219 ff., 231). There is neither the earth below nor the sky above us. There is nothing but the durational moment of complete freedom. The past no longer exists; and the future is not yet. There is just the pure self, what it feels, what it thinks, and what it desires. To the questions of others, *why* did you do it, the only possible answer is: "*Because I could.*" Fruitless to inquire into ethical justifications or scientific explanations.

In certain passages, Bergson holds that freedom can be directly apprehended by intuition. In other passages he offers a discursive argument for the freedom of consciousness, one grounded in the simplicity argument, by insisting on the unextended existence of "durational" moments "when" the whole self decides. "It is the whole soul, which gives rise to the free decision." This *freedom* Bergson calls *spontaneity*. The opposite of determinism is spontaneity; and he turns this dynamic conception against the associationist psychologists (*TFW*, 141–142, 216–217). The error of the associationists is that they have transferred the scientific paradigm of causal and mechanical relations, operating externally in space, as applying to the human body—and so have our current neurosciences by extending the model to the human brain. The physical causes become the stimuli and the bodily effects are the responses. Ideas become associated by experience. In opposition to active minds, behaviorism substitutes passive, receptive brains transforming the mental into the physiological and then proceeds to provide causal *explanations* based on empirical associative interactions. The associationist principle is engrained in the English empiricist traditions of Hobbes, Locke, Hume, the Mills, Bain, Hartley, Wundt et al., who collectively share the same limitations that Husserl later criticizes and labels as "psychologism."

There are two ways we can present Bergson's argument. First, qualities, as present within consciousness, are *both* simple *and* immediate existents. Being unextended, they cannot in principle exhibit or involve spatial relations; consequently, qualities cannot cause, effect, interact, influence, or determine each other. Since they are uncaused, they are spontaneous, *sui generis, causa sui*, and therefore independent of

Determinism and the consciousness of freedom   113

external causes, i.e., free. Second, pure time, i.e., *duration*, is temporally unextended. Because both (a) pure qualities *qua* sensations and feelings are immediately present to consciousness—given directly, intuitively to inner sense—and (b) *duration* is likewise, simple, temporally unextended, it follows that it is free from external conditions. Since internal, subjective time is non-dimensional, it cannot be directional in any sense; it cannot *point* to the next moment. Inner time is not a line consisting of transitive points, it is not an arrow indicating a future direction. It neither points to nor predetermines a predictable direction. Therefore, it follows that it cannot be causally connected or related to other times in an external or mechanical fashion. By a process of simple elimination, then, pure time, not being determined, must be the source of freedom (*TWF*, 224). It is the whole soul which gives rise to the free decision of a dynamic spontaneity (*TFW*, 167, 208, 219; cf. Robinet, 33).

We may well inquire in what sense Bergson can speak of a "whole self." The sense very importantly is this. Bergson is not denying that multiple qualities can be present to our awareness at the same time. Indeed, he insists on the intrinsically heterogeneous aspect of a consciousness aware of various qualities within the same moment. Obviously, this implies that our psychic states are if anything complex and not simple. But this is the point in the discussion where Bergson introduces his metaphors of "melting," "fusion," "blending," and "interpenetration." Both pure durational time and pure qualities are unextended; what is unextended can exist at once and interpenetrate, fuse, and "subsist" as a single, simple unity. "Duration has nothing to do with space" (*TFW*, 91).

Let me give an example of how this works. Consider a person who has lived in despair for many years and has frequently considered suicide. During each moment of his past life, when he actively considered killing himself, potentially, possibly he could have spontaneously consummated the act. But he did not; each moment ended in choosing survival; the decision, the final terminal act, could have been accomplished but it was not. All the previous dilemmas, to live or die, all the former decisions are completely irrelevant. But now, at this present moment of immediacy, of duration, his entire life, the complete history of his despair is directly, immediately before him. "To be or not to be." Within each instantaneous moment of duration, the

114 Determinism and the consciousness of freedom

deed is either done or not done. And yet each moment is uniquely different from every other. It can be accomplished in the morning or in the evening; publicly or privately; or indefinitely postponed. And each moment is critically spontaneous. Existence or non-existence; life or death?

After the suicidal consummation, a behavioral psychologist can always provide—*abstractly, retrospectively, after the fact*—a causal chain of motivations, as if he were weighing the balances of life and death on a scale. But that is not what faces the "real and whole" suicidal self. That is not the reality of the situation when it is presented in its *absolute* immediacy. The decision is perfectly compressed into a simple, single timeless moment. This is the same dynamic that repetitiously— with each instant as unique—continuously arises throughout life in Kierkegaard's paradoxical *Either/Or; faith/doubt; salvation/despair* decisions. Existential freedom has no antecedents. We immediately choose whenever we reflexively *consider* a choice.

For an insight into what Bergson means by "fusing" or "melting," we may turn for assistance to Descartes's and Spinoza's discussion of the medieval "Problem of Divine Attributes in God" (*TWF*, 208). Presented in its classic form, the problem is: *if* God possesses infinite and diverse attributes, *then* how can He be a simple Substance. And the answer is because of His absolute simplicity. The attributes are not "parts" on an immaterial Substance. God fuses all reality into an indivisible unity and identity. By the same token, God is not in time. He "exists" eternally. Similarly, in the above case of the depressed person's decisional, durational human act, immanent time-consciousness is analogous to eternity.

> But the principle of causality, in so far as it is supposed to bind the future to the present, could never take the form of a necessary principle; for the successive moments of real time are not bound up with one another, and no effort of logic will succeed in proving that what has been will continue to be, that the same antecedents will always give rise to identical consequents. Descartes understood this so well that he attributed the regularity of the physical world and the continuation of the same effects to the constantly renewed grace of Providence [so Malebranche]; he built up as it were, an *instantaneous* physics, intended for a universe the whole

duration of which might as well be confined to the present moment [as analogous to eternity]. And Spinoza maintained the indefinite series of phenomena, which takes for us the form of succession in time, was equivalent, in the absolute, to the divine unity; he thus assumed, on the one hand, that the relation of apparent causality between phenomena melted away into a relation of identity in the absolute, and, on the other, that the indefinite duration of things was all contained in a single moment, which is eternity.

(*TFW*, 208)

Abstract mathematical measurements distort reality by freezing it. The model of such perfect and absolute unity and identity, which Descartes and Spinoza conceive as manifested only in their versions of God, Bergson has transferred to the individual soul. The heterogeneity of qualities immediately present to consciousness can be compressed within the moment, within the individual self. And when this state of unity and identity is achieved, the *whole self* is attained and *in control of its self*, i.e., it is free. At that precise moment, man is free and knows himself to be free.

We should therefore distinguish two forms of multiplicity, two very different ways of regarding duration, two aspects of conscious life. Below homogeneous [i.e., scientific] duration, which is the extensive symbol of true duration , a close psychological analysis distinguishes a duration whose heterogeneous moments permeate one another; below the numerical multiplicity of conscious states, a qualitative multiplicity; below the self with well-defined states, a self which *succeeding each other* means *melting into one another and forming an organic whole* [i.e., self].

(*TWF*, 128; italics his)

Additionally, for Bergson, consciousness and language are radically opposed. Words and language are *indirectly* and empirically related by representations, by symbols, whereas duration is directly intuitional and non-verbal. Language is an artificial tool. Linguistic and analytic philosophers artificially distance, remove themselves from reality by using non-intuitive tools, and especially by their instrumental application of syntaxes as substitutes for synthetic *a priori* relations.

116 Determinism and the consciousness of freedom

Dictionaries separate meanings and concepts; grammar distorts duration.

> We necessarily express ourselves by means of words and we usually think in terms of space. Language requires us to establish between our ideas the same sharp and precise distinctions, the same discontinuity as between material objects. This assimilation of thoughts to things is useful [and artificial] in practical life and necessary in most of the sciences. But it may be asked whether insurmountable difficulties presented by certain philosophical problems do not arise from our placing side by side phenomena which do not occupy space and whether by merely getting rid of the clumsy symbols round which we are fighting we might bring the fight to the end. When an illegitimate translation of the unextended into the extended, of quality into quantity has introduced contradiction into the very heart of the question then contradiction must of course recur in the answer. The problem which I have chosen is one which is common in metaphysics and psychology, the problem of free will.
>
> (*TFW*, Authors Preface, ix)

As Bergson puts it in his summation, "Every demand for explanation in regard to freedom comes back, without our suggesting it, to the following question: 'Can time be adequately represented by space?'" And his answer is that real time, the durational moment of consciousness cannot be spatialized precisely because the *essence*, the *meaning* of duration cannot be conceived in terms of a spatial movement. In short, Bergson's entire "argument" is contained in a single *intuition:* spontaneity (*TFW*, 141–142, 217, 219–220).

Time and Free Will was originally published in 1889; *Matter and Memory* in 1896. In the later work, Bergson quixotically tries to reconcile quality and quantity, consciousness and matter through the conduit of memory. In the Introduction to the second study, he declares:

> This book affirms the reality of spirit and the reality of matter and tries to determine the relation of the one to the other by the study of a definite example, that of memory. It is then frankly dualistic.[9]

Determinism and the consciousness of freedom   117

Encouraged by the writings of the Scottish psychologist, Alexander Bain, Bergson sought to build a continuous bridge between consciousness-memory-and-brain, between physiology and epistemology. Basically, he fails; it is simply not possible to "fuse" brains and minds. His effort should be pronounced a failure and his strongest legacy remains unblemished as expressed in his earlier work. I have discussed Bergson at some length because he synthesizes the generally distinct concepts of freedom, time-consciousness, i.e., duration, and the unity of consciousness and fuses them into one.

Sartre

While Bergson holds that "nothingness" is inconceivable and consciousness is a qualitative plenum, Sartre, in turn, offers his own analysis of both nothingness and freedom.[10] Nevertheless, his definition of consciousness, like Bergson's, depends on the simplicity argument, as well as his commitment to the principle of cognitive spontaneity. According to Sartre, consciousness is the for-itself but it is a non-reflexive awareness. In other words, he is denying the Cartesian, Leibnizian, Kantian, and Husserlian concept of reflexivity as emphasized in the latter's *Cartesian Meditations.* Indeed, the self, i.e., the "me" is like any other object of transcendence, opaque and murky, whereas consciousness must be clear if there is to be a veridical cognition of transcendent intentional objects, the in-itself. An object, a being in-itself is extended; consciousness on the other hand, the for-itself, is unextended, simple, immaterial, translucent, and therefore empty.

> [T]he revelation of the spatiality of being is one with the nonpositional [non-thetic] apprehension by the for-itself [i.e., the ego-less consciousness] of itself as *unextended.* And the *unextended* character of the for-itself is not a positive, mysterious virtue of spirituality which is hiding under a negative determination; it is a natural *ekstatic* [i.e., spontaneous, transcendent] relation, for it is by and in the [intentional] extension of the transcendent in-itself that the for-itself makes itself known to itself and realizes its own non-extension. The for-itself cannot be first unextended in order to later enter into relation with the

118 Determinism and the consciousness of freedom

extended being, for no matter how we consider it, the concept of the unextended makes no sense by itself; it is nothing but the [Hegelian] negation of the extended ... In this sense extension is a transcendent determination which the for-itself has to apprehend to the exact degree that it denies itself as extended (italics and brackets mine).[11]

"Ek-staticity" *means* "beyondness," to reach *beyond* its self; it is a transcendence that absolutely outraces the sensory but momentary contents of consciousness. The for-itself exists as an unextended, indivisible, non-spatial existent. It exists out of itself in being a nothingness, "a hole in being" (page 96) whose concrete existence, its determinacy is supported by its own intentional activity of negation (again determination is negation; Spinoza, Hegel). The for-itself exists in a synthetic *a priori* relation with the in-itself (*Being and Nothingness*, Conclusion). Being, the in-itself is material, spatial, blobby, viscous, nauseating, and divisible, at least by the negative determinations of the for-itself. The for-itself by contrast is immaterial but it is actively *intentional*. Because it is a "yearning womb-like" nothingness, it potentially exists "out of itself," ek-statically (in time); it transcends itself, it is beyond itself, struggling to become what it is not, an object. For Sartre, as for Husserl, consciousness is intentional; but although it is a nothingness (for Sartre), it is permeated by a volitional spontaneity to escape beyond its "self" (*Transcendence of the Ego*); it is a pure freedom of active intentionality. Consciousness is defined by intentionality. It *desires* to unify itself in an object by escaping from its emptiness.

This transcendental sphere is a sphere of absolute existence; that is to say a sphere of pure spontaneities [i.e., acts] which are never objects and which determine their own existence ... The ego is not the owner of consciousness; it is the [transcendent] object of consciousness. To be sure, we constitute spontaneously our states and actions as productions of the ego. But our states and actions are also objects. We have a direct intuition of the spontaneity of an instantaneous consciousness produced by the ego.

(pages 96–97)

Notice that Sartre refers to Consciousness as a "sphere," thus indicating reflexivity whereas Being is an extended "realm." Generally, "sphericity" suggests *self*-consciousness.

Sartre, no less than Hegel and Bergson before him, employs the simplicity or immateriality *premise* as the ground for his conception of freedom. Consciousness is simple, immaterial. Nevertheless, it exists, and its essence is expressed in spontaneous acts of negation and determination. In Hegel, this dialectical negativity is inherent in the for-itself. Consciousness is the source of conceptual distinctions and discriminations, which constitute knowing our *inner* self as well as *outer* realities. It is only in so far as we cognize and re-cognize ourselves through thought that we achieve self-conscious freedom. We create the world we inhabit; we are its source; and we recognize our own product; we "own" it. We are the masters of our creations and therefore free— and it is a frighteningly responsible existential situation.

For Bergson, the essential indivisibility, the unity of the temporal ego conditions compressibility, the unification, the fusion of the immediate qualities present to consciousness *within* a single moment. The critical factor is that the qualities are unified by an identical self. It is this "whole self," which carries nothing forward from the past and expects nothing new from the future; it is completely self-contained; it endures on the brink of sheer possibility, a precipice of pure conceivability, in short absolute freedom. But, according to Sartre, this immaterial, unextended consciousness is a "nothingness," which not only (a) exists but it is (b) spontaneous, free, and intentional. And if it were not an existent nothingness, it could only be its opposite—a viscous, blobby, nauseating, undulating thing, e.g., the roots of the chestnut tree in *Nausea*. It is the active intentionality of consciousness, which introduces and supports the violent thrust of freedom into Being.

The previous passages are intended to reinforce my Weberian thesis that it is only human beings who create individual values for themselves alone.

> It follows that my freedom is the unique foundation of values and that *nothing,* absolutely nothing [i.e., no immanent Kantian or Husserlian structures of consciousness] justifies me in adopting this or that value, this or that particular set of values. As a being

to whom values exist, I am unjustifiable. My freedom is anguished at being the foundation of values while itself without foundation. It is anguished in addition because values, due to the fact that they are essentially revealed to a freedom, cannot disclose themselves without being at the same time "put into question" for the possibility of overturning the scale of values appears complementary as *my* possibility. It is anguish before values which is the recognition of the ideality of values.

(*B&N*, 46)

Again, Weber's principle. In short, I am condemned to freedom!

Because of the *individual* spontaneity of acts and their creation of subjective meanings and relations, each human experience is intrinsically unique and unrepeatable. Consequently, all attempts at psychological predictions and control are quixotically delusional. Plus, meanings are infinitely nuanced when turned loose in human consciousness. The infinite distance between a concept, its lived experience, and its existential value is immeasurable. That is why psychoanalysis, cognitive behavioral therapy, and the current neurosciences are impotent in their efforts to unravel human consciousness and determine human behavior. It would be paradoxical to say, "I predicted what I was going to do next."

My assumption regarding the relation between consciousness and loneliness is that in order to penetrate more deeply into the dynamics of human loneliness, it is necessary to acknowledge the subconscious hidden forces at work because by definition these submerged powers are well below the reaches of materialism, mechanism, determinism, empiricism, phenomenalism, behaviorism, and the contemporary neurosciences. And even psychoanalysis is unable to penetrate the forces of a Schopenhauerian *irretrievable subconscious well below the Freudian retrievable unconscious.* There are *personal* subterranean forces innate within human consciousness, which will ever remain inherently incapable of being *directly* accessed.

Notes

1 Martinich, A. P., *A Hobbes Dictionary* (Cambridge, MA: Blackwells, 1995), 56.

Determinism and the consciousness of freedom 121

2 Beck, Lewis White, *A Commentary to Kant's Critique of Practical Reason* (Chicago: University of Chicago Press, 1960), 200.

3 Hegel, G. W. F., *Philosophy of History*, translated by J. Sibree (New York: Dover, 1956), 9; hereafter cited as Hegel, *History.*

4 Hegel, G. W. F., *The Philosophy of Right*, translated by T. M. Knox (Oxford, 1969), 226.

5 Hegel, G. W. F., *The Philosophy of Mind*, translated by William Wallace (Oxford: Clarendon Press, 1971), which traces the physical and mental development of the newborn infant, Anthropology, Section 389 ff. and especially Sections 406, Zusatz and 408, Zusatz.

6 Schopenhauer, Arthur, *The World as Will and Representation*, translated by E. F. J. Payne (New York: Dover, 1969), I, 80, 122, 125, 131, 137–138, 140; II, 14, 249, 334. Schopenhauer also rejects Hume's empirical assumption that in terms of the causal relation, the object, the perception precedes the subject whereas in his philosophy, the subject precedes the object, *WWR*, 13–14, 68.

7 Bergson, Henri, *Time and Free Will: An Essay on the Immediate Data of Consciousness*, translated by F. L. Pogson (New York: Harper & Row, 1960), 6, 31–32, 90, 112, 130, 213. *TFW*, 208; cf. 219, 224; "it is the whole soul which gives rise to the free decision," 167; hereafter cited as *TFW.* The qualitative simplicity of sensations is directly derived from their mental, ideal, i.e., non-physical nature. Cf. Ben Mijuskovic, "Loneliness and Time Consciousness," *Philosophy Today*, 22:4 (1978). For Bergson's emphasis on dynamic psychiatry, as a "philosopher of life," on his *elan vital*, and his widespread influence on Pierre Janet, Alfred Adler, and Carl Jung, see Henri Ellenberger, *The Discovery of the Unconscious: The History of Dynamic Psychiatry* (New York: Dover, 1970), 354–355, 376, 624.

8 Robinet, Andre, *Bergson et les metamorphose de la duree* (Paris: Editions Seghers, 1965), 33, 40, 42. For Bergson, pure spontaneity or freedom *and* pure time or duration are identical; spontaneity is the ultimate source of intuitive freedom and it functions as the antithesis for determinism, *TFW*, 141–142, 217, 219, 220. The term dynamic in psychiatry means that the source of the psychic energy arises from within the self, as opposed to empiricism in which the conditioning cause lies outside consciousness.

9 Bergson, Henri, *Matter and Mind*, translated by N. M. Paul and W. S. Parker (London: George Allen & Kegan Paul, 1970), author's Introduction, xi.

10 Sartre, Jean-Paul, *The Transcendence of the Ego* (New York: Noonday Press, 1962), 21, 76, 79, 80, 91, 93, 96–97. Sartre attempts to distinguish Descartes's and Bergson's spontaneity from his own version. "Freedom is the human being putting his past out of play by secreting his own nothingness." For Sartre, consciousness must be empty for freedom to operate.

122   Determinism and the consciousness of freedom

11 Sartre, Jean-Paul, *Being and Nothingness* (New York: Washington Square, 1966); 218–219; italics his; hereafter cited as B&N

> As for the For-itself, if it is not in space, this is because it apprehends itself precisely as not being being-in-itself in so far as the in-itself is revealed to it in the mode of exteriority which we call extension. It is precisely by denying exteriority in itself and apprehending itself as ecstatic [i.e., intentional] that the for-itself spatializes space.
>
> (225)

Chapter 6

Descartes's bridge to the external world

The piece of wax[*]

Descartes's paradigm of self-consciousness requires the interplay of four formative, constitutive features: the given immediacy of sensations and feelings, the act of spontaneity, the immediacy of intuition, e.g., the cogito, and the mediacy of meanings, relations, and inferences. More than any other thinker, he institutes the clearest distinction between the immediacy of sensation and the mediacy of thought but by doing so he splits the self from the world. By contrast, neuroscience reduces "consciousness" to neuronal motions and electrical synapses in the brain and eliminates the mediacy of judgments and reduces the qualititative features of "consciousness" to neuronal interaction alone, i.e., solely to physiological sensations and feelings. The danger of Cartesian metaphysics and its epistemology is solipsism.

In the conflict between Materialism (Democritus), Idealism (Parmenides) and Dualism (Plato), any text, which aspires to provide both an accurate historical and philosophical account, couched in the history of ideas methodology, needs to address two pressing obligations. It must place the discussion in its larger contextual framework by clarifying the competing principles of disagreement between science and idealism, Plato's Battle between the Giants and the Gods.

The advent of modern skepticism

In 529 AD, the Christian Roman Emperor, Justinian, expelled all the Greek schools of philosophy from the Roman world and they migrated toward Moslem lands where they were preserved, translated, and studied. Avicenna commented on the dialogues of Plato and Averroes on the treatises of Aristotle. But in 1562, the works of Sextus

DOI: 10.4324/9781003156130-7

124 Descartes's bridge to the external world

Empiricus, and his exposition of Pyrrhonian skepticism, re-entered the Western world through Moorish Spain. Academic skepticism attacks all claims of certainty by challenging the twin criteria of truth, to wit, sensation and reason, contending that both inconclusively lead either to an infinite regress or to circularity with the result that both truth and doubt are equally balanced on a scale. There are two tendencies within skepticism. Dogmatic or academic skepticism, which categorically denies all truths—thus paradoxically violating its own assertion—whereas Pyrrhonian skepticism is mitigated. It holds not to know what is true or false but continues to strive toward the possibility of discovering truth. Descartes's goal is to meet the skeptical challenge by providing an indubitable criterion for truth, one which is applicable in testing all propositions tendered by science. Richard Popkin, in his extensive studies, beginning with *The History of Scepticism from Erasmus to Descartes*, and some 300 articles, deserves special mention.[1] Consider, for example, Montaigne's skepticism concerning external reality. What do we know and how do we know it?

> The first consideration that I offer on the subject of the senses is that I have my doubts whether man is provided with all the senses of nature. I see many animals that live a complete and perfect life, some without sight, others without hearing, who knows whether we too do not still lack, one, two, three, or many other senses? For if any one is lacking, our reason cannot discover its absence … We have formed a truth by the consultation and concurrence of our five senses; but perhaps we needed the agreement of eight or ten senses and their contribution, to perceive it truly and in its essence.[2]

Further, this skepticism is compounded by an equally cognitive limitation.

> Our conception is not itself applied to foreign objects [external to the mind] but is conceived through the mediation of the senses; and the senses do not comprehend the foreign object, but only their own [immediate] impressions. And thus, the conception and the semblance we form is not of the object, but only the impression made on the sense, which impression and the object are

different things. Wherefore whoever judges [i.e., doubtfully infers] by appearances judges by something other than the object. And as for saying that the impressions of the senses convey to the soul the *quality* of the foreign objects by resemblance, how can the soul and understanding make sure of this resemblance, having of itself no [direct] communication with foreign objects? Just as a man who does not know Socrates, seeing his portrait cannot say that it resembles him.

(ibid., 454; italic mine)

Notice in the above passage the implied distinction between the physical object and the *qualitative* mental features of the sensations. It is this primary epistemic difference that will continue to guide us throughout our text.

Montaigne is a major exponent of skepticism. His guiding dictum declares, "That there are no first principles for men unless the Divinity has revealed them; all the rest is but dreams and smoke" (ibid., 61). This is Descartes's intellectual challenge: to respond to skepticism without being forced to invoke religious faith.

Descartes and the Augustinian Oratory

The response to skepticism offered two possible avenues of advancement. Either (a) to continue the Platonic dualistic hierarchy of various qualitative substances and cognitive states initiated by Ficino's commentaries and promoted by the Cambridge Platonists; or (b) to encourage and pursue the growing appreciation in the direction of the empirical sciences.

Plato's metaphysical and epistemic Divided Line passage, in the *Republic*, offers a dualistic schema showing a hierarchy of ascending *qualitative* distinctions between two worlds: an independent realm of "objects" of knowledge corresponding to a matching relation to cognitive states of the mind. The lowest two tiers consist of *immediate appearances*, subjective images, shadows, echoes, and dreams matched with (a) varying opinions (*doxa*). Next a realm of visible and tangible physical objects matched with (b) epistemic beliefs (*pistis*). The following "transition" is *qualitatively* higher consisting in *conceptual intelligibles*, in mathematical and geometric definitions matched

126 Descartes's bridge to the external world

with (c) the cognitive discursive, mediate faculty of the understanding (*dianoia*) forming a "sort of bridge" between the lower world of human appearances and moving toward higher realms of knowledge consisting of (d) Ideas, i.e. universal *meanings* matched with intuitive knowledge (*episteme*). The entire superstructure is then "transcendently" unified by a supreme act of supra-intuitive comprehension, culminating in a coherent system of knowledge, by the Good (*noesis*; 509D-511B), not unlike Kant's ideal of the Unconditioned (A 666= B 694). *But Cornford's "sort of bridge" is left undefined and consequently epistemically suspect.* The critical issue, however, is the *transition* between the material world, with its sensory qualities and its corresponding spheres of human appearances and then proceeding on *into* the higher orders of reality. Presumably, it is mathematics and geometry that are able "to bridge," to serve as the transitional passage between appearance and reality. But what is troubling Cornford is that he believes Plato needs a "sort of bridge" connecting the worlds of human appearances to an independent reality.

> *Here is a sort of bridge carrying the mind across from the visible thing to the intelligible reality, which it must learn to distinguish.*
> (page 223; cf. *Rep.*, VI 510–511)[3]

The "bridge" is to be negotiated by the dialectical method.

> *The higher method is called Dialectic, a word which since Hegel has acquired misleading associations.*
> (ibid.)

But when we read Hegel's article on Plato in the *Lectures*, we realize that the "hypothetical" premise of the Forms in the *Republic* is only later to be concluded in the *Parmenides*. "The fully worked-out and genuine dialectic is, however, contained in the Parmenides—that most famous masterpiece of Platonic dialectic" (*Lectures*, II, 49 ff.). What I am suggesting is that for Hegel, it will be the dialectic method that *continually, uninterruptedly* "bridges" the dualistic schism between mind and matter, between consciousness and science, between the categories of Quality and Quantity. Whereas Kant imposes *distinct* formal categories, Hegel's dialectic method continually flows between two shores. The *Science of Logic* is the mind's unimpeded spiritual journey through its Qualities and its spilling into its subsequent Quantities. It is as if one added a colored die into a teeming pond full of life and the color saturated the entire liquid and denizens.

There are substances and there are methods. In the *Lectures*, Hegel discusses at some length Plato's dialectical method and suggests that method trumps metaphysics by reconciling the dualism between subject and object as well as its categorial Qualities and Quantities. We recall that in the *Critique*, in the Analytic of Principles, Kant categorically distinguishes the *quantitative* Axioms of Intuition from the *qualitative* Anticipations of Perception thus bifurcating the objective from the subjective forms of consciousness (A 162=B 202). There is no bridge; it is simply executed as a formal, i.e., transcendental distinction. However, Hegel, in the *Logic*, foregoes the "bridge" by phenomenologically *describing* Consciousness as a dialectical seamless constitutive "flow" of qualitative categories into quantitative measurements. There is no hiatus in consciousness and thus no "bridge" is required.

But in the Meditations, we observe Descartes trying to negotiate between soul and body, matter and mind. After acknowledging the Montaignian skeptical impasse of universal doubt in Mediation I, he invokes Augustine's principle of indubitability, the cogito from in *Contra Academicos*, in Mediation II, and Anselm's intuitive trust in God's goodness in not being a deceiver in Mediation V, while trying to do justice to the growing allure of mechanism inherent in the Scientific Revolution in Meditation VI. In effect, Descartes subsumes Plato's conflict between the God's and the Giants within his treatise and leaves it unresolved.

During Descartes and Hobbes' time, already the principle of mechanical causality was gaining scientific traction as Descartes sought to acknowledge and support the movement. His complex goal was to defeat skepticism; to process all knowledge through the cogito's criterion; epistemically to anchor the new science in clear (immediate) and distinct (definable) ideas; to depend on the beneficence of the Deity in assuring truth; prove the immortality of the soul; and endorse the mechanistic outlook of the new empirical sciences. On Descartes's considerable debt to Medieval theology, see Gilson.[4]

Descartes's genius consists in radically and conceptually separating the relation between matter and mind, thus completely bypassing the elaborate complexities of the entire Platonic system by severing at one stroke reality into two irreconcilable metaphysical substances, each with its own principles of operation, and by relegating the entire presence of the lower half of Plato's Divided Line passage to a realm of doubtful appearances, including mathematics, to a dream (First Meditation), thus abandoning each of us to our unique isles of desolation. Without God's beneficent intrusion, assuring us that an external world exists, the soul is absolutely *both* alone *and* lonely, as we are, each of us, abandoned to our intimate solipsistic spheres. But setting aside God's gratuitous disposition toward mankind, what is Descartes's "bridge" enabling him to "cross" from mind to matter? And is a bridge even necessary?

Cartesianism's Janus-like countenance reflects the past and anticipates the future. It represents the narrow stem of the philosophical hourglass, as he transforms everything that preceded as well as all that will follow. He also points toward two very different roads forward: *both* a concrete path of mechanical causality leading toward scientific certainties *but* also to an uncharted vista inclining toward the vast expanses of idealistic destinies soon to be traversed by Malebranche, Leibniz, Berkeley, Kant, Fichte, Hegel, Schopenhauer, and Bergson, as well as through the fields of Husserlian phenomenology and Sartrean existentialism. While the ancient Greek, Roman, Christian, and Renaissance thinkers essentially focused on three orders of metaphysical substances—God, soul, and matter—Descartes's egocentric revolution elaborately begins with a search for truth from *within the self alone*, as he seeks a universal criterion, one grounded in (a) clear, i.e., *pure immediate* non-sensory and (b) distinct, i.e., mediate *definable* conceptions, which will metamorphose into the immediacy of intuitions and the mediacy of judgments and inferences.

Descartes's soul possesses two critical attributes: immateriality and activity. The soul, as a substance, is both *simple*, i.e., *immaterial* and *actively* self-conscious. By contrast, he conceives matter as both extended and *inert*, while the *cause* of material motion is God (*Principles*, XXXVI). (Animal "consciousness" is reduced to mechanical automatons.) This radical distinction between mind and matter results in limiting any possible epistemic knowledge or physical interaction between soul and body, mind and matter. If the two substances share no attribute or predicate in common, then the twofold problem

Descartes's bridge to the external world 129

becomes how can the mind (a) epistemically acquire *knowledge* of the external world and (b) physically *interact* with it.

Initially, the Cambridge Platonists welcomed Descartes. But rather quickly his scientific flirtations with mechanism and determinism alarmed them and endangered their doctrine of an ethically free will. In their minds, Descartes's sacrifice of the entire Platonic hierarchical world of qualitative values resulted in chaining man to a deterministic materialism. He had severed reality into two disengaged substances, and in the process, he had cut lose any semblance of qualitative *values*, especially ethical, from the human sphere of self-consciousness.

And yet Descartes appears paradoxically determined to establish (a) a secure cognitive "bridge" from the mind to an external realm of material realities, a direct access into a scientific and independent realm of knowledge, while at the same time (b) demonstrating that the immaterial soul is immortal. To achieve the first goal, he needs somehow to "move" from the immediacy of sensation—and intuition (the cogito)—to the mediacies of scientific judgments. We recall that Plato also alludes to the mediacy of *judgments*, between thought and its affirmation, i.e., its mediate judgments (*Theaetetus*, 189e and *Sophist*, 263e). But in Plato, this issue is confined within an internal relation *within* the soul. He is not considering Descartes's problematic relation between his judgments *epistemically* connecting to an *external* referent; he is not concerned with "bridging" the separation between two *separate* but co-equal substances, mind and matter. Descartes, however, is in the middle of a scientific revolution and the growing battle between theology and science. At one point, in desperation, in his 1646 *Traite des Passions*, Section xxxi ff., he invokes the pineal gland in the brain as the physiological "bridge" between soul and body, which Spinoza will soon ridicule. Perhaps neuroscience can confirm this physically mediating and transitional role for us.

In Meditation II, Descartes ushers in his guiding principle of subjective idealism by announcing the clarion call of his cogito—"I exist only in so far as I reflexively think"; I could not exist without thinking and I could not think without existing. These *two* distinct conceptual elements—subject and predicate—are mutually implicative. And he insists that the mind "*is more easily known than the body.*" Then the problem becomes: how can he "move" from his doubt to assertions, to

130 Descartes's bridge to the external world

judgments reaching *beyond* and *transcendent* to the self? What is "the bridge"?

Descartes's dual goal then is first to establish an indubitable criterion of truth through the cogito, as it serves as a universal standard for all candidates summoned before the altar of truth. But his second, equally critical goal, is to escape from the prison of a solipsism that he has fashioned by whatever means and methods are conceptually possible and available.

For our contemporary neuroscientists, the issue of the "relation," the "dualism" between mind and body is non-existent, since the brain is *already* situated in the external world; it is biologically connected to it through the fetus-state and will remain so into adolescence and maturity. For neuroscience, there is only the immediacy of sensations, while the issue of "personal identity" is easily guaranteed via a person's unique DNA. Concerning any further issues concerning our personal identity, all we need to do in confirming who we are is to show our driver's license, social security card, and refer the questioner to our Facebook page.

The epistemic problem Descartes is juggling is the relation between (1a) the mind's passive sensations; (1b) acts of intuition (and/or spontaneity); (1c) the mediacy of judgments and inferences; and (2a) the mind's connection with and to an objective, independent scientific realm, an external world. Thus, the two critical questions looming before him is first *whether* he can escape the confines of epistemic solipsism, and second, if so, *how?* Is the soul forever prison pent, trapped within its own sphere of loneliness?

Descartes's only certainty lies in turning inwardly, within the self, within reflexive self-consciousness: "I think=I exist" is an existential, self-grounding *intuition*; an immediate, direct, and active apprehension of the self *within* its self as executed *by an act* initiated (spontaneously) by the self. The cogito's essence is defined as a circular act. But now it must reach "outer" things, independent objects.

Having moved so radically beyond Plato's (and later Hegel's) qualitative comprehensive vision, then the problem becomes how to cognitively relate, i.e., *bridge* the two substances to each other. How to reconcile and repair the original subtle but now utterly abandoned Platonic qualitative transitions: between appearance and reality; sensation and conception; *intuitive* immediacy and *temporal* mediacy; and ultimately *facts and values*. Plato had accommodated all these grades of reality by investing them with qualitative distinctions and significance, while Descartes disjoins them and leaves them dangling in the philosophical air.

We are now essentially left with four clearly irreconcilable metaphysical perspectives: (a) materialism (Hobbes); (b) truncated and neutered dualism (Descartes); (c) genuine Neoplatonic dualism (Cudworth and the British Platonists); and (d) subjective idealism (Leibniz). Science eliminates the qualitative aspects of reality by substituting quantitative factors alone and values are reduced to facts and subjective feelings while "judgments" of value are reduced to "emotive expressions" (Ayer, *Language, Truth and Logic*). Neuroscience remains implicatively two-dimensional—all that exists is material-motion. Gone is the meaning of life and its values.

Descartes's bridge to the external world

In Meditation II, Descartes offers his celebrated example of the piece of wax and asks us to consider it in the light of the conclusions he is seeking to establish.[5] Apart from Descartes's clear thesis that the knower is better known than what he knows, there are certain implications involved in the wax example, which commentators have misinterpreted as it underlies the critical junction between sensation and thought, immediacy and mediacy, and intuitions and relations.[6] Once more, these subtleties have no parallels in the neurosciences. Consciousness is multi-dimensional whereas science is three-dimensional (plus throw in time).

There are three possible interpretations implicated in Descartes's example of the "piece of wax." The usual interpretation claims that Descartes is seeking to prove that the essential nature of a material body lies in its defining attributes of spatial extension, infinite divisibility, and mathematical measurability. These predications are considered as primary, objective, i.e. intersubjectively verifiable. Motion, although measurable, is not a primary quality for Descartes because according to him (a) all movement depends on God's intervention (*Principle*, XXXVI); theoretically the universe could remain stationary. And second (b), he will argue, *contra empiricism*, that the *identity*, i.e., the *sameness* of a material body can only be grasped by the understanding, by the mind and not by the senses or the imagination.

132 Descartes's bridge to the external world

The first interpretation, as I shall argue, (a) is incorrect, whereas the second is obviously right. But beside denying thesis (a) and accepting thesis (b), I also want to offer a further interpretation by proposing that Descartes is concerned to show in Meditation II that (c), the human mind has the active power of making *mediate* and *relational* judgments and inferences; a capacity to *reach* mediately, discursively, indirectly (as opposed to intuitively, beyond the cogito, which is immediate and direct), toward an independent realm of existences. Plato's "sort of bridge" respected this distinction, namely the mediate nature of judgments, but he did not extend its *intentional* activity beyond the judgment itself. This third thesis enables Descartes to *reach* toward a transcendent world and other selves. This reach has *temporal* implications regardless whether or not it secures its intended goal (Leibniz). By contrast, according to materialists, empiricists, phenomenalists, behaviorists, and neuroscientists, this *mediate* activity of transcending intentional judgments does not exist in the arsenal of the brain. Both reflexive self-conscious and transcending intentional acts of consciousness are ruled out *ab initio* as metaphysical fictions thereby reducing and transforming all human cognition to Montaigne's sensory, subjective appearances. Nor is there any assurance that the "reaching beyond" is successful—that is why Descartes is forced to enlist the goodness of God. But for the neuroscientist, the distinction between immediate neurons and mediate neurons has no significance. The brain re-acts *passively, causally to external stimuli.*

A. E. Taylor in his influential study of Plato's *Timaeus*, which is cited repeatedly by S. V. Keeling and Norman Kemp Smith in their commentaries on Descartes, exemplifies the misinterpretation I intend to criticize. In his commentary, Taylor favorably compares Plato to Descartes in his discussion of Timaeus' point that "geometrical extension is the one universal and uniform invariant, which is always and everywhere the same" and he argues that both Plato and Descartes expound this identical conception of space.

> In the Second Meditation [Descartes] takes for consideration a lump of beeswax which is slowly melted, and points out that as it melts every sensible quality it originally had is lost, its shape goes, it expands in size, its colour and fragrance disappear, its hardness vanishes. What then do I mean by the thing I assume

Descartes's bridge to the external world 133

to be permanent throughout the process when I say that *it* was solid but now is fluid, was fragrant but is now scentless, and so on? Descartes says I can only mean that the one character that has not changed and that this character is that of being extended. The argument is so exactly that of Timaeus that we can hardly avoid believing that Descartes was writing with conscious or unconscious dependence on this passage of Plato.

(*Timaeus*, 50a-e)[7]

Similarly, S. V. Keeling in his interpretation of the wax passage follows the lead of A. E. Taylor, although in prefacing his discussion of the problem, Keeling warns us to distinguish, in the manner of Descartes, "questions of 'essence' from questions of 'existence.'" The problem concerning the wax belongs to the first category and Keeling is careful to caution us that in his analysis of the wax Descartes is *not* discussing an object in the external world *as yet*, i.e. up to the point of the Second Mediation. Nevertheless, Keeling goes on to observe that even as regards the essence of material things we have something to learn.

Yet careful analysis shows that, even beginning for such unclear ideas [as provided by the senses] as a basis, a definable meaning can be found for the term "material." This Descartes works out in his famous analysis of the essential character of the piece of wax, in Meditation II ... The argument presupposes what constitutes the "materiality" of a material thing is that (whatever it turns out to be) on account of which the body is "the same body" after undergoing alteration as it was before it was altered. So it follows that no determinate character the thing manifests at one moment, but fails to manifest at another can be, or be part of, what is meant by "being material," for we declare the thing to be "the same material body," when such transitory character is absent from it no less than when it is present. Now Descartes decides, the only characters that belong to the thing throughout the entire history of its alterations, and despite them, are a constant three-dimensional magnitude, susceptible under different conditions of assuming this or that determinate shape ...These determinate properties of being outspread in space [i.e., of being extended] ... are all that Descartes sees clearly [i.e., immediately] and distinctly [definably] to belong essentially and permanently to a material body. The characteristics the wax can lose without ceasing to be are, of course, smell, sweetness, softness, and so forth. Descartes here follows Galileo in dividing the qualities of things into primary and secondary ones, the former (the extensities and mobilities of bodies) belonging to them independently of being perceived, the latter not. Therefore extension must be the defining character of "matter"; it is on account of possessing this [attribute] that we call a thing "material" and that material existents are differentiated from those of other kind. This property of being extended can only be imagined vaguely and confusedly [versus clearly and distinctly] as, say, a more or less indefinite "spread" of some coloured homogeneous medium, but it can be *conceived* with perfect clearness and distinctness and is just what geometers call "space."

(cf. Keeling, op. cit., 125–126, cf. 143–144)

Thus, according to Taylor and Keeling, Descartes employs the melting wax experiment in order to show that the only attribute through which one can directly grasp or apprehend the wax *as identical, as remaining the same* is through its attribute of extension, which property alone allows it to be clearly (i.e. immediately) and distinctly (i.e. defined) conceived. After subjecting the piece of wax to the flame, Keeling contends only the primary quality of spatial three-dimensionality remains as the essential, defining characteristic of material bodies. The diverse secondary qualities, on the other hand, undergo a spectrum of modifications. Hence even such qualities as hardness are discovered to be *unessential* to "matter" as such, for if we imagined "that *every* body receded whenever our own body moved into contact with it, as in fact occurs with *some* bodies, e.g., water, air, we should never have come by the confused idea of hardness ... Hence hardness is not an essential [i.e., primary] quality of matter" (cf. Henry More, the Cambridge Platonist; Keeling, *op. cit.*, 143–144 note).

Gibson similarly interprets Descartes's example as an illustration of the principle that matter is essentially extended, infinitely divisible, and therefore intrinsically disunified.

Descartes shows in detail through the example of the piece of wax, every sensible quality of which changes before our very senses when it is exposed to the fire ... that its continued identity is explicable only in terms of a non-sensuous [conceptual] extension. All that is accidental must be stripped away, leaving only the essence without which it is impossible to conceive the object at all.

(Kemp Smith, op. cit., 23–24)[8]

Again:

There is no doubt, in view of Descartes's discussion of the piece of wax, in his belief that extension can be discovered in miniature at the base of every perception. It is these fragments of extension, and their compilations, which together form the objects of scientific knowledge.

All science can be reduced to two identifying conceptions: extended spatial matter plus physical motion. Matter in-itself is by definition inert. The motion, the movement is initiated by either falling motions or gravitational attractions, which together translate into a causal relation or sequences resulting in predictable outcomes, i.e., empirical science.

And finally, L. J. Beck echoes the same interpretation.

The point is that, in the analysis of the piece of wax, it was not by reliance of my sense or imagination that I got nearer to a more accurate knowledge of the nature of the wax; it was by turning to my intellectual powers that I was able to analyze it, to strip it of its accidental [secondary] properties ... [W]hat constitutes the reality, in this case the material reality, of a piece of wax is that which remains throughout all changes, or perhaps that on account of which the body remains the same body. [Descartes] is also making the point that certain properties of the wax (those that Locke will call secondary qualities) do not meet the requirements of enduring throughout the various changes from cold to hot, and that they must be considered as "accidental." They, however, are known to us through our senses ... [Thus] he is asking for a definition of what wax is, its essential nature. All in fact he is saying is that the essential property which persists throughout its modifications, and which is alone grasped by the intellect, is the determinable character of being extended. This thesis is not developed further for the very good reason that we have no right to assume the existence of the piece of wax or of any material object whatsoever.

(Beck, *opus cit.*, 99–102)

In other words, Beck recognizes that there is an improper violation of Descartes's own strict "order of reasons" if we are to consider the wax as an object in the external world before and until he has first authenticated the powers of the mind.

Nevertheless, Beck's contention is simply a repetition of the views of the preceding commentators already quoted, namely that Descartes recruits the wax example in order to demonstrate that we do not know an object in the external world by its variable subjective and sensory *mental* qualities but rather through a conceptual grasp, an immediate apprehension of its non-sensuous, i.e., its conceptual attribute of (mathematical) extension, which can only be conceived intellectually by the faculty of the understanding, *par l'entendement.* I do not disagree with these commentators that in the passage regarding the wax, Descartes is concerned with distinguishing the senses from the understanding. This contention is undoubtedly correct and beyond questioning. *But* what I am objecting to is their interpretation that he is *already* in Meditation II trying to demonstrate that the essential nature of a material body is extension. I am not of denying he *believes* that the essential attribute of a material body *is* extension. What I am denying is that he undertakes to show this as early as the Second Meditation. For it is manifestly clear that such an attempt would blatantly violate his exposition in view of his underlying commitment to a strict "order of reasons," his vaunted systematic, methodological principle stated in his "Rules for the Direction of the Mind." Descartes's method is, if anything, totally committed to unfolding his thought in a rigorously logical and disciplined manner. Thus, I would contend that in the Second Meditation, he is not assuming the existence of material objects, but neither is he concerned to show the nature or essence of physical bodies. Instead he is determined to describe, as he himself declares, "the nature of the human mind," the transcending powers of human consciousness.

But then the question naturally arises, a question obvious enough in light of the strong agreement between the preceding commentators: on what basis have they grounded their consensus on their agreed reading of Meditation II? And the answer is quite simply enough, on Descartes own words. For in the *Synopsis* to the Meditations, in the two paragraphs devoted to our subject, Descartes himself tells the reader that it was his intention and task to draw on the principle of the distinction "between the things which pertain to mind—that is to say to the intellectual nature—and those which pertain to the body." Similarly, he insists that "a distinct [i.e., separate] conception of corporeal nature" is given in the Second Meditation. *If* then this is Descartes's own view of the matter, on what possible grounds could one challenge the interpretation offered by the four Cartesian scholars cited above?[9]

The thesis I propose to offer is that Descartes's recapitulation of what occurs in Meditation II is highly misleading and despite his explicit utterances to the contrary in the introductory *Synopsis*, he is not in fact concerned with drawing the distinction between the essential conflicting attributes of mind and matter, soul and body in the Second Meditation but instead he is involved in depicting the fundamental powers of the human mind as the title indicates—and with that *alone.* But then how can one explain, I might as well say explain away, Descartes's imputed statements to the contrary?

The explanation, I believe, lies in the following account. Descartes originally titled his meditations—metaphorically a conflation of Augustine's *Confessions* and Montaigne's *Essays*, his "book of my self"—*Meditationes de Prima Philosophia in qua Dei existentia et Animae immortalitas demonstratur*, and it was originally intended in Descartes's own mind (a) to provide a basis for his twin *epistemological* criteria, of clarity and distinctness, as a foundation for his mathematical sciences; (b) proofs for *both* the *existence and* the *beneficence and veracity of God* (that He is not a deceiver regarding the reality of the external world and other souls, but also and foremost (c) as a revolutionary demonstration for the immortality of the soul. Thus, we may imagine his disappointment when we reflect that no sooner had he solicited Mersenne to gather a set of strategic "objections" to his work (we can only speculate as to how genuinely he wanted criticism) to realize his displeasure when at least the first two sets of *Objections*

138   Descartes's bridge to the external world

appeared so quickly. Regarding the Second Objections, Beck gives a vivid picture of Descartes's reaction.

> [The Second Objections] were collected by the Reverend Father Mersenne from the utterances of diverse Theologians and Philosophers. Descartes was rather surprised and annoyed to receive this set so quickly and did not hesitate to say so to Mersenne considering that the speed showed little application and study to his work.
>
> (Beck, *Descartes*, 40)

But what must have not only piqued Descartes but given him some considerable concern as well is the special criticism in the Second Objections, which accuses him of not having even attempted to demonstrate what he had set out to prove in his original title.

> Seventhly, you say not a word [in your Meditations] about the immortality of the human soul, which nevertheless you should above all things have proved and demonstrated as against those men—themselves unworthy of immortality—who completely deny it and perchance have an enmity against it. But over and above this you do not seem to have sufficiently proved the distinctness of the soul from every species of body, as we have already said in our first criticism; to which we now add that it does not seem to follow from the distinction you draw between it and the body that it is incorruptible and immortal. What if its nature be limited to the duration of the life of the body, and God has granted it only such a supply of force and has so measured out its existence that, in the cessation of the corporeal life, it must come to an end?[10]

But the author of the Second Objections was not the only reviewer who was critical of his proof, whether real or imaginary, that Descartes announced, but (perhaps) had not produced in his work. For in the Fourth Objections, Arnauld raises the same problem just mentioned.

> *Since M. Descartes has undertaken to prove the immortality of souls, it is right to ask if that follows evidently from this separateness of*

Descartes's bridge to the external world   139

existence. According to the principle of the vulgar philosophy that conclusion by no means can be drawn, for the common opinion is that the souls of animals are distinct from their bodies, but nevertheless perish with them.

However, as Arnauld observes in the next paragraph but one below this quotation, this does not present a problem for Descartes because he simply denies that animals have souls or the power of thought.

But he continues.

I had carried my criticism to this point and was intending to show how according to our author's principles, which I believed I had gathered from his method of philosophical inquiry, the immortality of the soul could be easily inferred from the distinctness of the body when a new work [viz., the Synopsis], a little treatise bearing the fruit of our author's reflections, came into my hands; and this work not only throws much light on the whole, but in connection with this passage brings forward exactly what I was to adduce with a view to the solution of the above passage.

(Arnauld, Objections IV, 85; italics his)

If we try to reconstruct what happened, we arrive at something like the following chain of events. Descartes after completing the Meditations asked Mersenne to procure some reaction to his work in order to test the current climate of philosophic opinion, and more specifically, in order to try to gauge the possible reception that would be accorded to his more scientific and anti-Aristotelian writings, e.g., *Le Monde*. In the eighteenth century, anyone in France who avowed allegiance to Aristotelianism was regarded as a pagan, i.e., an atheist. In the Meditations, Descartes assumes that proving the *absolute* distinction between soul and body *alone* is sufficient to prove the soul's immortality. But no sooner had he entrusted Mersenne with this mission than he received in the responses a vital criticism concerning his proof for immortality in the Second Objections. His reaction was twofold. First, he admitted it (although with some qualification); and second, he undertook to correct it in the *Synopsis*. Thus, in his *Reply to the Objections*, Descartes in answering the charge that he has not shown the soul to be indestructible declares that

140 Descartes's bridge to the external world

> In the synopsis of my Meditations I stated the reason why I have said nothing about the immortality of the soul. That I have sufficiently proved its distinctness from any body, I have shown above. But I admit that I cannot refute your further contention, viz. that the immortality of the soul does not follow from its distinctness from the body, because that does not prevent its being said that God in creating it has given the soul a nature such that its period of existence must terminate simultaneously with that of its corporeal life. For I do not presume so far as to attempt to settle by the power of reason any of the questions that depend on the free will of God.
>
> (Reply to Objections II, 47; cf. 85)

So, we may conclude that at this point (a) Descartes has proved that soul and body are absolutely distinct, but (b) he has not proved its immortality; nor (c) how soul and body are connected, related? Under pressure and in full retreat from what he considered to be justified challenges, Descartes composed the *Synopsis*. In it he qualifies the impression, which his original title might have given, and he commences his rejection of the expectation in the following apologetic terms.

> But because it may be that some expect from me in this place a statement of the reasons establishing the immortality of the soul, I feel I should here make known to them that I have aimed at writing nothing in all this Treatise of which I do not possess very exact demonstrations.
>
> (Synopsis)

Descartes does, however, in the *Synopsis* make one more attempt, a different one, to prove immortality. This "new" demonstration is sufficiently different that, as we have seen above, Arnauld claims himself to be satisfied with it, whereas he had expressed dissatisfaction with the proof based on the distinctness, the separation of soul and body. This proof is grounded in the "indivisibility," the immaterial simplicity of the soul. It follows that the soul is immortal.

It is not surprising then to find Descartes riding this old warhorse of an argument reluctant to commit himself to more than giving men the "*hope* of another life after death" (*Synopsis*). But perhaps the symbol of Descartes's admission of his failure to remain convinced he had provided an adequate proof for immortality in the Meditations is best reflected in his decision to change the original title and delete any mention of immortality from the heading.

In the *Synopsis*, he is already concerned in Meditation II in distinguishing matter from thought. He is setting forth his views in an ill-chosen and even false fashion. The reason is that he felt threatened by the Objections that he had not proved what he had promised (Gueroult, op. cit., 121–122). Reduced to a purely defensive position, Descartes cast about himself in the Meditations and lighted upon any and every passage where he uncovered intimating the distinction of the soul from the body and thereby implying a proof of immortality. His inconstancy in this matter is made quite obviously in the following quotation.

> Further [in order to establish immortality] we must have a distinct conception of corporeal nature, which is given partly in this Second [Meditation] and partly in the Fifth and Sixth Meditation. And finally we should conclude from all this, that those things which we conceive clearly and distinctly as being diverse substances, as we regard mind and body to be, are really substances essentially distinct from one from the other; and this is the conclusion of the Sixth Meditation.
>
> (Synopsis)

But certainly, this haphazard and sloppy method of exposition should not be taken as characteristic of the Meditations and Descartes in expressing himself in this fashion in the *Synopsis* is pronouncing utterances against his own best interests.[11] For in the "order of reasons," Descartes does not—and cannot—undertake to prove either the nature of extension or the existence of an independent, external world until he has *first* demonstrated the existence of God and His beneficence. For on Descartes' own principles, the malignant genius could just as readily deceive him regarding mathematical truths, as well as the external world. And the existence of God is not demonstrated until the Third Meditation; hence it would be futile for him to "prove" that the essential attribute of material bodies is allegedly undertaken in Meditation II. In Meditation III, Descartes, before beginning his

142 Descartes's bridge to the external world

proof for the existence of God, based on the principle that the idea of God cannot be created by the human mind, insists that the idea of extension may be contained within the soul "eminently" (Haldane and Ross, I, 165).

Starting from the cogito, in the strict order of reasons: (a) all our knowledge must first be grounded in the awareness of my own *active* mind, which then enables me (b) to grasp the *universal* criterion for all truth; and (c) our knowledge of a beneficent God, Who warrants the validity of my dual criteria of clarity and distinctness "so that these ... must be the most certain and most evident facts which can fall within the cognizance of the human mind" (Meditations, 143, 172). Clarity implies immediacy—the pain of a toothache may be clear, but it is not distinct, i.e., conceptually definable; and hence, it cannot be a universal item of knowledge or true. Truth can only reside in *both* immediacy, i.e., translucent clearness, *and* in conceptual distinctness, i.e., definability, as for example mathematical equations and geometric figures. Descartes, we recall, invented analytic geometry.

The new title includes the declaration that "The Distinction between Mind and Body Are Demonstrated." What remains to be further explored and determined—beyond the existential indubitability of the *intuition* of the cogito—is the *mediate* activity of the mind.

But up to this point, three considerations are at play. First, consciousness or the mind is simple, immaterial *and* there is *as yet* no consideration of an external world existing. Second, consciousness is spontaneous, *sui generis*, active; it appears to operate independently of an external world—*even in a dream* (Montaigne: "I have often in sleep been deceived"). Third, it entertains passive, given sensations. So now the question is exactly *how* does the mind function, what *are* its capabilities, its powers? What is the "bridge," if any, between "Mind and Body"?

For the purposes of this chapter, I shall not deal with the question whether Descartes is involved in a trap of circular reasoning concerning the criteria of the cogito and the goodness of God (Arnauld). My position is that the Cartesian cogito is an *existential* truth; the self cannot exist without thinking and it cannot think without existing precisely because all human thinking is reflexively self-conscious; i.e., even God could not deceive me that I exist; that I *appear* to sense, feel, and think, even without an external world.

Next Descartes announces that God has endowed me with a power of judgment.

> In the next place I experienced in my self a certain capacity for *judging* which I have doubtless received from God ... and as he could not desire to deceive me, it is clear that he has not given me a faculty that will lead me to err if I use it aright.
>
> (Meditation IV; italic mine)

In the structure of Descartes's argument, *at this point*, I only know that the mind exhibits an *active* power—in opposition to the passive nature of my sensations—of judging, of inferring, which is equally as important as the cogito and the criteria of certainty it provides. For even if the faculty of judgment deceives me, nevertheless it remains undeniably true that I experience an active *mediate, temporal* capacity along with and in addition to my active *immediate intuitive, spontaneous* cogito, *whether or not there is an external world.* But I must postpone the discussion of this faculty until I come to the final part of this chapter. Suffice it to say for the moment, that if we bear all these distinctions in mind, it should be clear why the previously cited commentators are wrong and why Descartes cannot be using the wax example to show that the essential attribute of material objects is extension. It would violate his rigorous method of reasoning, a method which critically enough itself rests on "a certain capacity of judging."

In the passage quoted below, we recall that Beck himself betrays the immanent conflict of his own interpretation.

> This thesis [namely that the essential nature of wax is constituted and defined by extension], however, is not developed any further for the very good reason that we have no right to assume the existence of the piece of wax, or of any material whatsoever.
>
> (Beck, 102)

That this sentence is not just a passing afterthought of the author but instead a crucial point in understanding Descartes may be gathered from Beck's following passage

> [Descartes] is, moreover making a point of capital importance for the study of his text; the whole work must be treated as a *single*

144   Descartes's bridge to the external world

argument and in this "order of reasons" lies the whole probative value. The *Meditations* will be an instance of those "long chains of reasoning" described in the *Regulae,* in which, even though we cannot embrace in one and the same vision all the intermediate links on which the connexion of the argument depends, we "know" the conclusion, provided we have seen *successively* all the links and their several connexions and provided we remember that each *successive* link, from first to last, was connected to its neighbour. We have been given here the clearest warning that to understand the metaphysical treatise of Descartes, we must in the words of the third rule "think in an orderly manner."

(ibid., italics mine)

One of Descartes's great irritations was the rapidity with which Father Mersenne was able to procure the Objections to the Meditations. For Descartes, this quick response was simply an unfortunate indication of the refusal of the critics to think through the problems in a sufficiently thorough and serious manner. Descartes was quite careful in titling his work—Meditations— and he expected that readers would study and reflect upon his treatise and not merely read it. Instead the objectors failed to process it in the systematic fashion in which he had expounded it and had neglected to meditate slowly and repeatedly on the sequence of results as he believed himself to have successively achieved.

But there is still another reason why we cannot take the wax example as intended to prove the extended nature of physical objects. The commentators discussed all fail to consider the second example Descartes considers—the one in which he discusses whether the men he sees *temporally* passing by in the street are really human beings and not automatons. Concerning the wax example, Descartes has just concluded in the preceding paragraph that he knows the wax by an inspection (the word is incorrectly translated in the Haldane and Ross edition as *intuition*) of the mind (*par la seule inspection de l'esprit*), by the *understanding* (Plato's mathematical *dianoia*). In the same way, he declares, I know that I see men and not machines covered with hats and coats, for it is the understanding, *l'entendement*—and *not* intuition—it is the *active mediate judgment* of the mind, it is an *inference* that comprehends (a) the wax as the *same* piece *after the mediate changes* in its appearances have occurred. It is a judgment, an inference—even if incorrect—that (b) the pedestrians are human beings and not robots. It is not, of course, the fact that both the wax and the men possess the attribute of extension. On the grounds of extension *alone*, wax and men would be indistinguishable. From the mere consideration that the wax can be conceived through the attribute of a conceptual non-sensuous extension, I could never know either that it is the same piece of wax or *judge* that the pedestrians are men and not automatons. But I *do successively, temporally infer* that it is the same piece of wax and I *do successively think* the strollers are not machines. Consequently, in this respect, the fact that wax and men are both extended tells me nothing. For these reasons we can conclude that both passages have nothing to do with the commentators' (or Descartes's own) claim that he is proposing to demonstrate that the essential nature of material bodies is extension intellectually conceived or otherwise.

But the critical consideration is that while the cogito is an immediate, direct, intuitive grasp, my judgement—whether it is true or not—*is a relational, temporal comprehension.*

> [W]hen looking from a window and saying I see men who pass by in the street, I really do not see them, but *infer* that what I see are men, just as I say that I see wax. And yet what do I see from the window but hats and coats which may cover automatic machines? Yet I *judge* these to be men. And similarly solely by the faculty of judgment which rests in my mind, I [mediately] comprehend that which I believed I saw with my eyes.
>
> (ibid.; italics mine)

Martial Gueroult, in his study of Descartes, suggests the same point I am making concerning the distinction between an immediate and a mediate power in the mind and he further states that the mediate knowledge of the world presupposes an immediate condition. He ushers in his remarks about the wax in the following terms.

> Ce que je croyais voir de mes yeux, je le comprends par la seule puissance de juger qui reside en mon esprit. Les corps ne sont pas connu de se qu'ils sont vus et touches, mais de ce qu'ils sont entendus ou bien compris par la pense. Par ou je connais que, les corps etant connus par l'intermediaire de l'ame, la connaisance de

> l'ame precede celle du corps comme l'immediat precede le mediat, la condition le conditionne. On retrouve ici par une autre biais, la conclusions directement en suivant l'ordre genetique des raisons.
>
> (Gueroult, op. cit., 121–122)

This is what constitutes mediate, relational, inferential, and *temporal* judgments. This is the *bridge* between consciousness and matter. This is what sensations alone and brain neurons alone cannot explain. Long ago, we recall that Plato described the *temporal quality* of judgments (*Theaetetus*, 189E) and (*Sophist*, 263E). Descartes's judgment is mediate, it reaches "outwardly" through a temporal conduit as it is actively, spontaneously initiated from within. But neurons are homogeneous; there are sensory neurons but no inferential neurons, no relational neurons. It is not only that Descartes separates soul from body, mind from matter—including brain neurons—immediacy from mediacy, but also sensations from judgments. To the best of my knowledge, there are no identifiable temporal neurons that are distinguishable from the *homogeneous* mass of blobby ones in neuroscience.

Why is this important? Because it is the juncture between the metaphysics of monistic materialism and qualitative dualism. I have argued that Descartes's illustration of the wax example is intended to demonstrate the fact that the human mind exhibits the twin powers of immediate apprehension, as exemplified in the cogito, as well as the power, the spontaneous activity to judge, infer, and guess about existences beyond and transcendent to its self. In so far as he is right, this supports my theory of subjective idealism and human loneliness. That is the positive part of his heritage. But what he has lost in his accomplishment is the infinite richness of Plato's and Hegel's qualitative realities.

The second issue is Descartes's metaphysical dependence on the goodness of the Deity in not deceiving mankind. But that is an inference without any support. Following Descartes, the mind-matter dilemma is bequeathed to Malebranche, who formulates a doctrine of divine intervention between God and man with his "occasionalist" theory in which God miraculously coordinates the interactions between human souls and their bodies. When I *think* of raising my arm, God *physically* raises it for me. Leibniz follows suit with his own theistic theory of a "pre-established harmony" coordinated by God between distinct "windowless spiritual monads, as He provides the *appearance* of contacts between separate souls. When I *think* or *perceive* I am communicating with an "other soul, actually the "other soul" in my mind thinks "he" is listening to me but there is no *real* interaction. And Berkeley's immaterialist theory holds that "We only see all things in God through the order of His natural laws"; we *ideally* participate through Him by experiencing "all the furniture of heaven and earth." Further for Berkeley, the soul only has a "notion" of activity, but it is not self-conscious. Accordingly, all three thinkers are forced to follow in Descartes's failing theistic footsteps in securing a "bridge" beyond the soul.

Why is Descartes's treatise called Meditations? First, because although both Plato and Christianity's theological thought, especially Augustine's, is metaphysically dualistic, no previous thinker had so distinctly separated the soul from reality. And second, once Humpty-Dumpty fell off the wall and was broken, not all the king's men and all their horses were unable to put him back together again. But third, and importantly, only Hegel's *Science of Logic* provides a meaningful, seamless, developmental solution to metaphysical "dualism" in his *Science of Logic*. There are two worlds, material and spiritual, but there is only one path that leads each of us by the way of self-consciousness to our subjective knowledge and correspondingly to our individual existential choices.

Notes

* Mijuskovic, Ben, "Descartes's Bridge to the External World: The Piece of Wax," *Studi Internazionali di Filosofia*, III: (1971); reprinted in *Descartes: Critical Assessments*, edited by Georges Moyal, (London: Routledge, 1996), II, 312–328.

1 Popkin, Richard, *The History of Scepticism from Erasmus to Descartes* (New York: Harper & Row, 1964). Professor Popkin was my dissertation director.

2 *The Complete Essays of Montaigne,* translated by Donald Frame (Stanford, CA: Stanford University Press,1968), 444.

3 Cornford, Frances MacDonald, *The Republic of Plato,* translated and with a running commentary (New York & London: Oxford University Press, 1968), 221 ff. Cf. *Hegel's Lectures on the History of Philosophy* (London: Routledge and Kegan Paul, 1968), translated by E. S. Haldane and F. S. Simpson), 43, 56–57, 61, 67. In both Plato and Hegel, it is the dialectic

148   Descartes's bridge to the external world

that functions as the *continuous* "bridge" unifying substances and cognitive qualities.

4   Gilson, Etienne, *Etude sur le Role de la Pense Medievale dans la Formation du System Cartesien* (Paris: Librairie Philosophique, J. Vrin, 1967), 191–201, 159–162. Cf. L. J. Beck, *The Metaphysics of Descartes: A Study of the Meditations* (Oxford: Clarendon Press, 1965), 212; S. V. Keeling, *Descartes* (Oxford, 1968), 119; and Norman Kemp-Smith, *New Studies in the Philosophy of Descartes* (New York: Russell & Russell, 1963), 18 note, 20, 23, 95 note, 194 note. Later, in the Objections, Arnauld criticizes Descartes's version of intuitive truth as circular since its certainty depends on *both* God's existence *and* his *goodness.* But His existence is in turn guaranteed by the veracity of our intuitions; *Philosophical Works of Descartes,* translated by E. Haldane and G. R. T. Ross (New York: Dover, 1955); Fourth set of Objections, II, 92.

5   Possibly the example of the wax was suggested to Descartes by a similar employment made by Augustine when he argues a substance can continue to be called by the same name despite a considerable change in its qualities.

> For if wax changes to a black color from white, it is none the less wax; and also it assumes a round shape after being square, becomes hard when it has been soft, cools after being hot. These are all in the subject, and wax is the subject. But wax remains more or less wax when these things [i.e., predicates] are changed. Therefore, some change of the things in the subject can occur, when the subject itself is changed with regard to what it is called.
>   (Augustine, On the Immortality of the Soul, Chapter Five)

Descartes, who, of course, expressed a deep interest concerning proofs demonstrating the existence of an afterlife, may have read Augustine's work, especially after coming under the influence of the Augustinian Oratory. Meanwhile Pope Leo X expressed his dismay that philosophers continued trying to prove immortality rather than simply accepting it on the grounds of faith.

6   Pierre Gassendi, in *Objections V,* correctly grasps that Descartes's main purpose in the wax example is to show that the mind is better known than the body, which interpretation Descartes readily acknowledges in his Reply. This interpretation is undoubtedly right and consequently I have not undertaken to discuss it as one of the possible interpretations but rather I have elected to concentrate on the wax's fuller implications. Interestingly, Hobbes is the author of *Objections III,* where he states, "From the fact that I am exercising thought it follows that I am, since that which thinks is not nothing ... For in the same way, I might say, I am walking; hence I am the walking." Here, in a nutshell, we have Plato's battle of the God's and the Giants, between the idealists and the materialists.

Descartes's bridge to the external world   149

7 Taylor, A. E., *A Commentary on Plato's Timaeus* (Oxford, 1962), first published in 1928); 322. Cf. S. V. Keeling, *op. cit.,* 125–126; cf. 143–144. Taylor, Keeling, and Kemp Smith are all convinced that Descartes was familiar with the *Timaeus.* We recall that Descartes withdrew the publication of his *Le Monde* following the condemnation of Galileo by the Church.

8 Gibson, A. B., *The Philosophy of Descartes* (New York: Russell & Russell, 1967), 9, 14–15, 24, 44–45, 55, 78, 100, 323. Cf. Todd Schmaltz, *Early Modern Cartesianism, Dutch and French Influences* (Oxford University Press, 2017), Chapter 3: "At La Fleche the study of mathematics delighted him more than any other subject 'because of the certainty of its proofs and the evidence of its reasonings'"; of course, the essence of the science of mechanics is mathematics; Keeling, *op cit.,* 6–9. Kemp Smith, *op. cit.,* 23–24; Gibson, *op. cit.,* 9, 14–15, 24, 44–45, 55, 78, 100, 109, 323. On Descartes's Platonism, cf. Keeling, *op. cit.,* 6–9.

9 We know that the *Synopsis* was composed before Arnauld submitted his criticisms to Descartes, since he tells us that a "little treatise" came into his hands while he was in the process of writing his objections. On the other hand, we also know that the composition of the *Synopsis* postdates Descartes's reception of the second set of objections, since he explicitly refers to some (unspecified) *Objections* and *Replies* in the *Synopsis.* Thus for example, Descartes already mentions another version of a proof for God's existence, which he offers in answer to the request of the author of the *Second Objections;* and we can hardly doubt that he is referring to his *Arguments Demonstrating the Existence of God and the Distinction between Soul and Body, Drawn Up in Geometrical Fashion.* In point of fact, the *Synopsis* was sent by Descartes to Mersenne fifty days after the Meditations had surfaced. *Philosophical Works of Descartes,* translated by E. Haldane and G. R. T. Ross (New York: Dover, 1955), 85, note 2.

10 This proof undoubtedly held a favorite place among the thinkers associated with the Neo-Platonic and Augustinian Oratory, to which circle Descartes belonged. Thus for example, the proof of the immortality of the soul, as grounded in its immaterial simplicity, *Phaedo,* 78b ff., is explicitly stated by Plotinus, *Ennead Four,* Tractatus Seven; cited by Augustine in *De Trinitate,* vi, 6; and resurrected by Marsilio Ficino, *Theologia Platonica,* Book II, 3 and Book XIV, 3, all of which works we can assume the Oratory to have been familiar with. Actually, Descartes had stated in the Meditations that the mind is "indivisible," i.e., simple because of its immaterial, unextended nature. But he had failed to explicitly relate it to a proof for immortality, precisely what subsequently satisfied Arnauld. I might further add that the assumed simplicity had traditionally certain inherent problems connected with it that implied a doctrine of reincarnation as in Plato. Indeed, the first edition was simply titled *First Meditations* (Haldane & Ross, I, 144,

note 1; cf. also, Descartes's letter to Mersenne, dated December 24, 1640 and Bernard Rochot's concluding explanatory note for support of this speculative hypothesis; P. M. Mersenne, *Correspondence,* edited by C. De Ward; Vol. 10, 344, 347 note.

11 Gueroult, Martial, *Descartes selon l'ordre des raisons,* where this thematic is fully elaborated, 18; see also 121–122; and Norman Kemp Smith, *The Philosophy of David Hume* (St Martin's Press, 1964), 117.

Chapter 7

Locke and Leibniz on personal identity

Without a substantial self, the issues of personal identity and lone-liness are meaningless. They disintegrate into phenomenalism, the "self" as a contingent construction of fleeting sense data. The anchors of time-consciousness and the unity of consciousness evaporate in the flux and fog of a disunified transiency. In Western thought, there are two avenues toward epistemic certainty. Rationalism maintains that there are some truths and ideas that are known independently of sensations and experience (Descartes, Spinoza, and Leibniz). By contrast, empiricism claims that all our ideas and truths are passively derived, i.e., caused by precedent sensations and experience (Locke, Berkeley, and Hume). It follows from the latter's premises that since the "self's" origin lies externally to the self, it is impossible to fashion a substantial concept of the self. This is true of Locke's uncertainty regarding the identity of the "self" as an "I know not what substance"(Essay); Berkeley's claim that "such is the nature of spirit or that which acts, that it cannot be, of itself perceived" (Principles); and Hume's "self" as "nothing but a bundle or collection of different perceptions" (Treatise). The same deficiency lies at the neuroscientific juncture of the brain.

Whatever Descartes's theoretical strengths and weaknesses might be, he certainly influenced both Leibniz and even Kant's forward paths.[1] Without a viable and substantial self, both loneliness as well as ethical responsibility are meaningless. But now I wish to turn to Locke's empiricist approach to selfhood and contrast it with Leibniz's idealist treatment.

Throughout three interweaving contexts, ethical, epistemological, and psychological, the issue of personal identity is critically important. Unless we can be certain that an individual, who commits a moral act at Time-1, is the same person, who is being

DOI: 10.4324/9781003156130-8

held accountable at Time-2, valuations of praise and blame are inoperable. Without a secure determination for personal imputability, reward and guilt are valueless. The second reason is that unless it can be shown that the self exhibits certain indubitable temporal and cognitive continuities over time, the reality of a self is questionable. And the third consideration is that in order to explore the deeper psychological motivational issues of an "abiding self," it is necessary to establish the first and second requirements and then the third concern will naturally follow.

In the seventeenth and eighteenth centuries, the simplicity premise and argument assumes a critical role in controversies between the empiricists, dualists, and idealists in regard to their opposing efforts to establish a criterion for personal identity. Locke is the first to address the issue as a special problem in its own right when he adds a chapter, at the request of his friend and correspondent, William Molyneux, in the second edition of his *Essay*, titled *Of Identity and Diversity*, dealing with the application of the "principle of individuation" in various contexts (*Essay*, II, xxvii). The concepts of personal and moral identity are mutually implicative and *mean* the same for Locke. The reality of the self is grounded in the establishment of two critical criteria: (1) a form of "intuitive" consciousness, presumably in the manner of Descartes, as well as (2) a biological organization of bodily parts with both together forming the necessary and sufficient conditions for holding an individual morally accountable.

In the *Essay*, Locke's conception of consciousness as "reflective" is quite different from Cartesian *reflexivity*. His ruling empiricist paradigm, his analogical metaphor that the mind is like a *passive* blank table upon which sensation and experience write, is actually "observational" and a clear violation of Descartes's principle of "intuitional circularity."

In terms of personal identity, Locke envisions two possibilities: (a) a version of Descartes's cogito, which he calls "reflection"; or (b) a plausible empirical base for bodily continuity. In the second case, we must be able to confirm the *continuity* of the bodily subject; that the agent of our predications is *temporally* the *same* subject through time. The problem, of course, is that the body undergoes a complete cellular transformation in a relatively short period of time. Basically, Hobbes had avoided the entire issue. For Hobbes, the continuity of the "self" is a nominalist fiction. And as a materialist, Hobbes is roundly criticized as an atheist by the Cambridge Platonists. But there were others at the time who promoted a more consistent bodily materialism along with a doctrine of natural mortality and a denial of immortality.

Locke, as a Christian, believes in the immortality of the soul on the grounds of faith. *But* because Locke is also committed to the theistic doctrine of the resurrection of the body in the afterlife, he becomes inextricably enmeshed in concerns regarding the immortality soul *and* the resurrection of the body in the afterlife. I say the body because he believes that after death, the body will disintegrate but following an unspecified interval of time, it will be restored to "somewhat" its prior state on the final Day of Judgment when all souls will be summoned before the altar and throne of God and ethically evaluated by Him.[2]

We recall that originally Plato, and indeed the entire Neo-Platonic Christian tradition, defines the soul as a *simple*, i.e., immaterial, incomposite, and indivisible but *active* substance as it is presented in the *Phaedo*.[3] In the Christian tradition, once created by God, the soul continues forever. Only God can create or annihilate the immaterial soul.

For Locke, all material bodies, including human ones, consist of parts external to each other and accordingly they are susceptible to decomposition and death. Death is simply the dissolution of the human compound and its resolution into its constituent now lifeless parts. And Locke proceeds to discuss the curious practice of mummification practiced by the ancient Egyptians but even then, the body is not indestructible (*Essay*, Section 8). Plato, of course, believes in the doctrine of metempsychosis, the reincarnation of the soul and the body with its subsequent transmigration into different forms of life (*Republic*, Myth of Er). Locke, however, is not interested in the Platonic doctrine of the soul's multiple metamorphoses, but he is concerned about the Christian account of the miraculous resurrection of the body. Indeed, he is implicated in the so-called "mortalist heresy," along with George Wither, Richard Overton, John Milton, and others, who, following Faustus Socinus, maintain that the soul is "naturally" mortal; that *both* the body *and* the soul terminate at death only later to be resurrected. In *The Reasonableness of Christianity* (1695), Locke

154   Locke and Leibniz on personal identity

stresses the reconstitution of the human body after death by quoting Scriptures with approval while maintaining that

> We must appear before the judgment seat of Christ, that everyone may receive the things done in his body, according to that he has done, whether good or bad; and that "all shall come forth from their graves, they that have done good to the resurrection of life. And they that have done evil, unto the resurrection of damnation."[4]

Thus, on the Day of Judgment, when the world ends, the dead, presumably, who have "lain in wait," who knows where, will be reincarnated. For according to Locke, without a physical body, rewards and punishments in either heaven or hell are meaningless.

In his new chapter, Locke discusses four distinct criteria matching an equal number of different sorts of "identities," each depending on the kinds of objects studied. First, he distinguishes nominal identities, merely material aggregates, without any real principle of unity, which he characterizes as a "cohesion of particles of matter any how united," as for example a heap of sand. Second, he considers mechanical identities in which the principle of unity lies in the mind of the artificer, as in a machine or a watch. Third, he discusses organic identities as discovered in plants, animals, and humans, in which the unity is derived from within the substance through "an organization of parts in one coherent body, partaking of one common life."[5] Fourth, he invokes the criterion of a seemingly "intuitive" consciousness. Thus "consciousness" represents the critical element in defining personal or moral identity and the establishment of the continuity of the self requires that it is the *same* self who committed a moral act and is now being evaluated. It is a necessary condition for holding someone morally responsible, as well as legally, since Locke assures us that the word *person* is also a forensic term. And he adds memory but that will play a more subservient role.

While Locke was living in political self-exile in Europe, he corresponded with Damaris Masham, the daughter of Ralph Cudworth, the leading figure of the British Platonist movement, and she was a strong advocate for her father's views. In 1691, upon his return to England, Locke took up permanent residence at Oates, Lady Masham's ancestral home, where he engaged in lively discussions

Locke and Leibniz on personal identity   155

with her and her frequent visitors, all of whom were familiar with the writings of the Cambridge men, including John Smith, Henry More, Benjamin Whichcote, Nathaniel Culverwell et al. but also importantly, Leibniz. Cudworth defines the soul in the following terms.

> A thinker is a *monade,* or one single substance, and not a heap of substances; whereas no body or extended thing is one, but many substances, every conceivable or smallest part thereof, being a real substance by itself.[6]

According to this line of reasoning, it follows that the identity of the person is twofold. It resides in an unchanging substantial soul or self that continues as a *reflexive* "center," i.e., as a monadic *self*-conscious "unity," but also it is one which is intrinsically active, as exemplified by the Cartesian cogito, and, most critically, it remains *temporally* present *as a continuous substance*, one which is always accessible despite its varying accidental or non-essential predications. Accordingly, the simple, unified, identical, and continuous monad is *constituted*—not materially caused—by its self-conscious activities emanating *within* the self, by and through its own internal resources, which form a permanent ground, a basis for human cognition, ethical responsibility, and immortality. And most importantly, its unity of consciousness.

> It is properly called, I My Self, not the extended bulk of the body, which is not one but many substances, but an unextended and indivisible unity ... one self-active ... substantial, or inside being.
>
> (ibid.)

After Locke, John Witty, Samuel Clarke—Isaac Newton's defender—and others followed suit along the same lines indicated by Cudworth. Thus, for example, John Witty insists that as thinking substances "are absolutely simple and infinitely removed from divisibility by a strict necessity, each of them must forever continue the same individual thing." Obviously, this premise exhibits a two-fold purpose: it establishes not only an inherent personal identity but, once created by God, the soul becomes endowed with an eternal existence as well.

Similarly, Samuel Clarke, in directing his objections against "Materialists and Mechanists" alike, is especially critical of Henry

Dodwell's thesis that man only exists as a *completely* material compound. For as Clarke insists,

> Your [Dodwell's] doctrine perplexes the notion of Personal Identity, upon which identity the justice of all reward or punishment manifestly depends; makes the resurrection in your way of arguing, to be inconceivable and impossible. And consequently your doctrine (which supposes the body to be the whole man), is destructive of all religion; leaving no room for reward or punishment, but in the present life only; and consequently giving men the liberty to do everything for their present pleasure or advantage ... which is the greatest mischief that can possibly befall mankind. But if the soul be, as we believe, a permanent indivisible immaterial substance, then all these difficulties vanish.[7]

The materialists, as opposed to the rationalists and the spiritualists, maintain that the identity of the self can be established by an appeal to bodily identity alone in this life. This notion is also implied by Hobbes' materialistic nominalism. According to Hobbes, we *call* a man the "same" man only insofar and as long as *we* arbitrarily choose *to name*, *to designate* certain physical appearances or groupings by a common term. "*This* is John Smith."[8] Again, what inclines Hobbes' conviction in this direction is the so-called "mortalist heresy," originally initiated by Faustus Socinus (the precursor of Socinianism and later Unitarianism), namely the doctrine that it can be *rationally* demonstrated that man is *naturally* mortal, as it was presented in England by George Wither, as well as in Richard Overton's anonymous pamphlet.[9] Accordingly, "mortalism" is a theoretical position Locke *inconsistently* sympathizes with because he believes it supports his doctrine of the resurrection as an article of Christian faith. For Locke, the immortality of the soul is secured by revelation, by faith. The collective claim of the "mortalists" is that the "soul" of man is reducible to the body and hence just as mortal as lower forms of life. And the only means by which man can be granted immortality is "conditionally," by God's "gift of grace," in so far as He *elects* to resurrect the human body on the Day of Judgment.[10]

Accordingly, Locke asserts, along empiricist lines,

> that we may be able, without any difficulty, to conceive the same person at the resurrection, though in a body not exactly in make or parts the same which he had in this present state, the same consciousness going along with the soul that inhabits it.
>
> > (*Essay*, I, II, XXVII, Section 15)

Nevertheless, it should be cautioned that Locke himself can also be interpreted as a rationalist and a metaphysical dualist.

> Locke regards the mind as a substance but a substance which is material. He accepts the usual dualism, the "two parts of nature," active immaterial substance and passive material substance, although he is most uneasy in his mind about the conception of substance itself, both material and immaterial ... It is a fundamental point with him that the universe cannot be explained in terms either of matter alone or mind alone. The one cannot be reduced to the other. Of the two, perhaps, mind is more indispensable, for mind is the active, productive principle. Matter produces nothing. In particular, to think of it as producing thought, Locke agrees with Cudworth, is to think an absurdity.[11]

We need to remember that despite all of Locke's "empiricist" convictions, *essentially* God remains a *spiritual* and *immaterial substance*. Locke's uncertainty regarding the possibility of securing certain knowledge concerning the concept of "substance," either material or spiritual, is evident when he describes substance "as an I know not what."

Of course, we cannot understand how matter could possibly think. But we also cannot understand how an immaterial substance can think either (so Hume later). On any view, thinking and knowing are mysteries. Nevertheless, it remains true that mere matter *alone* can never be the sole originating source of thought, even though material beings do happen to think. On the one hand, Locke maintains that each of us, as a human creature, possesses a sufficiently *substantial* material component to be *called* a "self." But on the other hand, he also insists

158 Locke and Leibniz on personal identity

on the necessary existence of a purely cogitative eternal Being in order to account for the presence of thought in mankind and even in lower orders of beings. We recall that by contrast, Descartes regards animals as robots lacking a soul.

Both criteria, the rationalist and the materialist, the latter in the guise of empiricism and phenomenalism, are extremes for Locke and he problematically seeks to mediate between them. The rationalists are wrong because as dualists they have completely severed any possible cognitive exchanges between soul and body, as well as any physical interaction between mind and matter. But the materialists, are likewise unable to plausibly make sense of "how senseless matter alone can think," which for Locke leads to certain puzzling theoretical difficulties concerning the transmigration of souls and transposed identities.

For example, Locke discusses the possibility of a prince waking up with his own continuous memories but in the body of a cobbler. The question then becomes which or "who" is the "true" person? A second difficulty entails such bizarre cases as men being turned into swine (the *Odyssey*?). Locke also considers an actual case, Prince Maurice's parrot, "who," or "which," reportedly had the ability to carry on rational conversations. The Prince had elaborately arranged to interview the parrot in the Brazilian jungle using an interpreter because the bird only spoke Portuguese and the Prince only spoke French (Section 8). Locke also considers the peculiar possibility of someone's little finger *alone* possessing the full consciousness of personhood.[12]

But eventually Locke declares that when we use the term "man" in our *language,* it essentially implies a natural combination and coordination between (a) organic bodily parts, e.g., arms and legs instead of wings; and (b) the ability to carry on rational discourses. Since the parrot does not have a human form, it cannot be *said* to be a man. The designation of humanity to the parrot would involve a complete violation of our ordinary ways of speaking, as well as an abandonment of our common sense. Traditionally, empiricism and language theory have always been mutually supportive, as all analytic and linguistic philosophers can vouch.

But basically, the shortcomings of the materialists, as Locke conceives it, is that anatomists and physiologists had already shown by his day that the human body undergoes a complete bodily transformation in material composition within a relatively short span of time. Hence personal identity cannot rest on bodily identity alone. Again, for our current reigning neuroscientists, the uniqueness and security of "personhood" protectively resides in the subject's DNA; it is not a problem; nothing could be simpler.

What then does Locke conclude from all this, at least in relation to Hobbes and Cudworth, the foremost English representatives of materialism and dualism during his time? What are the options, in terms of personal identity, as Locke conceives them to be? And more specifically, in terms of a *substantial* personal identity? Either it is the same individual, immaterial thinking substance; the same identical soul and nothing else. Or second, the same human body without any regard to an immaterial soul. Or third, the same immaterial spirit united somehow to an organic body (Section 21). But take which of these suppositions you please, it is impossible to make personal identity to consist in anything but consciousness or reach any further than it does. Hence, he offers an empirical criterion consisting of a threefold synthesis: (a) self "reflection," i.e., perceptual observations and personal memories; plus (b) a relatively stable continuing bodily presence, which (c) after death will eventually be sufficiently restored and recognized in the afterlife.

Accordingly, Locke's sense of personal identity is empirically secured by conscious reflection. Locke also assumes that without a "reflective" memory, which is to be extended into the afterlife, thinkers become entrapped in the absurdities of reincarnation. Faced with these radically divergent views, it is understandable why Locke felt uncertain in reconciling these conflicting positions.

Locke's solution to the problem of personal identity

Finally, it is *reflective* consciousness that is the critical determining criterion of personal identity. "It is impossible to make personal identity to consist in anything but consciousness, or reach any further than that does" (Section 21); "personal identity can by us be placed in nothing but consciousness (which is that alone which makes what we call *self*)"; and it is "that with which the consciousness of this thinking can join itself [to a body] makes the same *person* and is one *self* with it, and with nothing else, and so attributes to itself and owns the actions of that thing as its own, as far as consciousness reaches, and no further."

160 Locke and Leibniz on personal identity

Leibniz later went on to object that this position on memory implies a person could not be held morally accountable for what he has forgotten. But clearly for Locke, this shortcoming is countered by God's omniscience that on the Day of Judgment God's absolute knowledge guarantees that "the secretes of all hearts shall be laid open [and] ... no one shall be made to answer for what he knows nothing of" (Section 22).[13]

Locke's *Essay* was composed over a period of two decades, while he was basically a political refugee on the run and his thoughts underwent many modifications, including (a) his uncertainty in regard to his conception of the term "substance" as "an I know not what." But even more dramatically is his radical conceivability that (b) God could have created "thinking matter," which thesis explodes like a bombshell on the theological and intellectual fields of battle, and leads to his being accused of Socianism, deism, mortalism, and even atheism during his long-standing argument, virtually a feud, with Edward Stillingfleet, Bishop of Worcester, when Locke suddenly detonates his controversial thesis aimed against the Cambridge Platonists and indeed the entire Christian theological community in general.[14]

> We have the *ideas* of *matter* and *thinking* but possibly shall never be able to know whether any mere material being thinks or no; it being impossible for us, by the contemplation of our own ideas, without revelation, to discover whether Omnipotency has not given to some systems of matter, fitly disposed, a power to perceive and think, or else joined and fixed to matter, so disposed, a thinking immaterial substance; it being, in respect of our notions, not much more remote from our comprehension to conceive that God can, *if he pleases,* superadd to matter a faculty of thinking, than that he should superadd to it another substance with a faculty, since we know not wherein thinking consists, nor what sort of substances the Almighty has been pleased to give that power ... For I see no contradiction in it that the first eternal thinking being should, if He pleased, give to certain systems of created senseless matter, put together, as he thinks fit, some degrees of sense, perception, and thought: though, as I have proved, it is no less than a contradiction to suppose matter (which is evidently in its own nature void of sense and thought) should be that eternal first thinking being.
>
> (*Essay*, Book IV, Chapter III, 6, italics mine)

The issue centers on two considerations. First, the extent of God's unlimited power to produce metaphysical contradictions, e.g., *ex nihilo* to create "thinking matter" and bodily resurrections, etc. Second, the reference to God, "if he pleases," brings to the fore the Calvinist issues of God's pre-destinarianism and absolute voluntarism against the Cambridge men's counter-thesis that even God cannot violate the laws of reason. We recall Plato's *Meno* in this context, which asks whether something is good-in-itself, intrinsically, i.e. rationally or simply because it pleases the gods. Both issues become complicated by Locke's determination to account for man's immortality, while at the same time problematically trying to defend his doctrine of a bodily resurrection.[15]

Descartes's "reflexion" versus Locke's "reflection"; Descartes's intuition versus Locke's perception

Locke's epistemological theory distinguishes three grades of cognitive certainty and uncertainty: (a) "intuitive" (presumably) instantiated by the *immediate* certainty of our own conscious existence, allegedly Locke's "reflective" consciousness; (b) demonstrative or inferential knowledge, e.g., God's existence as exemplified in the cosmological argument, which may be fallible; and (c) sensory, perceptive awareness—not knowledge—of the sensory existence of particular things external to the mind, which is only probable at best. But the problem is with the term "perception." As soon as Locke has closed the door to any and all *active* innate principles or ideas, he has barred the path to *genuine* self-consciousness. "Let us then suppose the mind to be, as we say, white paper, void of all characters, without any ideas" (*Essay*, II, I, 2). *If* indeed the mind is like a *passive tabula rasa*, a blank tablet upon which sensations and experience write, *then* Cartesian reflexive self-consciousness is in principle impossible. Cartesian *reflexion* and Lockean *reflection* exhibit very different acts, powers, and meanings. First, Cartesian reflexion is self-referential, like the meaning intended by the French words *moi meme*; me myself. *Passive* sensations cannot be relations. Second, the 'I' and the 'think' are *relationally* unified; *my* substance and my changing *thoughts* are reciprocal predications. Later, Kant will define self-consciousness as a subject–object relation. Thus, Locke's term *perception* is a reflection, not a reflexion. In that regard, he is an empiricist.

162   Locke and Leibniz on personal identity

He begins by defining the mind as a "white paper, void of all characters, without any ideas" (Bk. II, Ch. 2). Next our perceptual responses to external objects are called SENSATION (*Essay*, II, I, 3).

> This source of ideas every man has wholly in himself; and though it be not sense, as having nothing to do with external objects, yet it is like it, and might properly be called *internal sense*. But as I call the other sensation, so I call this REFLECTION, the ideas it affords being such only as the mind gets by reflecting on its own *operations* within itself by reflection.
>
> (II, I, 4)

But here *operations* means *observations*. Locke's *empirical* "reflection" is directionally *perceptual;* it is empirically *other*-observational; it refers to something *other* than the self, *distinct* from the self that is being observed or noticed, e.g., visually looking *at* a bird but not aware of my self *as* looking *at* the bird *in* that moment (II, I, 24).

Locke's analysis of experience is twofold. First, he defines *ideas*; and then their *causes*.

> I must here in the entrance [of the *Essay*] beg pardon of my reader for the frequent use of the word *idea,* which he will find in the following treatise. It being that term, which, I think best to stand for whatsoever is the [immediate mental] *object* [i.e., the observational sighting] of the understanding [i.e., the mind], when a man thinks ... or whatever [object] it is which the mind can be employed about in thinking.
>
> (*Essay*, Bk. I, I, Sect. 8)

Here it is clear that the object is not the self but something else, an observation. The thinking and the object are separate. Notice that in this definition of an "idea," the idea is the "object" of a directed observation, a perception, which is triggered externally—not internally self-contained as in self-consciousness. It is *both* apart *and* observationally different from the self; it is activated by an external stimulus. Locke's reflection is perceptual. When one observes an object or a feeling, they are looking *at* but not thinking *about* their self. There is (a) consciousness—but it is not equal to *self*-consciousness; perception

Locke and Leibniz on personal identity   163

is not equal to self-perceiving; and (b) perceiving e.g., looking at a tree or feeling a hunger pang in my stomach but not the same as my self. The terms perception and observation go together but it sounds odd to utter the word "self-perception," whereas the word self-consciousness seems quite natural and common. Sometimes there is an effort to smuggle in the term "introspection" in substitution for circular self-reflexion but again they are *not* identical.

Again:

> Whatsoever the mind perceives in itself, or is the immediate [mental, phenomenal] *object of perception,* thought, or understanding, that I call *idea;* and the power to produce any *idea* in our mind, I call *quality* of the subject [i.e., the material external *object*] wherein that [causal] power is.
>
> (I, II, VIII, Section 8; italics mine)

The "object of perception" is a sensation other than the self. As to the *external cause* of the idea:

> The next thing to be considered is how *bodies* produce [i.e., cause] *ideas* in us; and that is manifestly by *impulse* [i.e., by an external physical motion causing a bodily stimulation], the only way which we can conceive bodies to operate in us [resulting in perceptions].
>
> (Section 11)

In other words, our *mental* ideas are *caused* by the cumulative effect of external *material* motions of minute insensible physical particles striking or impinging upon our sense organs from *without, externally*; but these bodies can and do exist independently of the mind. Reflective observation is outwardly caused. It is a re-action; it is the "bouncing" of a ball back toward from whence it came, like from a bright light. For Hobbes, we "push back" on the incoming sensations so that they *appear* as "outside" of us, thus *causing* us to think they are situated beyond us, they *appear* to be beyond us. By contrast, the principle or paradigm of Cartesian reflexive self-consciousness, attested to by dualism, rationalism, and idealism, are collectively committed in maintaining that there is an active *spontaneity* originating from *within* the soul or mind and it has *both* (a) the capacity to *actively*

164 Locke and Leibniz on personal identity

self-reflex (Kant) and (b) point outwardly, intentionally (Husserl). In short, Descartes's cogito is reflexive but Locke's passive perceptions are reflective, they are outwardly provided from without. Cartesian self-consciousness and Lockean perception *mean*, exhibit, and display very different features. I do not perceive my loneliness; I *know* it.

We recall Descartes's three major distinctions within consciousness: (a) *immediate* sensations, which are mechanically caused by the motion of external bodies impinging on our senses of sight and touch; (b) pure, i.e., immaterial self-conscious intuitions spontaneously generated from *within* consciousness, e.g., the cogito; and (c) *mediate, relational* thoughts, i.e., propositions, judgments, and inferences. But Locke's *passive* "reflection," his empiricist principle, consists of sensory observations passing "before" the blank tablet, the *tabula rasa* of a *receptive* mind—but it is not *self*-conscious. In his *Examination of Malebranche*, Section 46 (posthumously published in 1706), he categorically asserts that reflection does not give us knowledge of the mind itself but only of its operations, its perceptions. By contrast the Cartesian cogito is reflexively, actively self-conscious. Metaphorically it is the difference between passively watching an object or event versus actively participating within it. All dualists, rationalists, and idealists are committed to the principle that the *psyche*, soul, self, mind, or ego is *circularly reflexive.* The self knows what it knows and in the same moment knows its self. You cannot have one without the other. The knower and the known are distinguishable but inseparable in their activity. But in the empiricist paradigm, sensation precedes the observation. All materialists, empiricists, phenomenalists, and neuroscientists maintain that sense organs and brains are "*re*-active," "*re*-sponsive" to external physical stimuli. The stimuli precede the response. In Locke, the empirical emphasis is on the *content* of the mind—versus its *acts*— the focus is on the sensations that are *passively given to* the mind. But without *self*-consciousness, loneliness is meaningless.

Leibniz's monadic self-consciousness

In Leibniz, by contrast, the primary consideration is on the *activity* of the mind, on its *self-reflexion*. Empiricism concentrates on passive *contents* and subjective idealism focuses on *acts* constituting the reflexive unity of consciousness (Kant) and its transcendent intentionality (Husserl), as the latter *targets meanings* and not merely perceptual sense data. Empiricism observes; intentionality targets. Mirrors are reflective; they observationally record what is in front of them. But reflexion knows *both* that it is thinking *and* what it is thinking about. Metaphorically, figuratively reflexion can see both the front of the mirror and also the back as well in the same act.

One of the interesting features of Locke's empirical theory of consciousness (actually Hume's as well) is that consciousness is interrupted by deep sleep (*Essay*, Vol. II, I, 9 ff.) This means that Locke's criterion of personal identity involves a problematic implication concerning *continuous* identity; it stops at night and resumes in the morning. By contrast, for Leibniz's *dynamic* paradigm of the soul, it continually thinks. If it did not, then the self would both appear and disappear discontinuously.

Leibniz wanted to engage Locke in a discussion regarding their philosophical differences but unfortunately Locke died before he could and Leibniz was forced to abandon the project. It would have been instructive to compare and contrast Locke's *Essay* with Leibniz's *Monadology*. In the following I shall try to indicate some important differences between Locke's *tabula rasa* paradigm and Leibniz's model of the self-conscious Monad. The opening premises of the *Monadology*, paraphrased below, basically formulate his theory of *subjective* idealism. In fact, he calls himself "the first idealist." But of special significance, we notice the awareness of *change*, of the *temporality* of consciousness (first hinted by Descartes's Meditation II), but which later so impressed Kant.

> Paragraph 1: The Monad is an active "*simple* substance," i.e., an immaterial, unextended entity "without parts"; it represents an indivisible unity by virtue of its immateriality.

In Greek philosophy, the term *monas* denotes unity, oneness. As a substance, the Monad is *spontaneously* active from within.

> Par. 3: Where there are no parts, there can be no extension nor [Epicurean] *figure*. As a substantial unity, the Monad can be metaphorically described as an ideal or "spiritual atom." Along with God, Monads exist as the only realities; within the soul, monadic

perceptions are completely contained within consciousness; perceptions are predicates attributable to Monadic consciousnesses. And there are degrees and levels of consciousness spanning from the unconscious, the conscious, the self-conscious, and the rational (Par. 23; cf. the *Principles of Nature and Grace*, Par. 1 ff.).

Par. 4: Once created by God, Monads are continuous centers of activity, eternal, unified, and therefore immortal (*Theodicy*, 89).

Par. 6: Monads can only be created or annihilated by an act of God.

Par. 7: The Monad is absolutely solipsistic and self-contained; it is "windowless"; everything that happens to it is generated and contained within the Monad itself. Nothing can enter from "without" and nothing escape from "within."

Par. 8: Monads possess internal *qualities, predicates* that are expressed through *varying* perceptual differences thus accounting for self-conscious awareness of *temporal* changes. The Monads are not in space.

Par. 9: The universe is a plenum of self-contained Monads, each monadic existence—extended and unextended—reflecting the entire universe from its own unique perspective and monadic perceptions, as they *appear* to interact with each other, although all that occurs only actually transpires solely within the Monad itself as a self-contained substance.

Pars.10–11: All change in the Monad is continuous, from which it follows that monadic consciousness is a unity, an identity, *and a continuity* establishing its personal/moral identity. All "changes in the Monads come from an *internal principle* since an external cause can have no influence upon their inner being."

Par.14: Sensation or perception *qua* monadic consciousness is passive; animals have sensations/perceptions but not *ap*perception or self-consciousness; only humans are *ap*perceptive.

Par. 16: Self-consciousness is defined as a multiplicity in unity. Because the Monad is active, it has the capacity to unify diverse elements within itself in an *apperceptive,* i.e., self-conscious manner resulting in a "unity of self-consciousness."

Par. 17: "*Perception* and that which depends upon it are *inexplicable on materialist or mechanical grounds,* that is to say, by

[Epicurean] figures and motions. And supposing there were a machine so constructed as to think, feel, and have perception, it might be conceived as increased in size, while keeping the same proportions, so that one might go into it as into a mill. That being so, we should, on examining its interior, find only [mechanical] parts which work on one another, and never anything by which to explain a perception. Thus, it is in a simple substance and not in a compound or machine that perception must be sought for."[16]

As previously indicated, the *apparent* interaction between perfectly self-contained Monads is coordinated by a pre-established harmony instituted by God (Leibniz, *New System*, Third Explanation). Essentially then, we see Locke and Leibniz as fully engaged in Plato's Battle between the Giants and the Gods.

In summation, according to Leibniz, only if we assume as a first principle that the mind is *both* (a) immaterial, "simple" *and* (b) spontaneous, i.e., intrinsically active, can we account for the unity of consciousness, its identity, its continuity, and its immanent temporality. The Monad *always* thinks. By contrast, both Locke and Hume believe that in deep swoons and sound sleep the mind ceases to think. Leibniz also endorses unconscious thoughts, *petite* perceptions. But no empiricist can in principle affirm the unconscious—nor can a neuroscientist. Again, the neurons are homogeneous. Leibniz is also a precursor to *dynamic* psychiatry. The term dynamic connotes an *internal* source of energy and both he and Freud affirm the existence of a *forceful* unconscious consisting of forgotten or repressed memories, a retrievable mnemonic consciousness.

Notes

1 Weldon, T. D., *Kant's Critique of Pure Reason* (Oxford: Clarendon Press, 1968), 3–6.
2 Locke, John, *An Essay Concerning Human Understanding*, edited by John Yolton (New York: Dutton, 1964–1967), Book II, Chapter XXVII, 4, 6, 8, 15, 22, 26.
3 Plato, *Phaedo*, translation and running commentary by R. S. Bluck (New York: Bobbs-Merrill, 1955) 73–84.
4 Cf. Mijuskovic, Ben, *The Achilles of Rationalist Arguments: The Simplicity, Unity, and Identity of Thought and Soul from the Cambridge Platonists to*

168 Locke and Leibniz on personal identity

Kant (The Hague: Martinus Nijhoff, 1974), Chapter IV, "Personal Identity in the 17th and 18th Centuries," 94–99. Locke himself is of two minds. He believes the existence of God can be demonstrated by the cosmological argument but that the immortality of the soul is an article of faith.

5 Locke offers the metaphor of an oak tree as a case of identity, wherein the vital organization of all the parts combine in contributing to a common end, the life of the tree. This example later impressed both Anthony Ashley Cooper, the third Earl of Shaftesbury, in *Characteristics of Men, Manners, Opinions, and Times*, edited J. M. Robertson (Bobbs-Merrill, 1964), II, 69–70, 99–103, 276; and David Hume, *A Treatise of Human Nature*, edited by Selby Bigge (Oxford, 1955), I, 257), who both use it to advantage.

6 Cudworth, Ralph, *The True Intellectual System of the Universe* (Stuttgart-Bad-Cannstatt: Frommann, 1964; first published in 1678), 824 and 826. Notice Locke's assertion that "every conceivable or smallest part thereof, being a real substance by itself." Hume will later assign to each fleeting impression the same status of substantiality as long as it lasts.

7 Clarke, Samuel, *A Fourth defense of an argument made use of in a letter to Mr. Dodwell to prove the immateriality and natural immortality of the soul* (1708), 62; see also: 44–45. Clarke offers the example of the identity of Theseus' ship, whose every part and plank is substituted successively in his discussion of personal identity. Hume also cites the same instance in the *Treatise* (page 259). But these are analogies and fictions as Hume avows; as such they do not directly address the workings of an immaterial mind. See Leibniz, *New Essays on Human Understanding*, edited by A. C. Langley (Open Court, 1916), II, xvii, Sect. 4, passim and editor's note. Cf. also Sir Isaac Newton, *Mathematical Principles of Natural Philosophy and His System of the World*, translated by A. Motte and edited by F. Cajori (Berkeley: University of California Press, 1934), Bk. III, General Scholium, 545; George Berkeley, *The Works of George Berkeley, Bishop of Cloyne*, edited by A. A. Luce and T. E. Jessop (London: Nelson, 1948–1957), II, 231; and *Philosophical Commentaries* (Notebook B), I, Sections 14, 24, 200. Samuel Clarke was Newton's defender during the Leibniz-Clarke controversy over the metaphysical and epistemic status of space and time.

8 Hobbes, Thomas, *The English Works of Thomas Hobbes*, edited by W. Molesworth (11 Vols., London: 1839–1845), III, 147; cf. *Leviathan, of Man*, Chapter 16. For Hobbes, "Sensation is defined as a certain internal motion of animal bodies; it is identical with having a phantasm or idea" (*De Corpore*, 25.2); "all motion is generated [causally] by one body moving against another body. From this idea, Hobbes argues that

> the cause of sensation is a motion of an object (the sensed object) that moves [other] objects in a medium (usually air), that [in turn] move some external part of an animal (the sense organ), causing a motion of some internal parts of the animal (the sensation itself);

A. P. Martinich, *A Hobbes Dictionary* (Cambridge, MA: Blackwell, 1995), 271. For Hobbes, all reality is reducible to matter *plus* motion. An immaterial substance is a contradiction in terms.

9 Overton, Richard, *Man's Mortalitie, edited by Harold Fisch* (Liverpool University Press, 1968; first published in Amsterdam in 1643. Cf. Bryan Ball, *The Soul Sleepers: Mortalism from Wycliff to Priestly* (Clarke & Co., 2008), who discusses George Wither in the context of the "mortalist heresy," that man's soul is naturally mortal and terminates at death.

10 Locke, John, *The Reasonableness of Christianity as Delivered in the Scriptures*, edited by G. W. Ewing (Chicago: Regnery, 1965). Locke holds that it is through the sin of Adam that we have become mortal; cf. John Yolton, *John Locke and the Way of Ideas* (Oxford: Clarendon Press, 1968), 3–9, 147; and consult Augustine's doctrine of "divine grace," which is matched by the Calvinist "doctrine of the elect" along with predestination; God's omniscience foreordains even before we are born whether we are going to heaven or hell.

11 Aaron, Richard, *John Locke* (Oxford: Clarendon Press, 1955), 142–143, 144–146 ff. Cf. J. L. Mackie (Oxford: Clarendon Press, 1976), 38, 40–41. In Locke's *representational* theory of perception, the observer perceives an external, independent object. There is no sensation or perception of "resemblance" in Descartes's intuitive cogito. Resemblance is a relation.

12 Locke curiously suggests that consciousness of one's identity could be grounded in one's little finger alone (Section 16). Other passages, however, stress a melding of consciousness with the physical composition of man. *But the paradoxical problem remains unresolved, namely how to meld or fuse the physical body with the immaterial mind?*

13 Again, the reasoning behind this assertion in Locke is that rewards and punishments in the afterlife are meaningless apart from the bodies that feel them; pleasures and pains are necessarily connected to organs of sensation in this world as well as to the next. Accordingly, Locke alludes to a "spiritual body, one which does not require physical nourishment, but which nevertheless enjoys sensation through its organic and teleological organization of biological parts."

14 Yolton, John, *John Locke and the Way of Ideas* (Oxford: Clarendon Press, 1968), 10, 117, 137, 148–166; cf. Locke's controversy with Edward Stillingfleet, "Mr. Locke's Second Reply to the Bishop of Worcester," *Works*, IV, 303 ff.

15 Cf. the article on "Conditional Immortality," *Encyclopedia of Religion and Ethics* (New York: Scribners, 1961), Vol. 3, 822–823; and H. J. McLachlan, *Socinianism in Seventeenth Century England* (Oxford: Oxford University Press, 1950), 326.

16 *Leibniz: The Monadology and Other Philosophical Writings*, translated and edited by Robert Latta (Oxford: Oxford University Press, 1968), 217–228. Leibniz's deep commitment to the problem of personal identity

is obvious from his lengthy discussion of the issue in the Introduction to his *New Essays*, written after the main work, where he summarizes Locke's controversy with Edward Stillingfleet and agrees against Locke that even God could not have endowed matter with the power of thought (*Monadology*, 387–401). To appreciate Leibniz's influence on Kant in terms of the principles of the unity, identity, and continuity of consciousness, as he applies it in both of his two Transcendental Deductions (1781 and 1787); see Ben Mijuskovic, "The Structure of Kant's Argument in the Analytic," *The Southern Journal of Philosophy*, XII:3 (1974). See also: Ben Mijuskovic, "The Simplicity Argument and the Unconscious: Plotinus, Cudworth, Leibniz, and Kant," *Philosophy and Theology*, 1–2 (2008–2009); and "Kant's Reflections on the Unity of Time-Consciousness and the Unconscious," *Kritike*, 4:2 (2010).

Chapter 8

Shaftesbury and Hume on personal identity

The issue of personal identity and the nature of the self that Descartes initiates, and that we have just pursued in Locke and Leibniz, we will now address in Shaftesbury and Hume's treatment, while bearing in mind its intrinsic relevance to the issue of human loneliness. Metaphysically what is the self; is it really an independent substance; what is its relation to other selves; what are its ethical responsibilities—if any—to others of its kind; and most importantly what are the limits of self-knowledge; what can we establish for certainty about the self?

The tutor of Anthony Ashley Cooper, the Third Earl of Shaftesbury, is John Locke, so it is not surprising that he took a deep interest in the issues, problems, and the criteria regarding moral identity explored by Locke. Beyond that, along with Francis Hutcheson, Shaftesbury is credited with having formulated the "moral sense" doctrine in ethical theory, which not only influenced Hume's moral philosophy but his epistemological reflections as well according to Norman Kemp Smith. In his commentary, *The Philosophy of David Hume*, he argues that "What is truly distinctive and central in Hume's teaching is his reversal of the roles hitherto ascribed to reason and to feeling respectively," which essentially allows Hume to transform the mediacy of relations into the immediacy of feelings. In other words, the mediate, the connective aspect of the causal *relation*, for example, is transformed by Hume into a psychological *feeling* of anticipation. In effect, whereas rationalists were convinced that both intuitive (immediate) and rational (mediate) knowledge could be achieved, Hume shifts the entire center of discussion to psychological feelings and beliefs.[1]

DOI: 10.4324/9781003156130-9

172 Shaftesbury and Hume on personal identity

According to Shaftesbury (1671–1713), and later Hume, our sentiments of approbation and censure are engrained in our empirical human nature. Upon viewing an ethical action before us, one in which our own self-interest is uninvolved, i.e., "disinterested," we are guided by our sentiments alone as we depend on our *immediate* feelings in pronouncing the action as praiseworthy or blameworthy. For Christians, by contrast, the pronouncement of moral culpability or innocence rests on the determination of our individual free will and its degree of conformity to God's Will, as for example, in the rationalist doctrines proposed by the Cambridge Platonists.

> Those who affirm that virtue is nothing but a conformity to reason; that there are eternal fitnesses and unfitnesses of things, which are the same to every rational being that considers them; that the immutable measures of right and wrong impose an obligation, not only on human creatures, but on the Deity himself. All these concur in the opinion, that morality, like truth, is discern'd merely by ideas and their juxta-position and comparison.[2]

In this context, the Cambridge men were on the side of reason, and the Deity itself had to conform to the laws of reason. By contrast, the Calvinists preached and advocated God's power of the will over reason leading to His absolute commandments.

For Hume, by contrast, morality is essentiality the outcome of a natural sentiment or feeling, which is universally embedded in all mankind, in our common human nature, thus serving as an empirical criterion shared by all. It is the feeling of *sympathy* that allows us to "empathize" with others of our kind.

> Our affections depend more upon ourselves and the internal operations of our mind, than any other impressions; for which reason they arise more naturally from the imagination and form the lively idea we form of them. This is the nature and cause of sympathy; and 'tis after this manner we enter so deep into the opinions and affections of others, whenever we discover them.
>
> (*Treatise*, 319)

Shaftesbury and Hume on personal identity 173

In effect, Hume wishes to revolutionize the social sciences along the same lines that Newton had achieved in the natural sciences (*Treatise*, 10–11).

Later of course, Kant's own commanding ethical principle appeals instead to a synthetic *a priori* relational application, as it summons a universal law of reason, namely the categorical imperative. Kant also supports the concept of pure *duty*, the agent's *intention*, as originally envisioned by the Stoics, and he praises the virtue of sacrifice even when it fails.

Hume and Kant, however, despite engaging in radically different criteria for morality, nevertheless agree that ethical principles, unlike scientific ones, deal with the Ought and not the Is; with Values and not Facts.

> In every system of morality, which I have hitherto met with, I have remark'd that the author proceeds for some time in the ordinary way of reasoning, and establishes the being of God ... when of a sudden I am surprz'd to find, that instead of the usual copulations of propositions, *is* and *is not,* I meet with no proposition that is not connected with *ought* or *ought not.* This change is imperceptible; but is, however, of the last consequence. For as this *ought,* or *ought not,* expresses some new relation or affirmation, 'tis necessary that it should be observ'd and explain'd; and at the same time that a reason should be given, for what seems altogether inconceivable, how this new relation can be a deduction from others, which are entirely different from it.
>
> (*Treatise*, 469)

Both thinkers split science from ethics. For Hume, who is an empiricist, and Kant who is a rationalist, nevertheless both agree that science and ethics are distinct disciplines and rule independently of the natural sciences. This is important because I am arguing, explicitly following Max Weber that science deals with the *quantitative* aspects of matter plus motion, whereas both subjective idealism and existentialism address ethics from a principle that assumes the legitimacy of *qualitative* judgments of human value. The spontaneity prevailing in subjective idealism and the radical freedom inhering in existentialism

174 Shaftesbury and Hume on personal identity

allows for each individual to create qualitative values for herself or himself alone.

But what will occupy us in the following discussion will be Shaftesbury's speculations regarding the search for a criterion of selfhood and how his musings influenced Hume's own ruminations on the subject, while at the same time displaying the complexity of Shaftesbury's approach to the issues as they involve no less than half a dozen refractive facets: (1) the metaphysical tenets of Democritean and Epicurean atomistic materialism; its conflict with (2) Cartesian dualism, the latter essentially evolving from (3) strong Platonic and Neo-Platonic tendencies, which Shaftesbury admires and yet he nevertheless exhibits (4) a healthy dose of Pyrrhonian or mitigated skepticism, while (5) concluding with his own positive analysis of the self, which subsequently (6) influenced Hume's own reflections on personal identity.

During the period we are now considering, we shall once again be forced to navigate between the formidable cliffs of Charybdis and Scylla, between materialism and idealism, revisiting the philosophical voyages and scenes, which originally spanned two millennia, from the age of Epicurus to the time of Hobbes and paralleled the period from Plotinus to the time of British Neo-Platonism as the dueling criteria were intensely disputed within the halls of academia and science, as well as the sanctuaries of religion and humanism. The perennial issue always retains the same pivotal question balanced on the shifting pinnacles we have been pursuing all along: Can senseless matter *alone* think? It is on this metaphysical question alone that the whole criterion of personal identity is delicately balanced.

On the issue of metaphysical dualism, Shaftesbury is sufficiently cautious to consistently demur.

> As for what is said, "A material unthinking substance being never able to have produced an immaterial thinking one," I readily grant it, but on the condition that this great maxim of nothing being ever made from nothing may hold as well on my side as well as my adversaries ... The spiritual men may, as long as they please, represent to us in the most eloquent manner, "that matter considered in a thousand different shapes, joined and disjoined, varied and modified to eternity, can never, of itself, afford one single thought, never occasion or give rise to anything like sense or knowledge." Their

argument will hold good against a Democritus, an Epicurus, or any of the elder or later atomists. But it will be turned on them by an examining [skeptical] Academist, and when the two substances are fairly set asunder, and considered apart as different kinds, 'twill be as strong sense, and as good argument, to say as well as of the immaterial kind: "That do with it as you please, modify it a thousand ways, purify it, exalt it, sublime it, torture it ever so much or rack it, as they say, with thinking, you will never be able to produce or force the contrary substance out of it." The poor dregs of sorry matter can no more be made out of the simple pure substance of immaterial thought, than the high spirits or reason can be extracted from the gross substance of heavy matter. So let the [Academic] dogmatists make of this argument what they can.[3]

Again:

But if the defining material and immaterial substances, and distinguishing their properties and modes, is recommended to us as the right manner of proceeding in the discovery of our own natures, I shall be apt to suspect such a study as the more delusive and infatuating on account of its magnificent pretension.

(ibid., I, 188; see also 194–195)

Nevertheless, despite these cautious self-admonitions, Shaftesbury offers an uncertain mélange between the tenets of Cartesian consciousness and Lockean perception.

For let us carry skepticism ever so far, let us doubt, if we can, of everything about us, we cannot doubt what passes within ourselves [Descartes]. Our passions and affections are known to us. They are certain, whatever the objects on which they are employed [Locke]. Nor is it of any concern to our argument how these exterior objects stand: whether they are realities or mere illusions, whether we wake or dream.

(I, 336–337)

But when the question turns on the criterion of our presumed assurance that it is the *same* self, then the answer is not so secure as

176 Shaftesbury and Hume on personal identity

Shaftesbury confesses. The question is not whether we *believe* we are the identical self now that we were a moment before, but rather how do we *know* it? What is the guarantee that it is the *same* self that we hold morally responsible over time? And, second, beyond that, what is the principle, the criterion underlying the unity of consciousness even within the temporal span of some brief moments? Even new-born babes are "conscious," but are they *self*-conscious? Until they have developed the capacity to distinguish their *self as a separate and distinct entity* from a realm of inanimate objects and later from other animate selves, they cannot with certainty *reflexively* understand the meaning of a continuous "selfhood" and therefore be self-assured of their own personal identity. To be *immediately* aware of sensations is not identical to *knowing* that I am self-aware of my own thoughts, that I recognize them as my own and not someone else's. The question persists: does just being conscious *per se* mean that there is an identifiable *continuous* thinking substance. As A. J. Ayer famously challenges, in *Language, Truth, and Logic,* being conscious merely indicates that "There is a thought *now*." It demonstrates nothing beyond the immediacy of the utterance, its "specious present" (William James).

In any case, Shaftesbury's skeptical reflections on the metaphysical status of the self seriously piqued Hume's interest and influenced his own thoughts on personal identity.

> [A]ll knowledge whatsoever depends on this previous one, "and that we can in reality be assured of nothing till we are first assured of what we are ourselves." For by this alone we can know what certainty is. That there is something undoubtedly which thinks, our very doubt itself and scrupulous thought evinces. *But* in what subject [i.e., substance] that thought resides, and how that subject is [temporally] continued one and the same, so as to answer constantly to the supposed train of thoughts or reflections which seem to run so harmoniously through a long course of life, with the same relation still to one single and self-same person, this is not a matter so easily or hastily decided by those who are nice self-examiners or searchers after truth and certainty. 'Twill not, in this respect be sufficient for us to use the seeming logic of a famous modern, and say, "we think therefore we are." … Miraculously argued! "If I am, I am." Nothing more certain! For the Ego or I being established

Shaftesbury and Hume on personal identity   177

in the first part of the proposition, the *ergo,* no doubt, must hold
it [tautologically] good in the latter. But the question is, "What
constitutes the We or I?" and "whether the I of this instant be
the same with that of any instant preceding or to come?" For we
have nothing but memory to warrant us [as Locke maintained] and
memory may be false [as Leibniz later warned]. We may believe we
have thought and reflected thus or thus; but we may be mistaken.
We may be conscious of that as truth which perhaps was no more
than a dream, and we may be conscious of that as a past dream
which perhaps was never before so much as dreamt of. This is what
metaphysicians [e.g., Descartes and Locke] mean when they say,
"that identity can be proved only by consciousness, but that consciousness, withal, may be as well false as real in respect of what is
past." So that the same *successional* We or I must remain still, on
this account, undecided. To the force of this reasoning I confess I
must so far submit as to declare that, for my own part, I take my
being upon *trust.*

(Shaftesbury, II, 274–275; italic mine)

The influence of Shaftesbury on Hume is most strongly documented
in the commentaries of Charles Hendel, John Laird, and Norman
Kemp Smith.

This definitive passage produced a strong sympathetic response in
Hume, which in turn led to his own discussion *Of personal identity.*
Two key concepts will be endorsed by Hume: temporal succession
and psychological trust. But in the end, Hume, like Shaftesbury, will
express the same echoes of caution on the issue in his *Appendix.* For
Hume the expansive presentation of exegetical choices offered by
Shaftesbury, the healthy skepticism, the subtler recognition that the
problem is not merely consciousness but more critically the *continuity,
the temporal unity, and the consequent identity of the self through
time,* all are wonderfully laid out by Hume throughout the *Treatise*
and dramatically climaxed in his Appendix. But in the passage above,
Shaftesbury actually provides us with the Kantian key to the solution
of the problem of self-identity when he interposes the term "successional" (above) because it implies a grounding within an immanent
framework of internal time-consciousness, which can only transpire
if the self remains temporally *continuous.* The undeniable immanency

of temporal consciousness can *only* transpire, stream, or flow *if* (and only *if*) consciousness is endowed with an active, reflexive, *temporal*— as opposed to a Lockean *reflective—unity and continuity.*

Hume's discussion of personal identity shows Shaftesbury's influence and especially regarding the critical issue of a temporal *succession.* The complexities, the various conflicting strands, with which Shaftesbury is contending, are also Hume's. Like his forerunner, Hume criticizes the rationalists as dogmatists in a like manner as his predecessor, who argues that the simplicity premise and argument are insufficient to establish the self's unity, identity, and continuity (*Treatise*, 246–248).

But before presenting his own theory of the self, Hume first summarizes his opponents' position prior to disputing it. The argument and the metaphors are derived from the writings of Ralph Cudworth, the British Platonist.

> There is one argument commonly employ'd for the immateriality of the soul, which seems to me remarkable. Whatever is [materially] extended consists of parts; and whatever consists of parts is divisible. But 'tis impossible any thing divisible can be conjoin'd to a thought or perception, which is a being altogether inseparable and indivisible. For supposing such a conjunction, wou'd the indivisible thought exist on the left or on the right hand of this extended divisible body? ... Or if the thought exist in every part, it must also be extended, separable and divisible as well as the body; which is utterly absurd and contradictory. For can anyone conceive a passion of a yard in length, a foot in breadth, and an inch in thickness? Thought, therefore, and extension are *qualities* wholly incompatible and never can incorporate together into one subject.
> (*Treatise*, 234–235; italic mine)[4]

The reference to "a passion of a yard in length, a foot in breadth, and an inch in thickness" is gleaned from Cudworth. Once more, we discover a critical ontological distinction shared between idealism and rationalism—in contrast to materialism and empiricism—as it centers on the difference between the meanings of *quality* and *quantity. Mental, ideal qualities* are traditionally immaterial; they involve both *subjective* secondary qualities (colors, sounds) as well as tertiary judgments of value, e.g., aesthetic and ethical values, as completely dependent upon and inherent *within* the mind. *Material quantities*, by contrast, are described as *objective* (presumably) in the sense that their referents exist independently of the mind; and hence they are open to scientific determination, measurement, and intersubjective disputation. In turn, however, this deep conceptual divide between the two opposing principles of reality—subjective mental *qualities qua perceptions* and material objective spatial *quantities*—is precisely why these issues continue to bedevil analysis as they persist in the continuing conflict between Plato's Gods and Giants (*Sophist*, 246A-E), the disagreement between the idealists and the materialists. But it is important to note that all three classical *empiricists*—Locke, Berkeley, and Hume—not one of them is a *reductive* materialist in the manner of Hobbes. Locke is a dualist; Berkeley is an immaterialist; and Hume is a conflicted dualist, a dualist "with qualification" because—on the one hand—he attributes an *ideal*, a *mental status* to impressions, ideas and perceptions, since clearly his perceptions are not physical, "they exist nowhere" (*Treatise*, 235–236); but he stops short of being a metaphysical dualist in the manner of Descartes or Locke because he rejects the metaphysical reality of the self *as a substance.* Properly speaking for Hume, all that exists as immediately, directly present within awareness is a fleeting flux of Heraclitean *impressions* followed by anticipatory psychological *beliefs.* We *believe* the future will resemble the past, but we can never *know* it.

Four factors loom critically for Hume: (1) his perceptions are inconstant but they are all that exists; (2) he fails to notice the problematic relation between time-consciousness and the unity of self-consciousness; (3) his ambivalent dualist/anti dualist stance regarding the self as a mental "substance"; and (4) his concluding admission of uncertainty concerning the epistemic status of the unity of consciousness in the Appendix (*Treatise*, 633–636).

To understand Hume's position on the self, I need to anchor a quartet of assumptions. First, Hume assumes that both his "simple" impressions and their fainter copies, their ideas are generically one and all *perceptions*, unextended, mental, immaterial "entities." In short, Hume is basically a phenomenalist. Again, phenomenalism is the thesis that all "reality," including the external world, the causal maxim, and the "self" are composed of *contingent* sensory constructions grounded and patched together in the imagination.

Any reference to reason is unnecessary. The perceived patches of sight and the echoes of sound are pasted together and manufactured from secondary i.e., sensory *qualities*; or in the contemporary parlance of our analytic brethren, they are composed of "sense data" or "sense qualia," which means they are mental *appearances* "within" the mind. To describe perceptions as present "within" the mind is obviously a spatial metaphor but the mind itself is actually materially and physically "nowhere," as Hume declares. Second, he maintains that matter can "produce" i.e., *cause* immaterial thought, i.e., consciousness. Third, he denies that the self is a substance and instead he concludes that essentially it is a "bundle" of disconnected, atomistic impressions, his "atomistic psychology" paradigm. And fourth, he ends by pleading an ambivalent skepticism regarding the question whether the mind is a unity or merely a loose collection of random and unruly fleeting impressions (Appendix).

Let me begin with the first consideration. It is important to start here with Hume's own immaterialist premise. In the section of the *Treatise* titled *Of the immateriality of the soul*, directed against the materialists, he argues that the greatest part of beings, entities, or presences in consciousness, i.e., our perceptions do not exist in any *particular* place. Hence, he declares his "maxim is"

> *that an object may exist, and yet be nowhere;* and I assert that this is not only possible, but that the greatest part of beings do and must exist after this manner. An object may be said to be nowhere, when its parts are not so situated with respect to each other, as to form any [Epicurean] figure or quantity; nor the whole with respect to other bodies so as to answer to our notions of [spatial] contiguity or distance. Now this is evidently the case with all our perceptions and objects ... A moral reflection cannot be plac'd on the right or on the left of a passion, nor can a smell or sound be either of a circular or square figure. These [ideal] objects and perceptions so far from requiring any *particular* place, are absolutely incompatible with it, and even the imagination cannot attribute it to them. These objects and perceptions, so far from requiring any *particular* place, are absolutely incompatible with it, and even the imagination cannot attribute it to them.
>
> (Hume, *Treatise*, 235–236)

Shaftesbury and Hume on personal identity   181

Our impressions, ideas, and perceptions "are nowhere," i.e., they are only "in" the mind. But Hume grants that our visual sightings and aural hearings concerning material objects *do* exist *independently* of the mind. In short, he is a contingent immaterial/material dualist. Again, he is not a dualist in the traditional sense because he denies the *reality* of the self. Nevertheless, he is a dualist with an important qualification. Metaphysically and technically, Hume is classified as a Minimal/ Mental and Physical/Dualist. "Thus, the same individual subject can possess both mental and physical properties."[5]

What is troubling Hume is not the rationalist principle that thoughts (Hume's mental impressions, ideas, and perceptions) are unextended. This he accepts, and indeed as we have just seen above, he recruits this same principle in his argument against the reductively materialist accounts of perception. Rather what Hume wants to criticize is the rationalist inference that the self can be traced to a "simple," a pure intuition, an innate idea of the self. But although Hume wishes to argue this, properly speaking he does not do so in the present section, but rather foregoes his criticisms until he reaches the section *Of personal identity.* At this point in the *Treatise*, he is satisfied, like Shaftesbury before him, with simply treating both sides, both the materialist and the dualist arguments, as equally inconclusive. This skeptical attitude also mimics Montaigne's epistemically balanced set of scales, his metaphor for the suspension of judgment, his epoche, and his motto: "Que sais je?"

> But tho' ... we cannot refuse to condemn the materialists, which conjoin all thought with extension; yet a little reflection will show equal reason for blaming their antagonists [e.g., the Cambridge Neoplatonists], who conjoin all thought with a simple and indivisible substance.
>
> *(Treatise,* 239)

However, although this is the case, Hume nevertheless gives ample warning of the line of inquiry he intends to pursue as early as Part IV, Section ii, when he announces that

> We may observe that what we call a *mind,* is nothing but a heap or collection of different perceptions, *united together by certain*

> *relations,* and suppos'd, tho' falsely, to be endow'd with a perfect simplicity and identity. Now as every perception is distinguishable from another, and may be consider'd as separately existent [i.e., a substance]; it evidently follows, that there is no absurdity in separating any particular perception [i.e., impression] in the mind; that is, in breaking off all its *relations,* with that connected mass of perceptions, which constitute a thinking being.
>
> (Hume, *Treatise*, 207; italics mine)

The chief difficulty is that relations are not impressions, ideas, or perceptions. There are impressions of the color *blue* but no impression of *relation*. "Perceptions" are *immaterial*; they exist "nowhere," in no place—except "within" or "present to" consciousness—and precisely because perceptions are not in space, they cannot be nor are they material entities. Note also once more, that philosophically speaking, *any* single impression that exists for only a moment *is a substance.* To be distinct is to exist in separation from all other entities and that is the definition of an Aristotelian substance. In other words, Hume is loosening all simple impressions from each other—and consequently—all ideas from each other as well, which means that there can be no question of the self as a *unitary* substance. The self as a substance is a "natural" *fiction* of the imagination. Accordingly, Hume will invest in the "self" as a "natural belief," while excluding it from any real or metaphysical status. And by doing so, he will rely solely on the immediacy of *sentiment*, of *feeling*, and on our imaginary *belief* that we are a "self." We recall Shaftesbury's inclination to accept his own self upon trust, "to take my being upon trust." Just as the "causal maxim" is resolved by transforming it into a psychological feeling of anticipation, just so the "reality" of the "self" is assured by a sentiment, by an imaginary and psychological feeling of "succession." One *feels* that one *exists.* One also *feels* one exists with others through a sense of *sympathy* and empathic *resemblance* (*Treatise*, 318–319, 359). But there is no impression of "relation" or "contiguity" or "resemblance." Hume has no method, no means of accounting for the *mediacy* of consciousness. Notice also in the above passage Hume's phrase, "*united together by certain relations.*" There are *immediate* impressions and ideas of blue and red but no impressions of resemblance and relation. "Resemblances" are not colored; they are not sensory existents. Hume thus attributes a suffusing psychological force to sympathy and resemblance, which cannot in either case be reduced to impressions. But sympathy and resemblance—feeling *into* an other, projecting one's "self" into an other, or resembling an other self—are *mediate relations*—epistemically completely different from experiencing an "ouch."

Recalling the discussion in the preceding chapter on Locke and Leibniz, we remember that Leibniz argued that each monadic perception—entertained by the soul Monad—is related, connected within the same *unity of consciousness.* It is because they are all bound together, united by an *active* dominant soul Monad, that there *is*, there must *be* a self. *But* if we try to compare Hume's simple impressions with Leibniz's unique perceptual monads, we realize that Hume's are atomically separated, disunified. Leibniz posits an *active* unity of consciousness, whereas Hume describes a *passive* bundle of "associated" loose impressions, an untethered swarm and flux of simple disconnected impressions. But then the only possible *sentiment* is one of a fictitious "unity," a fortuitous "bundling," which can only be attributed to a psychological *feeling* of selfhood, a belief without continuity, instantaneously sustained but for a moment but never extended beyond each vanishing impression to an indubitable *act* of self-cognition. The "self" is merely a phenomenal appearance and yet he wishes to hold that these fleeting shadows are somehow morally responsible (Laird). But how can I have a bond of "sympathy" with another human being, if neither of us *is* a true self? Hume's empirical "sympathy" is based in human *feeling.* In the last chapter, we will revisit this issue in the guise of Husserl's phenomenological conception of "empathy" as an *eidetic* meaning when we discuss his Fifth Cartesian Meditation.

Thus, Hume never denies that we have a *feeling* of a "self." And it is only the rationalist account, the view that holds (a) the self can be intuitively grasped and (b) then inferentially pursued to conclude that once created by God, it will forever remain a unity, continuity, and identity and that we are continuously self-conscious of its indubitable presence; that we have an innate idea of the self every moment of our lives as a simple, continuous, identical being. It is all these expressions, conceptions, and arguments that Hume emphatically denies.

> There are some philosophers, who imagine we are every moment intimately conscious of what we call our SELF; that we feel its

existence and its continuity in existence; and are certain, beyond the evidence of a demonstration, both of its perfect identity and simplicity.

(*Treatise.*, 248)

This and this alone both Hume and Shaftesbury seek to deny. Against these thinkers, Hume asserts that

There is properly no *simplicity* [in the mind] at one time, nor *identity* in different; whatever natural propension we may have to imagine that simplicity and identity.

(Hume, *Treatise.,* 253; italics his)

Against these rationalists, the Scottish philosopher responds with his own paradigm of consciousness. Against the intuitional rationalists, Hume contends that at least he himself cannot discover any such idea continuously present within his own field of awareness.

But setting aside some such metaphysicians of this kind I may venture to affirm of the rest of mankind, that they are nothing but a bundle or collection of different perceptions, which *succeed* each other with an inconceivable rapidity, and are in perpetual flux and movement.

(Hume, *Treatise*, 252; italic)

To consciousness he will grant, nay, he will insist that it is unextended and that it exists "nowhere," i.e., solely in our immaterial minds; but against the demonstrative rationalists, he will insist that the indivisibility of thought—*qua* immaterial—does not allow them to infer that the soul is an *existing* substance; or further that by its simplicity it follows that it is an identity, unity, continuity and hence entitled to immortality.

What has always historically and conceptually divided metaphysical materialism and idealism into two warring camps is the inability to reconcile the fact that if the two opposing substances share no common attribute, then it is inconceivable for (a) the mind and (b) its bodily companion (c) to epistemically *know* each other and (d) to physically *interact* with each other.

Shaftesbury and Hume on personal identity   185

Once again, Hume's thoughts echo those of Shaftesbury:

> tho' every one must allow, that in a very few years both vegetables and animals endure a *total* change, and yet we still attribute identity to them, while their form, size, and substance are entirely alter'd. An oak, that grows from a small plant to a large tree, is still the same oak; tho' there be not one particle of matter, or figure of its parts the same. An infant becomes a man, and is sometimes fat, sometimes lean, without a change in his identity.
>
> (Hume, *Treatise.*, 257; cf. Shaftesbury, *Characteristics*, II, 99–100; and Locke, *Essay*, II, XXVII, 4)

Accordingly,

> We now proceed to explain the nature of *personal identity,* which has become so great a question in philosophy, especially of late years in England … And here 'tis evident, the same method of reasoning must be continu'd, which has so successfully explain'd the identity of plants, and animals, and ships, and houses, and of all the compounded and changeable productions of either art or nature. The identity, which we ascribe to the mind of man, is only a fictitious [imaginary] one, and of like kind with that which we ascribe to animal bodies. It cannot, therefore, have a different origin, but must proceed from a like operation of the imagination upon like objects.
>
> (*Treatise*, 259; cf. Shaftesbury, *Characteristics*, II, 100–101)

But this unifying and identifying feat is accomplished by "the artifice of the imagination" and not by any device of an immaterial simplicity. Whereas both Locke and Shaftesbury append an organic body as a "commonsense" attachment to our natural conception of personal identity, Hume transfers the entire "union" of both mind and body to the sole faculty of the imagination.

Locke had suggested that conceivably God could have "created thinking matter." But Hume's answer to the paradox of metaphysical dualism—the relation of soul and body, mind and matter—resides not in the miraculous intervention of an omnipotent Deity but rather he attributes it to the radical contingency of Nature. As far as material causes are concerned, anything can produce anything. Indeed, if we consider the matter *a priori,* any thing may produce any thing, and that we shall never discover a reason, why any object may or may not be the cause of any other, however great, or however little the resemblance may exist between them.

(Hume, *Treatise,* 247)

Earlier in the text, he had announced that in relation to material causes and their consequent effects

Anything may produce anything. Creation, annihilation, motion, reason, volition; all these may arise from one another, or from any other object we can imagine.

(*Treatise,* 173)

Similarly, the Epicureans, we recall, had attributed an element of chance, a "random swerve" to the paths of the atoms as they hurtled through the voids of space with unpredictable results.

Thus:

And should we inquire about the relation between soul and body, matter and mind I wou'd answer, that we must separate the question concerning the substance of the mind from that concerning the cause of its thought; ... we find by the comparing of their ideas that thought and [material] motion are different, and by experience, that they are constantly united; ... when apply'd to the operations of matter, we may certainly conclude, that [matter and] motion may be, and actually [are] the cause of thought and perception.

(*Treatise,* 248)

Additionally, in his *Enquiry Concerning Human Understanding*, he echoes the same principle, namely that as far as the contingencies of nature and "matters of fact" are concerned, "The contrary of every matter of fact is still possible; because it can never imply a contradiction" (*Inquiry*, Section V, Pt. I, 22).

This is a *metaphysical* dualism pure and simple. It is a dualism, however, that can only be *contingently, empirically* grasped as an "accident" of Nature.

Noam Chomsky has proposed a similar theme, while following up on my discussion of the Locke-Stillingfleet debate in the *Achilles of Rationalist Arguments.*

> In Hume's judgment, Newton's greatest achievement was that he seemed to draw the veil from some of the mysteries of nature, he shewed at the same time the imperfections of the mechanical philosophy; and therefore restored Nature's ultimate secrets to that obscurity, in which they ever did and ever will remain." On different grounds, others reached similar conclusions. Locke, for example, had observed that motion had effects "which we can in no way conceive motion to produce"—as Newton had in fact demonstrated before. Since we remain in "incurable ignorance of what we desire to know" about matter and its effects, Locke concluded no "science of bodies is within our reach" and we can only appeal to "the arbitrary determination of that All-wise Agent who has made them to be and to operate as they do in a way wholly above our weak understanding to conceive."[6]

What Hume maintains is that in the natural course of the universe, there are certain combinations of matter that are capable of "producing" or "causing" certain *immaterial, mental, ideal impressions, ideas, and perceptions.* Contingently, accidentally, i.e., empirically anything can cause anything; and "The contrary of every matter of fact is still possible; because it can never imply a contradiction" (*Enquiry*, Section IV). It is important to remember that the concept of a "predicate"—in relation to the term "substance"—is often substituted by the concept of an "accident." In other words, predicate, property, attribute, and *accident* can and are often used interchangeably. The *essential* attribute of the mind is its *active* reflexive self-consciousness and transcendent intentionality; *but* the human predication of seeing colors and hearing sounds are inessential "accidents," i.e., they could be radically different than they are or even non-existent (Montaigne). They are merely subjective qualities inherent in actual thinking substances. For aught we can imagine, humans could have been so constituted as to communicate telepathically rather that aurally.

Hume's famous skepticism about the self is grounded in his epistemic reduction of all perception=consciousness to the multiple

188 Shaftesbury and Hume on personal identity

compositions of single, indivisible, and compound *mental* impressions and their fainter and less vivid ideas. *Simple* impressions and ideas alone collectively form all our perceptions, as his analysis regarding the "self" shows.

> [W]e may observe that what we call a *mind,* is nothing but a heap or collection of different perceptions, *united together by certain relations,* and suppose'd, tho' falsely, to be endowed with a perfect simplicity and identity. Now as every perception is distinguishable from another, and may be consider'd as separately existent [i.e., a substance]; it evidently follows, that there is no absurdity in separating any particular perception from the mind; that is, in breaking off its relations, with that connected mass of perceptions which constitute a thinking being.
>
> (Treatise, 207)

When we compare Hume's paradigm of the "mind" as consisting of disconnected, i.e., distinct atomic impressions, it is readily comparable to the neuroscientific model of the brain as consisting of disconnected, i.e., distinct neurons. For both Hume and neuroscience, any possible "unity" is a crapshoot at best. And if we further compare both those implications with Hume's contentions regarding the suffusing force of the imagination and compare that with the neuroscience's electrical synapses, the predictability of human desires and thoughts appear completely undetermined. Using the empirical principle of the "association of ideas," try to "trace" your own thoughts for an hour to their origins and what you will find is that your thinking will be inundated by completely new intervening thoughts.

Once more we notice that Hume's reference to unifying relations—resemblance and contiguity—are left unaccounted for; relations are not immediate impressions, immediate ideas, nor immediate perceptions. Relations *mediately* connect. If we compare this passage with the claims of our current neuroscientists, namely that each single neuron is as isolated as Hume's simple impression, it follows that the mysterious unity (suggested above) still remains unaccounted for by neuroscience. There is no neuron of relation. Synapses are electrical discharges and not constitutive self-conscious relations. Differently expressed, just as Hume's "self" is reduced to a fortuitous "bundle of impressions," just so the neuroscientist's "self" can be reduced to a "bundle of brain neurons."

Thus, Hume declares:

> For my part, when I enter most intimately into what I call *myself,* I always stumble on some *particular* [simple, single] perception or other, of heat or cold, light or shade, love or hatred, pain or pleasure. I never can catch *myself* at any time without a perception. When my perceptions are remov'd for any time, as by sound sleep; so long am I insensible of *myself* and may be truly said not to exist. And were all my perceptions remov'd by death, and cou'd I neither think, nor feel, nor see, nor love, nor hate after the dissolution of my body, I shou'd be entirely annihilated, nor do I conceive what is further requisite to make me a perfect non-entity. If any one upon serious and unprejudic'd reflection, thinks he has a different notion of *himself,* I must confess, I can no longer reason with him.
>
> (Hume, *Treatise*, 252)

Clearly with Descartes in mind, Hume goes on to state, "He may, perhaps, perceive something simple and continu'd, which he calls *himself;* tho' I am certain there is no such principle in me."

> But setting aside some metaphysicians of this kind, I may venture of the rest mankind, that they are nothing but a bundle or collection of different perceptions, which *succeed* each other with an inconceivable rapidity, and are in perpetual flux and movement … There is properly no *simplicity* in it at one time, nor *identity* in different; whatever natural propension we may have to imagine that simplicity and identity.
>
> (*Treatise* 252–253; italic mine)

When Hume was on his deathbed, his devoted friend, Adam Smith, attempted to turn his thoughts to the afterlife and Hume gently declined.

Following Kemp Smith's *Commentary* on Kant, he suggests there are basically only three plausible candidates for an indubitable premise concerning human consciousness: (1) the independent existence of an external world (materialism); (2) the Cartesian cogito, the reality of self-consciousness; and (3) Kant's principle of immanent time-consciousness (as opposed to the scientific notion of time as the measurement of the motion of bodies moving through space). Clearly, Descartes challenges the first thesis and Hume the first and the second as well. But notice in the passage quoted above (as well as earlier in Shaftesbury), Hume admits to an indubitable *continuity* of a *temporal succession*, to the reality of a conscious *temporal transition, movement* of *his* own thought, the reality of *succession*, of a set of "different perceptions, which *succeed* each other with an inconceivable rapidity."

Kant's conclusive answer to Hume is that by acknowledging an immanent temporal *succession*, he has forfeited his entire argument against the reality of a substantial self. One cannot experience a succession of impressions unless the *same, identical self* is able to bind, to relate, to synthesize by its *acts* the different contents and moments into a "unity of *temporal* consciousness." It is worth declaring Kant's own principle regarding the indubitability of temporal consciousness.

> Whatever the origin of our representations, whether they are due to the influence of outer things, or are produced through inner causes, whether they arise *a priori,* or being appearances have an empirical origin, they must all, as modifications of the mind, belong to inner sense [to our temporal consciousness]. All our knowledge is thus finally subject to time, the formal condition of inner sense. In it, they must all be ordered, connected, and brought into relation. This is a general observation which, throughout what follows, must be borne in mind as being quite fundamental.[7]

This premise, and this alone, is sufficient to establish the indubitability of the self as a stand alone substance.

In many respects, the eighteenth-century is the century of the imagination. No longer does the faculty of *a priori* reason rule but rather it is the imagination. For Hume, the self is a natural fiction, which produces *belief*. The causal relation rests on a psychological feeling of anticipation. And Hume seeks to show how the identity we ascribe to plants, animals, ships, houses—and "the mind of man"—are phenomenal fictions as well.

But finally and precisely, how does Hume's skeptical assault on personal identity fare by his own frank self-appraisal?

> In short there are two principles, which I cannot render; consistent; nor is it in my power to renounce either of them, viz. *that all our distinct perceptions are distinct existences, and that the mind never perceives any real connexion* [i.e., relation] *among distinct existences.* Did our perceptions either inhere in something simple and individual, or did the mind perceive some real connexion among them, there wou'd be no difficulty in the case. For my part, I must plead the privilege of a sceptic and confess, that this difficulty is too hard for my understanding.
>
> (Appendix, 636)

The section *Of personal identity* was published in 1739 but the Appendix was written a year later in 1740 and obviously Hume reconsidered his entire position.

Nevertheless, despite Hume's reluctance to commit to the metaphysical reality of the self, in the end he heartily endorses and commends the one indisputable universal fact concerning human nature, one which is grounded in the innateness of human sympathy, when he declares our common need to avoid loneliness and secure intimacy.

> In all creatures, that prey not upon others ... there appears a remarkable desire of company, which associates them together without any advantages they can ever propose to reap from their union. This is still more conspicuous in man as being the creature of the universe, who has the most ardent desire of society, and it is fitted for it by the most advantages. We can form no wish, which has not a reference to society. A perfect solitude is perhaps the greatest punishment we can suffer. Every pleasure languishes when enjoy'd apart from company and every pain becomes more cruel and intolerable.
>
> (*Treatise*, page 363; cf. *Characteristics*, I, 299; II, 36–37)

He may have displayed a healthy cognitive skepticism about his metaphysical self, but he never doubted our deepest feelings and desires

192   Shaftesbury and Hume on personal identity

for intimacy, a sympathy with others of our kind, which can only be prompted by our desire to avoid an enforced solitude.

Finally, let me conclude with the overriding neuroscientific difficulty in all this. The *quantitative* collision of homogeneous neurons in the brain can cause physical sensations but they cannot cause or explain the *qualitative* essence regarding judgments of value. That is the problem. Although one can argue that human *sensation* is heterogeneous, as it consists of sight, hearing, taste, smell, and touch, and the feelings of pain and pleasure, nevertheless they cannot be used to reduce the *meanings* regarding human judgments of value to the immediacy of simple sensations because value judgments are mediate modes of reflexive self-consciousness and purposeful intentionality.

Notes

1   Kemp Smith, Norman, *The Philosophy of David Hume: A Critical Study of Its Origins* (London: Macmillan, 1964), 18–19, 23 ff. Cf. *Thomas Hill Green's Hume and Locke* (New York: Thomas Crowell, 1968), 196, 209, 241.
2   Hume, David, *A Treatise of Human Nature* (Oxford: Clarendon Press, 1973), 456–457; hereafter cited as *Treatise.* Hume is also an early exponent of utilitarianism. Moral standards are applied in terms of the salutary consequences gained, pleasure and pain in the case of Jeremy Bentham and happiness and unhappiness in the case of John Stuart Mill.
3   Cooper, Anthony Ashley, Third Earl of Shaftesbury, *Characteristics of Men, Manners, Opinions, Times* (New York: Bobbs-Merrill, 1964), II, 69–70; see also, 275–276; hereafter cited as *Characteristics.* For Shaftesbury's influence on Hume, consult Charles Hendel, *Studies in the Philosophy of David Hume* (Indianapolis, IN: Bobbs-Merrill, 1962), *passim*; Norman Kemp Smith, *Hume*, 138, 163, and 199; and Kenneth Winkler, "All Is Revolution in Us: Personal Identity in Shaftesbury and Hume," *Hume Studies*, XXVI:1 (2000), 3–40, Note 5.
4   Laird, John, *Hume's Philosophy of Human Nature* (London: Methuen, 1967), 164, 223, 241, 302. It is Cudworth who rhetorically challenges us to produce a thought a yard long and a foot deep.
5   Ibid, Laird, 157–158; and see Phillip Cummins, "Hume as Dualist and Anti-Dualist," *Hume Studies*, XXI:1 (1995), 47–56.
6   Chomsky, Noam. "The Mysteries of Nature: How Well Hidden?" *The Journal of Philosophy*, CVI:4 (2009), which cites my discussion of the Locke-Stillingfleet controversy in *The Achilles of Rationalist Arguments*,

as well as his references to the *Achilles* in his *New Essays in the Study of Mind and Language* (2000); *Chomsky Notebooks* (2007); and *What Kind of Animals Are We?* (2013).

7 Kant, Immanuel, *Critique of Pure Reason*, translated by Kemp Smith (London: MacMillan, 1958), A 97 ff.; and cf. William James, *Principles of Psychology* (New York: Dover 1950, I, 338–340).

Chapter 9

Hume on space (and time)[*]

> *The chapter is critical in the context of the historical and conceptual controversy between materialism and idealism. At the very dawn of the Scientific Revolution, the metaphysical and epistemic status of Space and Time are exposed to severe questioning. Newton and his defenders argue that both space and time are absolute, while Leibniz and Hume maintain that they are subjective formulations created by the mind. By contrast, for contemporary neuroscientists, the brain is situated in an independent material, spatial, and temporal external world and no issues concerning their derivation arise. But to this day, their origin within consciousness has not been satisfactorily resolved. If all living entities were fated to be terminated, would matter, space, and time still "exist"; would the planet Mercury still circle around the sun?*

The current neurosciences begin with the unquestioning conviction that space and time exist unproblematically and there is no issue concerning their *metaphysical* status; they exist independently of human consciousness, forever have and always will. However, in 1715–1716, both the independent reality and the subjective nature of space and time became hotly contested debates between Leibniz and the defenders of Newton.

But let me start with three general comments. First, according to Hegel, there is a genealogical family resemblance between philosophical skepticism, empiricism, phenomenalism, and a crude version of idealism. Consider the following comment from Hegel's *Lectures on the History of Philosophy*.

> With the ancients, scepticism is the return into individual consciousness in such a way that to it this consciousness is not the

DOI: 10.4324/9781003156130-10

truth, in other words, that scepticism does not give expression to the results arrived at, and attains no positive significance. But since in the modern world this absolute substantiality, this unity of implicitude and self-consciousness is fundamental—that is, this faith in reality generally—scepticism has here the form of idealism, i.e. of expressing self-consciousness or certainty of self as all reality and truth. The crudest form of this idealism is when self-consciousness, as individual or formal, does not proceed further than to say: All objects are our conceptions. We find this subjective idealism in Berkeley and another form in Hume.[1]

As Hegel continues, this form of *skeptical* idealism, i.e. *phenomenalism*, which begins with Locke, and infects Berkeley and Hume as well, reduces all consciousness to subjective appearances, i.e. *qualities*. First, it follows from Hegel's insight that not only colors and sounds are reduced to a secondary status, but even space and time as well. It is with this passage from Hegel in mind that we witness Hume seeking to account for our *ideas*—rather than our impressions—of space and time. Second, because of Newton's monumental accomplishment in the natural sciences, Hume, in the opening section in the *Treatise, Of the ideas of space and time*, and later Kant with his intuitions of space and time in the *Aesthetic*, both find it necessary to begin their major treatises with space and time as the basic foundations for the natural sciences. And third, I intend to establish Hume's familiarity with the famous Leibniz-Clarke debate and Hume's debt to a Leibnizian form of genuine "idealism."

There are three guiding influences on Hume. First there is Newton's postulation of gravitational forces operating in nature. This suggests to Hume that it may be possible to forge an analogous "attraction" in the mental sphere by appealing to the principle of "the association of ideas" in the mind, "to regard it as a gentle force, which commonly prevails in connecting our ideas to each other through resemblance, contiguity, and causality" (*Treatise*, 10–11). Hume accordingly proposes to pursue this phenomenalist theme by accomplishing within the mental sphere what Newton had achieved in the natural realm.

These are therefore principles of union or cohesion among our simple ideas, and in the *imagination* supply the place of that inseparable connexion, by which they are united in our memory. Here is a kind of ATTRACTION which in the mental world will be found to have as extraordinary effects as in the natural, and to shew itself in as many and as various forms.[2]

Hume claims, as an epistemic principle, that all our ideas begin first with impressions. In his discussion *Of the Ideas of space and time*, however, he begins with *ideas* and not impressions. And Hume's term "connexion" substitutes for the rationalist term "relation." But in empirical terms, there is no sensory impression or idea of "connexion." Hume's challenge, then, will be to account for space and time in terms of impressions—*minima sensibilia*—and provide an imaginary phenomenal substitute for his term "connexion." In doing so, I argue, he will be influenced by Leibniz.

By contrast, Newton posited the metaphysical reality of a preexisting empty space and time, created by God, in which absolute designations of left and right, up and down, as well as before and after, were taken to be meaningful descriptions independently of any presence of sensory objects, events, or human consciousness.

The second influence on Hume, as previously noted, derives from Shaftesbury's and Francis Hutcheson's moral sense doctrines, namely, that our *cognitive* judgments are ultimately based on our feelings or sentiments, as opposed to innate intuitions or reason. Hence truth, like ethics, is to be grounded in our psychological *sentiments, feelings, and* their *consequent beliefs.* This principle, as we observed in the preceding chapter, encourages Hume to turn *within the mind*, to *subjectivity*, to the *ideas* of space and time, unlike the naturalist philosophers of his time, who regard both space and time as independently "real" and "absolute" in the company of Newton, who was religious and believed that God was directly responsible for creating absolute space and time. Indeed, space and time represent God's sensoria; He is literally infinitely and eternally present everywhere and always. And further, theoretically, space and time precede the creation of the world and individual souls.

The third confluence comes from Hume's commitment to his immaterialist or mentalist theory of impressions, ideas, and generically his perceptions.

Philosophically, although not necessarily pragmatically, the critical problem impeding the progress of the scientific revolution required that some meaningful "definition" or account could be provided regarding the ontological and epistemological status of space and time. This is why Hume in the *Treatise*, and Kant in the *Critique*, felt obliged to begin in the first case with Hume's *ideas* of space and time, and in the second instance, with Kant's *intuitions* of space and time as "*pure* forms of sensibility*," respectively. But without establishing a secure theoretical foundation for both space and time, the entire edifice of science is erected on shifting sands. In Kant's case, it is to be noted that although the "pure forms of sensibility" of space and time are inherently *passive, intuitively, innately given* to consciousness, and although they are not mediate concepts, nevertheless, since Aristotle, the term "form" always suggests a modicum of activity in consciousness beyond mere potentiality, an accommodation. Kant's intuitions allow for their sensory "contents" to be spatially and temporally distributed on the purely empty canvasses of our intuitions.

Hume's labyrinthine analysis of space and time clearly testifies to his conviction of their central role in the physical sciences then making such fantastic progress in his day. Thus, quite early in the *Treatise*, Hume already indicates his ambition to accomplish a revolution in the mental sciences comparable to the one Newton had achieved in the physical disciplines. In pursuit of his investigation, Hume begins by repeating the principle that all our ideas are *first* derived and dependent upon antecedent simple, indivisible, impressions; and further that impressions *always* precede their corresponding ideas (*Treatise*, 4, 7). This distinction is not unlike that of Hobbes. There are only two elements, existents, i.e. contents before the mind: sensations and imagined "decaying sensations." Hume's ideas are analogous to Hobbes's "decaying sensations." Once this principle is firmly established, Hume then proceeds, paradoxically enough, to declare that our *ideas* of space and time are *complex, compound* ideas that lie beyond the nature of each of our *distinct*, i.e. atomistic simple impressions, i.e. ideas. Although both impressions and ideas are immediate, their primary difference is that impressions are more vivacious and forceful. Differently put, Hume is now insisting (a) that our *idea* of space (and presumably time), unlike our "simple" impression of a shade of blue (page 6),

198 Hume on space (and time)

are no longer *directly* and *unproblematically* given, as he had earlier contended; nor (b) are they derived from preceding *mental* impressions; nor (c) are they appearances *indirectly* derived via physiologically-caused sensations in the manner of Locke; but (d) rather they are the result of imaginary "connexions" (above). For example, the "unity" prevailing in our *idea* of space is the product of an imaginary connectivity, a "connexion," i.e., a relation (?), but not one that is *given* directly by either sensations (Hobbes, Locke) or impressions (Hume). In short, space (and presumably time) is a *mediated* idea dependent on imaginary "connexions." Thus, our idea—not our sensation—of space cannot be empirically caused; e.g., it is not traceable to an antecedent simple impression of blue; it is not caused by contact with an external blue object. Differently put, in the case of space, the "whole" precedes the "parts," the imagined "relations" precede the impressions, which is a clear violation of Hume's own empiricist principle that simple impressions *always* precede simple ideas.[3]

Hume's insistence that our *idea(s)*—not impression(s)—of space is non-sensational has perplexed numerous competent commentators. Even Kemp Smith has been puzzled "why it is that [Hume] did not take the more easy line of allowing 'extensity' to the sensations of sight and touch."[4] Or

> How is it that [Hume] has not taken what would seem to him the easier and more obvious course, at least as regards space—the course usually taken by those who hold a sensationalist theory of knowledge, namely that extensity is a feature of certain of our sensations (those given through the senses of touch and sight), and in consequence sensibly imaged?
>
> (*PDH*, 280)

Of this simpler more straightforward solution, according to Kemp Smith, both Hobbes (*Leviathan*, Pt. I, 1; *De Corpore*, Pt. II, 7, 8) and Locke (*Essay*, II, xiii, 27) had availed themselves prior to Hume. Hence Kemp Smith has found the section on the *ideas* space and time to be tough going indeed and has been content, to a great extent, in simply offering a number of historical appendices suggesting lines of influence on Hume, through passages discovered in the works of Pierre Bayle, Nicholas Malezieu, and Isaac Barrow. But, if we recall that in the *Treatise*, Hume argues "the maxim that our [sensuous] perceptions exist nowhere," then he is forced to lay the groundwork for our ideas of space—sans sensations—to be interpreted on idealist terms.

Accordingly, I intend to develop, in the following account, a strong "historical" influence on Hume initially offered by a student of Kemp Smith, Charles Hendel; and I shall extend Hendel's point by arguing a theoretical one, namely that Hume's "Hegelian idealism" in this critical section devoted to space and time, in the *Treatise*, is actually influenced by a form akin to Leibnizian idealism.

In 1925, Hendel argued that Hume was directly influenced by the Leibniz-Clarke debate concerning the ontological and epistemological status of space and time; and he believed that for Hume space and time, as mental appearances, were ultimately grounded in the associative power of the imagination.[5] Thirty years later, in a second edition, Hendel however disavowed his earlier claim concerning the imagination and avoided any discussion of his prior view connecting Hume with the famous *Leibniz-Clarke Correspondence.*[6] However, John Laird also intimates that Hume was familiar with the celebrated scientific controversy, but he did not further develop this claim nor say exactly *how* Hume was influenced by Leibniz.[7]

The twin theses I propose to defend are first that Hume was indeed aware of both Leibniz and Clarke's contending principles in the *Letters* and the correspondence between Clarke and Leibniz; and second that he sought to reinterpret Leibniz's theory along phenomenalist and indeed even idealist lines, which latter involve active *acts* of consciousness. In short, I wish to maintain that in the course of Hume's discussion of space and time, he ends up offering a Leibnizian version of the simplicity argument supporting Leibniz's thesis that the "elements," the "contents" of consciousness are the result of the active deployment, the ordering of unextended and indivisible *minima sensibilia*, as generated solely from *within* the mind; from a consciousness devoid of any reference to an external, extended, physical, or material world, thus concluding that space and time are essentially *ideal* imaginings.[8] What is important to note is that Hume's simple impressions are themselves unextended; they *are minima sensibilia*, which includes *minima tangibilia* (touch) and *minima visibillia* (sight). By the way, so are Kant's sensations. Once more, this is a direct consequence of the simplicity premise, namely that the soul or mind is unextend, non-spatial.

200 Hume on space (and time)

If the instrument of perception, i.e. the mind is immaterial, then the resulting observations cannot be extended and material.

Hume's knowledge of the Leibniz-Clarke debate could have been gained from a first edition, published in French, which appeared in 1720, under the editorship of Pierre Desmaizeaux (1673?–1745), a French Protestant refugee residing in England.[9] Hume may also have studied the *Letters* at La Fleche (1734–1737), where he had an easy access to an "excellent library" at the Jesuit College and also where the philosophies of Descartes, Malebranche, and Newton, as well as Leibniz, were being discussed and debated. Later he had ample opportunities to discuss the views of Locke, Bayle, and again Newton upon his return to England when he made the acquaintance of Desmaizeaux, who had been a close friend of Pierre Bayle, in fact editing the *Oeuvres diverses* and writing a biography of the great skeptic. In 1699, he came to England with Bayle, who was already there and introduced him to his own close companion, Anthony Ashley Cooper, the Third Earl of Shaftesbury, a writer whose works and opinions Hume followed closely.[10]

We know that Hume met with Desmaizeaux at least as early as March 1738, when Hume began residing at the Rainbow Coffeehouse, Lancaster Court, in London staying for over a year. The inn was a customary and popular meeting place for a group of religious exiles to which Desmaizeaux belonged. The close relationship between the two men is evidenced by the fact that in a letter of April 6, 1739, Hume asked Desmaizeaux for his opinion of the *Treatise*, the first two books of which had already appeared. Desmaizeaux penned a brief complimentary notice of the work, which, much to Hume's chagrin, compromised his anonymity by naming him as the author. And the short "review" surfaces again in a second quarter issue of the *Bibliotheque raisonee des savans de l'Europe* that same year.[11] Further it is quite likely the editor, Desmaizeaux, was preparing his second edition of the Clarke-Leibniz *Correspondence* at the time, which was published in 1740, and that Hume discussed the conflicting theories of Newton and Leibniz with his friend and I would argue that this led to Hume being directly influenced by the famous debate in processing his own views on space and time.[12]

In the proceedings, Samuel Clarke defends Newton by contending that infinite space and eternal time are absolute "quasi-substances"

Hume on space (and time) 201

and in effect representations of God's "divine sensoria" and consequently He is literally everywhere and always present. There is an absolute right and left as well as an absolute before and after even before the creation of the *material* universe and temporal events. By contrast, Leibniz argues against Newton that space and time are *subjective* forms of consciousness constituted by the mind's *active relational orderings of perceptual simples*; by the "manipulation" and "unification" of indivisible monadic points within consciousness, all occurring *within* the dominant Soul-Monad. Hume, however, in contrast to Leibniz, conceptualizes that the simple *minima visibilia* and *tangibilia appear* directly, immediately to consciousness *as a whole*; the whole *idea(s)* of space preceding the impressions of its distinct "parts." The critical difference is that for Leibniz, *perceptual sensibilia* need to be actively *worked* through, i.e., related, unified, and ordered, whereas Hume's "ordering" is empirically, phenomenally, passively, and directly *given* and therefore the *ideas* of space and time have *already* preceded the constitutive *acts of ordering* the impressions as in Leibniz. The issue is this: clearly Hume's impressions (*qua* ideas) are immediately, given, passive; and supposedly so are his ideas. *But* if the *idea* of space *precedes* the impressions, then clearly in some way or fashion, "relations," "orderings," "connexions" must have immediately usurped the original precedent role of the impressions.

Accordingly, Hume characterizes space as an *idea* and not an impression and certainly not a Hobbesian or Lockean sensation. He does this because, unlike Leibniz's rationalist approach, he does not distinguish the essential cognitive immediacy of impressions from the mediacy of conceptual thought, i.e., *relations*. And second, he regards the impressions, the "elements" or "contents" of our idea of space to be simple, unextended, and immaterial, i.e. *minima sensibilia*. This premise of course is completely consonant with the simplicity argument. In other words, the elements of space are composed of *minima sensibilia*; including the tactile *tangibilia* and the visual *visibilia*, which together consist of unextended, dimensionless points of touch and sight. It follows that these punctilist dots, comprising our idea(s) of space, are simple, indivisible, and only by virtue of their spatial— assumed *distanced*—ordering are they able to account, to produce, to result, to contribute—but not cause—the phenomenal, i.e. mental appearances of spatial extension.[13]

202 Hume on space (and time)

Once again, for Leibniz, the principle of the simple *qualitative*—as opposed to the compound *quantitative*—appearances of the *minima perceptions* can be traced back to our ancient and ubiquitous Neo-Platonic tradition, which defines the soul as an immaterial substance and holds that the contents predicated or attributed to the mind must also be immaterial and unextended. Accordingly, it follows that whatever engages the mind—either from the "inside" or the "outside"—must itself be ideal. Thus, if both soul and its thoughts are essentially immaterial, it at once becomes not only problematic but indeed inconceivable how an immaterial mind could possibly cognitively know, process, and/or interact with a materially extended world, which by definition is separate and distinct from the self. If so, then space can only be accounted for subjectively, immanently as consisting of *ideal* perceptions (Leibniz) or *phenomenal* imaginings Hume (cf. once more Kant's Fourth Paralogism, A 367 ff. *Of Ideality*, A 367 ff. and compare it with his Refutation of Idealism, B 274 ff.).

A fundamental commitment to the Achilles premise, I believe, similarly underlies Hume's invocation of the term "perception," which is clearly more "subjective" than the term "sensation" in the manner of Locke, since the latter term is infected with physicalist connotations. Following Berkeley, Hume endorses all the implications of the "way of ideas" path—that "to be is to be perceived by a mind" (*Treatise*, 67–68); and it is in the service of the imagination "that it produces the opinion of a *continu'd,* or of a *distinct* existence" (*Treatise,* 188). Once more, Hume is agreeing here with the dualists and idealists that our ideas, our perceptions are immaterial and therefore they "exist nowhere"; nor can their source be discovered independently of the mind in external, i.e., Newtonian space and time. "Perception" is a loaded mental term, a "mindful" term, and like the conception of an "idea," it is not the sort of existent we could describe as having length and dimensionality, although it can "produce" the *appearance* of both. When Hume is being strict and consistent, it is considerations such as these that prompt him to redefine Locke's term "sensation" and instead judiciously use the mental terms "impressions," "ideas," and "perceptions" (*Treatise*, 2). I can share universal concepts, meanings with others, but not my perceptions. They are purely subjective. By contrast, Locke's term "sensation" clearly implies a physiological source, an accompanying *tabula rasa*, and consequently a corresponding physicalist and causal account of sensations. But Hume develops an empirical theory in which our ideas and perceptions of space and time consist of sets of *immediate* "connexions"—generally a contradiction in terms—holding between unextended visible points.[14] Accordingly, Hume, like Leibniz, endorses a subjectivist and "relationalist" or idealist theory of space.

Further Hume agrees with the idealisms of Malebranche and Berkeley by viewing the primary qualities—space, extension, and motion—as reduced to the same ontological status as the secondary ones, as having only a subjective, that is to say, a mental existence. In conformity with his prior use of the terms "perception," "object," or "idea" as interchangeable, he states:

> If colours, sounds, tastes, and smells be merely [ideal] perceptions, nothing we can conceive is possest of a real, continu'd existence; not even motion, extension, and solidity, which are the primary qualities chiefly insisted upon. To begin with the examination of motion; 'tis evident this is a *quality* altogether inconceivable alone, and without a [relative, relational] reference to some other object. The idea of motion necessarily supposes that of a body moving. Now what is our idea of the moving body, without which motion is incomprehensible? It must resolve itself into the idea of extension or of solidity; and consequently the reality of motion depends upon that of other qualities. This opinion, which is universally acknowledg'd concerning motion, I have prov'd to be true with regard to extension; and have shewn that 'tis impossible to conceive of extension, but as compos'd of parts, endow'd with colour or solidity. The idea of extension is a [relational?] compound idea; but as it is compounded of an infinite number of parts or inferior [i.e. extensionless] points, it must at last resolve itself into such as are perfectly simple and indivisible [i.e. *minima sensibilia*]. These simple and indivisible parts, not being ideas of extension, must be nonentities, unless conceiv'd as colour'd or solid.[15]

In this manner, Hume reaffirms his conclusion, offered in Book I, Part II, that "our ideas of space and time … [are] founded only on that simple principle, *that our ideas of them are compounded of parts, which are indivisible* (*Treatise*, 38), which are "indivisible points or atoms"

(*Treatise*, 42, 58). Hume's idealist conclusion, then, is that "extension ... is nothing but a [relational?] composition of visible or tangible points dispos'd [or distributed] in a certain order" (*Treatise*, 62); and that "we have no idea of any real [i.e., independently existing] extension without filling it with sensible objects [i.e. ideal mental points] and *conceiving* [sic] its parts as visible or tangible" (*Treatise*, 64; italic mine).[16] Notice the shift from the term perceiving to conceiving. Perceptions are sensory; conceptions are universals, abstractions.

In another passage, Hume, after having argued that space cannot be composed of physical, i.e. sensory extended parts, nevertheless suggests that unextended "sensations result in extended ones" (*Treatise*, 19, 41). Hume can only argue this line of thought if he assumes Leibniz's relational theory of space and time; only if he intends that the points *appear* to be at relative distances from each other as opposed to contiguous to each other within consciousness.

If the *minima sensibilia* constitute the "content" aspect of space and time, what is the "formal" aspect? Hume's response corresponds in all essential respects to Leibniz's formulation, which is that the ideas of space and time consist in the "manner," in the "order" of the arrangement of visible and tangible points as perceived within consciousness. It is the *relational* ordering that constitutes the *idea* of distance that produces the *appearance* of space.[17] *If* there were only a single point in the entire universe, *then* there could be neither space nor time. And if there were only two points, it would be impossible to tell which point was moving if the distance between them was increasing.

In the 1720 edition, Desmaizeaux gives the following concise summary of Leibniz's doctrine: Hume was fluent in French.

> [I]l s'etendit particulierment sur la nature de l'Espace, du Tem & de la Duree. Il rejeta absolument le Vuide, ou l'Espace reel absolu: regardant l'Espace, comme une pure Relations. Ce n'est, dit il, que l'Ordre ou l'Arrangement du Corps; c'est l'Ordre de situations, ou de Coexistence, c'est a dire, des choses qui coexistent; comme le Tems est l'Ordre des Successions ou, des choses qui se succedent l'une a l'autre.
>
> (It dwells particularly on the nature of Space and Time, and Duration. It rejects absolutely the Void or real absolute Space: looking at Space as a pure relationship. It is not, he says,

but the order or the Arrangement of the body; it is the order of situations, or the Coexistence, it is to say, of things coexisting; like the Time is the Order of Successions, or of things succeeding one after another.)

This emphasis on the term "succession" may be why Hume incorporates the term "succession" in his discussion *Of personal identity*, when he describes the self: as "nothing but a bundle or collection of different perceptions, which *succeed* each other with an inconceivable rapidity" (*Treatise*, 252). We also recall Shaftesbury's inclusion of "succession" in his depiction of human consciousness.

Hume, like Leibniz, denies the perceptual possibility of a vacuum or an empty space. Indeed, in one important passage, he hints that perception consists of a plenum of sense impressions, that a man atop a mountain sees no more physical points than a man "cooped up in a room" (*Treatise*, 112), In other words, consciousness is completely filled with minimal points.

Leibniz, of course, denies that space is a thing-in-itself, an independent reality existing apart from human consciousness; or that it possesses any sort of truly ontological or metaphysical status as Newton and Clarke held. Rather, according to Leibniz, space is ideal. So Hume. But again, Leibniz's refutation concerning the independent existence of space and confirming its subjective ideality is grounded in his over-riding principle that the mind is itself immaterial; therefore whatever appears to the mind must be simple, unextended, indivisible, without parts despite its spatial appearance.

Finally, whatever the advantages and the disadvantages of the Leibnizian-Humean account of the generation of space and time, it is far superior to the naïve simplicity of the Hobbesian tenets as well as to the unreflective thought of our current neuroscientists. Both space and time—whatever they are—are inconceivable apart from a unified subjective self. As we go forward, we will learn that although *all* of us are physically privileged to share a common spatial world together, nevertheless *each* of us separately dwells within our own subjective enclosure of an intimate and personal time. Today, neuroscience unreflectingly, naively, dogmatically assumes that space and time exist unproblematically. By doing so, it totally disregards the powers and the creations of the solitary mind. But imagine if something as

206 Hume on space (and time)

seemingly unproblematic as space is in reality indecipherable, how much more so are the inner hidden workings of the self!

The secondary literature on Hume's discussion is virtually non-existent but the issue is not whether Leibniz and/or Hume are right but whether space and time are meaningful existents separately from human minds?

Notes

* Ben Mijuskovic, "Hume on Space and (Time)," *Journal of the History of Philosophy*, XV:4 (1977); reprinted in *David Hume: Critical Assessments*, edited by Stanley Tweyman (Routledge & Kegan Paul, 1994).
1 *Hegel's Lectures on the History of Philosophy*, translated by E. S. Haldane and F. H. Simson (London: Routledge, 1968), "Idealism and Scepticism," III, 363–364.
2 Hume, David, *A Treatise of Human Nature*, edited by L. A. Selby-Bigge (Oxford, 1973), 12–13; hereafter cited as *Treatise*. Later, in his *Enquiry Concerning Human Understanding* (1748), space and time are not discussed. Again, the secondary literature is virtually non-existent.
3 How problematic the whole issue of space is may be ascertained by examining Hobbes's inconsistent, actually contradictory, versions of whether space is independently real or subjectively fictitious.

   In an earlier work, *Anti-White*, Hobbes had asserted the existence of real space and had identified it with body itself. "So this space which, when inherent in a body, as the accident in its subject, can be called 'real,' would certainly exist even if there were no being to imagine it" (*AW,* p. 41).

   But according to the doctrine of *De Corpore,* space is simply the phantasm (that is the phenomenal image) of a body, absent its other properties that has an existence outside of the mind: "space is the phantasm of a thing existing without the mind simply; that is to say, that phantasm, in which we consider no other accident, but only that it appears without [i.e., as external to] us (*De Corpore,* 7:2). Since every body exists [independently] outside the mind, space is imagined as being external to the mind. But in fact space is only in the mind. Bodies are not literally in space. A. P. Martinich, *A Hobbes Dictionary* (Cambridge, MA: Blackwell, 1995), 287.

   Hobbes's metaphysical assumption that space would exist even in the absence of any mind is the same position as our current neurosciences. But how could you prove that? Notice the contradictory clash between scientific materialism and subjective phenomenalism, between physical objects and mental images. On Hobbes's phenomenalism, consult John Laird, *Hobbes* (New York: Russell & Russell, 1968), 123–156, 258–265.
4 Kemp Smith, Norman, *The Philosophy of David Hume* (London: Macmillan, 1964), 277; hereafter cited as *PDH*.

5 Hendel, Charles, *Studies in the Philosophy of David Hume* (London: Bobbs-Merrill, 1963), Chapter V, "Space, Time, and Reality," esp. 139–145, 500–504. Hume in deference to his English audience and in the interest of avoiding controversy, undoubtedly would have neglected citing Leibniz by virtue of the acrimonious exchange between Newton and Leibniz over the discovery of the infinitesimal calculus. Newton was convinced that Leibniz had plagiarized it from him pursuant to a personal visit.

6 *The Leibniz-Clarke Correspondence,* edited by H. G. Alexander (Manchester University Press, 1965). Hume alludes to Newton's views on the absolute reality of space and time and the existence of the void on pages 37 and 55 of the *Treatise.* For a summary of the debate, cf. Robert Paul Wolff, *Kant's Theory of Mental Activity: A Commentary on the Transcendental Analytic of the Critique of Pure Reason* (Cambridge, MA: Harvard, 1963), 2–8.

7 Laird, John, *Hume's Philosophy of Human Nature* (London: Archon Press, 1967), 64–65, 67, 73, 77.

8 Leibniz is the first to invoke the term of "idealism" and specifically in reference to himself in a metaphysical sense. And it clearly implies that *all* reality can be interpreted and contained within monadic spheres of subjective consciousness. For Leibniz, space is a *phenomena bene fundatum.* Ordinary *conscious* perceptions result from confused, "indistinct" conceptions ("sensations") in the human mind but in principle even these flawed perceptions can be purified into clear active *self*-conscious, rational conceptions. For Hume, as a phenomenalist, passively given images (impressions) are mental but obviously not pure, i.e., sensory as images. Thus, Leibniz is an idealist and Hume is a phenomenalist. In addition, Hume is not an idealist in the sense of one who interprets all reality as mental, mind-dependent, or spiritual (G. E. Moore); rather he assumes the existence of a material world external to the mind. And he accepts the existence of an independent physical world as a natural psychological *belief.* In the section on space and time, Hume switches back and forth without warning, as his purposes demand, from assuming a common sense view of the independent reality of external objects, i.e., real physical objects of sight and touch and his example of the spot of ink (*Treatise,* 42) to arguing a strict epistemological thesis that *only* mental perceptions exist as entities and occur as events (*Treatise,* 67–68).

9 The first edition, of Desmaizeaux's collected study was titled *Recueil de diverses pieces, sur la philosophie, la religion naturelle, l'histoire, les mathematiques, &C, Par MRS Leibniz, Clarke, Newton & autheurs celebres,* was printed in Amsterdam (1720).

10 Mossner, E. C., *The Life of David Hume* (Edinburgh, 1954), 102–103, 109. Apart from the French edition, the *Correspondence* was translated into English immediately upon Leibniz's death by Clarke as early as 1717. It was generally recognized at once as of the very first moment in contemporary

208 Hume on space (and time)

philosophical speculation. Hume would also have ready access to the principal tenets of Leibniz's thought through Bayle's *Historical and Critical Dictionary* article, "Rorarius"; see especially note H and following; hereafter cited as Mossner.

11 Greig, J. Y. T., *The Letters of David Hume,* 2 Vols. (Oxford, 1932), I, 29–30, Letter 10; and Mossner, 118–119.

12 Kemp Smith holds that Book I of the *Treatise* was composed after the last two books. It is also possible that the section on space and time is the very last portion to be written. Although I am not sure how far I am prepared to defend his modified "patchwork" thesis." But cf. Mossner, who quotes Hume as stating that Bks. I and II "were unquestionably completed in France" (page 74). Similarly, Hendel holds that the section on space and time to be very early Hume.

13 Cf., *Treatise,* 228. The strongest defense of this interpretation is to be found in Kemp Smith, *The Philosophy of David Hume,* Chapter. XIV; see also: John Laird, Hume's *Philosophy of Nature* (Archon, 1967), 68–69, 72; and B. M. Laing, *David Hume* (Russell & Russell, 1968), 112–113. Leibniz as well as Berkeley held this view on the *minima sensibilia;* cf. Ben Mijuskovic, *The Achilles of Rationalist Arguments: The Unity, Simplicity, and Identity of Thought and Soul from the Cambridge Platonists to Kant* (The Hague: Martinus Nijhoff, 1974), Chapter V; both Kant and Fichte, in the *Vocation of Man,* held it after Hume. Its ultimate origin once again is Leibniz. See Kemp Smith, *A Commentary to Kant's 'Critique of Pure Reason'* (Humanities, 1962), 51, 86–87 101, 103, 105, for a compendious background sketch of its history. The *minima sensibilia* only admit of *qualitative* differences, e.g., sight and sound but never quantitative or extended ones. See also Ivor Leclerc, *The Nature of Physical Existence* (New York, 1971), 243, ff. For the Platonic influence on Leibniz's doctrine of relations, confer Hector-Neri Castaneda, "Leibniz and Plato's *Phaedo:* Theory of Relations," in *Leibniz: Critical Interpretative Essays,* edited by M. Hooker (Manchester University Press, 1982), 124–125. Cf. Robert Paul Wolff, who argues in effect that Hume virtually invokes an active Kantian form of consciousness in his article, "Hume's Theory of Mental Activity," *The Philosophical Review,* 69:3 (1960); and consult, Ben Mijuskovic, *Consciousness and Loneliness: Theoria and Praxis* (Leiden: Brill, 2019), 128–130.

14 The simplicity premise, with its single assumption but various arguments and conclusions, remains at the very center of endless discussions engaged on both sides of the question, namely whether senseless matter alone can think, as it was pursued after Descartes by Malebranche, the Cambridge Platonists, Locke, Bayle, Clarke, Shaftesbury, and Berkeley? Hume was keenly aware of many of these disputations and makes a lengthy reference to these discussions on pages 234–236 of the *Treatise.* It bears emphasizing that with the exception of the scholastically inclined Cambridge

Platonists, it was not an inclination for authors at the time to cite or quote sources, with the exception of Bayle's dictionary. As mentioned, it is important to remember that in the case of the *minima sensibilia,* Hume distinguishes between *impressions,* which are "*no where,*" as opposed to the *experience* of "those of sight and feeling," which are induced by external physical motions (Hume, *Treatise,* 235–236). Hume is a dualist; matter is real and so is the mind.

15 Hume, *Treatise,* 228; cf. Berkeley, *Principles of Human Knowledge,* Sections 9–15, 42–43, 67. Previously Malebranche theorized that:

> C'est que ces grands espace que vous voiez, ne sont que des espaces intelligible qui ne remplissent aucun lieu. Car ces espaces que vous voiez sont bien differens des espaces materiel que vous regardez. Il ne faut pas confondre les idees des choses avec les choses meme. Souvenez-vous quon ne voit point les corps en euxmemes, et que ce n'est que par leurs idees qu'ils sont visible. Souvent on en voit, quoiqu'il en ait point: prevue certaine que ceux qu'on voit sont intelligible et bien differens de ceux quon regarde (*Entretiens sur la Metaphysique et sur la Religion suivi des Entretiens sur la Mort* (Paris, 1961), IV, x, 137).

Hume alludes to Malebranche in the *Treatise,* 84, 158, 171, 248–249 and in the first *Enquiry,* Sects. 4, 54–55, and 58 note. Although the section on the ideas of space and time is omitted from the *Enquiry Concerning Human Understanding,* nevertheless in a footnote to Section 124, Hume continues to insist that there are points or images that are "absolutely indivisible." Cf. B. M. Laing, *David Hume* (New York: Russell & Russell, 1968), 106, 112–113.

16 The "idea of extension is nothing but a copy of these colour'd, points and the manner of their [relational?] appearance" (*Treatise,* 34). Hume's clearest expression of his argument is given in relation to time.

> The idea of time is not deriv'd from a particular impression mix'd up with others, and plainly distinguishable from them; but arises altogether from the manner [i.e., order?] in which the [simple] impressions appear to the mind, without making one of their number. Five notes play'd on a flute give us the impression [sic] and idea of time; tho' time be not a sixth impression, which presents itself to the hearing or any of the other senses. Nor is it a sixth impression, which the mind by reflection finds [i.e., observes] in itself ... But here it only takes notice of the *manner* in which the different sounds make their appearance.
>
> (Treatise, 36–37)

17 *The Leibniz-Clarke Correspondence,* Leibniz's First Paper, Sect 4; Third Paper, Sect 12; Fourth Paper, Sect. 35; Fifth Paper, Sects. 24, 47, 84, 87, 106. The references are identical in the Desmaizeaux and Alexander editions. In the 1720 edition there are explanatory appendices excerpted

from Leibniz's works, e.g., the *Theodicy* (App. 5), that would have offered Hume considerable insight into Leibniz's principles. Also in the second volume, Leibniz in a dialogue examines Malebranche's philosophy and offers a phenomenalist interpretation as the logical conclusion of the Oratorian's principles. For this phenomenalist interpretation regarding space and matter, confer Desmaizeaux 1720 ed., I, 226 ff.). Only Monads are substances; "matter" only exists in the form of monadical perceptions within the soul Monad. Soul Monads are active principles of unity and indivisibility. Matter (le corps), on the other hand, is merely "un etre de raison ou plutot d'imagination, un phenomene" (pages 227–228). Again, the soul is immaterial and therefore the appearing "bodies" are likewise simple, immaterial. As we can dream of bodies without bodies being present, so we can mentally entertain the appearances of bodies. Thus, should God annihilate the alleged material world, we would still continue to experience the same phenomena. For Philarete, who basically represents Leibniz's views, the material world drops out and an immaterial God acts directly on human souls (pages 243–244). Obviously at this point, Philarete seems to represent a conflation of both Malebranche and Leibniz's views (Desmaizeaux, 1724, II, 508 ff., 521, 525, 530–531, 533). What is important in all these discussions, however, is that given the exigencies of metaphysical dualism, and the incompatibility of reconciling body and soul, matter and mind, thinkers are forced to turn to God in order to bridge the chasm between the two substances: Descartes to the goodness of an undeceiving God; Malebranche to God's continuous occasionalist miracles and direct interventions; Leibniz to a pre-established harmony instituted by God; and Berkeley to the principle "that we see all things in God." *But we recall that Hume turns not to the Deity in his solution to the problem of dualism but to the contingencies of Nature. This is my prejudice as well.*

Chapter 10

Kant's two premises in the transcendental deductions

> *What an incredible wealth of contents, acts, and structures within consciousness, including the immediacy of sensations and feelings; the mediacy of conceptions, meanings, relations, judgments, and inferences; distinctions between quantities, qualities, and values; constitutive levels and stages; spontaneity, reflexivity, intentionality, temporality; a subconscious and an unconscious; scientific facts and formal laws; ethical principles; aesthetic expressions; and even "the sheer nothingness of consciousness," and all the flood and flux of our emotions and moods! And by contrast, in stark opposition, neuroscience informs us that all this can be causally explained by turning to the quantitative collisions of some one hundred billion brain neurons and electrical synapses. What can we know for sure? Where should we begin?*

Aristotle defines philosophy as the search for "first principles." All arguments, in any serious discipline or endeavor, must start with an "undisputed," i.e., *assumed* basic premise. But Kant's *Critique of Pure Reason* offers two quite different candidates as starting points in his two Deductions: immanent time-consciousness in the first edition *Critique*, A 99–104 (1781) and the transcendental unity of apperception in the second edition, B 131–132 (1787). The following discussion further deepens the problem by involving Kant's distinction between the problematic relationship of the unity of consciousness treated in the second edition Deduction (above) and the first edition Second Paralogism, *Of Simplicity*, in the Dialectic (A 351–352, 1781); and more specifically as the Second Paralogism is compromisingly involved in the on-going conflict between materialism and idealism, which is at the heart of all

DOI: 10.4324/9781003156130-11

four Paralogisms in the first edition, namely "whether senseless matter *alone* can think?"

Robert Paul Wolff, in his study of Kant's Transcendental Analytic, proposes an interesting way of approaching the argument in the first edition Deduction in the *Critique of Pure Reason*.[1] Wolff, following the commentaries of Erich Adickes and Hans Vaihinger, which in turn conclude in the interpretation expounded in Kemp Smith's *Commentary*, is convinced that there are four distinct stages of *logical* argumentation developed in the Deduction in the first edition of the *Critique*. Kemp Smith argues at length that these four levels are not only chronologically but also developmentally distinguishable, the first dating back to a period as early as Kant's *Inaugural Dissertation* of 1770, a period during which Kant believed it was possible to have knowledge of metaphysical things-in-themselves.[2] In fact, Kemp Smith holds that Kant's concept of the *transcendental object=x,* occurring in the first stage (A 107-A 110), is a reference to a noumenal reality. This would be consistent with Leibniz's monadic subject–object relation. The fourth stage of the Deduction, which develops the account of the threefold transcendental syntheses produced by the creative and generative imagination, resulting in immanent time-consciousness, was just completed on the very eve of publication.[3]

Wolff, who is following the work of Kemp Smith, refuses to commit himself to the chronological version of the theory concerning the four levels, but he does agree that the Deduction can be broken down on logical grounds into four ascending levels of argumentative sophistication.[4] What Wolff does share with his exegetical forerunner, Kemp Smith, is the conviction that the second edition Deduction constitutes the heart of the Analytic and that it is in this section that Kant either (a) establishes his grounding premise and proves his transcendental argument, concerning the possibility of synthetic judgments *a priori* as conditioning both ordinary consciousness, as well as Newton's science of gravitational mechanics, or (b) fails.[5]

According to Wolff:

> In each of the four versions of the argument of the Deduction [and a fifth version given at the end of the Second Analogy [on page 278], the premise consistently remains the same. The starting point is the *cogito,* "I think," of Descartes. Or rather it is a revised

Kant's two premises 213

form of the *cogito,* which expresses what Kant believes to be the most general fact about any [human] consciousness: its unity.[6]

Wolff then proceeds to explain what Kant means by the "unity of consciousness," which is the empirical manifestation of its underlying epistemological condition, "the transcendental unity of apperception" (Wolff, 187). He initiates his discussion with a quotation from Kant, which, disconcertingly enough is a citation from the second edition and not from the Deduction in A (1781), which Wolff is purporting to explain.

> *The Unity of Consciousness.* "It must be possible for the 'I think' to accompany all my representations; for otherwise something would be represented in me which could not be thought at all, and that is equivalent to saying that the representations would be impossible, or at least would be nothing to me" (*Critique*, B 131–132). In this way Kant introduces in the revised version of the Deduction the idea of the unity of consciousness. Following Descartes, though with very different results, he adopts the "I think" as the absolutely first principle of philosophical speculation. But Kant does not only assert "I think." Rather he states that the "I think" can be attached to each of my mental contents. Thoughts are not like stones in a heap, or rabbits in a hat. They do not simply lie in the mind as an aggregate of unconnected contents. They are all bound up together as the thoughts of *one* mind. They are all *my thoughts* and only mine. The force of this statement, however, is not on the face of it obvious. "All my mental contents are my mental contents" is merely a tautology and an "I think" attaches to my mental contents does not seem much better. What is the characteristic to which Kant is trying to call our attention? Light may be thrown on the problem if we take a trick first suggested by Brentano.

Wolff then proceeds by imagining that we have two pieces of paper on which we write two identical sentences. The example he chooses is "The unicorn is a mythical beast." The first piece of paper is divided among six men, Jones, Brown, etc., each knowing a single word. The second piece is left intact and given to a seventh man, Smith. It follows that

Every word of the sentence is contained in the consciousness of some member or other of the group of six. Similarly, every word of the sentence is contained in Smith's consciousness. But the two cases are absolutely different, for while in the former it is true that the separate parts of the sentence are contained in *some* consciousness, they are not contained in the *same* consciousness, and hence there is no *unity of consciousness* of them as there is in the case of Smith. William James puts the point in the following way. "Take a sentence of a dozen words and take twelve men and tell to each one word. Then stand them in a row or jam them in a bunch and let each think of his word as intently as he will; nowhere will there be a consciousness of the whole sentence." The fact is that one consciousness of twelve words is not the same as twelve consciousnesses of one word each. Following Kant's terminology, we may characterize the difference by saying that one consciousness of all twelve words binds them together, conceives them as a unity.[7]

The point is that whatever you do with the *bodies* of the twelve men, materially, you will be unable to manufacture a unified self-conscious meaning of the entire sentence. According to Wolff, the ultimate and undeniable premise of the Deduction is the proposition "All the contents of my consciousness are bound up in a unity." What Kant intends by this he has just tried to make clear in his example of the seven men. In doing so, he has reinforced his interpretation with a passage from James and he mentions that particular quotation is also cited by Kemp Smith in his *Commentary*.[8] But what Wolff fails to explain, and what is puzzling in all this, is that Kemp Smith uses his reference to James in order to offer the reader an insight into Kant's metaphysical—and essentially Leibnizian—Second Paralogism, *Of Simplicity*, which is grounded in Leibniz's principle of monadic immateriality; the fallacy based on the rationalist and "dogmatic" argument, which *discursively* demonstrates*, on purely *a priori* grounds, that the unity of the soul follows from its unextended simplicity. The problem then is that Kant attacks the very example and argument Wolff is attempting to impute to Kant as an indubitable premise. The reader will readily notice the similarity between Wolff's "trick" and the example I have italicized from Kant in the quotation below from the Second Paralogism as Kant presents it as a *metaphysical* fallacy.

> This is the Achilles of all dialectical inferences in the pure doctrine of the soul. It is no mere sophistical play, contrived by a dogmatist [i.e., rationalist] in order to impart to his assertions a superficial plausibility, but an inference which appears to withstand the keenest scrutiny and the most scrupulously exact investigation. It is as follows.
>
> Every composite [material] substance is an aggregate of several [physical] substances, and the action of a composite, or whatever inheres in it as thus composite, is an aggregate of several actions or accidents, distributed among the plurality of the [divisible material] substances. Now an effect that arises from the concurrence of many acting [physical] substances is indeed possible, namely, when this effect is external only (as for instance, the motion of a body is the combined motion of all its parts). But with thoughts as internal accidents belonging to a thinking being, it is different. For suppose it be the [material] composite that thinks; then every part of it would be a part of the thought, and only all of them taken together would contain the whole thought. But this cannot be consistently maintained. *For representations (for instance the single words of a verse), distributed among different beings, never make up a whole thought (a verse), and it is therefore impossible that a thought should inhere in what is essentially composite.* It is therefore possible only in a *single* [immaterial] substance, which, not being an aggregate of many [material] substances, is absolutely *simple* [i.e., immaterial]. The so-called *nervus probandi* of this argument lies in the proposition, that if a multiplicity of representations are to form a single representation, they must be contained in the absolute [immaterial simplicity and] unity of the thinking subject.
>
> (Second Paralogism, *Of Simplicity*; A 351–352)[9]

All four metaphysical Paralogisms have but one goal, namely, to *rationally* demonstrate on *a priori* principles that "senseless matter *alone* cannot think!" Traditionally this is a theme that all dualists, rationalists, and idealists alike assume as their first principle and share

216 Kant's two premises

in common. Obviously, the same objection can be levelled against the neurosciences.

Kemp Smith comments on the eulogy with which Kant introduces the argument and remarks "that it may well seem a quite invulnerable argument."[10] Indeed! And that is one important consideration. But the second implication, namely Wolff's, is much more troublesome, since if Wolff is right, it would then follow that the ultimate principle, the grounding premise of the Deduction(s) would be an *a priori* metaphysical argument, which properly belongs to the Dialectic.[11] The difficulty is that in B 131–132 (above), Kant is offering a positive *transcendental* synthetic *a priori—i.e., a universal and necessary—*principle as a condition for *both* the possibility of ordinary human experience *and* Newtonian science.

The rationalist argument for the unity of self-consciousness, which initially passes from Plotinus to Ficino, on to the Cambridge Platonists, and then Descartes via the Augustinian Oratory finally settles with Leibniz. In Kant, it serves as the basis for all four Paralogisms in the A edition. First, for the establishment of the soul as an independent thinking substance; second, for its reflexive self-conscious unity; third, for its continuous unique personality; and fourth, as the constitutive condition grounding a metaphysical form of subjective idealism, for if the soul is the only instrument available for cognition, then whatever appears to consciousness must also be immaterial and "ideal." But if so, then the Achilles premise and arguments cannot *both* succeed in defending, in "proving" a quartet of noumenal conclusions in the Paralogisms in 1781 *and* also in the same moment double as the ultimate transcendental premise for the Deduction in B in 1787. In the second edition, all four original Paralogisms are deleted and newly replaced by a proof for the immortality of the soul.

But it is more than a curious fact that in rewriting the *Critique* for the second edition, there were only two sections, which were completely recast for the second edition. They were the Transcendental Deduction in B *and* also the single Paralogism written anew in the Dialectic in B focusing on the immortality of the soul.[12] In the Preface to the First Edition, Kant is clearly desirous of putting to rest all those writers who "profess to prove the simple nature of the soul" (A xiv). But in preparation for writing the Preface to the Second Edition, in which the key theme is his Copernican Revolution, he must have reread the passage where he speculates about penetrating *below* his transcendental arguments (A xvi–xvii, as we previously mentioned in Chapter 2). It seems that during the intervening period of a half-dozen years between the two editions, Kant pondered his original intention to explore a "Subjective Deduction," which would seek to establish *how* the "faculty of thought itself is possible?" by speculating, by "hypothesizing" that there may be *subconscious* acts below his formal transcendental categories. This would certainly involve a heretofore hidden dynamic, undoubtedly a deeper, perhaps an inaccessible spontaneous activity operating *below* his transcendental categories and principles; a *subconscious* force—as opposed to a Leibnizian mnemonic and unconscious realm. It may be that when he reconsidered his speculative ruminations regarding a deeper investigation of "how thought itself is possible?" he realized that he was in effect juggling three issues: (a) the possibility of subconscious activities; (b) validating his transcendental, i.e., formal, "logical" conditions presupposed for the possibility of human experience; and (c) its outcome in terms of justifying the empirical sciences.

It is important to remember that Kant originally—and seriously—suggested that there may be *subconscious* activities, which make "thought itself possible." This would be very different from Leibniz's (and later Freud's) unconscious mnemonic recollections and quite different from the formative *transcendental* synthetic *a priori* categories and principles constituting his Copernican Revolution. In other words, I am suggesting that there may be three distinguishable levels of consciousness: subconscious; transcendental; and phenomenal in contrast to his unreachable noumenal realm of realty. And, as a further speculation, I would venture to propose that Schopenhauer's irrational noumenal Will is the inheritor of this third and irretrievable force, which finds expression in his version of a noumenal irrational Will. Kant's noumena are transcendent; Schopenhauer's are subconscious.

In any event, Kant's promise, "though, as I shall show elsewhere," is never fulfilled. I believe what transpired during the intervening half-dozen years between the two editions is that Kant wanted to plumb more deeply into the subterranean levels of the subconscious mind and more specifically by reconsidering the creative, i.e., "spontaneous" aspects of the "productive imagination" (A 97–98, A 50=B 74, A 51=B 75, A 68= B 93) in order to unravel the more hidden, what he describes as the "hypothetical" levels of consciousness, but that he was

218 Kant's two premises

dissuaded from attempting to do so because of the bewildered scholarly response of many of his early critics to the first edition *Critique* and consequently he was discouraged from pursuing this more difficult endeavor. *But* while pondering these obviously problematic issues and delayed goals, he realized that the second edition transcendental unity of apperception (B 131–132, 1787) is not only seriously compromised, but indeed *invalidated* by the first edition Second Paralogism (A 351–352, 1781). And his "solution" was to completely rewrite both sections. In fact, as we have seen, in the second edition, he only offers a single Paralogism as he veers from the "unity of self-consciousness" to criticizing Mendelssohn's proof for immortality based on his version of the *Phaedo*. But the problem remains. Which serves as the premise for the Deduction, the paralogistic argument offered in A 351 or the terse statement provided in B 131?

Kemp Smith proposes that there are actually three possible premises: (1) the independent existence of the world; (2) the reality of the self; and (3) immanent time-consciousness.[13] Descartes challenges the first; Hume both the first and second, but he is unable to challenge the third.

My own view follows Kemp Smith's lead in his *Commentary* on Kant. I am persuaded that Kant's first edition A Deduction is the stronger of the two because the argument rests on the indubitable conviction that "consciousness of time is an experience whose actuality cannot be questioned; [and that] by its actuality it will therefore establish the reality of everything that can be proved to be its indispensable condition." I am further convinced that it also grounds the self's nature as fundamentally a form of subjective idealism. To repeat:

> Whatever the origin of our representations, whether they are due to the influence of outer things, or are produced through inner causes, whether they arise *a priori,* or being appearances have an empirical origin, they must all, as modifications of the mind, belong to inner sense. All our knowledge is thus subject to time, the formal condition of inner sense. In it they must all be ordered, connected, and brought into relation. This is a general observation which, throughout all that follows, must be borne in mind as being quite fundamental.
>
> (A 99–104)

Kant's two premises   219

But without an empirically unassailable premise, Kant's transcendental argument cannot proceed and succeed.

Nevertheless, A. J. Ayer finds the premise of consciousness alone as fatally flawed. Whether we summon Descartes or Kant, Ayer's issue exemplifies one of the great divides between Consciousness and Science, immediacy of sensation and the mediacy "thought."

> But even if it were true that such a proposition as "there is a thought now" was logically certain, it still would not serve Descartes' purpose. For if "*cogito*" is taken in this sense, his initial principle, "*cogito ego sum,*" is false. "I exist" does not follow from "there is a thought now." The fact that *a thought occurs at a given moment* [i.e., immediately] does not entail that any other thought has occurred at any other moment, still less that there has occurred a series of thoughts to constitute a single self. As Hume conclusively showed, no one [immediate] event intrinsically points to any other. We *infer* the existence of events which are not actually observing, with the [empirical] help of general principles. But these principles must be obtained *inductively.* By mere deduction from what is *immediately* given we cannot advance a single step beyond. And consequently, any attempt to base a deductive system on propositions which describe what is *immediately* given is bound to be a failure (italics mine).[14]

Ayer's argument is empirical, "inductive." But he admits "we infer" without realizing that inferences, qua judgments, are not immediate. He reduces consciousness to Hume's *immediacy* of impressions. And he acknowledges the distinction between the self and its thoughts. But he fails to consider Hume's *own* admission to a *temporal succession*, to "different perceptions, which *succeed* each other with an inconceivable rapidity" within consciousness (*Treatise*, 252). For Kant, the essence of consciousness is constituted by the *mediate* synthetic *a priori* relation between the subject and its conceptual object (A 107–110). The subject, temporally active unifies the contents. But even more importantly, as our analysis of Descartes's Second Meditation has shown, the human mind intrinsically possesses the ability to *actively* transcend sensory immediacy by enlisting judgments, inferences, and even guesses. That is precisely the difference between *active* minds and *passive* brains.

220 Kant's two premises

To the question, "what is the self?" Ayer's answer is

we have solved Hume's problem by defining personal identity in terms of bodily identity and bodily identity is to be defined in terms of the resemblance and *continuity* of sense-contents.

(page 127)

But "continuity" means temporal *succession*!

Notes

1 Wolff, Robert Paul, *Kant's Theory of Mental Activity* (Harvard, 1963), 105–111; excerpts from this book also appear in a "A Reconstruction of the Argument of the Subjective Deduction," *A Collection of Critical Essays*, edited by R. P. Wolff (Garden City, NJ: 1967), 88–133.
2 Kemp Smith, Norman, *A Commentary to Kant's 'Critique of Pure Reason'* (New York: Humanities, 1962), xx ff.
3 Ibid., 202 ff. It is this version of Kemp Smith's four-pronged interpretational thesis that H. J. Paton criticizes as a revival of Erick Adickes and Hans Vaihinger's "patchwork thesis in its extreme form"; H. J. Paton, *Kant's Metaphysics of Experience* (New York: Humanities, 1963), I, 38.
4 Wolff, *op. cit.*, 81–84, 101–103.
5 Kemp Smith, *op. cit.*, xxiv, Wolff, op. cit., 78–80.
6 Wolff, *op. cit.*, 105.
7 Wolff, *op. cit.*, 105–106.
8 Kemp Smith, *op. cit.*, 459, note.
9 Kant, *Critique of Pure Reason*, A 351–352; italics mine. In the passage, Kant identifies simplicity and unity as he often does. Of course, what is simple must be a unity although the converse does not necessarily follow.
10 Kemp Smith in his *Commentary*, however, declares that it is the temporal character of consciousness, which forms the starting point of the transcendental argument and not the unity of consciousness; *op. cit.*, 458 ff.
11 Interestingly, Ewing in his study of Kant maintains that it is open to Kant to accept the argument of the *Second Paralogism* "for the transcendental unity of apperception but he will not accept it as an argument for the view that the self is a simple substance." A. C. Ewing, *A Short Commentary to Kant's Critique of Pure Reason* (University of Chicago, 1967), 203. But I am still at a loss to understand in what sense Ewing intends that Kant "would have accepted it as an argument" and I remain perplexed as to how a transcendent, noumenal proof can yet have *transcendental* validity. *If* the argument is sufficient to "account for" (in however broad a sense we allow to the term) the unity of apperception, *then* on what possible grounds could Kant continue to deny that it is *also, in addition*, a perfectly

adequate demonstrative proof for the other three Paralogisms, as well as all the previous metaphysical and rationalist arguments tendered from Plotinus to Descartes, the Cambridge Platonists, and Leibniz, all of whom had exploited the simplicity argument to extend, to apply not only to the unity of consciousness but even to Kant's Copernican Revolution, which is based on the Fourth Paralogism, *Of Ideality.* Cf. T. D. Weldon, *Kant's Critique of Pure Reason* (Oxford, 1968), 201. In any event, the active immateriality premise functions as the foundational principle for all five Paralogisms, four in the A edition and one in the B edition. This said, at least the question remains *why* Kant deleted the first edition Paralogisms.

12 It should be pointed out, however, that in the Appendix to the *Prolegomena*, Kant had already expressed some dissatisfaction with the first edition Deduction and with the Paralogisms (*Prolegomena*, Sections 380–381). The rewritten second edition Paralogism in 1787 was a complete throw away, an unsophisticated criticism of Moses Mendelssohn's proof, in his *Phaedon*, for the immortality of the soul based on Plato's ancient dialogue, Kant arguing that even what is perfectly simple, e.g., the soul nevertheless could disappear by "elanguescence," by a gradual (qualitative?) diminution. How can any substance that is absolutely simple and indivisible able to diminish by "degrees"?

13 Kemp Smith, *Commentary*, 243; see also 239 ff. Kemp Smith holds that Kant has three possible starting points open to him: experience of objects; experience of self; and experience of immanent time-consciousness. Descartes rejects the first; Hume the second; and admits the third 252–253.

14 A. J. Ayer, *Language, Truth, and Logic* (Dover, 1946), 46–47.

Chapter 11

Brentano's intentionality of consciousness

Brentano's concept of intentionality derives from St. Augustine's intentio, essen intentionale *in his work,* On the Trinity, *Chapter 10. It describes an active striving will, a* voluntas, *a mental act directed at or targeting some entity beyond its self. Unlike the act of reflexivity, which circularly relates, pairs the subject with an object, it is meant to signify an intentional movement* toward *an object. But there is also a strong Aristotelian component as well, a teleological tendency ingrained in the conviction that human consciousness is always directed at a final cause (the four causes in the* Physics). *Thus, the ultimate origin of intentionality is Aristotelean. For Aristotle, mechanism and teleology are not mutually exclusive. This dovetails with Brentano's, Weber's, and my thesis that man's ultimate desire is to be guided by qualitative values; that the essence of man, the peculiar virtue of humans is to create value-laden goals for one's self alone; and that we are the only creature displaying this unique mode of consciousness. We also recall that for Aristotle, man's highest virtue is to intellectually contemplate the Unmoved Mover's thoughts* (Metaphysics). *For Brentano, intentionality is ultimately teleological; and in the end he hopes it will lead to immortality. This chapter is important because I seek to synthetically a* priori *unify the acts of Kantian reflexivity with Brentano's principle of intentionality.*

I now wish to discuss Brentano's principle of intentional consciousness by examining an illuminating number of inconsistencies involving the simplicity argument, as presented in his *Psychology from an Empirical Standpoint.*[1] I shall also seek to put into proper perspective and balance the current interpretation of Brentano as an Aristotelean realist—without denying these obvious themes in his writing—by emphasizing certain underlying immaterialist assumptions and Kantian influences

DOI: 10.4324/9781003156130-12

on his work as well (*PES*, 180–181). Thus, since ample justice has been done to the Aristotelean elements in his thought, I wish to concentrate on his more neglected tendencies.[2]

Brentano is best known for his ground-breaking and influential definition of consciousness as an *act of intentionality* borrowed from scholastic philosophy and which he describes as embedded in all our cognitive acts thus securely connecting his theoretical principle within a history of ideas context.

> Every mental phenomenon is characterized by what the Scholastics of the Middles Ages called the intentional (or mental or ideal) inexistence of an object and what we might call, though not wholly unambiguously, reference to a content, direction toward an object (which is not to be understood here as meaning a thing [in the external world], or immanent objectivity. Every mental phenomenon includes something as object within itself, although they do not all do so in the same way. In presentation something is presented, in judgment something is affirmed or denied, in love loved, in hate hated, in desire desired and so on.
>
> (PES, 88; and consult note 11 and 89)

Intentionally I can see a goat, imagine a goat, hate a goat, feed a goat, buy a goat, etc. and all within my "field" of mental empirical consciousness. Unlike reflexion, the act is not self-referential but rather transcendent. It is *about* or *of* something *other* than the self. The important consideration is that unlike phenomenalism, which is a construction of secondary sensory qualities e.g., patches of colors, sounds, tastes, etc., by contrast, phenomenology actively targets empirically or fictitiously given objects, "so what we are concerned with is the sheer having something as object, as the distinguishing feature of any act of consciousness" (*PES*, 79).

> Thus, contents are treated as analogues to objects, among which we distinguish some which have their being only in a loose and improper sense in the mentally active subject, and some which have their being in the strict sense outside of the subject, where they belong to the realm of real things.
>
> (PES, 292)

224 Brentano's intentionality of consciousness

Brentano's intentionality is active; phenomenalism's sense data are passive. Further:

> Psychology is distinguished by the fact that it has to do with phenomena which *are known immediately as true and real in themselves.* This, and nothing else, was and is Brentano's doctrine (*PES,* translator's comment, page 20).
>
> This intentional inexistence is characteristic exclusively of mental phenomena. No physical phenomenon exhibits anything like it. We can therefore define mental phenomena by saying that they are those phenomena which contain an object intentionally *within* themselves.
>
> (PES, 89; cf. translator's footnote 11 and
page 79, footnote 1)

And again:

> [T]he term "consciousness," since it refers to an object, which consciousness is conscious of, seems to be appropriate to characterize mental phenomena precisely in terms of its distinguishing characteristic, i.e., the property of the intentional inexistence of a [mental] object, for which we lack a word in common usage.
>
> (PES, 102)

The intentional "object" is *immediately*, *directly given* "within," "before," or "to" consciousness, what Husserl was later to focus on as the *meaning* grasped in an *eidetic* intuition (*PES,* 271). Critically important is the assertion that intentionality is a conscious *activity.* This at once removes it from the sphere of empirical *passivity* in the manner of Hume's phenomenalism.

But the problem is that the act and the content are *both* immediately apprehended, intuitively; the unity is not a relational, not a mediate connection of a subject with its object (Kant).

> What is characteristic of every mental activity is reference to an object. In this respect, every mental activity *seems* to be something relational. And in fact, Aristotle enumerates the various main classes of his categories of relation, he mentions mental reference

... In other relations both terms—both the fundament and the terminus—are real but here only the first term—the fundament is real.

(*PES*, 271)

This makes it sound as if the fundament, "the object," is alone and in-itself active. It is one thing to say that consciousness is intentional and quite another thing to say the object in-itself is intentionally active.

Nevertheless, the foundation for Brentano's empirically based "descriptive psychology" is similar to classical empiricism in the sense that sensations, e.g., colors and sounds, are directly "presented" or "given" to consciousness; the connection is *immediate* between the *act* of consciousness and its *content*. What is important to emphasize, however, is that Brentano's principle of a *descriptive*—as opposed to a genetic—psychology is grounded in the immediate moment, so to speak, in direct descriptions of object/meanings, whereas by contrast, Freud's psychology, for example, is genetic, developmental, and dynamic, i.e., the source derives from the self-conscious ego.

By contrast, for Kant, the cognitive *relation*, *structure* between the self<>act<>conceptual object/content is mediate, relational, and synthetically *a priori*. The act is thought *through* a mutual, reflexive reverberation between a subject in relation to a conceptual "object"; it is a self-conscious act; circular rather than linearly intentional. Both Brentano and Kant posit an active "unity" between subject and object and both assume that all consciousness is expressed in judgments but that is where the similarity ends. Self-conscious reflexion and transcendent intentionality, although they are both acts, "travel" in different directions. But more importantly Brentano is wrong in maintaining that intentionality intrinsically derives directly from the experience of the immediately given mental phenomena. Intentionality arises from the mind, not from the intended sensation, the "intentional in-existence" (*PES*, 88 note, 89 note). By contrast, for Husserl, intentionality is meaning-intending, it is directed at immediate *eidetic* intuitions beyond the self, transcendent to the self.

The other problematic implication of this targeting act is that there is no archer. The arrows are shot but there is no bowman. That is why and how later Sartre validates his version of the "transcendence of the

226 Brentano's intentionality of consciousness

ego;" the "ego" as a "nothingness"; only the intentional act is real; the "self" is transformed into an object, a "me."

For Brentano presumably the three distinguishable elements of consciousness are: act, content, and object. My problem is that Brentano identifies or fuses the act with the content, which is precisely what Kant distinguishes. For Brentano to invoke the targeted aspects—seeing a goat—*as per se active* is a complete begging of the question. For Kant the *relation* of subject to conceptual object is a synthetic *a priori* one, it is actively, mediately relational (*Critique*, A 107–110 ff.). For Brentano, it appears the object *is* the act.

Consider the following string of quotes as *"Examples" of mental phenomena.*

> Brentano understands "mental phenomena to mean the same as 'mental activity' … since every such activity, at least in men and animals, is a *passio,* a [sensory] affection in the Aristotelian sense. So what we are concerned with is the [immediate] sheer 'having something as object' as the distinguishing feature of any act of consciousness."
>
> (commentator's remark, PES, 79, footnote 1)

This is the problem: For Brentano, "mental phenomenon" means "mental activity." This identification denies the very distinction between content and act. I have the power, the potential, the *dynamis* to actively use my arm. But it is not until I have grasped an object—the content—in my fist—that I have mediately completed the action, its *energeia*.

The effort to attain "introspection" is invalidated because it is not an *immediate* perception but rather a mnemonic "observation," a reflection on or about something *past*. In this regard, Brentano simply assumes that phenomenal mental "in-existences" are intrinsically active and unified (*PES*, 96–98, 155). And although he criticizes Kant's principle of a synthetic relational *mediacy*, he fails to realize that Kant appeals not only to (a) acts of *spontaneity* (*Critique*, A 97, A 50=B 74, A 51=B 75, A 68=B 93) but also (b) to its mediate, i.e., relational results. Synthesis can only occur on the condition that there are at least two terms to connect. In other words, Brentano regards the unity of consciousness as intrinsically immediate, as opposed to Kant's relational mediacies. Brentano also has little to say about time-consciousness

Brentano's intentionality of consciousness 227

in the proper text but he satisfies himself by simply mentioning both Kant and Schopenhauer's intuitions of space and time (*PES*, 358), whereas Husserl, of course, has a great deal to say about internal time-consciousness, while Brentano is content with merely "classifying" certain misconceptions, including Kant's and Schopenhauer's limitations (cf. Brentano's Appendix, XVI, *On* Ens Rationis, Section 8, 358 ff.).

However Brentano is also anxious to confirm (a) the Kantian *ideality* of the unity of self-consciousness on his own terms as "a fusion" (*PES*, 130–131), while at the same time (b) struggling to preserve the multiplicity of extended shapes in perception, and (c) also accommodating brain "activity" into the mix (*PES*, 61–62). Expecting to benefit from a Kantian *reflexive*—as opposed to an *intentional*—paradigm of the unity of consciousness (*PES*, 126, 127, 130, 133), he declares that "Every mental act, therefore, is accompanied by a twofold inner consciousness, by a presentation, which refers to it and a judgment which refers to it, the so-called inner perception, which is an immediate, evident cognition of the act" (*PES*, 143, 153–154, 155 and note 1). For Kant, metaphorically speaking, the act of *reflexive* self-consciousness is circular whereas Brentano's and later Husserl's acts of transcendent intentionality are (inconsistently *taken* to be) linear. This is *both* possessing a reflexion *and* in the same moment (b) targeting its intentionality without realizing the difference or resolving the contradiction between a circle and a line. In short, in having it both ways. Reflexivity and intentionality, to be sure, are both acts but *not the same act.* As far as recruiting "fusions" are concerned, Bergson can appeal to interpenetrations because he is describing *contents* and *not* acts.

Put differently, Brentano claims he is faithful to an Aristotelian principle but avoids Aristotle's conflicting declarations concerning his empirical commitment to the principle of (1) the *tabula rasa*, the mind as a blank tablet in *De Anima*, 430a, and its inconsistency with (2) the immaterial and reflexive nature of a *relational* self-consciousness exemplified by the Unmoved Mover in *Metaphysics* (1075a). Consult passages *PES*, 126, 127, 130–131, 133), which indicate genuine Kantian reflexivity.

What I do agree with is that both reflexivity and transcendence are *acts*, activities of consciousness, but they are separate, i.e., distinguishable *acts* from their presentational *contents*; they are as different as a circle is from a line, although both are geometric figures. But further,

228 Brentano's intentionality of consciousness

what I wish to hold is that both self-consciousness and intentionality are *a priori* synthetically related within consciousness, both are necessary. But Brentano identifies the two as if they share the same activity, as if they are the same act. If the essence of intentionality is targeted outwardly, directionally, then it cannot circularly turn on its self without providing a phenomenological descriptive account of the process, which he does not offer. Lockean empiricism, we recall, is "outwardly" observational and passive, and reflection and reflexion are not synonymous acts. For both Kant and Brentano, consciousness is judgmental. He criticizes Kant's synthetic *a priori* version (pages 211, 305), but he affirms the unity of consciousness (pages 97–98, 160, 163, 165) but he also affirms a Kantian reflexivity: "That is to say, we have something as our primary object and at the same the mentally active subject has himself as object, as someone who is mentally active" (155 note).

Brentano, in referring to the traditional distinction between mental and physical phenomena also asserts the following.

> People have tried to formulate a completely unified definition which distinguishes all mental phenomena from physical phenomena by means of negation. All physical phenomena, it is said, have extension and spatial location, whether they are phenomena of vision or of some other sense, to products of the imagination, which presents similar [Aristotelian corresponding?] objects to us. The opposite, however, is true of mental phenomena; thinking, willing, and the like appear without extension and without spatial location. According to this view, it would be possible for us to characterize physical phenomena by saying they are those phenomena which appear extended and localized in space. Mental phenomena would then be definable with equal exactness as those phenomena which do not have extension or spatial location. Descartes and Spinoza could be cited in support of such a distinction. The chief advocate of this view, however, is Kant who explains space as the form of the intuition of the external sense.
>
> (*PES*, 85)

The weak point of this distinction is that, yes, if you are describing the *contents* of the two substances, matter and mind, but not if you are defining the *acts* of reflexion and intentionality.

Brentano's conception of intentionality is designed to undercut the distinction between (a) an act and (b) its content by an identification of a/b; an identity of the act with its content, as it forms a judgment; it serves to negate this allegedly naïve bifurcation within dualism by confining the *act/inexistent object* into a single, a "fused" unity. That is why in certain versions of phenomenology, the self can be bracketed; "put out of gear." But the question remains whether he is successful?

Accordingly, Brentano's characterization in the passage above is correct but merely as far as it goes. In the quotation, Brentano cites Descartes, Spinoza, and Kant. But for rationalists, dualists, and idealists, a critical distinction is that matter is (allegedly) inert—and sensations are passive, a *passio*, as he admits above (*PES*, 79)—as in the over-arching principle that senseless matter alone cannot think precisely because sensations are *passively* given to consciousness. They are *not* phenomenal activities; that would be a contradiction in terms. Hume's impressions and ideas are not acts; they are merely "given." Brentano, by referring to "phenomenal activity," has conflated two incompatible "elements"—acts and contents—and simply assumed what he requires to demonstrate. This is *the* critical difference between sensations and thoughts, body and soul, mind and matter. If one merely assumes that mental phenomena are intrinsically active, that is a presupposition that can be challenged like any other "first principle" or definition by its contradictory. If immediate sensations are intentionally conscious, then fleeing insects as well as humans would be creatures endowed with meaningful cognitions and intentions.

And yet Brentano declares "Nothing distinguishes mental phenomena from physical phenomena more than the fact that something is *immanent* as an object in them [i.e., *within* consciousness]" (*PES*, 197; italics mine). This admission is strongly supportive of a dualist metaphysic.

Brentano's own version of intentionality, of course, later influences Husserl, who studied under him from 1884–1886, and who is similarly often guilty of shifting between the two "principles," between *both* acts of reflexivity *and* acts of intentionality in his writings. On my account, both are legitimate modes of consciousness, like opening your eyes and listening to an orchestra, and shutting your eyes and muting the musicians.

230 Brentano's intentionality of consciousness

For Kant, in the Aesthetic, the pure *form* of spatial sensibility is *given* as an intuition but as a *form* it is a *potentially* active *constitutive* element of consciousness, without which human consciousness would not be possible (or at least radically different). All *forms* in idealism—by definition—are potentially active (Aristotle's *dynamis*) but not necessarily relational. Similarly, inner sense, *qua* temporal, is likewise (1) a *form* of intuition, as in the Aesthetic, where it is transcendentally *given*—rather than *constituted*. But in the Analytic (2), "inner sense," time-consciousness is a creative, productive, synthetic *process*; it is *constituted—not* caused—by a threefold temporal *series* of acts; by synthetic *a priori* acts of apprehension (intuition), reproduction (imagination), and conception, recognition (synthesis); *Critique*, A 99–104 ff.). Again, note that the mediating force of the imagination is *both* passively sensuous *and* actively free.

Immanent time-consciousness serves Kant as a recurring "first principle" in varying contexts as it punctuates the critical *act* of relational mediacy. By contrast, Brentano obscures this "dimension," this temporal "feature" of consciousness" by an "absorption," an "identification," a "fusion" of act and content. Once more, Bergson can do this because he is describing contents and not their "fusing" acts. This is also why and how Husserl can concentrate on directly given *eidetic* meanings alone and also bracket, put out of gear both the entire external world, metaphysical issues, the empirical sciences—*and even on certain occasions the nomadic ego.*

Later Husserl, in his *Phenomenology of Internal Time-Consciousness*, in criticizing Brentano (Section 3, Par. 36 ff.), recruits Kant's conception of "constitutive acts" making it clear that all cognitive acts involve an immanent temporal "flow," a "stream of consciousness," when he describes how the separate notes in a melody are related in creatively constituting the *meaning*, the intentional meaning of listening to a song. And in Appendix XIII, he concludes his treatise by rather inelegantly but concretely titling it, "The Constitution of Spontaneous Unities as Immanent Temporal Objects." An act, any act intrinsically means a spontaneity, a novelty, a beginning, and a creation of an existence and an event that previously did not exist. Every song becomes constituted—not caused—as a creative immanent temporal event. Thus consciousness exhibits an inner, temporal dimension but not an outer, external, and spatial dimension, while the scientific conception

Brentano's intentionality of consciousness 231

of time, by contrast, measures the motion of objects in space. And finally, Brentano believes psychology could become an exact science but not in terms of a "genetic" pursuit but rather only as a descriptive or phenomenological discipline.

By comparison, Husserl grounds his own principle of intentionality on Brentano's version only later to be forced to acknowledge, while under the combined counter influences of Descartes, Leibniz, and Kant, his own egological compatibility with a "transcendental" reflexive idealism in the *Cartesian Meditations*, a text wherein he fails to solve the problem of solipsism by appealing to the concept of empathy (*Cartesian Meditations*, Fourth and Fifth Mediation).

> As beginning philosophers, we must not let ourselves be frightened by such considerations. Perhaps reduction to the [reflexive] transcendental ego only *seems* to entail a *permanently* solipsistic science … As a matter of fact, we shall see that, in a certain manner, a transcendental solipsism is only a subordinate stage philosophically.
>
> (*CM*, Section 13)

The escape route is proposed in the Fifth Meditation when he undertakes to recruit the concept of empathy as the solution to solipsism by appealing to a descriptive *bodily "mediate appresentation," "an analogical apperception," a "mirroring" of my body with or to the body of the "other"* (Sections, 44, 50). The entire enterprise is a failure. And the paradoxical dilemma of solipsism entirely collapses into a form of unsustainable subjective idealism.

By contrast, Paul Ricoeur believes it is successful. In any case, Husserl later triumphantly carries empathy over into *The Crisis of the European Sciences and Transcendental Phenomenology.*[3]

But that the immateriality of the human soul continues to percolate in Brentano's mind is obvious by his resumption of the ancient and long-standing discussion regarding the Platonic battle between materialism and empiricism versus dualism and idealism.

> Our investigation has shown that whenever there is mental activity, there is a certain multiplicity and complexity. Even in the simplest mental state a double object is immanently present. At least one of these objects is conscious in more than one way: it is not simply the

object of a presentation but of a judgment and (a feeling) as well. But this lack of simplicity was not a lack of unity. The consciousness of the primary object [i.e., subject] and the consciousness of the [existing] secondary object are not each a distinct phenomenon but two [relational?] aspects of one and the same unitary phenomenon.

(*PES*, 155)

This is pure Kant; moreover:

Our investigations leads to the following conclusion: the totality of our mental life, as complex as it may be, always forms a real unity. This is the real well-known fact of *the unity of consciousness,* which is generally regarded as one of the most important tenets of [theological] psychology.

(*PES*, 163)

Regarding the immaterial nature of the mind, Brentano rather suggestively credits Aristotle with the following formulation.

[Aristotle] draws a distinction among mental phenomena by considering some of them as activities of the *central organ* (*sensus communis*) and others as incorporeal, hence as phenomena of the moral and immortal parts of the soul, respectively.

(*PES*, 179; cf. Tassone, note 2)

Notice the connection between "the moral" and the "immortal parts of the soul." We recall that Brentano remained a priest. This classification of two different kinds of phenomena, Brentano informs us, "remained dominant throughout the Middle Ages and its [dualistic] influence extends into modern times" (*PES*, 179, 181). Indeed! Consequently, according to Brentano, this distinction between two kinds of consciousness leads to implications both in terms of dualism as well as to the immortality of the soul.

For Aristotle believed that certain faculties of the soul were the exclusive property of man and were immaterial, whereas he held that the faculties which are common to all animals are faculties of a bodily organ. Consequently, supposing that the Aristotelian theories are correct, this classification divides into two groups of phenomena which occur in isolation from others in nature, too. And the fact that the latter are functions of an organ, while the [immaterial] former are not, allows us to assume the existence of important common characteristics and laws in each of these two classes of phenomena.

(*PES*, 195)

But this remains an open question. Brentano will not undertake *to prove* that Aristotle is correct in this dualist assertion, that demonstration he hopes to postpone for a future volume of the *Psychology*, one which however was never completed. Nevertheless, he ventures to envision that the metaphysical theories of Aristotle deserve endorsement not only by the already existing validations of the Medieval thinkers but also by the Moderns and presumably by his contemporaries as well. And he greets all this as a welcome confirmation of the traditional twofold distinction between soul and body, initially heralded by Aristotle (*PES*, 195), and he applauds it because of its essential connection to the promise of an afterlife (*PES*, 14–17, 25–27, 72–73, note 5). As an interpretational issue, most commentators on Aristotle believe that it is man *as a species* that is immortal and not the individual soul.

If we summarize Brentano's varying themes, we discover that his conception of the unity of consciousness is grounded in the immaterial nature of consciousness; "All that can be determined now is that all mental phenomena really appear to be unextended"; and "Further we found that the *intentional in-existence,* the reference to something as an object is a distinguishing characteristic of all mental phenomena. No physical phenomenon exhibits anything similar" (*PES*, 97). These positions, I believe, are tantamount to an admission of a dualistic *pairing* between the reflexive nature of self-consciousness and its intentionality, which in turn can be viewed as directly leading to an *a priori* synthetic *binding* of the two principles thereby further committing both to a form of metaphysical dualism. The virtue of this interpretation is that we can conclude that in terms of the twin acts constitutive of human consciousness, namely Kant's reflexive self-consciousness and Brentano's transcendent intentionality, the twin streams of this

234 Brentano's intentionality of consciousness

temporal activity can then be *a priori* synthetically coalesced, unified, combined, and fused in phenomenologically describing why and how we sense, feel, act, and think both reflexively and intentionally.

Otherwise, the alternative is that Brentano's "acts" of sensory intentionality simply reduce to a species of empirical phenomenalism. And why? Because if one *separates* acts and contents within awareness *but* fails to account for their *relational* unification, then they will have failed to *separate* the self *from* the world, which, in the last analysis, is the only way in which loneliness can function as the most meaningful of all cognitive and motivational concepts.

Finally, Brentano's attraction to the dualisms of Plato and Aristotle, and their issue regarding "the question of continued existence after death" and "whether the soul is composed of parts or whether it is simple," is declared as the most important question in philosophy because of its connection to human immortality" and by virtue of the soul's immateriality, it constitutes the necessary condition for its immortality" (*PES*, 14–17).[4] In short, Brentano is a traditional dualist.[5]

Notes

1 Brentano, Franz, *Psychology from an Empirical Standpoint*, translated by Anton Rancurello, D. B. Terrell, and Linda McCallister (New York: Humanities Press, 1973; originally published in 1874); hereafter cited as *PES*. For the religious origins of the intentionality principle, consult Victor Gaston, "Connecting Tradition: Augustine and the Greeks," vgaston@umich.edu

2 Tassone, Biaggio, "Franz Brentano's Phenomenological Transformation of Aristotle's Theory of Judgment," *Journal of the British Society for Phenomenology*, 42:3 (2011), 305–328; cf. Tim Crane, "Brentano's Concept of Intentional Inexistence," *The Austrian Contribution to Philosophy*, edited by Mark Textor (London: Routledge, 2006), 1–20.

3 Ricoeur, Paul, *Husserl, An Analysis of His Thought* (Evanston, IL: Northwestern University Press, 1967, 64–65). Ricoeur's defense of Husserl is weak and apologetic. Ricoeur holds that in the *Cartesian Meditations*, Husserl successfully *projects*, connects the subject's ego pole *within* the pole of "the other ego"; as a *sharing* entry into the other's field of consciousness, by employing the device of an empathic intersubjectivity between the two egos. But the other's penetration is not acknowledged; it is not only one-sided but a *bodily* immersion; it is not an eidetic *meaning*. His effort to escape solipsism by invoking the *meaning* of *bodily* "empathy" is a failure and so is Ricoeur's invocation of empathy in Husserl's behalf equally

unpersuasive in "solving" the problem of solipsism (Ricoeur, 64–67). Nevertheless, Husserl continues to assume that he has proved intersubjective "empathy" in *The Crisis of European Sciences and Transcendental Phenomenology: An Introduction to Phenomenological Philosophy*, translated by David Carr (Evanston, IL: Northwestern University Press, 1970), 163–164, 184–185, 209, 231, 238, 243, 255, 258. The same inability to rescue Husserl occurs in Gaston Berger, *The Cogito in Husserl's Philosophy* (Evanston, Il: Northwestern University Press, 1972), 88–89. But consult Herbert Spiegelberg: "It is a very revealing fact that originally, i.e., in the first edition of the *Logische Untersuchungen*, Husserl rejected the conception of an identical subject over and above the intentional acts of consciousness, very much in the manner of David Hume and other empiricists. But by the time Husserl published the *Ideen* (1913), he had completely reversed himself, a reversal which he acknowledged frankly in the second edition of the *Logische Untersuchungen*," quoted in Herbert Spiegelberg, *The Phenomenological Movement: A Historical Introduction* (The Hague: Marinus Nijhoff, 1965), "From the very start Husserl admitted that all our knowledge of others is to some extent indirect. The other is given us not in direct presentation but only by way of *Appresentation,* a process which acquaints us with aspects of an object that is not directly presented" (I, 87–88, 158–159). In short, it was not an *eidetic* intuition. Cf. Ben Mijuskovic, *Consciousness and Loneliness: Theoria and Praxis* (Leiden: Brill 2019), 440–442. However, Ricoeur, in an article, also interprets Husserl's struggle with transcendental solipsism as leading "to the embarrassment of Husserl in the constitution of the *alter* ego" over the issue of spontaneity; "Kant and Husserl," *Philosophy Today*, 10:3 (1966).

4 Franz Brentano, google: "Catholicism, Idealism, and Immortality"; Southern Nights"; google: https://socialecologies.wordpress.com. For my part, I would contend that Aristotle also assumes that the soul is both bodily and mental but when death intervenes the soul vanishes and memory ends. For Aristotle, the agent intellect survives but only as a universal species, not as an individual. Cf. Ross, W. D. *Aristotle: A Complete Exposition of His Works and Thoughts* (New York: Meridian, 1961), 149–150.

5 Frechette, Guillaume," Brentano on Perception," *Hungarian Philosophical Review*, 62:4 (2018), 27.

Chapter 12

The science of matter and the philosophy of mind

> *Imagine that I am reading this chapter in an empty auditorium. Meanwhile, down the hall, in a classroom, a group of students is observing a blank wall upon which the jerking motions tracking the gyrations of an electroencephalograph attached to my head are transmitting brain waves to the class. There are no audible sounds accompanying the lecture, no images of moving my lips. How meaningful would that be? People could surmise that I am thinking but little else.*

I now intend to show that the simplicity premise and argument grounds a paradigm of consciousness that directly challenges D. M. Armstrong's materialist theory of the "mind"=brain as proposed in his study.[1] In opposition, I intend to defend a subjective idealist model of consciousness by emphasizing the twin constitutive acts of self-conscious reflexion and transcendent intentionality as innate and emanating from within a genuine, substantial self.

According to Armstrong, "the mind is nothing but the brain ... man is nothing but a material object having none but physical properties" (*MTM*, 1). It is composed of cellular filaments and tributaries, which he further defines as "the physico-chemical workings of the central nervous system" (*MTM*, 32–34, 43–47, 77–78, 89 ff.). "Inner processes" and "mental states" are not denied, rather they are reinterpreted as "purely [sic] physical states of the central nervous system" (*MTM*, 273, 337, 355–356). The mind is "a computer" (*MTM*, 344), which is physically programmed and operated, i.e., activated as re-sponsive to externally caused environmental stimuli thus resulting in both specific and dispositional behavioral patterns (so Gilbert Ryle, B. F. Skinner, and J. J. C. Smart). Causes can be either "mental" or physical (*MTM*, 349). In principle, then, Armstrong contends that "internal thoughts"

DOI: 10.4324/9781003156130-13

put into motion overt bodily behaviors that are completely determined and "the future is predictable" (*MTM*, 49). And one must assume controllable as well. There is no "freedom"; freedom is merely an ignorance concerning the precipitating causes involved. ("We are aware of our desires but not their causes," Spinoza). The external physical world exists along with the receptive human brain, which passively re-sponds and re-acts, i.e., pushes back against the external material motions of objects in space. Armstrong's causal schema of *explanation* is diagrammed by the following sequence.

Physical World
matter in motion→impinging on bodily sense organs→brain→ behavior
or
Physical Brain
The brain "re-sponds, re-acts" to physical stimuli, which in turn cause→sensations= "mental" effects, i.e., perceptions resulting in overt public behaviors

This is obviously a reductionist theory of the "mind"=brain (*MTM*, 32–34, 269). As a cognitive paradigm, it exhibits certain "scientific," "causal," or "explanatory" advantages obvious to everyone as it depends on particularizing physical movements striking the brain, a conception, which I will call the *unidirectional* theory of consciousness. This will be contrasted with Brentano's (and later Husserl's) *intentionality* dynamic. Armstrong criticizes Brentano's paradigm (*MTM*, 40–42, 264–265) but does not mention Husserl.

I will discuss three theories of consciousness, which I shall designate as the "unidirectional," the "intentional," and the "reflexive.

The first view is classically represented by the ancient atomic materialism of Leucippus, Democritus, Epicurus, and Lucretius. Everything in nature is reducible to matter *plus* motion, including human and animal sensations and behaviors. Hobbes represents its modern counterpart. In Hobbes, primary reality consists solely of matter *plus* motion. The residual effects on the bodily organs, e.g., seeing colors, hearing sounds are alternately called sensations, ideas, and/or "phantasms" by Hobbes; sensations, ideas, and perceptions by Locke; and impressions, ideas, and generic perceptions by Hume. The lingering images of the

238 Science of matter and philosophy of mind

imagination are termed "decaying sensations" by Hobbes. Not once is the brain mentioned in Hobbes's *De Homine*, or Hume's *Treatise*. In short, all these modes of consciousness are *appearances*, distortions of "realty" caused and transmitted by the external motions of material objects striking.

Hobbes's basic principle is then carried forward into our contemporary period by Armstrong. "Before the modern [and the present] revival, the most conspicuous defender of Central-state theory was Thomas Hobbes. But the theory lacks philosophical sophistication" (*MTM*, 11; cf. 121, 182). Armstrong simply adds a brain to Hobbes's previous account. The material causes impinge on our sense organs and are then transmitted to the brain as its *passive* receptor, the effect (MTM, 144). In short, Armstrong defends Behaviorism (Skinner).

The mind also depicts certain *dispositional* attributes. If certain conditions are present and certain causes or stimuli occur, then certain predictable effects inevitably follow. If I am driving my car and someone jumps in front of me, I immediately slam on my brakes. If I hit a piece of glass sharply, it shatters. The point is that everything human and natural is determined and predictable. Glass is dispositionally brittle and I am on "the alert" when I am driving a car; I am not self-consciously thinking all the while what shall I do if someone jumps in front of my vehicle? It is simply a behavioral dispositional reaction.

Armstrong's theory of "introspection" (a) makes reflexive self-consciousness inconceivable and therefore (b) he denies the *substantial* reality of the self (*MTM*, 258). As he asserts, in his Acknowledgement in the book, "Professor J. J. C. Smart converted me to the view that mental states are nothing but physical states of the brain" (*MTM*, xi), which basically amounts to *explaining* self-consciousness away (*MTM*, 94–95, 112–113). The critical passage follows.

> In the case of perception, we must distinguish between the perceiving, which is a mental event, from the thing perceived which is something physical. In the case of introspection, we must similarly distinguish between the introspecting and the thing introspected. Confusion is all the more easy because *both* are mental states of the same mind. Nevertheless, although they are both mental states,

Science of matter and philosophy of mind   239

it is impossible that the introspecting and the thing introspected should be one and the same mental state. A mental state cannot be [reflexively] aware of itself, any more than a man can eat himself up. The introspection may itself be the object of a further introspective awareness, and so on, but, since the capacity of the mind is finite, the chain of introspective awareness of introspections must terminate in an introspection that is not an object of introspective awareness. If we make the materialist identification of mental states with material states of the brain, we can say that introspection is a self-scanning process in the brain. The scanning operation may itself be scanned, and so on, but we must in the end reach an unscanned scanner.

(*MTM*, 324)

In "the end," it seems, ideally it would be birth I suppose. A similar thesis is proposed by Auguste Comte, who argues that introspection is impossible because *both* the instrument *and* the object of introspection cannot be one and the same. Therefore, psychology should be replaced by sociology.

Here we see that the scanning process is essentially an *observing* one; the observer views something that is "independent" of the self. Hume's analysis of personal identity is a good example (*Treatise*, 251); it is a perception but not a self-perception. The "unscanned scanner," *qua* observer, shifts from observation to observation, from perception to perception as the environment moves or his thoughts wander. Accordingly, the problem is that *observational* perceptions cannot be *self*-perceptual. In principle, sensory observations and self-consciousness, or reflection and reflexion are different *modes* of consciousness. The direction is from the world to the brain thus causing the brain to be "outer" *observant* while the second is circularly coiled, revolving, cyclical, and reflexive. Although they both *belong* within and to *my* field of consciousness, they are not the same acts; they are two very different *modes* of consciousness, just as seeing and hearing are two different modes of sensation and yet both are connected to the same human organism. Both are present in consciousness, but as cognitions implementing thoughts and behaviors, they are radically different.

But imagine an observer watching a baseball game and an outfielder chasing a fly ball. If perceptions are reducible to "physiological brain processes," i.e., minute motions in the brain and central nervous system, as Armstrong hypothesizes, *then* it follows that we should be able to identify which particular physically connected neurons and synapses correspond to "nice catch" or "error" in the baseball example. The baseball situation exhibits two quite different "aspects;" both (a) a physical and *quantitative*, i.e., *sensory* as well as (b) an aesthetic and *qualitative*, evaluative appearances. But we cannot *match* the synaptic firings in the brain to specific qualitative meanings and relations in the brain. Feeling pleasure and displeasure are sensations but "nice catch" and "error" are evaluative *judgments*. Electro-chemical and neuronal synapses can be traced to sensations of pleasure but not to evaluations of beauty. Although to be sure *empirical*, physiological, and "causal sequences" can be *explained* as triggering physical and behavioral patterns in reaction to sensory stimuli, I submit that the capacity, the ability to capture *qualitative* nuances and subtleties are not decipherable on an electroencephalograph. *That* a person's brain is physically reacting can be inferred and determined by observing a machine but *what* a person is thinking cannot be so concluded. The "process" of thought may be "indicated" by the jagged lines traced on a metal appendage attached to a machine, but the gyrations of a mechanical arm are not *thoughts*. Thoughts, states, stages, and levels of consciousnesses—subconscious, unconscious, conscious, self-conscious, and evaluative—intrinsically imply not only quantitative complexity but even more complicated qualitative nuances and subtleties. And if we ask a neuroscientist to decipher and interpret the jerking movements of the machine, if we ask in what manner they "represent" *the meanings and relations constituting*—not causing consciousness, it simply won't work. There is no neuron for "relation." Further, the *particular* sensation of *this* red is meaningless apart from the spectrum of rednesses; the relation of this red to other rednesses. Sensations *alone* are not meanings nor relations. And Armstrong thus states, "the capacity of the mind is finite." Granted, but self-consciousness is circular and self-sufficient unto its self. All rationalists, dualists, and idealists are committed to this principle of circularity, of self-reference.

Neurons are homogeneous. There are no neurons of immediacy as distinct from neurons of mediacy. Judgments are not reducible

Science of matter and philosophy of mind 241

to sensations. We can disagree about our judgments, but it would be meaningless to disagree about our sensations.

For behaviorism, fear is equivalent to sweating palms, the quickened pulsations of the heart, the tremor of the hands, heavier breathing, etc., and although these behaviors do accompany fear, an "accompaniment" is not an identification any more than correlation is identical with causation. Rather fear is a *meaning*, a relation between a subject and a dangerous object or event; it is a *meaningful* object or event that is not only cognitively but also evaluatively invested with human significance by a thinking self-conscious subject. Emotions and values are completely different modes of consciousness.

Active intentionality is purposeful; it *intends* human purposes; the relation is one of interest. I am *concerned* in what I am thinking and experiencing; I *care*. Behaviors are simply descriptive. Insects behave— they respond to external stimuli—but they do not think. Meanings and relations are not simply reducible to little bits of material particles crashing around the skull. Although thoughts and brain pressures coexist, they are not the same *thing*. Historically, Greek rationalism from the beginning smuggled in a teleological element (Plato, Aristotle).

The problem of a criterion concerning the establishment of personal identity is a difficult one as Armstrong recognizes. He criticizes Hume as a "Bundle Dualist" (7, 16) and a phenomenalist (218), thus clearly distancing himself from both principles, while aligning himself to Central-State Materialism (73–125). Armstrong also suggests that "a group of happenings constitute a single mind because they are all states, processes, or events in a single [material] *substance*" (337), i.e., the brain and therefore "there is indubitable knowledge of mental states" (109–111). Further he states, "I suggest that the solution is that the notion of 'a mind' is a *theoretical* concept: something that is *postulated* to link together all the individual happenings of which introspection makes us [me?] aware" (337). Indeed, he labels his position "Monistic Materialism" (361). Apparently, I simply postulate that I am a different self from other selves. Perhaps I can also postulate that I am altogether someone else.

One obvious obstacle to this view—as Locke, Shaftesbury, and Hume already knew—is that the body undergoes a complete biological transformation in a relatively short span of time. Consequently, a criterion

242 Science of matter and philosophy of mind

of personal identity grounded in bodily continuity won't do because the body of an infant and that of the man he becomes is not the same. And precisely how does a sensory neuron, as it biologically expires, transmit its "knowledge" to a receiving memory neuron? Is it like a father transmitting the family history to his children? Hobbes alludes to the imagination in terms of "decaying sensations," but how would a "decaying neuron" pass its *meaning* on to a newly born neuron? Do parental neurons have obligations to their neuronal children?

Armstrong also suggests that as a theoretical concept, the self may be similar to Wittgenstein's notion that personal identity is like a rope, which consists in the interweaving of interconnected single fibers rather than being held together by a single continuous thread running throughout the entire length of the rope (*Philosophical Investigations*, Section 67). All these efforts, of course, are simply attempts to explain away not only self-consciousness but also the "integrity," the reality of the self.

Further, according to Armstrong, human freedom is an illusion. Both in nature and in man the future is completely predictable (*MTM*, 49–50, 160–161). He believes that behavioral psychology, as a science, will someday be refined, simplified, and reduced to physics through the intermediary science of physiology.

Often there is confusion when one conflates the meaning of "the unity of consciousness" with the conception of "personal identity." And Armstrong is guilty of just this muddle (*MTM*, 16–17, 336–337). The best he can do is the following.

> Consciousness is no more than *awareness* (perception) of inner mental states by the person whose states they are. If this is so, then consciousness is simply a further mental state, a state directed towards the original [scanned] inner states.
>
> (*MTM*, 94)

Consciousness of "internal" time is never mentioned by Armstrong; it is replaced by external causation. But one way to untangle the confusion is to focus on the *temporal* continuity of personal identity. Importantly, the temporal *nature*, the *quality* of the *immanency* of consciousness is something, that the materialist account is unable to explain away or to account for. Time for the empirical sciences always consists of

Science of matter and philosophy of mind   243

a one-dimensional external observation of motion. According to the physicalist doctrine, time is grounded in the awareness of the movement of objects in and through space; it consists in an awareness of change. It is based on perceived *motional*—not relational—transitions between sensory data. For science, space is primary, and time is derivative. Think of a photograph. It represents space but not time. But for the *continuity* of consciousness, time becomes primary and space is derivative.

This now brings us to the consideration of the second model of consciousness, the intentionality principle and thus to the theories of Brentano and Husserl as defined by their similar principles of intentionality.

(self)-consciousness→intentional act→"inexistent object" (Brentano) and

(ego)→constitutive   noetic   acts→noema=transcendent   eidetic meanings (Husserl)

The second model of consciousness, unlike Armstrong's, is characterized by a mental or ideal *act of intentionality*, an activity generated from within the mind rather than from the "outside" (Brentano, Husserl). Like the first, it is unidirectional, however the activity "travels" in the opposite direction; from *acts* of consciousness, toward *transcendent* objects or meanings of investiture; toward what we are conscious *of* and *about*. For Brentano, consciousness is directed at mental phenomena, "at objects intentionally within themselves," including thinking, judging, inferring, loving, hating, and so on, as opposed to Armstrong's mental *introspections* of *particular* physical sensations, of sensory data, and stimuli. Brentano's targeting acts are aimed at "inner perceptions of our own mental phenomena … this inner perception is not to be confused with inner observations of our mental states, since anything of that sort is impossible."[2]

Whereas Armstrong posits sensory contents, Brentano posits *inexistent objects* and Husserl *eidetic meanings*. Consciousness thus features the principle of *intentionality*—in opposition to Armstrong's behavioral principle. In contrast to Armstrong's materialist principle, consciousness is immaterial, ideal, but above all significantly active. The transcendent acts are "outwardly" directed. I leave aside for the moment the issue of the (possible) "bracketing" of the ego. In Sartre,

244 Science of matter and philosophy of mind

the intentional acts are "projected" beyond the "nothingness" of an unstructured consciousness.

For Brentano, the dynamic of intentionality generates and dictates a *descriptive* phenomenological approach—as opposed to a causal, explanatory, i.e., scientific one. Intentionality thetically posits objects *beyond the self, transcendent* to its self; by and through constitutive, structural acts, i.e., judgments. Consciousness is intrinsically object (or meaning) intending in contrast to empirically sensory. We have something as our primary object and in the same moment the subject acknowledges the object as its own. Every mental act is conscious; it includes within the self a consciousness of its self. Therefore, every mental act, no matter how simple, has a double-object, a primary and a secondary object (Brentano). The simplest act, for example the act of hearing, has as its primary object the sound, and for its secondary object, its self, the mental phenomenon in which the sound is heard. Consciousness of this secondary object is threefold; it involves a presentation, an act of transcendence *toward* it; and a cognition.

According to Brentano, the intended *"inexistent object is in consciousness."* Consciousness actively *intends* objects and events; it targets mental phenomena. Similarly, for Husserl, all *meaningful* states of consciousness—at their most basic judgmental level—are acts *directed at meanings.* Initially, in their purest form, the implementation of the methodological device of the epoche allows the researcher to bracket, to put out of gear all "existing" metaphysical, scientific, and empirical positing concerning an independent "external existence." Again, the contrast between the two principles/paradigms/models of consciousness is that Armstrong's is passively unidirectional, i.e., receptive, while Brentano and Husserl's are actively intentional.

If we interpret Hume as a phenomenalist, all impressions and ideas, including objects, the external world, causality, and the self are basically contingent *imaginative* constructions of passive perceptions. But as contents, they *represent* those entities. But for Husserl, by contrast, phenomenological meanings are *immanent*; and they are not analyzable, reducible to Hume's passive *hyletic*, i.e., intrinsically meaningless impressions. Impressions alone are meaningless. Rather Husserl transforms Kant's "unity of consciousness" into a "unity of meaning"; meanings are (a) ideal unities, which (b) remain continuous *epistemic* identities, universals, while yet (c) possessing the inherent potentiality of accruing further meaningful "enrichments" through halos, horizons, nuances, and the fringes of consciousness. In addition, they can be tested and amplified by "free imaginative variations," which are embedded in synthetic *a priori* relations, which in their turn are capable of generating, e.g., entire fields of theoretical, ethical, and aesthetic *systems* (Husserl, *Experience and Judgment*). Hence to say that meanings "remain identical" is not to deny that meanings may increase in significance on the peripheries of consciousness and eventually form entire systems as they relate to other synthetic *a priori* meanings.

Originally, when *Loneliness in Philosophy, Psychology, and Literature* was first published (1979), I based my theory of loneliness entirely on Kant's principle of reflexive self-consciousness. It was three-and-half decades later that I realized that I needed *both* Kant *and* Husserl; not only were they compatible but indeed they were mutually required in order to adequately complete my own theory of consciousness in relation to human loneliness. I realized that Husserl's principle of intentionality added a "dimension" of *purposiveness* to human existence—and especially in connection with the *value* of shared intimacy—and that I needed to synthetically *a priori* unify both Kant's self-consciousness and Husserl's intentionality *together;* *both* were needed in order to provide insight and understanding into the dynamics of loneliness and intimacy.

According to Husserl, the transcendental ego, "the wonder of all wonders," "the pure ego and pure consciousness" remains as an irreducible residue after all other reductions have been subjected to phenomenological reductions.

> Whether convenient or inconvenient, and even though (because of no matter what prejudices) it may sound monstrous to me, it is the *primal matter-of-fact to which I must hold fast,* which I, as a philosopher, must not disregard for a single instant. Whether we like it or not, whether … it may sound monstrous or not, this (the 'I am') is the fundamental fact to which I have to stand up, which, as a philosopher, I must never blink for a moment. For philosophical children this may be the dark corner haunted by the specters of solipsism or even psychologism and relativism. The true philosopher,

246 Science of matter and philosophy of mind

instead of running away from them, will prefer to illuminate the
dark corner with light.

(Formal and Transcendental Logic, Section 95, 237)

But notice the interesting equation Husserl makes between psychologism and relativism. It is not subjective solipsism that leads to
valuative relativism but scientific psychologism. We recall Weber's
admonition, in *The Vocation of Science*, that the empirical sciences
are constitutionally incapable of addressing questions of value. After
the *Cartesian Meditations*, Husserl's purpose in the *Crisis* shifted
from the transcendental ego to the goal of establishing a description of the ways in which our *communal* experiences come to be and
the criterion for their coherence. But, basically for Husserl, ethical
values are grounded in experience and he paid little attention to ethical issues and valuations.[3] Under the influence of Heidegger, his
guiding beacon was the establishment of a coherent and comprehensive *Lebenswelt* and "*the ego cogito as transcendental subjectivity*"
was left far behind.

Again, the question regarding the *substantial* reality and the *nature*
of the self is obviously a highly contested philosophical issue of the
time. In the *Logical Investigations* (1900–1901), Husserl essentially
"brackets" the ego by putting "out of play" any and all metaphysical, scientific, and psychologistic assumptions by concentrating on the
acts and *contents* of consciousness. However, as we saw in the previous
chapter, by the time of the *Cartesian Meditations* (1931), the transcendental ego is unambiguously asserted in the Fourth Meditation; and
the failing "solution" to solipsism is proposed in the Fifth Meditation
through the path of empathy.[4]

In terms of existential intentionality, in Sartre's *The Transcendence
of the Ego*, as the translators note, "The phenomenology of Husserl
was a reflexive inquiry, or a philosophy of consciousness ... Thus
characterized, however, the phenomenology of Husserl would be
difficult to distinguish from Kantian epistemology, which was also
a philosophy of consciousness."[5] This interpretational comment is
important for my purpose because I believe when both Brentano and
Husserl's intentionality principle allows reflexivity to seep in between
the cracks.

Science of matter and philosophy of mind   247

But Sartre rejects Husserl's ego-structuring activities as leading to an opacity within consciousness. It is like having something in your eye spoiling the clarity of your vision.

> The ego is not the owner of consciousness; it is the object of consciousness. To be sure, we constitute spontaneously our state and actions as productions of the ego. But our states and actions are also [transcendent] objects.
>
> (*TOE*, 97)

Accordingly, he attempts to stay faithful to a pure intentionality through his ontological descriptions of a "me"—rather than an "I," as an object in the external world of Being, the in-itself, when he offers the example of someone running to catch a street car in which the "I" is not intentionally present but rather consciousness is entirely consumed and immersed in the object of its pursuit, the vehicle. In this situation, I am said to be pre-reflectively conscious; "I" am not even there. But when I stop, consciousness observes "me" at a distance, so to speak— simply as another object in the world—chasing the streetcar. Properly speaking, "I" am reflecting but not self-consciously reflexive; I am merely telling a story about someone who happens to be "me."

Sartre defends the "nothingness," the "non-being," the vacuity of consciousness. The for-itself is an "existential" emptiness, immaterial, a translucent medium (not dissimilar to Descartes pure cogito) in or through which objects appear and disappear. Both *The Transcendence of the Ego* and *Being and Nothingness* (passim) affirm the power of nothingness masquerading as consciousness. Again, we are reminded of Marjorie Grene's trenchant criticism of Sartre's elimination of the reflexive ego when she critically challenges his account of the relationship between consciousness and intentionality. Without the reflexivity of consciousness, intentionally is completely loosened from its moorings and moral responsibility evaporates. It is freedom without subjectivity, without a self.

We recall Sartre positing nothingness as potentially endowed with pure acts of freedom, of spontaneity, an *ek-stasis*, a transcending power reaching *beyond* itself (Chapter 2). In the earlier work, Sartre describes this spontaneity as operating in a vacuum in opposition to

248 Science of matter and philosophy of mind

Bergson, who conceives his freedom as acting within and through a plenum of qualities (*Time and Free Will*).

What I am proposing is that *both* reflexivity *and* intentionality are required for a true reading of the dynamics of consciousness.

This brings us to the third paradigm of consciousness, which is, like the second, one of an active consciousness. The reflexive model has dominated Western philosophy since its clear formulation was first unfolded in Plato's *Theaetetus* (189E and *Sophist*, 263E); Aristotle's description of the Unmoved Mover in *Metaphysics* (1075a); and reinforced by Plotinus in the *Enneads* (IV, 6, 7). According to the classic principle of a dynamic reflexion, all consciousness is self-consciousness; it is circular; it curls back on itself; it is anchored by an intrinsically active co-relation between subject and *the conceptual object within consciousness*; between knower and known. Metaphorically it is represented as a circle without beginning and continuing temporally as long as the thought lasts. The entire dualist-rationalist-idealist tradition from Plato to Plotinus, Augustine, Descartes, Leibniz, Kant, and Fichte is committed to it.

Throughout the present text, I have tried to recapture some of the significance of the perennial war between materialism and idealism, of this never-ending conflict. But the difference is that our current neurosciences and biosciences, the latter of which merely add Darwinian evolution to the equation, have been unable to account for the *qualitative* values promoted by intellectual, ethical, aesthetic, and humanistic modes of consciousness—and systems—that alone make life worth living.

From the beginning of Western thought, materialism's explanatory accounts of both nature and mankind have been expressed ever since the Pre-Socratic atomistic philosophers and it persists today in Armstrong's crude Central State Materialism, especially in behavioral psychology. The same reductionism is observable in our current neurosciences and evolutionary biosciences. The paradigm has remained *qualitatively* unchanged since time immemorial. Basically, an amoeba and a human brain are homogeneous. This crude materialistic simplicity has degraded and reduced the highest pursuits of humanity, especially the efforts in formulating ethical and aesthetic ideals and standards. Materialism and the current neurosciences herald an age of extreme *moral* subjectivism, relativism, and skepticism. Our higher aspirations become subservient to environmental and cultural forces.

Science of matter and philosophy of mind 249

And all distinctions between fact and value, science and ethics, and the Is and the Ought become eclipsed.

Science is essentially grounded in material quantitative motions and measures; it deals with Facts, with the Is. But Consciousness, by contrast, qualitatively *opens* the possibility of introducing values, ideals, with what *should* be, with "oughts." This is the Battle between the Giants and the Gods elevated to a higher human level. Existentially humans are the only creatures who guide their lives by creating, choosing, and committing to values, each for himself or herself alone.

When Parmenides, Leibniz, Schopenhauer, and Heidegger each chimed in as a chorus and asked, "Why is there something rather than nothing?" they paid homage to this eternal question within the very heart of Being itself. And when William James declared that the never-ending clock of metaphysics is kept running because the conceivability of the non-existence of this world is just as possible as its existence, he too sensed the power of absolute nothingness.

The answer begins with Aristotle's declaration that philosophy consists in a search for first principles, grounding assumptions. In Western thought, there are three metaphysical choices: materialism, dualism, and idealism. The problematic one is dualism. *If* matter is defined in terms of bodily extension (and/or inertness); *and* consciousness is characterized by immateriality and activity; *and* they share no attribute, predicate, or property in common, *then* it is inconceivable how matter and mind can *know* each other or *interact* with each other. Following Hume, I have agreed with his first principle: "when apply'd to the operations of matter, we may certainly conclude, that motion may be, and actually is, the cause of thought and perception" (*Treatise*, 248). This is a clear doctrine of metaphysical dualism, when he states as his first principle, in the *Enquiry concerning Human Understanding*, that "The contrary of every matter of fact is still possible; because it can never imply a contradiction, and is conceived by the mind with the same facility and distinctness, as if ever so conformable to reality" (Section IV, Part I). In agreement, I can conceive *both* a materially extended object *and* with the same facility consider a thought as not being a foot in length, six inches wide, and two inches deep (so Cudworth and Hume). Neither can I *explain why* both gravity and electricity exist; or *how* hydrogen and oxygen mix to produce water; nor why men do what they do.

250   Science of matter and philosophy of mind

How does one arrive at first principles? According to Pascal, "The heart has its reasons, which the head does not know" (*Pensées*); Fichte attributes them to "our most basic inclinations and interests" (*Science of Knowledge*); and William James credits them to our "passional natures" ("The Will To Believe"). In short, first principles are not innate; one creates them. Can one change their first principle? Indeed, one can, just as Augustine does in his conversion from Manichean materialism to Christian spiritualism by positing the existence of an immaterial God and souls (*Confessions*, chapter 7).

Beyond this, however, what remains critically important is Max Weber's admonition, delivered after the First World War, when he elucidates that the moral responsibility required in determining ethical values is completely lacking in both science and politics.[6] In the light of his radical Kantian orientation, Weber seeks a "positivistic conceptual separation of 'facts' from 'values'" (page xiv).

> Thus famously in the *Critique of Pure Reason* Kant established that reason was itself limited and that this limitation was not a fault of reason but rather made it possible for rationality to exist at all ... Weber will attempt the construction of a noumenal realm for the purposes of making social science possible. It is for this reason that we call his understanding "heuristically transcendental."
>
> (pages xvi–xvii)

Citing Kant, Weber sought to link the concept of value to scientific activity in the modern world, but his ultimate *negative* claim is that *empirical* science is constitutionally unable to answer questions of value. His *positive* argument rests on his distinction between causal explanations versus the insights of the understanding (*Verstehen*); that empirical scientific inquiries into social phenomena are not capable of settling disputes about ethical and cultural issues. He emphasizes that evaluative choices cannot depend on merely technical considerations when applied to moral and the factual foundation of scientific studies; the separation of scientific *facts* in opposition to evaluative ethical judgments.

Whereas Weber's moral principle endorses Kant's noumenal realm, by contrast, I believe each of us existentially chooses valuative meanings. What makes human life meaningful and worthwhile is the ability to perform qualitative distinctions, to recognize the differences between them, and consequently to pursue the meanings of our lives in terms between excitement and boredom, strength and weakness, altruism and egoism, good and evil, beauty and ugliness, sloth and energy, and loneliness and intimacy as each is embedded in our ability to create and recognize qualitative differences. The ongoing skirmish between science and determinism, on the one hand, and religion's defense of free will and idealism's positing of spontaneity, on the other hand, promises to continue forever. What Christians conceive as moral free will, idealists regard as epistemic spontaneity. Each person has an inalienable access to create their own unique teleological images so long as they are reflexively and intentionally conscious. Each of us is flung into the firmament of reality to shine brightly or dimly as are the innumerable stars in the heavens. Each monadic sphere of consciousness, whether shining dimly or brightly lasts but a lifetime. But during that brief span of existence, it has the privilege of spontaneously creating its own reality for itself alone *in its own image* for better or for worse.

> The anxiety of meaninglessness is anxiety about the loss of an ultimate concern, a meaning which gives meaning to all meanings. This anxiety is aroused by the loss of a spiritual center, of an answer, however symbolic and indirect, to the question of the meaning of [one's personal] existence.[7]

In the end, we create meanings for our selves alone. We have no common essence but for better or for worse a unique one.

> What kind of chimera then is man? What novelty? what monster, what chaos, what subject of contradiction, what prodigy? Judge of all things, imbecile worm; a depository of error and truth, and a sewer of error and doubt, a sink of uncertainty, glory and scum of the earth. Who will unravel this tangle? Certainly, it surpasses dogmatism and Pyrrhonism; and all human philosophy.
>
> (Pascal, *Pensées*)

The issue between Materialism and Idealism hangs on Plato and Hegel's distinction between the quantitative categories of science and

252 Science of matter and philosophy of mind

those of qualitative consciousness, as first announced in the *Republic's* Divided Line passage and second, in Hegel's *Science of Logic.* Monistic Materialism, as Armstrong declares, offers a single reality. By contrast, both Plato and Hegel envision multiple activities and levels of consciousness and realities. When Hegel introduces his triadic opening in the *Logic*, the quality of Parmenides's Being is transformed into Buddhism's Nothingness and Heraclitus' Becoming. These *qualitative* beginnings constitute the reflexive and transcendent essence of human consciousness presented in dialectic form.

Notes

1 Armstrong, D. M., *A Materialist Theory of Mind* (London: Routledge & Kegan Paul, 1971); hereafter cited as *MTM*.
2 Brentano, Franz, *Psychology from an Empirical Standpoint*, translated by Antos Rancurello, D. B. Terrel, and Linda McAllister (New York: Humanities Press, 1973), 34; see also, 153–154, 155 Note 1; hereafter cited as *PES*. My point is that not only are reflexion and transcendence compatible, but they are both essential acts of consciousness.
3 Smith, David Woodruff, *Husserl* (New York: Routledge, 2013) 369–373.
4 Cf. Husserl, Edmund, *The Paris Lectures* (The Hague: Martinus Nijhoff, 1964), 25–28; and Husserl, Edmund, *The Idea of Phenomenology* (The Hague: Martinus Nijhoff, 1964), xix–xx.
   On Husserl's failure to solve the problem of solipsism through the path of empathy, see Mijuskovic, Ben, *Consciousness and Loneliness: Theoria and Praxis* (Leiden: Brill, 2019), 91–92, 440–442.
5 Sartre, Jean-Paul, *The Transcendence of the Ego: An Existential Theory of Consciousness*, translated by Forest Williams and Robert Fitzpatrick (New York: Noonday Press), 12.
6 Weber, Max, *The Vocation Lectures: "Science as Vocation" and "Politics as Vocation"* translated by Rodney Livingstone (Cambridge: Hackett, 2004), cf. xiv–xvii. In an article, I offer a schematic table of ethical principles and criteria, from relativism to absolutism, from skepticism to rationalism, empiricism, fideism, and existentialism, and from immediacy to mediacy; cf.
   Ben Mijuskovic, "Ethical Principles, Criteria, and the Meaning of Life," *Journal of Thought*, 2005) and "Virtue Ethics," *Philosophy and Literature*, 31:1 (2007).
7 Tillich, Paul, *The Courage To Be* (New Haven, CT: Yale University Press, 1952), 47.

Chapter 13

Loneliness

An interdisciplinary approach[*]

Thus far, I have concentrated on the subjective modes or aspects of consciousness, the sensory elements, the spontaneous, synthesizing acts, and the formative structures involved in human self-awareness and intentionality, on the underlying epistemic theory, as opposed to its affective dynamic, and how it is resolved in the formation of a unique personal identity in each of us. But now I wish to approach loneliness through its more emotional and motivational dimensions and demonstrate how the *feelings* and *meanings* of loneliness permeate all our moods and lives, how they "shape" all human existence.[1] Loneliness has been recognized and dwelled upon ever since mankind mastered the ability to record human thought. It is synonymous with human existence.

The following chapter is strongly influenced by Frieda Fromm-Reichmann's groundbreaking posthumously published paper, "Loneliness," which appeared in the journal *Psychiatry* in 1959. I was impressed by two distinctive features. First, by her interdisciplinary approach and second, by her interpersonal emphasis as opposed to Freud's intrapsychic focus.[2]

Psychological principles addressing *why* human nature is what it is; theories by which we seek insight, understanding, explanations, and even sympathy into our feelings of enforced solitude but above all in trying to learn how to connect with others of our kind. What a variety of possible principles has been offered by philosophers and students of human nature! All men seek happiness announces Aristotle (*Nicomachean Ethics*). Just as all men delight in imitation (*Poetics*) and human beings take pleasure in knowing (*Metaphysics*), in that same sense it may be said that the *arche* of human conduct and action

DOI: 10.4324/9781003156130-14

derives from the human desire to achieve a state of social well-being with others of our species. According to Hobbes, each human being is motivated by self-interest and self-preservation; Bentham regards man as under the twin masters of pleasure and pain, whose dominion extends over the entirety of human conduct. Freud retraces the path of our problematic symptoms to a fund of repressed sexual and libidinal energy whose fettered strivings result in neurotic tendencies. Adler invokes a Schopenhauerian and Nietzschean "will to power" principle as a model for understanding our inherited feelings of inferiority, whose ultimate origin is grounded in the inadequacies of infancy. And Jung cavalierly splits the human race into introverts and extroverts, the islanders and the cosmopolitans.

What I have chosen as my concern in what follows is not simply a rough survey of conceptions concerning human nature—whether man is good, bad, or indifferent; primarily a rational creature or a sentient one; whether his nature has ever been the same or if "man creatively makes himself" through his means of production (Marx). Rather I am seeking to uncover what *motivates* man; I am searching for a universal first principle through which we may understand *why* humans do what they do and *why* they are *who* they are. Obviously, the commitment we make in terms of human motivation will guide us in forging a corresponding description of human nature; it will ultimately show us what motivates us in all our endeavors, in all that we feel, think, say, and do. I am seeking a universal motivational principle, but whereas Freud grounds his dynamic foundation in libidinal energy, aggression, and the impetus toward sexual pleasure and proclivities, I propose instead to base it on the fear of loneliness and the concomitant desire to secure intimacy with other self-conscious beings whether animal, human, or divine.

But let me make clear what I am *not* trying to do. In the seventeenth- and eighteenth-centuries, philosophers considered the emotions as the precipitating *causes of human behavior*, as "the springs of human conduct," and provided catalogues listing and defining the emotions. For example, Descartes in the *Passions of the Soul*, offers a mechanical account of how the body operates; Hobbes in *De Homine*; Spinoza in the *Ethics*; and Hume in his *Treatise*, in Book II, *Of the Passions*, all seek to establish a "science of human nature." Often it is claimed that Psychology is a very recent science. It is not. Both Plato, in the

Republic and Aristotle in *De Anima* and the *Nicomachean Ethics*, discuss the soul in the light of its motivational factors. But rather what I am seeking is a universal principle animating all mankind. I am concerned to portray human loneliness in much broader strokes as our primary existential condition; loneliness as a ubiquitous and pervasive mood that colors all aspects of our feelings, thoughts, and conduct. My thesis is that the universal motivational principle guiding humankind is the fear of loneliness; it anchors all our anxieties. Once man has satisfied his primary biological drives and secured the necessities of air, water, nutrition, and sleep—*and before sex*—he strives to reach others, to forge intimate contacts with others of his kind. Emotionally we seek to penetrate, to project our "self," our "identity" within the consciousness of the other self; within the other's sphere of existence and values; to connect with other self-conscious beings. It is not so much a fact, then, correcting Jung, that we can be dichotomized into extroverts and introverts but rather that we all begin by aspiring toward human communion, recognition, and affection, a goal that requires a continual struggle. Those of us who fail are the frustrated extroverts, the retreating introverts.

In the following, I propose to discuss loneliness from a variety of interdisciplinary perspectives. The critical theme toward which all these aspects converge as lines drawn toward a common center, however, remains essentially a meaning-nucleus, a noematic, phenomenological center (Husserl). It consists in what A. O. Lovejoy defines as a *unit-idea*, as it retains an *identical meaning, the same core significance* throughout its myriad historical manifestations. As Lovejoy comments, in *The Great Chain of Being*, the conception of God in Aristotle, Augustine, and Spinoza is not the same God. By contrast, I wish to maintain that loneliness remains a unit-idea, its *meaning* endures as it preserves the same historical and conceptual definition throughout the various ages of Western thought and culture. In short, the feelings, the meanings, and the dynamics of human loneliness have ever remained the same.

Loneliness is both a *feeling* and a *meaning*. As a feeling, it is indefinable, just as G. E. Moore suggests that yellow, as a color, as a sensation is simple, indefinable. You either see it or you do not. Loneliness is like that; you either feel it or you do not.

The psychological desire to secure nurturance first arises from the earliest stages of human infancy when the child experiences the feelings of neglect, abandonment, and rejection, generally by the mother. *As an immediate feeling, as a sensation*, it cannot be conceptually defined, and neither can it be *conceptually* communicated and shared with another person by the means of language. It is intimately personal. Each person's feelings are their own and not someone else's. Just as a person congenitally blind cannot *experience* the color red.

But in terms of cognitive and emotional development, the child yearns to *mediately*, to *relationally* connect *to* and *with* other conscious beings as soon as it realizes the presence of other *responding* entities; there is a "reaching out" attempt; an intentional, transcending, purposeful instinct; a teleological drive to be recognized, affirmed by a reciprocating consciousness; by an other-than-its-self, again at first generally the mother. The infant becomes cognitively aware of other animate beings. Just as the experience of gravity is both internally felt as well as externally visible, so does the feeling of loneliness, of emotional deprivation become acknowledged inwardly as well as outwardly, publicly. The child begins to dualistically realize that the feeling and the meaning of loneliness affects her within her own psychological *sphere of selfhood* as well as in her relation to an *external social realm* beyond her.

As a feeling, loneliness is driven by a self-conscious desire to be intimately related to a special other self but in the same moment fearing rejection, being unable to achieve and sustain that desired unity, that yearning for intimacy. All meanings are dualistic; they intrinsically imply their opposite. As a universal, as a conceptual *meaning*, loneliness is mediately shareable through language and other means of communication. But again, as a subjective *feeling*, it is immanently unshareable and incommunicable because human beings are metaphysically subjectively distinct.

At a much deeper level, often lonely people describe it as a sense of nothingness, an emptiness, a feeling of meaninglessness in their lives. Metaphysically this recalls our discussions of Parmenides's, Hegel's, and Sartre's conceptions of the nothingness of consciousness, which can only be assuaged by a replenishment of human intimacy and values. But there are no *identifiable* neurons assigned as *causing* a sense of meaninglessness and emptiness.

Since loneliness is a significant concept, it must have a meaningful opposite. If everything were orange, then nothing could be orange. The opposite of loneliness is *intimacy*. Others might propose that its contrary is love. But love can be one-sided. I can love someone who does not love me. But intimacy must be *mutually* supportive, reciprocal. It is grounded in a dual empathic relation between two feeling-thinking beings. It is said that Aristotle described friendship as one soul sharing two bodies. This more fully captures the meaning of intimacy.

Loneliness *precedes* love; the babe in the crib first experiences the sense of something lost; something missing within its self; an emptiness; a lack before it can *feel* the fulfillment of a relational alliance with an other *distinct* being; a sense of being nurtured, cared for, which is embedded in a dependence upon the *other* responding self, again generally the mother. Nevertheless, when it does reach the stage of feeling nurtured, this is not yet intimacy because it is not reciprocal; it is nurtured but it does not nurture in return; it can desire nurturance and care but it does not as yet reciprocate. It is because the essential primary *quality* of primitive narcissism intrudes. This is important because intimacy is a highly developed stage, and it is grounded in a mutuality of feelings, meanings, and values. There is a singular *intensity* within loneliness, and it can only be adequately addressed and conquered by the equal *intensity* of intimacy.[3]

Most researchers studying loneliness claim it is passively *caused* by external conditions and circumstances, familial, environmental, cultural, situational, and even chemical imbalances in the brain and therefore that it is essentially transient, curable, and avoidable. By contrast, I argue that it is actively *constituted* by the synthetic *a priori* relations inherent within reflexive self-consciousness (Kant) and transcendent intentionality (Husserl) and therefore permanent, incurable, and unavoidable.

We clearly have a need to breathe, drink, eat, and sleep. But my interest in the drive to avoid isolation and secure intimacy stems from regarding it as both innate and developmental. Loneliness generates *internal* psychological feelings of yearning and longing, of filling the existential emptiness of meaninglessness, and seeking the security that the other self will respond in kind. It is embedded in a desire to be cared for and nurtured. That is why it is so painful when it does not happen. But there is also a *dynamic* motivation to be acknowledged *at the expense of the other self*, what Hegel describes as a *desire for unilateral recognition* (*Phenomenology of Spirit*, "Lordship and Bondage" section), which Freud denotes as narcissism. There dwells within the first stage of primitive consciousness an aggressive insistence demanding a one-sided recognition of one's self. Narcissism is engrained in the self's innate desire for *individual* recognition. Its more primitive expression is succinctly described by Hobbes, the master of psychological egoism.

> So that in the nature of man, we find three principal causes of quarrel. First, competition; second diffidence; thirdly glory. The first maketh man invade for gain; the second for safety; and the third for reputation. The first use violence to make themselves masters of other men's persons, wives, children and cattle; the second to defend them; the third for trifles, as a word, a smile, a different opinion, and many other signs of undervalue, either direct in their person, or by reflection on their kindred, their friends, their nation, their profession, or their name.
>
> (Hobbes, *Leviathan*, chapter XIII)

The sense of loneliness intervenes whenever one experiences rejection. To be sure, the feeling and self-awareness of loneliness may be accompanied by physiological factors but *its essence, its meaning* dwells within self-consciousness and not in its bodily reactions and external manifestations. The rapidly beating heart, the tightening stomach muscles, the tears are merely accidental accompaniments. This is not to deny that external manifestations are present, but *alone* they are not *meanings.*

There are two challenging dynamical forces that are constitutive elements within loneliness that we must first learn to negotiate between in order to understand their "interplay" when the self begins to *separate*, to *distinguish* its "self" from the surrounding world of alien objects; as it starts to want *things.* And second, how to adjust to the increasing anxiety engendered by the sense of separation between the self from other selves. Psychologically the awareness of separation, the sense of forced and unwanted isolation, becomes projected and expanded not only in terms of the world in general and its objects but more poignantly from the painful sense of separation from other selves. The consequence of this internal conflict produces first anger, then fear, then depression—*in that order.*

Loneliness in Western culture

We begin with a critical question whose answer will have far reaching consequences. Is loneliness really engrained in the reflexive and transcendent structures of individual consciousness? Perhaps it is merely a recent aberration caused by a systematic and dissociative falling away from our ancient traditional tribal communities; our rural village orientations; the more recent collapse of our extended families; the increasing divorce rate; our migratory job relocations, as we are all thrust forward into a progressively tightening job market; an economic survival of the fittest; and forced into individual competition; pushed toward impersonal, alienating, bureaucratic, and technological modes of "social interaction"; shallow media outlets; and simple-minded Facebook internet exchanges. If so, then one could argue that loneliness is neither a necessary nor a universal structure of human consciousness but merely a contingent, unfortunate, temporary but correctible aberration.

But when we turn to our earliest literary writings in the West, we are reminded of the lost friendship and the grief portrayed in the Sumerian *Epic of Gilgamesh*; God's concern that man should not live alone in *Genesis*, that he requires a helpmate; the lonely punishment of Job before his friends; Abraham's terrifying command from God to sacrifice his only son; Achilles grief in the *Iliad* and Odysseus's homeward journey in the *Odyssey*. Western culture has emphasized the solitariness of the self from the very beginning. And when we turn to the Greek myths and dramas; the tragedy of Oedipus, whose search for the murderer of the King ends with himself, Antigone's duty to her brothers ending in her sentence of being entombed alive, we begin to discern the darker visage of the Greek *psyche*. The Greek myths are an eloquent testimony to the force of loneliness among both men and gods. Jung cites the story of Prometheus the Titan, who violated the edict of the gods and aided man by gifting him with the use of fire and paid for it by being chained to "the lonely cliffs of the Caucuses mountains," where daily a ravenous eagle tears at his bowels as a symbol of suffering loneliness. In the myth of Deucalion and Pyrrha, after a punishing global flood cleansed the world of all its evil by decimating the entirety of mankind, it left the marooned couple all alone in the world. When Zeus viewed their utter desolation, he took pity on them and allowed them to reestablish the human race by throwing stones behind their backs. There are the tales of the solitary labors of Sisyphus in the Underworld and the separation of Orpheus and Eurydice in Hades. And, of course, the Greek dramas, especially those of Sophocles, are replete with expressions of loneliness and despair. In *Oedipus Rex*, we are presented with a man, "nobler than ourselves," who is fated in the end to suffer the most extreme forlornness, doomed to wander in self-inflicted blindness with his two children as his only companions. It symbolizes the consuming quest of every human to plumb to the depths of their own identity. Oedipus solved the riddle of the Sphinx by discovering that the solution lay in the realization that man has arisen beyond his animal nature into genuine self-consciousness (Hegel, *The Philosophy of History*, chapter III, "Transition from the Egyptian to the Greek World"). Oedipus realizes that the *essence* of man lies in his singular possession of *reflexive* self-consciousness. But he had not as yet (mercifully) achieved the deeper reality of his own vulnerability and guilt. The tragedy fills us with pity and fear. As Aristotle enlightens us in his *Poetics*, whereas history deals with the particular, art deals with the universal. Oedipus thus initiates a search whose goal is complete *self*-knowledge. He unwittingly initiates a search for which he is his own end, a circle which ends with himself. This is what captures Hegel's admiration in the myth, since it symbolizes mankind's reflexive search for self-knowledge only to find that it begins and ends with himself. In his desperate driving search, Oedipus pitilessly subjects Tiresias, Creon, Jocasta, and the old shepherd to remorseless questioning. Oedipus's tragic flaw is his lack of pity and his hubris; in the end he turns that flaw even against himself by condemning himself to utter darkness, aloneness, and self-exile. His self-sentence is much harsher than what the Olympian god had demanded. The drama concludes with the plea of a once powerful king not to have his children taken away. Oedipus accordingly refers to himself as "the last man," a phrase which will find a haunting echo in Nietzsche's self-expression, "I am the loneliest of the lonely." And there are the tragedies issuing from the House of Atreus, Agamemnon sacrificing his daughter, Iphigenia, so that the Greek fleet could sail to

Troy; Clytemnestra killing her husband in revenge; and Orestes killing his mother in turn. This was the deeper Greek culture! Every bit as dark as the Christian conception that man is born in original sin! And more human than mythical is Socrates's election to drink the hemlock rather than be exiled from Athens.

The earliest discussion concerning the dynamics of human loneliness first surfaces in Plato's dialogue, the *Symposium*, which examines the essence of Love against the background of our innate loneliness. Describing the essential *quality* of loneliness as a sense of *separation* from a cherished other self, Plato recounts the speech of the comic playwright, Aristophanes, and his myth regarding our early human ancestors, who are depicted as roly-poly creatures consisting of four legs, four arms, two visages facing in different directions, and two sexual organs: both female and male but three genders, sexual identities, male-male, female-female, and a hermaphroditic, female-male. Originally these creatures were so powerful, aggressive, and troublesome that Zeus was finally forced to split them into two, and ever since then each half has desperately searched for its other half.

> Now when the work of bisection was complete, it left each half with a desperate yearning for the other, and they ran together and flung their arms around each other's necks and asked for nothing better than to be rolled into one again. So much so that they began to die of hunger and general inertia, for neither would do anything without the other. And whenever one half was left alone by the death of its mate, it wandered about questing and clasping in the hope of finding a spare half-woman—or a whole woman, as we should call her nowadays—or half a man. And so the race was dying out ... So you see, gentleman, how far back we can trace our innate love for one another, and how this love is always trying to reintegrate our former nature to make two into one, and to bridge the gulf between one human being and another.
>
> (*Symposium*, 189c–191d)

Freud discusses Aristophanes's myth at some length but attributes the sense of loss to an *organic* and *cellular* separation, while also intimating that the original eviction of the fetus from the womb, forced at birth and torn apart, leads to its consequent striving to reintegrate through

262   Loneliness: an interdisciplinary approach

the sexual instinct with an other being (*Beyond the Pleasure Principle,* Part, VI). He believes the separation is primarily a biological issue rather than a psychological one in the manner of Plato. Significantly, however, it represents "the first great anxiety-state of birth and the infantile anxiety of longing—the anxiety due to separation from the protecting mother" (*The Ego and the Id*, V). But Freud also appeals to a metaphor of life returning to a state of inanimation, death consisting of a return to an original biological state, as his view on death is more inclined toward physiology rather than psychology. Freud, of course, originally began his career as a neurologist.

> If we are to take it as a truth that knows no exception that every-thing living dies for *internal* reasons—becomes inorganic once again—then we shall be compelled to say that *'the aim of all life is death'* and, looking backwards, *'that inanimate things existed before living ones.'* ... In this way the first instinct came into being: the instinct to return to the inanimate state.
>
> (*Beyond the Pleasure Principle*, IV)

For Freud, the Greek myths symbolize man's sexual, aggressive, and instinctual desires; they herald the self-destructive impulses of Thanatos, death, the separation from Eros, and the desire for unity and intimacy. But for me, the Greek myths rather symbolize the universality of human loneliness. In any case, the ancient Greek myths and dramas eloquently testify to the fact that loneliness is not simply a modern and a merely contemporary malaise.

Psychology as a distinct discipline, as opposed to the study of Nature initiated by the Pre-Socratic philosophers, begins in Greece. It appears as early as Plato's *Republic*, which distinguishes the three "parts" of the soul: the rational; the spirited; and the appetitive or desiderative. Correspondingly, in the *Phaedrus*, the tripartite soul is metaphorically represented as a heavenly charioteer struggling to control a pair of steeds, the first is amenable to guidance, while the second is unruly (246a-b). These forces have been compared to Freud's distinction between the id, ego, and superego. Aristotle's approach to human happiness is also primarily psychological. It is concerned with human feelings and actions that are accompanied by pleasure and pain. By practice and the training of good habits, we establish a

Loneliness: an interdisciplinary approach   263

virtuous disposition that is most conducive to society. The attainment of friendship is the highest virtue and the surest antidote to loneliness (*Nicomachean Ethics*, Books VIII–IX). "But he who is unable to live in society or who has no need because he is sufficient unto himself, must be either a beast or a god" (*Politics*, 125a)—but he is not human. Psychology and loneliness have been a focus of interest and study ever since the dialogues of Plato and the treatises of Aristotle.

Later, in the Roman period, the theme of an ideal friendship among a select few becomes the ethical goal of Epicureanism. For the Athenian citizen, the good man could only exist on the condition that the state was good. Plato's ideal *Republic* is an "organic unity." But with the dissolution of the Greek city states, first with the Republic and then the Roman Empire, "the organic bonds, which had until then essentially constituted the good life of the earlier Hellenic Greeks, were systematically loosened."[4] For both Plato and Aristotle, the "virtuous man" is inconceivable apart from the good of the polis. Subsequently, however, during the Hellenistic period, we find men fragmented from their fellows. Their mode of existence, along with their quest for *personal*—as opposed to communal—salvation becomes radically different. There is a sudden shift from the organic and communal paradigm of the Greek polis to an atomistic model of society. Individuals assume a mode of existence that increasingly resembles self-contained and unrelated physical atoms. Both the Epicurean and Stoic "schools" of philosophy are implicated in metaphysical materialism. Consequently, the struggle for wellbeing increasingly assumes the characteristics of a struggle for *internal* self-sufficiency against the background of a disintegrating social order. It was, as George Sabine has emphasized, a time during which men were beginning "to make souls for themselves." No longer is the good of the individual grounded in the larger unit of the whole; henceforth the path to salvation is to be progressively conceived as a personal, and therefore by implication, a lonely journey. The Stoics still yearned for an ideal of human companionship, for a cosmopolitan approach, one in which "all men are brothers," "that no man is *born* a slave," and that we are together citizens of one world, that each of us has an ethical duty to others. But this was more of an ideal than a reality. Hegel was later to criticize this as a naïve abstraction. Meanwhile the Epicureans turned to small groups of friends thus reflecting the atomicity of individual existence, while the Skeptics, with their own distinctive, nihilistic frustrations, elected to deny both truth and social permanence, while seeking for the singularity of intellectual self-sufficiency as a protection from the dangers of societal loneliness. But by insisting on their own imperious power to disbelieve, the Skeptics, in their own ironic fashion, sought to withdraw within themselves by doubting in the reality of both the external world and the existence of other selves. In their unique fashion, each ended by only affirming the nucleus of their own doubting selves. Through an insistence on a limitless power to deny all other realities, they managed to establish a complete reliance on themselves alone, a form of negative self-sufficiency. According to Hegel, Pyrrho of Elis even went so far as to doubt the existence of the external world to such an extent that his friends were required to prevent him from walking into the paths of horses because he was uncertain of their existence.[5] But philosophically, Pyrrhonian skepticism initiated a subjective concentration with problems both *issuing* from and *contained* within the self; issues emerging from an opaque central nucleus of selfhood and toward a vague sense of "personal identity," a concentration confined within their own subjective selves. The fundamental question thus became what can be known—if anything at all—and if so how? But while the Skeptics turned toward a restrictive self-sufficiency, for others, the pressing consideration was to seek for a more secure personal and intimate relationship, toward a spiritual salvation, which promised the Christian soul a refuge from loneliness through an eternal companionship with God.

Loneliness in Christianity

In the early small Christian community, fidelity to God becomes the only true way to eternal salvation and protection against the throes of earthly loneliness. Through faith, devotion, shared spiritual companionship, and the promise of an everlasting life, the Christian millennium offered a promise of a perfect communion, an intimacy selectively awarded through God's Grace. It was a promise of an eternal intimacy with a Being that knows the soul's every feeling, thought, and most of all its *intentions*.

> Who will give me help so that I may rest in you? Who will help me, so that you will come into my heart and inebriate it, to the end that I may forget my evils and embrace you, my one good? What are

you to me? Have pity on me, that you command me to love you, and grow angry and threaten me with mighty woes unless I do? Is it but a small affliction if I do not love you? Unhappy man that I am, at your mercy, O Lord my God, tell me what you are to me. Say to my soul I am your salvation. Say this so that I may hear you. Behold my heart's ears are turned to you, O Lord; open them and say to my soul, "I am your salvation."

(Augustine, *Confessions*, chapter 5)

In the meantime, during the intervening extended period of Christianity until the Renaissance, between monasticism and the advent of the modern age, all these questions and issues concerning "personal identity," instead of being addressed, were avoided and put in abeyance. Christianity simply took the metaphysical existence of the soul for granted, unproblematic, and unchallenged during the Age of Faith. Once created by God, the absolute reality of the self was assumed to provide a protective shield against the ravages of plagues, wars, barbarity, and the surrounding universality of human loneliness then desolating the Western world. Christianity offered a permanent solution amid the chaos of the prevailing warring conditions and factions and the extreme social and political isolation so common during the period of the "dark" Middle Ages. Given mankind's desperate need to alleviate their burgeoning feelings of utter abandonment, the Church offered an eternal omniscient Being, intimately familiar with mankind's every desire, thought, intention, and deed. What more secure guarantee that each of us is not alone? But then, of course, the deepest suffering and estrangement would result in displeasing God (Hegel's Unhappy Consciousness in the *Phenomenology*). But it also engendered a troublesome schism between finite man and an infinitely unknowable transcendent Being. This sense of separation developed into what Jacob Loewenberg, in his commentary on Hegel's *Phenomenology*, describes as the schizoid attitude of medieval monastic man, an internal strain between our awe of God and the fear of His abandonment.

The advent of theological and epistemic skepticism

Eventually all this culminates in the rediscovery of the skeptical writings of Sextus Empiricus in 1562 and Michel de Montaigne's soliloquies

266 Loneliness: an interdisciplinary approach

symbolized by his epistemically balanced scale of yea or nay coming to the fore in Descartes's revolutionary doubt elaborated in his First Meditation. We recall Descartes's terror at the possibility of his mortality and the sense of his threatened non-existence during his Three Dreams in 1619 (chapter II). There is also Pierre Bayle (1647–1706) with his skeptical and erudite back and forth philosophical discussions in his encyclopedic *Historical and Critical Dictionary* questioning all human assertions to truth and Hume's *Treatise* challenging scientific causality and the reality of a substantial self. Thus, after the Middle Ages, a powerful shift asserts itself as man increasingly turns inwardly seeking to alleviate his sense of isolation by turning away from God and instead toward other men, toward man as a universal essence, e.g., Hegel's Spirit of nationalism impregnating the State; Feuerbach's notion of man as universal species-being; Marx's concept of a unifying *class*-consciousness; and Comte's idealization of a positivist science, of *Le Grand Etre*, not as a transcendent God, but as Universal Man, while advocating for a Religion of Humanity blessed with a calendar of scientific saints.

But as we proceed, we begin to uncover the deeper psychological roots of loneliness, we will discover that the Tree of Knowledge indeed bears a very bitter fruit. As we descend more deeply toward the subterranean filaments of the subconscious soul and the mind of man—far deeper than any Freudian unconscious—toward the utmost depths of human consciousness; as we further excavate the ultimate sources of our affective fears, impulsive aggressions, and lusts, we will be forced to encounter our own innermost "shadow self" (Jung) inhabiting the secret and hidden passages of the soul; a Conradian *Heart of Darkness*, as it serves as more than a match confronting the exterior darkness of the primitive jungle—a moral vacuum—and the unexamined forces in each of us, as we confront the interior darkness harbored within the human soul and heart.

Loneliness and psychology

Hobbes' *modern* psychological outlook is unique. Although Descartes formulates a list of human passions, it is Hobbes who is foremost in asserting a universal psychological *principle* of human conduct: self-preservation, self-interest, and basically what Schopenhauer later identified as egoism. But what defines *contemporary* psychology as a "science" is its inflexible commitment to provide causal explanations—which Hobbes does—but also by offering predictive outcomes. Therapeutic interventions can only be proposed if both human thought and conduct are assumed to be causally structured. Physical causes move toward the physical body until they impinge on our sense organs and are then transmitted to the consciousness.

In terms of human loneliness, although the existential writings of Kierkegaard and Nietzsche highlight the quality of subjective loneliness in mankind, oddly enough, psychologists have had relatively little to say about loneliness. And there is but a slight mention of it in Freud. The following passage is one of the few he offers.

> In children the first phobias relating to situations are those of darkness and solitude. The former of these often persists throughout life; both are involved when a child feels the absence of some loved person who looks after it—its mother that is to say. While I was in the next room, I heard a child who was afraid of the dark call out: "Do speak to me Auntie. I'm frightened!" "Why, what good would that do? You can't see me." To this the child replied: "If someone speaks to me it gets lighter." Thus, a longing felt in the dark is transformed into a fear of the dark.[6]

The symbol of light represents the possibility of communication with another consciousness. Light is a connecting spatial medium serving as a *tertium quid* between two consciousnesses during which the subject can *see* that s/he is not alone, while by contrast darkness confines us to an inner solipsistic temporality, a sense of psychological separation. The desire to communicate with an "other" responding awareness constitutes a mutual reassurance that we are not alone. Loneliness begins at birth and early infancy as Bruno Bettelheim similarly connects separation, darkness, and loneliness along with Freud. Loneliness and separation are *a priori* synthetically related.

> During periods of sleep, the infant experiences his first separation from the mother, which is bearable to him only if his cry brings her presence and a consequent relief from tension. As she appears when needed during the night, the infant learns to expect with certainty her reappearance in the morning, and thus becomes

268   Loneliness: an interdisciplinary approach

> more able to relinquish her for longer periods of time during the night ... Similarly, disturbed children, who are chronically under the pressure of fearful expectations, become more tense at night ... To such children the darkness of night is a constant threat ... They feel deserted, and the pressure of their anger, as well as their longing wishes, adds to their sense of isolation. This arouses the fear of being separated from human contact. Children struggle to keep awake because they cannot tolerate the threat of loss of contact. Darkness means helpless abandonment to their own hostile tendencies, which a child can hold in check only in the immediate presence of protective figures who visibly demonstrate to him that his angry feelings do not lead to actual destruction.[7]

Epistemically darkness eclipses not only light but space as well. The child is forced to temporally *feel* the loneliness alone in the dark. The primordial need for human reassurance arises at the very dawn of consciousness within the individual ego. Severe emotional neglect directly entails physical and psychological developmental issues that will follow throughout the sufferer's lifetime. Its origin lies in the affective deprivation of emotional nurturance in infancy, the withholding of adequate recognition of the child's narcissistic value as a human being. The psychoanalytic passages above represent the child's vital need for communication with another consciousness. Virginia Satir, a family therapist, is especially sensitive to this need for verbal connectivity.

Children are terrified of the dark because it symbolizes the singularity of isolation and the absence of an assuring consciousness confirming that they do not exist alone. They are often afraid of going to sleep at night, not because they fear never awakening again, but because they are horrified by the prospect of being *both* self-conscious *and* alone. Infants are not at first afraid of death because they cannot comprehend or imagine what a permanent loss of consciousness might mean. But they are frightened by a feeling of being awake and left all alone long before they begin to understand what death might possibly entail. Young children initially assume they will live forever.

What horrifies the child when the specter of death first invades consciousness, however, is the possibility that its consciousness will continue but that it shall be the only one. It imagines its self as a solipsistic awareness existing alone within a dark universe, wandering the solitary expanses of space and time in unending desolation, the sole monadic consciousness dumbly reflecting from sightless windows of awareness a soulless universe—save for one soul all alone: "One soul was lost; a tiny soul: his. It flickered once d went out, forgotten, lost. The end, black cold void waste" (James Joyce, *A Portrait of the Artist as a Young Man*, chapter III).

For philosophers, the issue of loneliness only came to the fore with the existential writings of Kierkegaard and Nietzsche, as both described intensely personal expressions of a deep inward loneliness. But it was after the Second World War that existential authors concentrated on the themes of loneliness, the absurdity of human suffering, the contingency of human life, and death in the essays and novels of Camus and Sartre. Original sin is one thing but the possibility of a systematic extermination of the entirety of all human beings is *qualitatively* something quite different. And now—today—humanity faces multiple national arsenals of nuclear weapons threatening global destruction.

In an early study on loneliness, George Weiss describes loneliness as if it were a disease like any other. "Severe loneliness is almost as prevalent as colds during the winter." By classifying it as an illness, it implies that it is merely a transient condition, one which may be avoided when certain precautions are undertaken. Indeed, the slim volume adds a litany of remedies and cures for the orphaned, the divorced, the aged, and the like, who may avail themselves in order to abate or conquer their affliction. On this model, loneliness is conceived as a medical problem. Just as malnutrition is defined as a lack of food, loneliness is regarded as a lack of companionship.[8] When the slim volume was first published, it created quite a stir, but it was two psychoanalysts who realized earlier and much more significantly the true nature of the danger. Nevertheless, for many Weiss's impression became the common and essentially public view of loneliness, as it was considered as a medical or sociological "disorder," a sort of societal flu. It was published by MIT Press, the official herald of the neurosciences—and the neurosciences have never looked back.

Gregory Zilboorg, a psychoanalyst, is the first researcher to discuss loneliness as a subject matter in its own right. Basically, he commandeers the Kantian conception of a synthetic *a priori* formula, its structure by connecting the ego's narcissistic vulnerability to loneliness as intrinsically connected to hostility. Following Freud, the initial state of the ego is narcissistic, whether it is engaged in self-preservation or self-aggrandizement. The ego continually compares its self against those subjects which surround it. As soon as it has developed the epistemic capacity to realize the distinction between its self and the other self, it strives for dominance over the other, whether the rivalry is against the mother, siblings, other children, or persons at large.

> Man pries into his neighbor's business not because of any altruistic sense, but because he feels the need of showing others up *sub rosa,* of showing himself off. It is a form of unabated self-love, a special form of it, in which he indulges himself … and not always devoid of malice, which gratifies an inherent self-admiration as elemental as it is constant. This type of sheer self-admiration is called narcissism … it denotes specifically that state of mind, that *spontaneous* attitude of man, in which the individual himself happens to choose only himself instead of others to love.
>
> (page 46; italic mine)[9]

Drawing on the Greek myth, he emphasizes the narcissist's vulnerability to feelings of loneliness but above all its sense of emptiness, the insatiable need to be fulfilled by the constant drum of adulation—but also its inherent self-destructiveness. In the original Greek myth, there is an intrinsic implication of self-destruction. Once more, we see that emptiness and loneliness are synonymous and in fact closely related to boredom. But it all begins in infancy as Zilboorg turns to the dynamics of the child's nurturance in the crib as s/he is enveloped in affection, pampered, played with, and the fortunate recipient of a love that does not need to be redeemed for quite some time.

> It learns the joy of being admired and loved before it learns anything about the outside world. It knows emotionally that everything is serene, that it is always protected, always indulged; the baby is constantly vibrant with the delight of living. Here we have the quintessence of what will later become the narcissistic orientation: a conviction that life is nothing else but being loved and admired— hence self-centredness, self-admiration, which are difficult to keep in abeyance in later life when adulthood asserts its allegiance.
>
> (page 53)

As circumstances change in the relationship between mother and infant, as social rules prevail over the infant's desires, and practical interventions come into play, e.g., toilet training and enforced delays begin to irritate and burden the developing child, it progressively begins to realize the limitations of its power. Older siblings only increase the frustrations and force the embattled infantile ego to retaliate (Alfred Adler).

> He is restless, unhappy, anxious, angry. The tragedy resolves itself, and the battle with and for life comes to a standstill with the first eager aggressive suck of milk. The world is reconquered; it pays to squirm, cry, kick and be angry. Here is the nucleus of hostility, hatred, impotent aggression of the lonely and abandoned. Here is the beginning of that intolerant anger which some day civilization will have to subdue, or mental illness will discharge again into the open. And if we continue on from the crib to the nursery and to the kindergarten, we can observe, scene by scene, the enactment of the story entitled 'megalomania, narcissism, loneliness.' It is therefore as interesting as it is impressive to note that the overprotected, overindulged and therefore seemingly overly happy children develop not infrequently into lonely depressed self-centered adults who in the depth of their personalities unwittingly but forcefully crave to return to the good overproviding and ever protecting mothers.
>
> (pages 53–54)

Zilboorg is here tracing the emanation of a progressive emotional sequence as the narcissistic ego reacts, first with hostility when its desires are unmet; then anxiety as it loses the battle; and only then depression as the ego surrenders and withdraws within its self. In early infancy cases, it can lead to a regression, a retreat toward the womb and death. According to Zilboorg, when unduly intensified or prolonged, the anger engendered by acute or chronic loneliness can result in murder and/or suicide. Narcissistic vengeance and reprisal are often the underlying motive in many allegedly "senseless," "meaningless" acts of domestic violence; it fuels the desire to punish others for one's perceived abandonment or betrayal.[10]

Zilboorg is writing this in 1938. German Nazism is already clearly on the political and military horizon in 1933. Germans, furious at

272 Loneliness: an interdisciplinary approach

what they perceived as their humiliation, punitive treatment, and the reparations imposed after the First World War, still convinced they are a "master race," and guided by a dangerous megalomaniacal narcissistic leader, the world was unprepared to deal with the onslaught and the concentration camps that were to last until 1945. Hannah Arendt, in *The Origins of Totalitarianism* (1948), following Zilboorg, agrees that narcissism, loneliness, and aggression are not only present in individuals but in groups and even nations as well.[11]

There are two motivational forms of narcissistic destruction in response to acute and/or unduly prolonged loneliness. First pure revenge often coupled with suicide. Consider for example, the cases of Eric Harris and Dylan Klebold on 4/20/1999 at Columbine High School; Lufthansa pilot Andreas Lubitz on 3/24/2011, who plunged his jet into the Alps killing 125 passengers; Adam Lanza on 12/14/2012 at Sandy Hook Elementary School; Elliot Rodger on 5/23/2014 in Isla Vista, CA; Stephen Paddock on 6/17/2015 at Las Vegas's MGM Mandalay Bay Hotel; Omar Mateen on 6/12/2016 at the Pulse Nightclub in Florida; and Nicholas Cruz on 2/4/2018 in Parkland, Florida; and so on. The second variation on destroying others issues forth from an extravagant conceit, a messianic delusion of martyrdom, motivated by a self-aggrandizing desire to be a leader; to symbolize an "ideal," as for example in calling for a racial or political call to arms, to rally others to their mission, as instanced by the cases of Anders Breivig on 7/22/2015 in Oslo, Norway; Dylann Roof on 6/17/2012 in Charleston, South Carolina, at a black church; and Brenton Tarrant on 3/18/2019 at a Black Muslim mosque. Often, in these cases, the perpetrator elects to live in order to fulfill his role as a leader. These examples are basically case studies on destructive narcissism.

But to be philosophically and psychologically realistic, narcissism will forever remain as the absolute indispensable core of subjective self-consciousness because it is required for self-survival. And every human creature must be in varying degrees narcissistic; it is both a liability and a protection. In Hobbes's version, it represents the instinct for self-preservation. As he declares, "the life of man is solitary, poor, nasty, brutish, and short" and "a war of all against all, where every man is an enemy to every man" (*Leviathan*, chapter XIII). Often our sports are disguised as "healthy" competitive outlets for our energy;

Loneliness: an interdisciplinary approach   273

but dare to look beneath the surface; dare to peer more closely. Seeking to win without aggression is a contradiction in terms.

Whereas Freud's analyses strongly promote an *intrapsychic* approach to psychological issues, Harry Stack Sullivan and Frieda Fromm-Reichmann instead favor an *interpersonal* perspective in understanding loneliness. Drawing on Zilboorg's contribution, she points out that essentially until the time of her writing, in 1959, there had been no sustained discussion of loneliness in the field of psychological studies. The situation also exhibited a glaring deficiency in the related disciplines of psychiatry and sociology. This, she believed, was not merely a theoretical oversight but clearly in the nature of a methodological tragedy. And not because it was a disavowed illness—like syphilis, a social embarrassment—but one which desperately needed to be both recognized and addressed. For although we shall never be able to "cure" it, we will be better able to alleviate its suffering by gaining insight and understanding into its dynamics in relation to our own limitations. Fromm-Reichmann offers a decidedly more "humanistic" perspective as she begins her article with an interview of an institutionalized catatonic patient. She describes how at first the woman is completely unresponsive, until she raises her index finger and utters the question: "That lonely?" And then the flood of words erupts. Again, illustrating how critically important human communication is. Often, we are lonely because we believe no one is listening to us; no one understands; and therefore no one cares. While Zilboorg connects loneliness and hostility, she relates it both to a lack of communication and more critically to anxiety and panic, to a sense of abandonment and failed intimacy.

> The longing for interpersonal intimacy stays with every human being from infancy throughout life; and there is no human being who is not threatened by its loss.
>
> (page 3)[12]

The only individuals who seek solitude are those who are not condemned to it. A joy unshared is no joy at all, but a sorrow experienced in solitude is inexpressible anguish. As Gabriel Marcel expresses it: "Il n'y a qu'une souffrance, c'est d'etre seul."

As she goes on to suggest, the extremely unnerving "experience of real loneliness also has much in common with some other quite serious mental states, such as panic. People cannot endure such states for any length of time without becoming psychotic" (page 5). Following Ludwig Binswanger and Harry Stack Sullivan, she agrees that our defenseless state of "naked existence," our "naked horror of loneliness" creates a more intense and compelling drive than any of the more commonly recognized psychological needs of man.[13]

> Anyone who has encountered persons who are under the influence of real loneliness understands why people are more frightened of being lonely than of being deprived of sleep, or having their sexual needs fulfilled.
>
> (page 7)

Echoing Zilboorg's sentiments, she declares:

> If the omnipotent baby learns the job of being admired and loved but learns nothing about the outside world, he may develop a conviction of his greatness and all-importance which will lead to a narcissistic orientation to life—a conviction that life is nothing but being loved and admired. This narcissistic megalomanic attitude will not be acceptable to the environment which will respond with hostility and isolation of the narcissistic person. The deeply seated triad of megalomania and hostility will be established, which is, according to Zilboorg, at the root affliction of loneliness.
>
> (page 5)

Equally illuminating are the insights of Erich Fromm, who adds guilt and shame to the dynamics of loneliness.[14] Once more we find the all-too familiar themes we have already investigated: the need for the individual to intimately attach himself to a world of others beyond himself. "To feel completely alone and isolated leads to mental disintegration just as physical starvation leads to death" (page 19). But Fromm adds something new to the equation as well. He defines "moral aloneness" as the inability of the individual to relate, not necessarily to other human beings, but to *values and ideals* in general. In this regard, Fromm points out how the monk in his monastery, who believes in God, or the political prisoner in his cell, who feels the solidarity of a common—albeit "abstract"—cause is not alone. "Religion and nationalism, as well

Loneliness: an interdisciplinary approach 275

as any custom and belief however absurd and degrading, if it only connects the individual with others [even if indirectly, abstractly], are refuges from what man most dreads: isolation" (page 20). But this "connection" is not conceived as an interpersonal one; rather the relation attaches to a *value*, to an *ideal*; to the martyr on the cross, to the patriot in a dungeon. Accordingly, Fromm traces the feeling of extreme loneliness to "the subjective nature of self-consciousness, to the faculty of thinking by which man is aware of himself as an individual entity, different from nature and other people" (page 21). Man, once having attained the level of individual self-consciousness, once having reached a state of his own distinct personal identity, is suddenly confronted by the consequence, by the realization of his extreme and complete aloneness. But just "as a child can never return to the mother's womb physically, so it can never reverse psychically the process of individuation" (page 30). We find a symbolic allusion to enforced solitude as early as Dante's *Inferno*, in the ninth sphere of Hell, where the sufferers are depicted as entombed in ice, unable to touch, to speak, to communicate as they are condemned to an absolute isolation. Here in frozen incommunicable agony are they, who, like Cain, were treacherous against those to whom they were bound by special ties (page 9). The infidelity of these souls was denial of love, represented by God, and of all human warmth. As they denied God's love, so are they removed from the suffusing light and warmth of his sun. As they denied all human ties, so are they bound alone by the unyielding ice. In Balzac's *The Inventors Suffering*, we find the following passage.

> Man has a horror of aloneness. And of all kind, aloneness is the most terrible. The first hermits lived with God, they inhabited the world which is most populated, the world of spirits. The first thought of man, be he a leper or a prisoner, a sinner or an invalid, is: to have a companion of his fate. In order to satisfy this drive, which is life itself, he applies all his strength, all his power, the energy of his whole life. Would Satan have found companions without this overpowering craving.
>
> (quoted by Fromm, p. 20)

The citations from Fromm are singularly important for two reasons. First, if we reconstruct Zilboorg's emphasis on the relation between loneliness and the emotion of hostility, Fromm-Reichmann's inclusion of anxiety and the inability to communicate, with Fromm's "symptoms" of guilt and shame, we realize that they are *intrinsically* interrelated to each other as constituent synthetic *a priori* elements within loneliness. Elsewhere I have argued that loneliness is an umbrella concept that covers beneath its enveloping folds a rich multiplicity of both feelings and meanings directly deriving from loneliness. It is the genus, which encompasses the active species of jealousy, revenge, rejection, avoidance, panic, abandonment, betrayal, alienation (Marx), estrangement (Kierkegaard), etc. As Freud subsumed and organized an entire psychological system under the principle of libidinal energy, I believe it is possible to emulate his insight and actively systematize an equally coherent discipline based on the universal principle of loneliness. The same could be done for human intimacy.

Second, following Fromm's suggestion, I agree that many seek to alleviate their loneliness by *intentionally* being guided by the tertiary qualities of value. Loneliness seeks consolation not only in committing to individuals but to ideals as well, to existential values.

This is what cognitive behavioral psychologists, psychoanalysts, and neuroscientists fail to acknowledge. Fromm's instinct is right. Consider a higher order animal, a dog for instance. It certainly has the capacity to experience loneliness but obviously it does not have the ability to communicate its feelings verbally or explicitly, through language. But that is not the critical difference between animal and human consciousness. To Weber's point, the difference between man and beast is that man self-consciously creates transcending, intentional *qualitative values*. Humans are the only creatures who have the capacity *to intentionally, teleologically formulate, and commit to judgments and principles of value*. Dogs simply do not think that way.

The dilemma of man, the paradox of human existence is that one must first strive to distinguish the self from its amorphous field of consciousness, from Hegel's Sense-Certainty, James' "buzzing, blooming confusion," and Freud's "oceanic feeling." But once that is achieved, the infant is then rudely confronted by the realization that it has been self-evicted from a secure and unchallenging abode; the babe is no longer secluded in her mother's womb; instead "she" must fend against an inhospitable and challenging world of objects and other selves. Then the lifelong task and trek to re-establish a sense of lost unity is undertaken.

Loneliness in sociology

As far as insights into loneliness are concerned, sociology has lagged far behind psychology and that is because it concentrates on group dynamics rather than individuals. Nevertheless, as Zilboorg, Marx, Arendt, and others have maintained, loneliness can also be experienced not only in groups but in nations as well.

In *The Lonely Crowd*, David Riesman et al. interpret loneliness within a communal context as an institutional dysfunction maintaining that it is symptomatic of certain identifiable societies. For example, in India, the formation of the hierarchic caste system predetermines a tradition-oriented segment of society, which is essentially regulated by an inflexible social order, to a lower standard of human existence. Structured by past generations, it imposes on the lower caste severe limitations on both its financial and social advancement, thus leading in turn to a heavier burden of loneliness as it falls on the lower caste unequally. By contrast, the inner-directed man is essentially guided by a personal commitment to his own subjective principle of individual, as opposed to social, conscience, much in the manner of the adherents described in Max Weber's *Protestant Ethic and the Spirit of Capitalism*, which forged the Robber Baron class in the crucible of competition during the period of the Industrial Revolution in America. According to Weber, Calvinism's theistic pre-destinarianism becomes transformed into the doctrine of the "elect," that God has preordained a select few for the gift of immortality, for the Giants of Industry and the Lords of the Manor. In this context, the chosen few are the fortunate recipients at the top of the economic and social scale, as it is programmed to favor them. The rest are relegated to toil for their economic survival as they compete with each other in a prevailing atmosphere of social Darwinism (William Graham Sumner). "Working men of the world unite; you have nothing to lose but your chains" (Marx, *Communist Manifesto*, 1848). Only the strong survive, which leaves the exploited working classes abandoned to struggle for economic and social survival.

Marxist aestheticians, like Leszek Kowalkowski, maintain that the novel form had its roots in the depiction of the alienating structure

278 Loneliness: an interdisciplinary approach

of modern society, with its attendant growth of economic inequalities. In this regard, the novel quickly evolved into a means of explicitly portraying the ills of industrial society in order to condemn them. With this sociological interpretation in mind, Defoe's *Moll Flanders*, Dickens' novels, as well as D. H. Lawrence's works, are cases in point.

In the outer-directed society, by contrast, the premium is on popularity, to be well-liked by the mass of "others," led by a conformity to public fads, ephemeral values, and a criterion of outward social success as it exposes the inner self to a feeling of emptiness. The strength of "inner conscience" gives way to the superficial facades and fads of popularity.[15]

By contrast, according to Emile Durkheim,

> Egoistic suicide results from the fact that society is not sufficiently integrated at all points to keep all its members under its control. If the sense of personal disenfranchisement increases inordinately, it is because the State, on which the individual depends, has itself excessively expanded out of his reach; it is because society, weak and disturbed, allows too many persons to escape too completely from its influence. Thus, the only remedy for the State is to restore enough consistency to social groups for them to obtain a firmer grip on the individual and for him to feel himself bound to them. He must feel in himself more solidarity with a *collective* existence, which precedes him in time, which survives him, and which encompasses him at all points. The real Hegelian substance is the State. When this occurs, he will no longer find the only aim of his conduct in himself, and, understanding that he is the instrument of a purpose greater than himself, he will see that he is not without significance. Life will resume meaning in his eyes because it will recover its natural aim and reorientation. But what groups are best calculated constantly to re-impress on man this salutary sentiment of solidarity? [Unfortunately] not political society. Especially today, in our great modern States, it is too far removed from the individual to affect him uninterruptedly and with sufficient force. Whatever connection there may be between our daily tasks and the whole of public life, it is too indirect for us to feel it keenly and constantly.[16]

Interestingly, Durkheim draws on Hegel's dialectic of the immediacy of family feeling, of unity; the mediacy of egoism in civil society; and the sublation of the nation state to resolve loneliness. But the world has evolved into a pandemic of loneliness. Eight billion highly mobile and untethered individuals. The scattered, impersonal, and atomistic configuration of the modern state, the extreme rootlessness of contemporary "political" man, the primacy of motivational cut-throat competition, the weakening bonds of marriage, the diminution of the extended family, the higher divorce rate (fortunately encouraged by the rights of women to economically fend for themselves after the Second World War), all have guided us into an increasing void between humans, which in turn has inevitably led to consequent hostilities between not only individuals but also societies at large and racial iniquities. The centering value of belonging to "something greater than one's self" that Durkheim extols is considerably weakened if not extinguished. Today, there are eight billion atoms inhabiting the world with indeterministic mobility—rootless atoms, a pandemic loneliness.

Currently there are national and even global movements to address loneliness. England has instituted a Minister of Loneliness; Japan, Finland, and Poland have instituted international conferences to address the problem.

Loneliness in literature

Beginning with the reflexive essays of Montaigne at the close of the Renaissance, we start to see a deeper concentration on our innermost self as originating from within consciousness and a more explicit concentration on "personal identity." Correspondingly, the Cartesian positing of the cogito brings into higher prominence our individual confrontation with metaphysical aloneness, an inviolable egocentric predicament accompanied by the specter of solipsism. Henceforth the inexplicable relation between the self, the external world, and other selves becomes progressively more problematic: the insoluble separation between the immediacy of self-consciousness and the inferential and dubitable awareness of a questionable realm of existence beyond the certainty of the self.

But it is the modern novel that most powerfully ushers in the strengths and virtues of personal narration in expressing the uniquely

280   Loneliness: an interdisciplinary approach

intimate features of loneliness. In *Loneliness in Philosophy, Psychology, and Literature,* I appended a long list of novels that I believe provide invaluable insight and understanding into the feelings, meanings, and dynamics of loneliness. But here I will briefly recommend the novels of Thomas Hardy, Joseph Conrad, and Thomas Wolfe. For more specialized orientations, I would suggest Somerset Maugham's *The Razor's Edge*, Radclyffe Hall's *The Well of Loneliness*, Richard Wright's *Black Boy*, Arthur Machen's *The Hill of Dreams*, and Carson McCuller's *The Heart Is a Lonely Hunter.* But it is Joseph Conrad who captures the essence of loneliness best.

> [T]he tremendous fact of our isolation, of the loneliness impene-trable and transparent, elusive and everlasting; of the indestruct-ible loneliness that surrounds, envelops, clothes every human soul from the cradle to the grave and perhaps beyond.
>
> > (*An Outcaste of the Islands*, IV)

Who of us has not felt—if not expressed so eloquently and profoundly—these sentiments? And even if we have experienced it but once in our lives, why do we think that it is not in truth our prim-ordial condition, which we continually but futilely strive to escape? Why do so many of us persist in dismissing it as merely a momentary aberration? We may choose to consider it as a transient psychological and exaggerated melancholic form of hysteria found in certain unique cases and individuals, but surely not in more well-balanced and saner social natures. But the fact is we are born alone; we breathe alone; and we die alone. Perhaps Thomas Wolfe expressed it best in his first novel as he described Eugene Gant's dawning self-consciousness.

> And left alone to sleep in a shuttered room, with the thick sun-light printed in bars upon the floor, unfathomable loneliness and sadness crept through him; he saw his life down the solemn vista of a forest aisle, and he knew he would always be the sad one; caged in that little round of skull, imprisoned in that beating and most secret heart, his life must always walk down lonely passages. Lost. He understood that men were forever strangers to one another, that no one ever comes really to know any one, that imprisoned in the dark womb of our mother, we come to life without having seen

her face, that we are given to her arms a stranger, and that, caught in that insoluble prison of being, we escape it never, no matter what arms may clasp us, what mouth may kiss us, what heart may warm us. Never, never, never, never, never.

(Look Homeward, Angel, chapter 4; compare Of Time and the River, chapters 7, 14, 25, 30)

In Wolfe, the centering dynamic of loneliness constitutes the essential unifying theme in all his works. It is an isolation, which he conceives as forever continuing within the *temporal* structures of consciousness, within each individual life. Although we communally exist in an open and shared social space, we dwell alone in a personal, unique, and enclosed immanent frame of time-consciousness.

Naked and alone we came into exile. In her dark womb we did not know our mother's face; from the prison of her flesh have we come into the unspeakable and incommunicable prison of the earth. Which of us has known his brother? Which of us has looked into his father's heart? Which of us has not remained prison-pent? Which of us is not forever a stranger and alone?

(ibid.)

But lest we think that Wolfe is merely describing an idiosyncratic state of consciousness, he goes on to make it clear that he regards loneliness as the universal condition of all mankind.

Loneliness, far from being a rare and curious circumstance, is and always has been the central and inevitable experience of every man.

(You Can't Go Home Again, Bk. 4, Ch. 31)

And we die alone (Tolstoy, "The Death of Ivan Ilyich").

Existential literature

Should we wish to have the universal feelings and meanings of loneliness expressed in the context of our human condition, we can do no better than turn to the writings of Pascal and Kierkegaard. In theological texts, it is the theistic existentialism of Pascal and Kierkegaard that best captures the fear of the soul's estrangement from God.

According to Pascal, man is thrown completely alone into a meaningless existence and in terror he confronts his solitude against the background of a soulless universe. The sense of complete isolation, which we observe in certain exaggerated pathological states, is but the finger in the wound of each of us as we singly realize our radical contingency and metaphysical exile.

> En regardant tout l'universe muet et l'homme sans lumiere abandonne a lui-meme comme egare dans ce recoin de l'uinverse sans savoir qui l'y a mis, ce qu'il deviendra faire, ce qu'il est venu faire, ce qu'il deviendra en mourant ... j'entre en effroi comme un homme qu'on aurait porte endormi dans une ile desert et effroyable, et qui s'eveiallerait sans connaitre et sans moyen dans sortir.[17]

Similarly, in the atheistic writings of Nietzsche, we find that the death of God proclaims and seals the utter aloneness of human existence. In *Thus Spake Zarathustra*, "the last man" announces that we are each of us separately condemned to an irredeemable solitariness, "the terrible loneliness of the last philosopher." Zarathustra and Dostoyevsky's Grand Inquisitor share more than a striking resemblance through their self-imposed isolation from mankind.

> I call myself the last philosopher because I am the last man. Nobody talks to me but myself, and my voice comes to me like that of a dying person!... Through you I conceal my loneliness from myself and make my way into the multitude and into love by lies, ... for my heart cannot bear the terror of the loneliest loneliness and compels me to talk as if I were two.
>
> (Nietzsche)

For Nietzsche, each man is the creator of values for himself alone, which is the principle I am trying to declare. The prison is the self but the key to the cell is the creation of a value.

Which of us have not felt—if not uttered so eloquently, profoundly, and desperately—these sentiments of Nietzsche. And even if we have experienced it but once in our lives, why do we not think that it is the truth of our primordial condition, which we continually strive to escape?

Empiricism and human nature

But we can also cite the empiricist philosophers of human nature, Shaftesbury, Hume, and Burke, who collectively affirm the distress of a denied sociability.

> How wretched it must be, therefore, for man, of all creatures, to lose that sense and feeling, which is proper to him as a man? How unfortunate must it be for a creature whose dependence on society is greater than any others, to lose that natural affection by which he is prompted to the good of his species and community? Such is man's natural share of this affection, that he, of all creatures, is plainly the least able to bear solitude. Nor is anything more apparent than that there is naturally in every man such a degree of social affection as inclines him to seek the familiarity and friendship of his fellows.
>
> (Shaftesbury, Characteristics of Men, Manners, Opinions, Times, I, 315)

Equally Hume declares that "A perfect solitude is, perhaps, the greatest punishment that we can suffer" (*A Treatise of Human Nature*, II, ii, v). Similarly, Edmund Burke announces in no uncertain voice that an

> absolute and entire solitude, that is, the total and perpetual exclusion from all society, is as great a positive pain as can almost be conceived ... an entire life of solitude contradicts the purposes of our being, since death itself is scarcely an idea of more terror.
>
> (*A Philosophical Enquiry into the Origin of Our Ideas of the Sublime and the Beautiful*, I, xi)

Collectively, these eighteenth-century students of human nature have identified the common ground we all share through our humanity, our sense of loneliness, as it defines and delimits the constant parameters of our existence, as they expound a "science of human nature." The foregoing declarations together express the single guiding motivational principle of all mankind. For Shaftesbury and Hume these avowals directly follow from their "moral sense" doctrine, from an immediate sentiment of sympathy and natural affection for our fellow man, which serves as the key to assuaging the despair of our sense of isolation.

284 Loneliness: an interdisciplinary approach

But consider also this passage from Bertrand Russell's *Autobiography.*

> Throughout my childhood I had an increasing sense of loneliness and of despair of meeting anyone with whom I could talk. Nature and books and mathematics saved me from complete despondency.
>
> (I, 30)[18]

Loneliness, religion, and society

Interestingly, the Hegelian movement of religious estrangement (*Entfremdung*) from God, splits into two movements, a right and a left. On the right, the section on the Unhappy Consciousness in the *Phenomenology* portrays man's fear of separation from God. Clearly no religious thinker has ever advocated for a solitary immortality, none has ever expressed a desire for an absolutely singular existence, rather it is always conceived as an immersive companionship with other self-conscious beings or a supreme Being, it is always an afterlife *with* God and/or other consciousnesses. While for the left Hegelians, Feuerbach's dialectical version represents God as man's own alienating psychological self-projection and impoverishment. Man has fashioned an alien image of God as an independent substance—omnipotent, omniscient, and omnibenevolent—only to realize that it is in reality man as *universal species-being, as class-conscious being*, who possesses the predicates of power, knowledge, and goodness. Man psychologically projects an alien being in order to escape his utter sense of loneliness; in order to assure him that there is an eternal Being caring for him, only to return to himself realizing that this ideal is a product of his own insecurity and desperation (Feuerbach, *The Essence of Christianity*). Meanwhile, Hegel's concept of alienation (*Entausserung*) becomes Marx's watchword for the workers' sense of separation, externalization, and objectification from nature, his labor, his products, his profits, and his fellows in forced competition for economic survival.

My own view is that these social ideals of unity will always fall far short of success because of the force of our innate monadic spheres of consciousnesses. Against Hegel's conviction that the immediacy of feeling in family unity will dialectically evolve into a period of atomistic particularity, fragmentation, and egoism as engrained within civil society, and only then will it be reconciled, sublimated into the higher organic unity of the nation state is naive. Hegel trumpets the historical virtue of the German modern state, while Bruno Bauer, Feuerbach, and Marx extol the social freedom of man. But these are superficial "solutions" to loneliness, efforts to immerse the self within an "absolute system," "humanity at large," or by depending on a restructuring of political and socioeconomic systems. It is only an evasion from recognizing human isolation with supplanted pipe dreams. Marx, mercifully sheltered by his immediate family and devoted friend, Engels, never pondered that loneliness may be ingrained in consciousness rather than in his abstract socio-economic system, itself an "ideological construct," as it hides from an underlying psychological reality. As Freud complained of Marxism, it is not systems that are bad but men.

Not only are we alone in relation to others but we are even strangers to ourselves. Bergson's discontinuous immersions in *duration* last but a moment. There is reflexive awareness but anything much beyond that is a mere remembrance. If I split my self into two persons, as I am now and as I once was as a child, and if I could converse with the child I once was, the enormous abyss that separates me from my former self would surely bewilder "me." Who has not revisited a former friend or haunt and realized that his "self" has changed through time; that the former qualitative features and structures of each present moment are intrinsically unique and unrepeatable and hence that the past is gone forever, irretrievable, and unrepeatable. Certainly, we try to imagine that it is the friend or the place that has changed. But is it? We are not only strangers to others but, even more frighteningly a dark mystery to our own selves. Contemporary man is deeply concerned with issues regarding his uniqueness; he desperately searches for his "identity" and he fears its loss. He yearns for an integrated self. Against the external world, the ego struggles to maintain its own unique selfhood despite the immanent "infections" of those other earlier "selves."

Notes

* Mijuskovic, Ben, "Loneliness: An Interdisciplinary Approach," *Psychiatry: A Journal for Interpersonal Processes*, 40:2 (1977); reprinted in *The Anatomy of Loneliness*, edited by Joseph Hartog, J. R. Audy, and Yehudi Cohen (New York: International Universities Press, 1980).
1 Mijuskovic, Ben, *Loneliness in Philosophy, Psychology, and Literature* (Bloomington, IN: iUniverse, 3rd edition, 2012); *Feeling Lonesome: The*

Philosophy and Psychology of Loneliness (Santa Barbara, CA: Praeger, 2015); "Cognitive and Motivational Roots of Human Loneliness," Chapter 2, edited by Ami-Sha'ked and Ami Rokach in Addressing Loneliness: Coping, Prevention, and Clinical Interventions (New York: Routledge, 2015); and Consciousness and Loneliness: Theoria and Praxis (Leiden: Brill, 2018).

2 Fromm-Reichmann, Frieda, "Loneliness," Psychiatry: A Journal of Interpersonal Processes, 22:1 (1959); hereafter cited as Fromm-Reichmann. Essentially, the journal served as a sounding-board for Harry Stack Sullivan's interpersonal psychoanalytic approach.

3 Mijuskovic, Ben, "Loneliness and Intimacy," Journal of Couples Therapy (1991); reprinted in Autonomous Intimacy: Intimate Autonomy, edited by B. J. Brothers (New York: Haworth Press, 1991).

4 Sabine, George, A History of Political Theory (New York: Holt, Rinehart, and Winston, 1961), 131 ff., 141: "Men were slowly making souls for themselves, turning inwardly." Contemporaneously, according to Hegel, the small Christian community was establishing a shared spiritual value through Christ, while in turn the Epicureans turned to the shared values of friendship, and the Stoic's to an ideal of a communal brotherhood.

5 Hegel, G. W. F., Hegel's Lectures on the History of Philosophy (London: Routledge and Kegan Paul,1968), II, 336; The Phenomenology of Mind, translated by A. V. Miller (Oxford: Clarendon Press, 1977), on "Skepticism," Section 202 ff.; cf. Jacob Loewenberg, Hegel's Phenomenology: Dialogues in the Life of Mind (La Salle, IL: Open Court, 1965), 94–95; and Jean Hyppolite, Genesis and Structure of Hegel's Phenomenology of Spirit (Evanston, IL: Northwestern University Press, 1974), 187–188.

6 Freud, Sigmund, Introductory Lectures of Psycho-Analysis (1971); cf. Stanford Ed. Psychol. Works, Vol. 16; Hogarth, 1963, 407.

7 Bettelheim, Bruno, Truants from Life (London: Macmillan, 1955), 33.

8 Weiss, George, Loneliness: The Experience of Emotional Isolation (Cambridge, MA: MIT Press, 1973.

9 Zilboorg, Gregory, "Loneliness," Atlantic Monthly (February, 1938), 45–54. Freud introduced the concept of narcissism as early as 1913 and it continued as a focus of interest in his later writings as well, including Beyond the Pleasure Principle, Civilization and Its Discontents, Totem and Taboo, Group Psychology and the Analysis of the Ego, The Ego and the Id, and The Future of an Illusion.

10 Mijuskovic, Ben, "Loneliness and Hostility," Psychology: A Quarterly of Human Behavior, 20:3 (1983); "Loneliness, Hostility, Anxiety, and Communication," Child Study Journal, 16:3 (1986); "Loneliness and Adolescence," Adolescence, 21:84 (1986); and "Adolescence and Alcoholism," Adolescence, 23:92 (1988).

11 Arendt, Hannah, The Origins of Totalitarianism (New York: Harcourt, 1968; originally published in 1948), 474–476 and Preface to the First Edition.

Loneliness: an interdisciplinary approach 287

12 Mijuskovic, Ben, "Loneliness and Communication," in *Man and His Conduct* (University of Puerto Rico Press, 1980).

13 Sullivan, Harry Stack, *Interpersonal Theory of Psychiatry* (New York: W. W. Norton, 1953), 290.

14 Fromm, Eric, *The Art of Loving* ((New York: Harper & Row, 1956), 6–7 on the relation between self-consciousness, loneliness, and separation; cf. *Escape from Freedom* (New York: Avon Books, 1969), 34–36.

15 Riesman, David, Denny, Reuel and Glazer, Nathan, *The Lonely Crowd* New Haven, CT: Yale University Press; 1950), v-vi, 68–69, 373. Cf. Ben Mijuskovic, "Marx and Engels on Materialism and Idealism," *Journal of Thought: An Interdisciplinary Journal,* 9:3 (1984).

16 Durkheim, Emile, *Suicide: A Study in Sociology* (Glencoe, IL: Free Press, 1958), 373–374), 405; cf. Mijuskovic, Ben, "Organic Communities, Atomistic Societies, and Loneliness," *Journal of Sociology and Social Welfare* (1992); "Loneliness and Suicide," *Journal of Social Philosophy,* XI:1 (1980); reprinted in *Geriatrics and Thanatology,* edited by Elizabeth Pritchard (Praeger, 1984).

17 Pascal, Blaise, *Pensées,* Section 194; Nietzsche quoted by Karl Jaspers, *Nietzsche: An Introduction to the Understanding of His Philosophical Activity* (University of Arizona Press, 1965), 56; cf. 58 ff., 70, 74, 81, 84–87, 402, 436. As Jaspers indicates, Nietzsche wrote this in 1876, while he was still a young professor and surrounded by friends. *Zarathustra* was not yet on the literary horizon. But again, this is offered as a personal fact about Nietzsche rather than as the universal essence of human individuality. But confer *The Gay Science,* Section 50; *The Will to Power,* Sections 985, 988, 993. See also Soren Kierkegaard, *The Concept of Dread,* translated by W. Lowrie (Princeton University Press, 1944); *The Sickness unto Death,* translated by W. Lowrie (Princeton University Press, 1955); *Fear and Trembling,* which describes the loneliness of Abraham as he struggles with the paradox of faith that he must *both* murder *and* sacrifice his son on the altar of God, a command so contradictory that words cannot express it. cf. Josiah Thompson, *The Lonely Labyrinth, Kierkegaard's Pseudonymous Works* (Carbondale, IL: Southern Illinois University Press, 1967), for a portrait of existential self-consciousness and loneliness. Sartre, in "Existentialism Is a Humanism," clearly defines loneliness as an essential descriptive "category" of the human condition.

18 Russell, Bertrand, *Autobiography of Bertrand Russell* (New York: Simon & Schuster, 1967), Volume I, 30; cf. 4, 43, 51, 64; II, 35–36, 234; cf. R. W. Clark's *The Life of Bertrand Russell,* which stresses the intense affinity between Russell and Joseph Conrad because of their mutual understanding of loneliness as its bond.

Chapter 14

Loneliness and the dynamics of narcissism

Plato and Aristotle define man in terms of reason; Christians in terms of faith; Hobbes and Schopenhauer in terms of egoism; Freud in terms of sexual proclivities; linguist and analytic philosophers in terms of language. My inclination favors the dynamics of loneliness. In any case, the stakes in terms of life's values during our sojourn upon this transitory earthly realm are incredibly high: happiness or misery; goodness or evil; altruism or egoism; and intimacy or loneliness.

The first year of infancy is critical in the development of the personality. Both loneliness and narcissism are deeply rooted from the very beginning by the constitutive—not causal—acts forming each personality as a unique individual. The best early childhood development studies in relation to infantile loneliness were performed by the psychoanalyst, Rene Spitz, who concentrated on the first year of infancy. During World War II, his subjects were children removed from their mothers' care as a requirement for them to work in factories for a year in order to help in the war effort.[1] In the previous chapter, we concentrated on Zilboorg's thesis regarding the synthetic *a priori* connection in the development of childhood aggressiveness as intrinsically related to narcissism, loneliness, and hostility.

Now I propose to explore the deeper connection regarding subjective idealism, especially as promoted by Fichte, in gaining both insight and understanding into the principles of dynamic psychiatry a well as narcissism. The term *dynamic* signifies that the source of energy arises from within the ego rather than from external causes. In the context of primary narcissism, and indeed psychoanalysis in general, Freud's theory of the unconscious and Schopenhauer's theory of the subconscious offer insights into the effects of loneliness gone woefully

DOI: 10.4324/9781003156130-15

awry. Beginning with Leibniz's principle and paradigm of the self, as a completely self-enclosed "windowless Monad," from which nothing escapes from within and nothing invades from without, the force of narcissism draws breath and vigor by developing fantasies of success and the accompanying fears of rejection. In Henri Ellenberger's monumental study, several philosophers, including Leibniz, Fichte, and Schopenhauer, assume leading roles in the history of dynamic psychiatry.[2] Together they contribute to the principle of dynamism.

> [Dynamism] is the same process that drives the entirety of living nature from the first living cell of mankind and to the present world, a striving to challenge and conquer death itself.
>
> (Ellenberger, 624, 628)

In Fichte, spontaneity is explicitly tied to an originating creative act *alone*: "In the beginning was the *Act.*" Thus, Fichte starts with the immediacy of consciousness itself—hence phenomenologically, i.e., descriptively—with the ego's spontaneous act of thetic self-positing: "I am I." This absolute positing of the ego is narcissistically creative. It means that the ego creates its own reality independently of the natural environment and other selves. It is the "First, absolutely unconditioned principle."

> The self's own positing of its self is thus its own pure activity. The *self posits its self,* and by virtue of this mere self-assertion it *exists;* and conversely, the self *exists* and *posits* its own existence by virtue of merely existing [sic]. It is at once the agent and the product of the action; the active and what the activity brings about; action and deed are one and the same; and hence the 'I am' expresses an Act.[3]

In this fashion, Fichte's self-positing Ego—"I am I"—initially assumes the aspect of an uncompromising narcissism (Ellenberger, 517). Although Fichte's ostensive moral goal is to ground an autonomous principle for his absolute ethical idealism, his extreme metaphysical and dynamic voluntarism deludes the self into an illusionary aura of self-sufficiency, power, and narcissism only later to be betrayed into the arms of loneliness. According to Fichte, the ego first posits its own existence in an absolutely "creative" way, i.e., spontaneously. There is a defining *qualitative* schism between our biological birth and the narcissistic origins of our assertive self-consciousness. Fichte's primordial *thrust of spontaneity, this impulse of creativity, this inexplicable sui generis act* of positing its self as absolute, as an unconditioned first principle centered within human consciousness, directly leads to an enshrinement of the self as primarily motivated to act only *for* its own sake. The self's own positing of its self is thus its own pure unconditional activity.

> It is only through this act, and first by means of it, by an act upon an act itself, which specific act is preceded by no other whatever, that the self originally comes to exist for itself (page 34).
>
> However, we shall not merely argue here, but we will cite the words of Kant himself. At B 132 he says, "But this representation (I think) is an act of *spontaneity,* that is it cannot be regarded as belonging to sensibility.
>
> (page 49)

According to Jon Mills,

> Fichte understood that self-consciousness cannot be adequately explained by a reflection thesis whereby the self reflects upon itself for the reflection is inherently circular. This is because there is not a necessary criterion for identification that allows for self-consciousness to re-cognize its own image in the mirror reflection of the other. The reflection model of cognition presupposes what it sets out to explain. For Fichte, self-consciousness is given in a spontaneous act of positing and thus escapes circularity.[4]

This is an interesting way to present the difference between Kant and Fichte and it anticipates the distinction between reflexion and intentionality in Brentano. Perhaps a different way of putting it is that Kant *assumes* human experience and then his *transcendental* argument outlines the *indirect* formal conditions for its empirical possibility. By contrast, Fichte *directly* invokes the act of spontaneity; it is self-sufficient unto its self. Just as Descartes asserts "I think," Fichte declares "I act." From that initial starting point, it follows that all non-egos—both objects and other "selves"—must dependently follow upon the "I"s, the ego's initial declaration. Expressed in this fashion, Mills is right. Synthetic acts must follow rather than (formally) precede. Descartes's cogito is *reflexive*; Fichte's spontaneity is *intentional.* Dynamic forces always mean that the energy emanates from within as opposed to being causally determined from without. When we connect Zilboorg's psychological chain of conceptual inter-relations binding (a) narcissism, with its overpowering feelings of omnipotence, megalomania, delusions of grandeur, entitlement issues, and self-adulation; (b) with the ego's failure to gratify its desires and fantasies; which result (c) in the generation of an increasing loneliness; then (d) hostility inevitably intervenes. It is only then that we realize how dangerous and destructive narcissism can be both to the self as well as to others. And if we further connect all this with the absolute spontaneity of consciousness, we realize that man is capable of anything and everything spanning a spectrum from good to evil. Futile to search for "motivational causes" or "ethical justifications." The simple answer is: "I did it because I could."

For Freud, by contrast, the ego comes into being as an undifferentiated unity, i.e. his "oceanic feeling" as antecedent to grasping its self *as* a self; prior to becoming fully self-conscious; and before apprehending its self against the background of inanimate objects and other selves. Unlike the gradual evolution and development of an indeterminate consciousness as it gains mastery over its own ego, as described by Hegel in his *qualitatively* prefaced passage on Sense-Certainty as it ponderously moves, develops toward Perception (a subject–object distinction) in the *Phenomenology*, Fichte's version is analogous to God's spontaneous creations. It is self-creative.

This active trend empowers the dominance of the self above everything else as it stokes the fires of an insatiable narcissism. All four thinkers, Leibniz, Kant, Fichte, and Schopenhauer strongly endorse a paradigm of the self as spontaneously emanating from within. In Fichte's view—and certainly Schopenhauer's and perhaps Freud's as well(?)—the (absolute) ego first posits its self and then it dynamically proliferates into negative reactions *against* outward pressures, while in the same moment generating a recalcitrant alien realm of objects and other egos in *opposition* to its self. Fichte thus adopts a subjective idealist model of consciousness accounting for the relation between the ego's own private sphere of consciousness in opposition to a foreign realm of non-egos. I would venture that a corresponding "philosophy of mind," without its deeply idealistic prejudices, serves Freud as well with a strikingly similar conceptual basis for his own investigations into the sphere of the individual mind and the ego's pre-disposition toward narcissistic and egotistic drives, fantasies, and lusts. Freud was certainly aware of these circulating idealist paradigms of consciousness swirling around him during his time. Although it cannot be conclusively demonstrated that he was influenced by Fichte, Henri Ellenberger certainly suggests as much when he writes that Fichte and Freud shared an undeniable respect for the powers of the ego and narcissistic impulses (Ellenberger, 516–517).

For Freud, nevertheless, the ego develops, comes into being as an undifferentiated unity antecedently to grasping its self *as* a self and thus prior to becoming fully self-conscious; before apprehending its self against the background of inanimate objects and other selves. But whether Fichte's narcissism is sudden, while Freud's is developmental and delayed, the result is the same: absolute self-absorption leading to self-entitlement.

Freud's starting point is the "oceanic feeling," that singularly amorphous self-sufficient consciousness. In a significant way this is when and how it all starts.

> Originally the ego includes everything, later it detaches itself from the external world. The *ego-feeling* we are aware of now is thus only a shrunken vestige of a far more extensive *feeling*—a *feeling* which embraced the universe and expressed an inseparable connection of the ego with the external world. If we may suppose that this primary *ego-feeling* has been preserved in the minds of many people—to a greater or lesser extent—it would co-exist like a sort of counterpart with the narrower and more sharply outlined ego-feeling of maturity, and the *ideational* content belonging to it would be precisely the notion of limitless extension and oneness with the universe—the same feeling as that described by my friend as "oceanic." But have we any right to assume that the original type of feeling survived alongside the later one which has developed from it? Undoubtedly we have (italics mine).[5]

Loneliness and the dynamics of narcissism   293

The emphasis is first on feeling before cognitive states. And second, on the primitive delusion of self-sufficient omnipotence. Accordingly, the critical question becomes how far do our feelings and impulses control our lives as opposed to "reason" and "common sense"? How powerful are the affective forces? To what extent does the id dominate the ego? Are the whims of fantasy and lust more powerful than the fictions of a manageable "reality"? Freud's id is essentially instinctual and affective as opposed to cognitive, epistemic, and meditative. Later in the text, Freud alludes to "the narcissistic man, who inclines to be self-sufficient [and] will seek his main satisfactions in his internal mental processes."

Intrinsic to the "oceanic feeling," lies the bundle of incipient forces pregnant with promises of future fantasies, which will eventuate in the richness of delusional grandeur, omnipotence, self-assertion, and megalomania, as they begin to permeate and percolate through the ego's sense of ubiquitous entitlements; its over-weaning confidence that the ego's desires will develop and rule well beyond the infantile ego as it continues into childhood, adolescence, and adulthood. In Freud's *Totem and Taboo* discussion regarding the "omnipotence of thoughts," he declares

> The narcissistic subject behaves as if he were in love with himself; his egoistic instincts and his libidinal desires are not yet separable ... [and] we suspect already that this narcissistic organization is never wholly abandoned. A human being remains to some extent narcissistic even after he has found external objects for his libido.[6]

And he further emphasizes that this is a continuation of "the original narcissism in which the childish ego enjoyed self-sufficiency." This conception is repeated in his 26th Lecture, titled "The Theory of the Libido: Narcissism" (1926), where he announces that

> it is probable that this *narcissism* is the universal original condition, out of which *object-love* develops later without thereby necessarily effecting a disappearance of the original narcissism ... Thus it appeared that the auto-eroticism was the sexual activity [i.e. the dynamic source of energy] of the narcissistic phase of direction of the libido.

294 Loneliness and the dynamics of narcissism

Two points are worth commenting upon. First, although Freud's language is mental, his roots remain physiological, instinctual, and sexual. The libido is ultimately a bodily force disguised in mental garb, whereas my appeal to the loneliness principle is philosophically conceptual and ideal. Nevertheless, Freud also at times *assumes* a dual reflexive self-conscious paradigm, which agrees with his introspectionist perspective and by deliberately neglecting the "physiological" factor and building on a *purely* ideal psychological foundation, although for Freud the dynamism remains mainly unconscious.

> First, how is the concept 'narcissism' distinguished from 'egoism'? In my opinion narcissism is the [dynamic] libidinal complement of [cognitive] egoism When one speaks of egoism, one is thinking only of the [cognitive] *interests* of the person concerned; narcissism relates to the [intentional, pursuant] satisfaction of [acquiring] libidinal needs.[7]

Narcissism is affective; egoism is cognitive, it rationally plans how to secure its desires. This is the paradoxical problem. Freud wishes to be an empiricist, a scientist, and much of what he says is compatible with phenomenalism, namely that consciousness is a construction of sense data or sense qualia. Clearly, however, his mental language is reflexively "introspective." But by definition, his conception of the *unconscious* cannot serve as an agency that is directly, immediately given in consciousness. That would be a contradiction in terms. Phenomenalism has no room for an unconscious.

My guess is that Freud, who began his medical career as a neurologist, wanted to ground his dynamic theory as early as possible within mankind's "mental" nature, in consciousness, and he judiciously chose the Greek myths. Their primitive and sexual undertones directly led to a depiction of powerful and dangerous underlying sexual desires and aggressive instincts. And when he "processed" that viewpoint, a more literary style or mode of expression was required. As a persuasive writer, he is singularly gifted. The Greek myths singularly appeal to affective forces.

Although Freud denies being influenced by Schopenhauer and merely asserts a passing and belated awareness of his philosophy later in his life, there is ample evidence of a strong theoretical "sympathy" with Schopenhauer's *subconscious* "irrational Will' and Freud's theory of the *unconscious*.[8] Both authors are committed to an ego-centered, i.e., egoistic/narcissistic approach. We must remember that German idealism dominated both German and Austrian thought.

In its primordial Freudian state, the oceanic feeling, the ego just *is*; it *exists*. It does not distinguish, within its own bounds of consciousness, between its self, the external world, or other centers of conscious activity. For Fichte, it is spontaneously grounded in the requirement that for any possible state of awareness to occur, the non-reflexive ego must be first "given" and/or posited; it acts absolutely, self-aware *only* of its self, 'I am,' without any cognizable specifications. Once more:

> *To posit one's self* and *to be* are, as applied to the self, perfectly identical. Thus the proposition, "I am because I have posited my self" can also be stated as: "I am absolutely because I am."

If indeed this is the defining motivational first principle of human consciousness, then obviously it is but a short step for the ego to view the world through narcissistic lenses. This conceptual positing is synonymous with spontaneity, i.e., dynamism; it means an arbitrary, creative beginning as it grounds the ultimate origin of psychological narcissism. But whereas Fichte terms this origin as absolutely *spontaneous*, without preconditions, Freud rather recruits a *developmental* dynamic source in order to accommodate his "three-fold paradigm of id-ego-superego" (Ellenberger, 147). Only later and developmentally is the ego able to become "introspectively" conscious of its self as a distinct entity negating other entities within its own sphere of apprehension. Again, negation is determination (Spinoza, Hegel). But it is also the dynamic force behind self-conscious *separation* and thus human loneliness. For Freud, there lurks a more dangerous conflict, between psychic separation and unity, loneliness and intimacy symbolized by Freud's god of Death (Thanatos) and the goddess of Love (Eros).

If Fichte is right, then from the very beginning of human consciousness, the absolute ego will proceed forward by a *feeling*, by a *desire* that (a) it has a privileged status against all other conscious existences; and consequently (b) it has an absolute power to express its idiosyncratic desires in any fashion it chooses.

> We can now see perfectly how the self should be able to determine its [sensuous] passivity through and by means of its activity and how it can be at once both active and passive. It is *determinant* in so far as it posits itself, through absolute *spontaneity* in a determinate sphere [i.e. within its own consciousness] and among all those contained in the absolute totality of its [subjective] realities ... We have discovered the original synthetic act of the self, whereby the proposed contradiction [between sensation and act] is resolved and have thus lighted on a new synthetic concept.
>
> (Fichte, 135)

The opposite of psychological determinism is spontaneous activity. Causality belongs to the realm of materialism. Fichte is an extreme voluntarist; the ego has nothing to do with causality. Its freedom is immanent. That is why during a variety of human situations and decisional contexts, "motivational" factors cannot be attributed as "causes." The realm of the other(s) is *allegedly* solely created for the purpose of bringing into existence a moral world in which the ego is free to display its own ethical principles and decisions. In this manner, Fichte manages to fashion an ideal world (presumably) constituted by other "free" egos. As a domineering personality during his lifetime, Fichte was regarded as a difficult person to deal with.

When Freud appeals to temporal and spatial metaphors, such as the possibility of "two" egos—both the oceanic and the mature ego—surviving alongside and co-existing with each other at the same time (as above); or he compares the mind to an iceberg consisting of a dangerous and submerged unconscious force along with a visible surface presence; or he analogizes the hidden repressed ancient cities of Rome coexisting along with its present municipality, we realize a deliberate epistemic duality. And all this in order to describe how mental and psychological states of consciousness co-exist and interact in order to account for how the ego operates.[9] He is in effect committing himself—at least in part—to an idealist theoretical construct of the mind, one which abandons his original dependence on physiological neurons alone. He can only recruit such metaphors in so far as he considers that the mind is not entirely dependent on or reducible to a scientific determinism but that it shares in something ideal and mental. Significantly, his many allusions to Greek mythology betray much deeper figurative meanings and insights indicating a truer commitment to at least an epistemic dualism within the ego.

But the ensuing subsequent *personalized* sense of narcissism can only develop *after* the ego "center" has progressed beyond the stage of the non-reflexive, absolute ego to that of the empirical "self" or "me" as an "object" in the world as it developmentally moves forward to a conception of the self as essentially determined through and by a *confrontational* opposition against other selves as its determinative background (thus once more Hegel's Lordship and Bondage passage in the *Phenomenology*). Narcissistic feelings soon develop into feelings of entitlement; demands that one's desires be recognized at everyone else's expense; other selves merely serve as mirrors for the narcissist's self-aggrandizement. Differently put, during the stage of the oceanic feeling, there is just a "need" for physical indeterminate comfort without a definite object of desire. At the later stage of narcissism, the self recognizes the desiderative aspects of *self*-love, what Hegel calls *amour propre*, i.e., love of one's self, while engaged in competitive struggles *for narcissistic recognition* first within the confines of the self-mother relation and later within the sibling-sibling relation. In Hegel, the activity of separation by which consciousness particularizes, individualizes, and subjectivizes its self can only occur when it is able to differentiate itself from the oceanic feeling. In turn, negation is defined by a separation, which serves as the "mechanism" of an existential separation of the self from other selves. Both affectively and cognitively negation fosters distinctions and separations directly leading to loneliness, hostility, anxiety, and depression.

The origin of loneliness arises from the intrinsic paradox of human existence. At first the ego is an undifferentiated totality but not a self-conscious unity. Next the ego is violently awakened from its amorphous reveries as it is forced to acknowledge the intercession of an alien undesired "element"—Freud's reality principle; the realization that there are opposing existents beyond and separate from its wish-fulfilling desires and hence beyond its control. This results in an increasing awareness within the ego of a dissonance between the self and a discordant reality. And yet the ego yearns and longs for a reunification with its original primal conditions. But it is too late; Eden is lost forever; its protective, isolative seclusion is gone forever. The desire to return is the original anxiety. To be forced to do so would entail giving up all the *cognitive* achievements it had already forcefully secured from the external world at such a great emotional expense. The ego is alone and it both feels it and knows it. To overcome its feeling of isolation, it must curb its overwhelming selfish desires in order to have any hope of capturing the holy grail of eventual domination over others. A dialectic is thus engendered: to remain alone, master of one's own identity or force others—through the various devices of power, fame, wealth, glory, even love it matters little—to *recognize* its narcissistic desires and yearnings. *Man's original sin is narcissism.*

But unfortunately, of course, it is also important to realize that narcissism is our most basic human feature, which we all share in varying degrees and if we did not, we could not psychologically survive. However, when it becomes severely dysfunctional, it is clinically diagnosed as a chronic personality disorder (*DSM*, 301.81). The narcissistic individual does not want therapy. Unlike symptoms such as anxiety and depression, the narcissist does not believe there is anything amiss or wrong with her or him. Often there is an accompanying and pronounced lack of empathy for others and it often exhibits features of an antisocial personality; such individuals frequently demonstrate a disregard for the rights of others (*DSM*, 312.81, 301.7), which makes them doubly unpleasant and possibly dangerous.

In the "healthier" structuring process of individual ego-development, the infant begins to realize that its own ego is influenced by and develops in relation to and with a primary "other," usually the mother, who as an opposing "pole" of consciousness molds and influences—but does not determine—the child's orientation to the world and to others.

Notes

1 Spitz, Rene, *The Psychoanalytic Study of the Child*, 1:1 (1945); "Hospitalism: An Inquiry into the Genesis of Psychiatric Conditions in Early Childhood," *Psychoanalytic Study of the Child*, 1 (1945a), 53–74; "Overt Primacy Rejection in Infancy" and "Emotional Deprivation in Infancy," 1952 videos; and *The First Year of Life: A Psychoanalytic Study of Normal and Deviant Development of Object Relations* (New York: International Universities Press, 1965); the terms "object relations" signifies Spitz's commitment to Harry Stack Sullivan's principle of interpersonal relations as opposed to Freud's intrapsychic emphasis; *No and Yes: On the Genesis of Human Communication* (New York: International

Universities Press, 1957). Cf. Ruch, Floyd, *General Psychology and Life* (Chicago: Scott, Foresman, 1953, 134–136; and consult the many articles by John Bowlby on attachment disorder theory published in the 1950s. Cf. also Margaret Mahler, Fred Pine, and Anni Bergman, *The Psychological Birth of the Human Infant* (New York, Basic Books, 1975), passim; Ben Mijuskovic, "Loneliness and Narcissism," *Psychoanalytic Review* (1979–80); and Erlich Shmueli, "On Loneliness, Narcissism, and Intimacy," *The American Journal of Psychoanalysis*, 58:2 (1998). Cf. Lane Degregory, The Tampa Bay Times, *Face in the Window*, Google video, which documents the devastating arrested development of basically a "feral child" over a ten-year span, 2005–2015.

2 Ellenberger, Henri, *The Discovery of the Unconscious: The History and Evolution of Dynamic Psychiatry* (New York: Basic Books, 1970). The roots of dynamic psychiatry go back to Leibniz, 321, 624, 628; Fichte, 517; Schopenhauer, 208–209, 312, 628; and Bergson, 624, 628. Interestingly, Ellenberger even cites Plato's *Symposium* (203–204, 503), and Jakob Boehme (a Christian mystic, who Hegel credits as the first German philosopher (209, 312). Together they all contribute to the principle of dynamism.

3 Fichte, J. G., *Science of Knowledge* translated by Peter Heath (New York: Appleton-Century Crofts, 1970), 97; as an absolutely unconditioned first principle, 99, 104; this is a *sui generis* synthetic act, 135, 262.

4 Mills, Jon, *The Unconscious Abyss: Hegel's Anticipation of Psychoanalysis* (Albany: State University of New York: (2002), 137–138, and passim for important and insightful psychoanalytic discussions on the Fichtean and Hegelian influences on Freud. In *Origins: On the Genesis of Psychic Reality* (Montreal: McGill's-Queen's University, 2010), Mills describes "Fichte's notion of the absolute 'I' that posits itself into existence and declares its being *ex nihilo*," page 8.

5 Freud, Sigmund, *Civilization and Its Discontents*, translated by Joan Riviere (New York: W. W. Norton, 1955), 13–14. Freud's description of the immediacy the infant's "oceanic feeling" is paralleled by Hegel's description of Sense-Certainty in the *Phenomenology* and James' description of the "baby assailed by eyes, ears, nose, skin, and entrails at once, feels it all as one great blooming buzzing confusion" in the *Principles of Psychology* (New York: Dover, 1950), I, 488.

6 Freud, Sigmund, *Totem and Taboo*, translated by James Strachey (New York: W. W. Norton, 1952; originally published 1913), "Omnipotence of Thoughts," 89 and 90, note 1. "Original narcissism" is signaled by Freud as a stage "in which the childish ego enjoyed [total] self-sufficiency."

7 Freud, Sigmund, *A General Introduction to Psychoanalysis*, translated by Joan Riviere (New York: Pemabooks, 1958), 7, 424–425.

8 R. K. Gupta, "Freud and Schopenhauer" in *Schopenhauer: His Philosophical Achievement*, edited by Michael Fox (Sussex: Harvester Press, 1980), 226–235; and cf. Andrew Brook and Christopher Young,

"Schopenhauer and Freud," in the *Oxford Handbook of Philosophy and Psychoanalysis*, edited by Richard Gipps and Michael Lacewing (Part 1, 1994), who credit Schopenhauer's *direct* influence on Freud's treatments of sexual drives, repression, free association, the id, will over intellect, and the disposition toward human evil and narcissism. For his part, Freud offers that he only became aware of Schopenhauer late in life.

9 MacIntyre, Alisdair, *The Unconscious* (London: Kegan Paul, 1958), 64–71, 96–98. But consult the author for some serious criticisms concerning Freud's theoretical construct.

Chapter 15

The limits of self-knowledge

I now wish to concentrate on the issue of personal identity in relation to the limits of our self-knowledge. Selfhood is not only the province of philosophy but of novelists and psychologists as well. The highly subjective form of narration in the novel is singularly suited for expressing the inner feelings of subjective consciousness. Interestingly, the first novel, as a shared vehicle of social communication, was authored by Murasaki Shikibu, an eleventh-century Japanese noblewoman and its dominant theme is loneliness accompanied by its intrinsic connection to boredom (so Pascal and Schopenhauer). *The Tales of Genji* consists of 1,100 running descriptions of human isolation threaded throughout with its rich tapestry chronicling the universality of the human condition.

> What legacy do we bring from our former lives
> That loneliness should be our lot in this one? (page 139).
> There are no words—"lonely" and "forlorn"—seem much too weak—to describe his feelings (page 250).
> The young women were happy enough to be finished with country life which had mostly been loneliness and boredom, but this seacoast did after all have a hold on them (page 320).
> "Parting is the way of the world. It cannot be avoided; but the grief is easier to bear when you have a companion to share it with. I must leave it to your imagination how hard it is for me to go off without you knowing that you are alone" (page 806).
> Sadness, loneliness—they are what life brings.
>
> (page 807)[1]

DOI: 10.4324/9781003156130-16

302 The limits of self-knowledge

Her father, an intellectual, taught her how to read and write, which was highly unusual at the time, and she was well-stationed and respected at her court and her writings greatly esteemed. Interestingly today there is a global concern about loneliness and England has even appointed a Minister of Loneliness. In Japan, the elderly have become pathologically reclusive and only wish to be cared for by their adult children, to live with them, and they rarely venture out in public. No doubt a reaction to the atomic bombings of Hiroshima and Nagasaki resulting in a form of holocaust victimization. The Japanese social work authorities have required that their elderly read the book for its therapeutic effects. Ever since I was an undergraduate, my own experience has been that by reading the classics, it has saved me from imagining that I am the only human being in the universe that is lonely and in my clinical practice I have encouraged subjects—not "patients"—to read certain classic novels for insight. I have cited her work for two reasons: first because it reinforces my thesis that there is a close natural relationship between the temporal narrative form of the novel and human loneliness and second because a thousand years ago a woman was wise enough to be the first to record her feelings, thoughts, and moods in such an elegant and insightful style.

In European literature, *Don Quixote* (1616) is generally credited as one of the first novels and we discover that loneliness can be subjectively illustrated in either the first or the third person narrative form as it portrays the knight errant's solitary search for personal meaning through his delusions. There is also Daniel Defoe's diary of the marooned sailor's isolative experience in *Robinson Crusoe* (1709), initiated Alexander Selkirk's argument with his sea captain, followed by his impetuous request to be put ashore on the next island, which lasted for five years. And there is Emily Brontë's poignant soliloquy in *Wuthering Heights* portraying Catherine's fear of separation from her lover.

> But surely you and everybody have a notion that there is or there should be an existence beyond you. What were the use of my creation if I were entirely contained here? If all else perished, and he remained, I should still continue to be; and if all else remained, and he were annihilated, the universe would turn into a might stranger. I should not seem part of it ... I am Heathcliff—he's

always, always in my mind—not as a pleasure, any more than I am
a pleasure to my self—but as my own being—so don't talk of our
separation again—it is impracticable [i.e., inconceivable].

(chapter X)

We will return to this passage and its dominant theme in our last
chapter because it signals the essential connection between the fear
of isolation and the consequent desire for intimacy. It stresses the
mutuality, the reciprocity of two individuals feeling and thinking as a
single soul.

But let me turn to the more extreme and dynamic states of chronic
and intense loneliness and show how they impact our limited and
narrow path toward self-understanding. The four writers I discuss serve
to illustrate a variety of inherent impediments in attaining adequate
self-knowledge and thus overcoming loneliness. The self will always
be trailed by a worrisome shadow, a dark penumbra surrounding our
loneliness. There will always exist a clinging residue of more work to
be done, more secrets to be controlled lest we discover who we really
are. At the back of each mind, at the bottom of each soul, there will
always remain a feeling of uncertainty, a sense that "I'm not quite there
yet" and "do I wish to press any further?" A hidden voice murmuring
psychological obscenities. Plato's "Know thyself" is fraught with
disturbing forebodings.

I shall present four authors, who describe their crises when forced
to confront their deepest self, their critical Oedipal moment, as it
threatens further disintegration and the realization that perhaps we
are even strangers to our selves.

First, there is the reality that the "self" intrinsically displays a deep
disunity within our "self," that it actually consists in a multiplicity
of separate and irreconcilable selves that are at odds with each other
(Hesse). Second, the self, "at its core," consists of a dark, opaque,
and unfathomable center at the very heart of our "being" (Golding).
Third, that throughout our ordinary and mundane lives we have never
dared question *who* we really are and *why* we exist at all. We have not
confronted the ultimate *meaning* of our own individual existence. That
it is much safer, easier not to question what we may be capable of; that
it is better to "continue living our lives in quiet desperation" (Auden);
better to leave the sleeping dogs of our conflicted values well enough

304 The limits of self-knowledge

alone, as we continue to habitually transpire in modes of unreflective and meaningless obscurity without ever having the courage to consider our unique existential condition (Camus). And fourth, that the ego is ultimately permeated by tangled and knotted filaments of an irretrievable *subconscious*—as opposed to a Freudian unconscious—that it is vulnerable to spontaneous acts that are so deeply submerged that they cannot be accessed under any circumstances; a lurking shadowy antithetical personality, deeply hidden, vying for expression with our surface "self"; a noumenal irrational Will that unknowingly uses us for its own inexplicable devices of furthering what appear to be upon reflection evil acts, excused in the self-utterance, "I was not my self."

Hermann Hesse's novel, *Steppenwolf*, challenges the traditional Western prejudice of regarding the self as a oneness, a unity. Instead, he proposes a radical a *multiplicity of distinct selves*—not merely moods—*but separate selves.* Whereas the tenets of dualism, rationalism, and idealism have assumed the stable predication of a unity, identity, and continuity to self-consciousness, it is precisely this Western misconception that Hesse is disputing.

> It appears to be an inborn and imperative need of all men to regard the self as a unit ... In reality, however, every ego, so far from being a unity, is in the highest degree a manifold world, a constellated heaven, a chaos of forms, of states and stages, of inheritances and potentialities. It appears to be a necessity as imperative as eating and breathing for everyone to be forced to regard this chaos as a unity and to speak of this ego as though it were one-fold and a clearly detached and fixed phenomenon.[2]

And he concludes:

> For there is not a single being ... who is not so conveniently simple that his being can be explained as the sum of two or three principal elements. [The Steppenwolf] consists of a hundred or a thousand selves ... And if ever the suspicion of their manifold being dawns upon men of unusual powers and unusually delicate perceptions, so that, as all genius must, they break through the allusions of the unity of the personality and perceive that the self is made up of a

bundle of [distinct, separate] selves, they have only to say so and at once the majority puts them under lock and key.

Man is neither simple nor a unity. Rather he is a disunified multiplicity, a manifold constellation of complex drives, desires, lusts, instincts, fantasies, vices, and virtues. For Hesse, as for the richest characters in Dostoyevsky's *Notes from Underground*, Ivan and Dimitri in the *Brothers Karamazov*, and Raskolnikov in *Crime and Punishment*, the self is a contradiction, a multifarious conglomeration of inconsistent and even contradictory "tendencies," of both good and evil. For Dostoyevsky, the internal paradox of the multiple self is both its curse and its salvation. Raskolnikov the murderer is a completely different being from Raskolnikov the repentant. It is this spontaneous duality that makes possible the radically religious transformation that provides Dostoyevsky with his existential conviction that even the worst of us can save himself. The Steppenwolf, like the lonely Raskolnikov, is a Nietzschean duality of good and evil, divinity and bestiality, saint and sinner, reasoner and madman, scholar and criminal, as well as the damned and the redeemed. Each *act* and *intention* at the moment of its inception symbolizes the entirety of a distinct and unique personality. There is no measuring and weighing of the good and the bad and coming up with an ameliorating sum. Both Gide's *The Immoralist* and Hesse's *Steppenwolf* present their provocative expressions, regarding the complexities of loneliness, by illustrating their characters, who are never at peace within their own interiority, with feelings and thoughts, that do not "belong" to them in any secure manner. Loneliness proliferates into forms of self-alienation. Theoretically each self can be phenomenologically bracketed and described.

We recall that both Locke and Hume summon memory in their efforts to anchor the self's empirical continuity by recruiting an allegedly chronological restructuring of one's autobiographical and biographical recollections. But William Golding's *Free Fall* rejects this misleading manufactured fiction. As Golding conceives it, a deeper and unstable self is discovered when reflexive loneliness intervenes and intrudes. The anchor of identity, which originally appeared to be tethered to an earlier "self," becomes completely loosened when I seek to secure it to "the boy 'I' once was." I am as an adult, neither temporally continuous with nor contemporary to the child I once was. Indeed,

306 The limits of self-knowledge

when I look back, I am no longer the same person I once was. What or who am I *really* then?

> I see now what I am looking for and why these pictures are not altogether random. I describe them because they seem to be important. They are important simply because they emerge. I care about them. I am the sum of them. I carry round with me this load of memories. Man is not an instantaneous creature, nothing but a physical body and the [stimuli] reaction of the moment. He is an incredible bundle of miscellaneous memories and feelings, of fossils and coral growths. I am not a man who was a boy looking at a tree. It is the difference between the time, the endless row of dead bricks and time, the retake and coil. And there is something even more simple. I can love the child in the garden, on the airfield in Rotten Row, the tough little boy at school because he is not I. He is another person.[3]

I can only love objects and other selves that are different and distinguishable from my self. I am not a subject to my self except when I am telling a story to my self about a boy, who happens to have been "me" (Sartre). That is a child—a different person from my self—that I can love just as I love another being, one distinct from me. And, of course, it follows that "We cannot know about ourselves" (page 139) and therefore that "I don't understand my self" (page 143). For the self is basically both a discontinuity and a disunity "because each consciousness is a dozen [separate mnemonic] worlds" (page 249). Since the lonely ego is not a simplicity but rather a multiplicity; not a unity but a disunity; and not a continuity but a discontinuity, we can conclude that there are ineluctable limits beyond which the individual is incapable of grasping his own "personal identity." Once more, I am a stranger to my "self."

The themes of personal identity and loneliness coupled with the opacity of consciousness are also powerfully interwoven throughout Golding's *Pincher Martin*, a novel dedicated to the Crusoean motif of a disintegrative solitude. It is, as its famous forerunner, the story of a shipwrecked sailor clinging to life on a solitary crag in the ocean, as he is assailed and ravaged by the effects of an indeterminately prolonged isolation. Both the seaman's lonely plight and his determination to hang on to his definable identity as Christopher Hadley Martin's

The limits of self-knowledge   307

lest "he" is reduced to a "black centre of consciousness." Identity or madness?

> The centre cried out, "I'm so alone. Christ! I'm so alone" ... The centre felt the gulping of its throat, sent eyesight on ahead to cling desperately to the next light and then the next—anything to fasten the attention [of consciousness] away from the interior blackness.[4]

Intentionality disregards reflexivity. The powerful dissociative features directly point toward a fragmentation that so readily and often develops into prolonged states of psychosis. Any semblance of a unique or recognizable personality completely disappears under the duress of extreme loneliness, as the intense subjugation of the self eventually leads to a complete loss of identity and psychosis intervenes. An identity, which is comfortably couched in normal social circumstances, a protection which is the product of a complex interlacing of human factors, including societal intercourse, grudging mutual collaborations, unsatisfying companionships, unpleasant intimate exchanges, and so on, which nevertheless all contribute to the establishment of a superficial social identity. But without this societal network, it all collapses when the self is subjected to a complete social isolation.

> How can I have complete identity without a mirror? Once I was a man with twenty photographs of myself—myself at this and that—I could spy on myself and assess the impact of Christopher Hadley Martin on the world. I could find assurance of solidity in the bodies of other people by warmth and caresses and triumphant flesh. I could be a character in a body. But now I am this thing [i.e. consciousness] in here, a great many aches of bruised flesh, a bundle of rags and those lobster arms [i.e. his pinchers] on the rock. The three lights [i.e. his two eyes and consciousness] of my window are not enough to identify me however sufficient they were in the world. But there were other people to describe me to my self—they fell in love with me, they applauded me, they caressed this body, they defined it for me. There were people I got the better of, people who disliked me, people who quarreled with me. Here [on this rocky crag], I have nothing to quarrel with. I am in danger of losing my definition.
>
> (page 132)

308   The limits of self-knowledge

Having worked with psychotics for many years, it has been my experience that loneliness plays the most significant role in the disorder. One simply—and desperately—spontaneously creates an alternate reality. Clinically I spent time with a young man who had undergone five years of solitary confinement in prison; he was only twenty-four. He could only come in with his girlfriend because his hold on reality was so fragile that he needed a constant reaffirmation of "who" he "is" let alone "who" he "was" and even "why" he was there.

In Albert Camus's existential novel, *The Stranger*, the avoidance of a confrontation with one's own loneliness is avoided by the character's habitual diversions and sexual dalliances. The protagonist, Mersault, is virtually a human automaton, as he represents an unreflective consciousness, whose entire existence is confined to his daily habitual routines and his valueless reactions to an external parade of neutral circumstances, as he superficially functions oblivious to his own happiness or unhappiness. The deeper existential meaning of his life slumbers on until one day he essentially commits a purely gratuitous, senseless killing. Without a sufficiently discernable motive, he kills an Arab, a complete stranger, on a beach without any apparent reason, justification, or motive, except for the fact that the sun was shining. At the ensuing trial, the prosecution portrays him as a habitually uncaring person, even disinterested at his mother's funeral. His disengagement during the trial further corroborates his "character" as a murderer. But once sentenced to death, he is compelled to confront the significance of his unique existence. Only then does he finally realize that human companionship is the only means of personal salvation from loneliness and that a single strand of his mistress's hair has infinitely more value than all the abstract conceptions of a priest's God. But now it is too late, and he is sentenced to death. Having lost any semblance or hope for understanding, the only recognition he seeks to receive is a public display of hatred.

> All that was left to be accomplished for me to feel less lonely [*moins seul*], all that remained was that on the day of my execution there would be a huge crowd of spectators and that they should greet me with howls of execration.[5]

The juxtaposition between Mersault's daily uneventful mode of existence, his habitual routines, his continual uncaring attitude, all of which symbolize our own tendencies, in each of us, to mechanically "exist" throughout our lives without ever questioning *either* the meaninglessness *or* the value of our individual existence; our avoidance in assuming responsibility for creating our values or in making decisions, commitments in the face of our "naked existence," confronting our loneliness and our imminent death. We will not get a second chance.

The same criticism that we take our existence uncritically for granted is at the heart of Kierkegaard's voluminous writings. The ethical man goes about his business without reflection, without ever thinking about the terrifying paradox of faith. He attends church punctually every Sunday and leaves it at that. He fulfills his Kantian duty to his fellow man without ever confronting what it truly means to be a Christian— the uniquely paradoxical *either/or* demands of faith.

More sympathetically, Camus's the *Myth of Sisyphus* shows how the rebellious existential hero overcomes the "absurdity" of his mortality and suffering by asserting his human dignity, by opposing his sentence at each moment of his life. It is symbolized by Sisyphus' sense of pride, bravery, and dignity as he repetitiously and endlessly rolls his boulder uphill, reaches the summit of his toil, and reflexively looks back on his labors. It is an existential "attitude," comparable to Nietzsche's "eternal affirmation," continually willing to repeat one's life and values—regardless. It is the self alone that can invest meaningfulness and purpose in one's own existence. Values are not the sort of *meanings* that can be transmitted by God's written commandments; values are not engrained in our allegedly common and universal human nature; nor are values simply given to us by our artificial social environments. Ethical values are the creations of our lonely selves and they remain absolute only as long as we choose to affirm them. At critical moments in our lives, we are confronted with our eventual death and we are forced to face it existentially and alone. This is what disturbed Sartre about Freudian psychoanalysis, namely that we blame others for our unhappiness and misery. Children blame their parents for their unhappiness and the parents in turn blame their parents. In the end, no one is to blame. But the responsibility for the meaning of our values is circumscribed for each self alone to create. Who I am and what I value is my responsibility alone. Superficial sentiments may on the face of it *appear* as shared with others, but the deepest meaning of one's existence and eventual death can only be faced alone. It is incumbent on

310 The limits of self-knowledge

each of us to assume the responsibility for our investitures in our own existence, within the confines of our own solitude; to seek the *meaning* of who we are and what it was "all about." Beyond that, each of us dies alone (Tolstoy, *The Death of Ivan Ilyich*).

We have already discussed *The Plague* in an earlier chapter with its optimistic message of hope suggesting how physical suffering, loneliness, and death can be vanquished by communal cooperation through the strategy of a concerted human rebellion against the "absurdities" of the plague, by unifying with others of our kind thereby exemplifying a common bond within our mutual humanity. *But* should we not counterpose that perhaps the visitation of "plague" itself may be of human origin; perhaps it is the Nazi occupation of France.[6]

Its optimistic outlook is mistaken, and it is in error precisely because humans in groups are unable to sustain each other for extended periods of time due to "conflicts of self-interest." In the final analysis, their narcissistic impulses invariably intervene and prevail. The erroneous perspective in Camus's outlook is generated by his commitment to a false Cartesian paradigm of a shared *group-consciousness*, one which assumes a stable "ethical" clarity, distinctness, and unity within the aggregation; the delusion of a group consensus on what should be done and how over an extended period of time. In the novel, Camus is persuaded that if we "rationally," reflexively engage in a common enterprise, we shall not only discover our true "common selves"—a contradiction in terms—but also a clear and lucid idea of our legitimate desire for human companionship and cooperation. Group intimacy is a contradiction in terms. This was also Marx's error in trusting in the fiction of a homogeneous proletariat class-consciousness. It is also Sartre's mistake in his late straying toward communism. Class-consciousness and self-consciousness are *qualitatively* radically different. The salvation of intimacy is personal; group movements are fraught with collective egoism and politics. On this issue, Freud was clearly right. However one manipulates economic equality as one pleases, individual aggression and narcissism will prevail. It is not systems that are bad but individuals. This is also Weber's point: moral issues cannot be solved by political—or economic—means. Political ethics is a contradiction in terms.

Joseph Conrad traces the immanent journey of the soul as it plunges into its own innermost depths, through the darkest recesses of

The limits of self-knowledge 311

consciousness, as it confronts our deepest solitude, as it is consumed by the unbridled power of the Schopenhauerian subconscious while fraught with unchecked desires and lusts.[7] Perhaps the ablest and, certainly from my exegetical perspective, the most congenial of Conradian interpreters, Albert Guerard, has described the gloomy novel as a Jungian descent into the depths of the individual soul, a study of dark introspection, a perilous nocturnal journey toward the center of the soul, a visit within "the black inward abyss of the self." The book compels us to look "into the deeper regions of the mind," through those "great dark meditations" of reflexive thought, which, if sufficiently intensified and prolonged, will eventually discover within each self "what no other man can ever know." The novel exposes the deepest and darkest meanings inhabiting the nether regions of the soul, when its thirst for self-knowledge is loosened within the labyrinthine recesses and depths of his own consciousness and deceptive heart. "The mind of man is capable of anything—because everything is in it, all the past as well as all the future. What was there after all … but truth … truth stripped of its cloak of time." While Marlow is precariously tied to the world of commerce with its fragile civilization, he ponders Kurtz, who has obviously slipped beyond—or beneath—human comprehension. By its very nature the inquiry into truth assumes the aspect, the quality of a dream; a Dionysian exploration receding back into a timeless and primitive subconscious, through impulses long-hidden and controlled, and erupting without constraint. As Marlow expresses it:

> I am trying to tell you a dream—making a vain attempt, because no relation of a dream can convey the dream sensation…No, it is impossible; it is impossible to convey the life-sensation of any given epoch of one's existence—that which makes its truth, its meaning—its subtle and penetrating essence. It is impossible. We live as we dream—alone.

(page 44)

Granted that we are incapable, as Bergson warns, of translating the subjective intuitional qualities of a dream into the hard and brittle precision of an abstract, public language, still isn't there something we may succeed in communicating regarding the ultimate depths of human existence? And the answer is no. Self-consciousness is qualitatively

312 The limits of self-knowledge

subjective, intimate, and highly personal. Like the deepest ocean depths, it is teeming with various forms of life, each variety surviving by grotesque means. This is the reality, which Kurtz realizes within himself. The symbolic meaning of the jungle darkness stands for both the evil permeating it as a moral vacuum where anything can transpire; but it also mirrors, just as surely, the unfathomable aloneness that Kurtz has chosen for his unobserved abode of secrecy through his self-imposed isolation. Kurtz is desperately alone and lonely but he has willingly chosen his situation. "Is [Kurtz] alone there?" "Yes" (page 52). "Kurtz wandered alone far into the depths of the forest" (page 94); "how can you imagine what particular region of the first ages of man's untramelled feet may take him into by way of solitude—utter solitude" (page 82); "there was nothing either above or below him … he had kicked himself loose of the earth" and by implication from his fellow man and all ethical values; "he was all alone" (page 112). Kurtz's existence transpires not only within the emptiness of a moral vacuum, symbolized by the primitive and lawless jungle, but at the same time he exists in the midst of a psychological void as well. And what he realizes is the utter horror of his absolute loneliness: "his soul had gone mad. Being alone in the wilderness, it had looked into himself, and, by heavens! I tell you, it had gone mad" (page 113). His own self-condemnation on his inner vision—like Oedipus'—is to pronounce it as "The horror; the horror" (page 118). And the horror is simply that each of us, separately transpires through life alone and lonely. But rather than recognize this primeval Orphic truth, we mask our condition from our selves by exploiting false ideals and foisting Idols of the Cave and the Tribe (Bacon) lest we encounter the dark visage of our isolation, lest we confront the darkness, which gnaws within that is more than a match for the jungle blackness without. This is "the naked horror of our irredeemable loneliness," to borrow a phrase from Ludwig Binswanger, which Kurtz visualizes in his last earthly moments.

A similar barrier to self-knowledge can be found in Carl Jung, who, like Conrad, equally falls under the sway of the Schopenhauerian subconscious with his concept of the "shadow self." As an archetype, it represents the evolutionary surfacing of our animal instincts and the need to guard against our subconscious desires. It is also the mythical source of our tendencies toward unchecked evil and our theistic

The limits of self-knowledge 313

conception of "original sin," as well as the darkest side of the Freudian Id, which never appears before the light of self-consciousness. Its essence is to be self-unaware of its own self, as a *persona* it performs its acts while wearing the anonymity of a theater mask, all the while masquerading through life under the guise of "false colors" and discreetly hiding even from its own deeper self.

> The *shadow* is the sum of those personal characteristics that the individual wishes to hide from the others and from himself. But the more the individual tries to hide it from himself, the more the shadow may become active and evil-doing. An example from literature was "The Dark Monk," which accompanied the monk Medardus in Holman's novel *The Devils Elixirs*. This was the literary example of the "shadow" emancipating itself from the control of the conscious personality to commit evil actions behind its back. But the shadow can also be projected; then the individual sees his own dark features reflected in another person whom he may choose as a scapegoat. At times too, owing to the influence of alcohol or some other cause, the shadow can temporally take hold of an individual, who might later be surprised that he was capable of such evil behavior. The Jungian concept of the shadow should not be confused with the Freudian concept of the repressed; it is related to the phenomenon of [subconscious?] *unawareness* as opposed to unconsciousness. To unawareness belong those aspects of the world and oneself that an individual does not see, although he could if he honestly wanted to. A man can visualize himself as a good husband and father, who is liked by his subordinates and respected by his fellow citizens, and yet he ignores the fact that he is a selfish husband, tyrannical father, and hated by his subordinates and more feared than respected by his fellow men. This negative side of which this man is unaware is precisely what Jung calls the shadow.[8]

We "justify" scapegoating others by projecting our worst desires and our flaws unto others.

Again, unlike the Schopenhauerian subconscious, Freud's unconscious is theoretically *retrievable* in principle—otherwise psychoanalysis could not be therapeutic. We must be able to relive, in some significant

314 The limits of self-knowledge

sense, to re-experience, our traumatic and repressed experiences. Freud is a psychological determinist He believes he is conducting a scientific enterprise. All psychological sciences rely on *causal predictability*. The cause is the traumatic event, which is first repressed and then resurfaces as the symptomatic neurotic effect. But, according to Jung, the dynamic of the unconscious involves to a marked degree what he describes as a "hypothetical" limit to adequate self-knowledge because there will always remain a residue of untruth even from the very "center" of consciousness, which nevertheless forcefully "influences" the ego (Golding, *Pincher Martin; Lord of the Flies*). Nevertheless, despite this interior complexity, the ego remains a center, a principle of unification, whether sighted or blind, a binding, a synthesizing of the self within its self (Jung, 1960c). Thus, Jung defines the ego as "a continuous center of consciousness, whose presence has made itself felt since the days of childhood." In his memoirs, *Memories, Dreams, Reflections*, Jung asserts that next to Kant, Schopenhauer is the first philosopher "who had the courage to see that all was not for the best in the fundaments of the universe." Instinctual psychology begins with Fichte and Schopenhauer, with voluntarism—and with desires—as opposed to cognition.

> Just as Schopenhauer's will is not rational, purposeful volition but a blind and involuntary force, Freud's [and Jung's] id, too, is 'a primitive irrational quality,' not accessible to rational admonishment, 'the obscure part of our personality,' 'a chaos, a cauldron of seething excitement.' Like the will, the id does not think, it only wishes and acts. Like the will, again, it is insatiable—an endless, restless, tormented striving for satisfaction. The power of the id expresses the true purpose of the organismic life. This consists in the satisfaction of innate needs. The id 'has no organization and no unified will, only an impulsion to obtain satisfaction for the instinctual needs in accordance with the pleasure principle.' It stands for the untamed passions, it is the seat of the instincts, it is similar in its basic irrationality to the imperious will in Schopenhauer. Jung points out this crucial similarity. In suggesting that the unconscious drives for boundless and immediate satisfaction without regard for others, Jung agrees with Schopenhauer, 'who says of the egoism of the blind World Will that it is so strong

The limits of self-knowledge   315

that a man could slay his brother merely to grease his boots with his brother's fat.[9]

But again, we cannot let ourselves be confused. Either the unconscious is retrievable, or it is not. If it is retrievable, then psychology can give it a universal causal structure and it can be a predictive science. If it is irretrievable, then psychology cannot be a predictive science. As we observed in "Kant and Schopenhauer on Reality," Schopenhauer cannot have it both ways; either the irrational Will—if it affects mankind—cannot be causally structured; and if it cannot, then it is virtually meaningless and merely noumenal in the Kantian sense. In short, it is human, all-too human.

Nevertheless, Jung speculates on whether the ego is continuous throughout the span of our lives? Apparently not because "It is a fact that in the early years of life there is no continuous memory; at most there are islands of consciousness, which are like single lamps or lighted objects in the far flung darkness" (Jung, Volume 8, 390). May we not then legitimately, in our role as critics, question whether there is anything more permanent after adolescence or even after maturity? Jung's attempt to ground personal identity is no better than Locke's effort in summoning memory. In so far as Jung's meta-psychological theory is concerned, it seems that no one can truly know one's self and thus to that extent each of us remains separately alone and lonely.[10]

The present chapter argues that we are lonely because of the limits of our own self-knowledge. It follows that if there are limits in relation to our own selves, it would be unlikely that we could know others better than our selves. No wonder Schopenhauer opted for the soporific Buddhist denial of the self as an antidote to self-discovery.

Notes

1 Shikibu, Murasaki, *Tales of Genji*, translated by E. G. Seidensticker (New York: Alfred A. Knopf, 1978), *passim.*
2 Hesse, Herman, *Steppenwolf* (New York: Holt, Rinehart & Winston, 1972). Psychiatrically speaking, there are Dissociative Identity Disorders (*DSM*, 300.14), which symptoms include "The presence of two or more identities or personality states each with its own relatively enduring pattern of perceiving, relating to, and thinking about the environment and the self." Years ago, "multiple personality" disorders were a favorite literary topic.

Cf. Corbett Thigpen and Hervey Cleckley, *Three Faces of Eve* (1957); F. R. Schreiber, *Sybil* (Warren Books, 1973), in which the text documented sixteen *distinct* personalities; and Daniel Keys, *The Minds of Billy Milligan* (New York: Random House, 1981), which claimed twenty-four personalities. In all three cases, the victims suffered severe sexual abuse and learned to dissociate from the pain during the abuse. The different "selves" were allegedly aware of each other, but the core personality was unaware of the "selves." The trances were primarily in the nature of fugue states, a sort of "spacing out" conditioned by dissociating while the abuse was occurring.

3 Golding, William, *Free Fall* (New York: Harcourt Brace, 1959), 46; 8–12.

4 Golding, William, *Pincher Martin: The Two Deaths of Christopher Martin* (San Diego: Harcourt, Brace & Co., 1956), 7, 161, 174, 176, 180–182, 186, 188, 194.

5 Camus, Albert, *The Stanger*, cf. Albert Maquet, *Albert Camus: The Invincible Summer* (New York: George Braziller, 1958), 84, 94, 108.

6 Camus, Albert, *The Plague* (1947), 74, 81, 84, 108, which deals with the classic "problem of evil," and published soon after the Second World War. During the conflict, there were over one thousand concentration camps in seventeen countries in Europe, from 1939–1945, with some of the worst—if that adjective has any meaning in this context—at Buchenwald, Dachau, Ravensbruck, Auschwitz, Treblinka, and especially Jasenovac. Now the difference is that if a third effort at world supremacy unfolds, there are several nations with nuclear weapons and narcissistic leaders, so the hostilities should end quickly.

7 Conrad, Joseph, *Heart of Darkness*, Introduction by Albert Guerard (1971); cf. Bruce Johnson, *Conrad's Models of the Mind* (Minneapolis: University of Minnesota Press, 1971) offering illuminating contextual discussions of Conrad's involvement with psychoanalytic, existential, Freudian, Jungian, and Sartrean but especially Schopenhauerian themes, 41–53.

8 Ellenberger, Henri, *The Discovery of the Unconscious: The History and Evolution of Dynamic Psychiatry* (New York: Basic Books, 1970), 707, 664–665.

9 R. K. Gupta, "Freud and Schopenhauer," 227–228, in *Schopenhauer: His Achievement*, edited by Michael Fox (Sussex: Harvester Press, 1980).

10 Jung, Carl, *The Collected Works of C. G. Jung* (London: Routledge & Kegan Paul, 1960), (a) Vol. 7, 156–157, note 1; (b) Vol. 8, 119, 171–172, 310 ff.; and (c) Vol. 9, Pt. 2, 4–5, 8–10, 218–219.

Chapter 16

The dynamics of intimacy and empathy

I have sought to show (a) *that* the motivational drive to avoid loneliness is universal; it constitutes the existential human condition; (b) *why* this is so by offering a unified Kantian and Husserlian theory of consciousness; (c) the generated *consequences* of anger, anxiety, depression, shame, and guilt, and so on. But now I wish to address (d) its possible therapeutic *remedies.*

Loneliness can be incredibly intense. Therefore, its resolution must be correspondingly intense. In the following, I outline six possible *dynamic* modes of human separation. By "dynamic," I mean that the originating source lies in consciousness instead of the external world. First, developmentally there is the painful ejection of the fetus from the womb (object-object; biological separation). Freud describes it as the initial state of anxiety. Second, Freud's "oceanic feeling," which is the conditioning stage for primary narcissism, as the incipient ego mistakenly identities with the totality and boundlessness of "reality"); "it" is everything as it starts its separation from inanimate things and realizes it *desires* a specific "object," its mother's breast as an independent object (self-conceptual object separation; epistemic; intrapsychic). This represents the most primitive version of what Kant posits as the minimal *relational* requirement for self-consciousness to appear. Third, the separation of the self from the other self, usually the mother, which produces a *dialectic* of self-other than self separation, thus generating a narcissistic conflict between the child and the mother (interpersonal separation; Hegel's Lordship and Bondage relation). The fourth is not properly a developmental stage but rather a form of *internal* self-separation, the self in conflict within its own self, a form of intrapsychic separation in response to acute or chronic loneliness

DOI: 10.4324/9781003156130-17

318 The dynamics of intimacy and empathy

(psychosis), although Hegel describes insanity in his Anthropology as an early stage of development (*Philosophy of Mind*, Sections 408, *Zusatz*). Fifth, the separation of the self from cherished *values*, usually the result of disillusionments. Philosophers distinguish (a) primary "qualities," i.e., extensive quantities, always matter and often motion, from (b) subjective qualities, sensations and feelings; and both from (c) the tertiary qualities of *value*. *Humans are the only higher order animals capable of creating and committing to value distinctions*: from goodness to evil (ethics); from beauty to plainness (aesthetics); and from intimacy to loneliness. And sixth, the realization of the separation of the self from life in death, and the knowledge that the world will blithely move forward in the absence of one's life without missing a beat. Of special note, these are all constituted as relations within consciousness.

All *emotional*—as opposed to cognitive—separations involve anger, anxiety, depression, i.e., withdrawal issues. Throughout the previous text, I have suggested that we should view the present study in the context of a philosophical Battle between the Giants and the Gods. Just as momentously, we can interpret it as Freud's conflict between the God of Death, Thanatos, and the God of Unity, Eros, or between the dynamics of separation versus intimacy.

But we need to look more closely at the fifth form of separation, the self from its own created values because it is intrinsically connected to intimacy and empathy. I have emphasized Max Weber's thesis that both politics, i.e., ethics and science are constitutionally incapable of addressing issues of qualitative values. Humans alone are the only species capable of formulating *explicit* principles and judgments of *value* and the ability to establish criteria in applying those judgments to the self as well as to others. Although both secondary qualities, sensations and feelings, are subjective and variable and so are tertiary qualities, the latter serve as cognitive judgments and motivating principles, as guides in determining the direction we wish our lives to take. And as spontaneous creations, they can pivot at will. Sensations and feelings are immediate and incorrigible—neither true or false; judgments, however, are mediate cognitive assertions and we can argue about them.

Intimacy promotes a sense of belonging, togetherness, closeness, in short, a feeling of unity. In fact, this feeling is so strong that it can overcome our illusion of solipsism. The "problem of solipsism"

The dynamics of intimacy and empathy   319

cannot be "solved" epistemically; it must be addressed emotionally, just as Catherine expresses it in *Wuthering Heights* (Chapter 15). As previously discussed, Husserl's cognitive effort to recruit intimacy in his Fifth Meditation fails because he violates his own epistemic principle that *eidetic* meanings must be intuitive, immediate. But I shall argue that the solution to solipsism cannot run along a cognitive track but rather an *affective* one. It is grounded in the emotional path of empathy leading to intimacy as a value.

Currently the term "empathy" is often misused, it amounts to sympathy or even pity. Originally it was coined as an aesthetic concept by Theodor Lipps. According to Lipps, empathy is defined as a *projection* of one's feelings into an aesthetic object. For example, in watching a dancer, the observer projects his own sense of balance, beauty, freedom, rhythm into the dancer's *expressive* movements (Croce, *Aesthetic*). My valued qualities are projected and fused into the artistic *expression* of the dancer. The emotions *seem* to interpenetrate, *appear* to fuse and belong to and within the other self. The intentional transmission of aesthetic value is *projected* beyond my self into the person of the other (Feuerbach).

> Empathy is the fact that the antithesis between my self and the object disappears...I feel active in the movement or in the moving figure and through projecting my self into it, I feel myself striving and performing the same movement ... I am transported into it. I am, so far as my consciousness is concerned, entirely and wholly identical with it. Thus feeling my self active in the observed human figure, I feel also in it free, facile, proud. This is esthetic imitation and this imitation is at the same time esthetic empathy.[1]

But the flaw is that in Lipps's account, it is one-sided. The affections, feelings, and the expressions must be shared, mutual, and reciprocal. It is the difference between merely watching a dancer and emotionally dancing with her. In the *Cartesian Meditations*, Husserl sought to recruit empathy as a solution to the problem of solipsism. But the difficulty in his attempt is that he violates his own criterion of eidetic intuition by employing *mediate* relations, "analogical presentations," "mirroring," appresentations," and worse a "bodily" identification, as a placing of my body into the spatial place of the other's body, thereby

320 The dynamics of intimacy and empathy

violating his own criterion of eidetic intuition. Hence the effort is a failure. Solipsism is a theory that claims only my mind exists. It has nothing to do with bodies; it is about consciousnesses. True empathy must be mutual, reciprocal. For example, it would be odd for a mother to say, "I empathize with my newborn baby."

Consider two genuine examples of empathy. A young couple experiences the death of their only child. Their grief and sense of loss is qualitatively the same, the memories, the aspirations are mutual. Or imagine a loving older couple, after a long and happy marriage, being told that one of them has been diagnosed with terminal cancer. *Empathy* dynamically involves a *mutual* sharing of (a) feelings; (b) meanings; and (c) affection. And *intimacy* means a second and deeper reciprocal sharing of mutual (d) trust; (e) respect; and (f) values. This sharing can be between (a) equals (above); or (b) age-appropriate; or (c) status-appropriate to and with dual selves. By age-appropriate, for example, I mean the relation of sharing between a father and his son with both exhibiting a mutual relation of trust, respect, and values. But it also occurs in more complex status-appropriate intimacies, for example in the relation between the finite human soul and a transcendent God through the mediation of Christ. For instance, for a Christian, the desire for communion and intimacy with God *mediates* through the intermediary agency of Christ and it is "brokered" through passion. The human soul *empathizes* with Christ's suffering on the Cross, with his poignant plea to God not to be forsaken, and in turn his suffering resonates through Christ's love for mankind to God. The symbol, the figure of the crucified Christ on the Cross, is one of loneliness and the fear of abandonment. There is an intensity of sharing, of empathy through Christ to a communion, an expression of intimacy with God, a mutual relation connecting the faithful soul of the believer through Christ to God.

Kierkegaard distinguishes three orders of existential values: first, hedonistic aesthetic values, the physical pleasures of Don Juan; second, the ethical values embodied in Kant's universal categorical imperative; and third the individual's values exemplified in Abraham's paradoxical faith.

All shared intimacies are answers to solipsism. Without intimacy, both solipsism and loneliness are unanswerable and ineradicable. One *feels* a mutual sense of belonging; one feels the unity of two souls belonging to and with each other. The solution is *affective* rather than cognitive. Intimacy promotes a sense of belonging, togetherness, closeness, a feeling, and a meaning of unity so powerful that it intentionally and reflexively overcomes our delusion of solipsism. The "problem of solipsism" cannot be "solved" epistemically; it must be addressed emotionally, just as Catherine expresses it in *Wuthering Heights*.

Kant's second formulation of the categorical imperative is a good guide for achieving intimacy. "Always treat the other self as if they had infinite worth and dignity and never as a means for your own selfish or utilitarian ends." If two individuals respect that rule with each putting the other's wellbeing foremost, then intimacy will have been achieved.

Years ago there was a theoretical movement promoting philosophical counseling. The idea was that actually many crises are philosophical in nature, as opposed to psychological. Philosophical counseling was being promoted for individuals and groups by concentrating on certain intellectual themes and writings. Loneliness was one of those themes. Seeing it through the eyes of great writers, one can achieve insight and understanding, a therapeutic perspective. As Aristotle advises, history deals with particulars whereas philosophy treats universal truths.[2]

Notes

1 Lipps, Theodor, "Empathy, Inner Imitation, and Sense Feelings," in *A Modern Book of Esthetics: An Anthology*, edited by Melvin Rader (New York: Holt, Rinehart, and Winston, 1960), 375. Cf. Edith Stein, *The Collected Works of Edith Stein*, edited by Sister Benedict (Washington, DC: ICS Publication, 1989), "On the Problem of Empathy," III, which offers a physico-psychological approach in contrast to Husserl's "idealistic" account provided in the *Cartesian Meditations*.

2 Mijuskovic, Ben, "Some Reflections on Philosophical Counseling," in *Essays on Philosophical Counseling*, edited by Ran Lahav and Maria da Venza Tillmanns (Lanham, MD: University Press of America, 1995), Chapter Five; "Theories of Consciousness, Therapy, and Loneliness," in *Philosophy, Counseling and Psychotherapy*, edited by Elliot Cohen and Samuel Zinaich (Newcastle on Tyne: Cambridge Scholars Press, 2013); Chapter Four; and "Further Reflections on Philosophical Counseling," *Zeitschrift fuer Phiosophie Praxis*, 2 (1996).

Index

Achilles argument 202, 215–216; *see also* simplicity premise
Adler, Alfred 254, 271
animals: consciousness 22, 87, 128, 166, 226; identity 154, 185; incapable of value distinctions 5, 276, 318; sensation 101, 124; souls 139, 232–233
Anselm 10, 33, 87–88, 89, 127
Aquinas, Thomas 28
Arendt, Hannah 272
Aristophanes 261–262
Aristotle: Being 94; *Categories* 9; conflicting declarations 227; *De Anima* 9, 227, 255; definition of philosophy 211, 249, 321; *dynamis-energeia-entelecheia* distinction 27, 35, 37; empiricism 25; friendship 257; happiness 253, 262–263; intentionality 222; metaphysical dualism 9, 36, 232–233; *Metaphysics* 9, 21, 27, 35–37, 94, 105, 222, 227, 248, 253; *Nichomachean Ethics* 27, 253, 255, 263; *Physics* 21, 222; *Poetics* 253, 260; polis 263; *Politics* 263; psychology 255, 262–263; spontaneity 35, 37; unity of self-consciousness 105; Unmoved Mover 35, 36, 37, 38, 92, 102–103, 248
Armstrong, D. M. 236–237, 238–240, 241, 242, 243, 244, 248
Arnauld, Antoine 138–139, 140
associationism 101, 112
atomism 6, 50, 100, 237, 248
Augustine: creation 22; first principle 250; free will 22, 27, 28; "I believe so that I may understand" 10; intentionality 222; loneliness 31;

Original Sin 29, 46; principle of indubitability 127
Ayer, A. J. 176, 219, 220

Bacon, Francis 91
Bain, Alexander 55, 117
Balzac, Honoré de 275
Barrett, William 84–85
Bauer, Bruno 285
Bayle, Pierre 200, 266
Beck, L. J. 135–136, 138, 143–144
Beck, Lewis White 39, 104
behavioral psychology 1, 4, 102, 112, 114, 238, 241, 242, 248, 276
Bentham, Jeremy 103, 254
Bergson, Henri-Louis 50–51, 109–117, 119, 227, 230, 248, 285
Berkeley, George 17, 66, 147, 179, 195
Bettelheim, Bruno 267–268
biosciences 1, 60, 102, 248
Boehme, Jacob 91–92
Brentano, Franz: immateriality of the soul 231–233; intentionality 222, 223–229, 233–234, 243, 244; psychology as a science 231; time-consciousness 226–227, 230
British Platonists *see* Cambridge Platonists
Brontë, Emily 302–303, 319
Buddhism 87, 252
Burke, Edmund 283

Calvinism 10, 30, 161, 172, 277
Cambridge Platonists 125, 129, 131, 154, 155, 160; rationalist doctrines 161, 172
Camus, Albert 29, 308–309, 310
Catholicism 10, 30

Index   323

causality 4, 28, 44, 50–51, 78, 86, 101, 103, 110–113, 114–115, 127, 128, 195, 244, 250; neuroscience 6, 68, 102, 112, 132, 237, 240; psychoanalysis 25, 26; psychology 27, 102, 112, 114, 267, 296, 314, 315
Central-State Materialism 238, 241, 248
Cervantes, Miguel de 302
Chomsky, Noam 187
Christianity: Age of Faith 10; definition of the soul 153; free will 27–28, 172, 251; and loneliness 259, 264–265; role of intimacy 320; role of spontaneity 28, 29–30, 31–33; *see also* Calvinism; Catholicism
Clarke, Samuel 155–156, 199, 200–201
cogito 32, 33, 49, 52, 127, 129–130, 142, 143, 145, 152, 155, 164, 189–190, 212–213, 219, 279, 291
cognitive behavioral therapy 1, 120
coherence theory of truth 9, 24, 25, 105
Collier, Arthur 65–66
color 23, 24, 40, 53, 79, 101, 110, 187, 255
Comte, Auguste 239, 266
Conrad, Joseph 48, 280, 310–311, 312
Cooper, Anthony Ashley, Third Earl of Shaftesbury: influence on Hume 200; and Locke 171; loneliness 283; metaphysical dualism 174–175; "moral sense" doctrine 171, 172, 196; personal identity 175–178
Cornford, Frances MacDonald 126
correspondence theory of truth 25
creation 21–22; *ex nihilio* 21, 28, 34, 92, 161
Cudworth, Ralph 131, 154, 155, 178

Dante Alighieri 275
Defoe, Daniel 278, 302
Democritus 6, 9, 100, 102, 237
Descartes, René: cogito 32, 33, 49, 52, 127, 129–130, 142, 143, 145, 152, 155, 164, 189–190, 212–213, 219, 279, 291; emotions 254, 266; God 17, 141–142, 146; intellect and will 28; loneliness 31–32, 33, 146; mediate judgment 146; *Meditations on First Philosophy* 14, 28, 30–31, 33, 127, 137, 139–142, 143–146, 147, 165, 266; mortality 266; piece of wax 129–130, 131–137, 143, 144–145; "Problem of Divine Attributes in

God" 114–115; qualitative values 129, 130–131; simplicity premise 11; skepticism 124, 125, 127; soul 128, 139–140, 141; spontaneity 30–33, 130, 142, 143, 146, 163–164
Desmaizeaux, Pierre 200, 204–205
determinism 26, 28, 44, 48, 62, 68, 112, 296, 314; and free will 71, 100, 111, 129, 251
Dickens, Charles 278
Dodwell, Henry 155–156
Dostoyevsky, Fyodor 305
Durkheim, Emile 278–279

egoism: collective 310; distinguished from narcissism 294; Hegel 279, 284; Hobbes 102, 258, 266; Schopenhauer 45–46, 266, 314–315; *see also* narcissism
Ellenberger, Henri 289, 292
empathy: concept of 319; and intimacy 19, 320; lack of 298; and solipsism 231, 246, 319–320
empiricism 24, 25, 50, 65, 76, 82, 92, 112, 132, 167, 194, 225; Hume 173, 179, 198, 283; Locke 152, 157, 158, 161, 164, 165, 179, 228; and loneliness 283–284
Epic of Gilgamesh 259
Epicureanism 21–22, 100, 186, 263
Epicurus 21, 100, 237
Ewing, A. C. 65, 66
existentialism 83, 84, 173–174, 267, 281–282
extroversion 254, 255

Feuerbach, Ludwig 266, 284, 285
Fichte, J. G. 40–41, 250, 289–292, 295–296
Ficino, Marsilio 10, 125
First World War 250, 272
free will 22, 27–28, 30, 34, 39, 61, 72, 116, 172, 251; and determinism 71, 100, 111, 129, 251
Freud, Sigmund: and coherence theory 9; Eros and Thanatos 318; Greek myths 261–262, 294; hedonism 106; loneliness 267; narcissism 46, 71, 258, 292, 293–294, 295, 310; "oceanic feeling" 276, 291, 292, 293, 295, 317; as phenomenalist 60; principle of libidinal energy 25, 26, 254, 276;

324 Index

reality principle 297; repressed energy
254; unconscious 48, 167, 288–289,
295, 313–314
friendship 263; *see also* intimacy
Fromm, Erich 274–276
Fromm-Reichmann, Frieda 253,
273–274

genius 26, 27
Gibson, A. B. 134–135
Gide, André 305
God: as creator 32, 34, 196, 291;
estrangement from 265, 275, 281–282,
284; existence of 10, 33, 61, 87–88, 89,
90; rationalist view 77; unknowability
89–90; *see also* Calvinism; Christianity
Golding, William 305–307
gravity 45, 77, 102, 105, 106, 107
Greek dramas 260–261
Greek myths 259–260, 261–262, 270,
294
Grene, Marjorie 53, 247
Guerard, Albert 311
Gueroult, Martial 145–146

Hardy, Thomas 280
Hegel, G. W. F.: and Aristotle 27, 36–37,
105; coherence theory 24; criticism of
83–85; criticism of Kant 82, 85, 104;
criticism of Stoicism 263; desire for
unilateral recognition 258; dialectic
method 126–127; freedom 103,
104–108; God 90–91, 94; idealism
76–77, 79, 80, 81, 92–93; *Lectures on
the History of Philosophy* 36–37, 77,
80, 87–88, 89, 90–91, 126, 127,
194–195; loneliness 95–96, 107–108,
297; metaphysical dualism 147;
nationalism 266; Oedipus myth
260; pantheism 85, 86, 88, 89,
92; phenomenalism 194–195;
Phenomenology of Spirit 42, 43, 76,
77, 78, 80, 81, 85, 86, 92, 93, 95–96,
105, 258, 265, 284, 291, 297; and Plato
105; Quantity and Quality 42–43, 75,
77, 80–81, 82, 85–86, 87, 94–95, 127,
251–252; *Science of Logic* 42, 43, 75,
76–77, 78, 80, 81, 82–83, 84, 85, 86,
87, 88, 89, 91–92, 93, 94, 106, 127,
147, 252; Sense-Certainty 42, 43, 76,
78, 80, 92, 93, 276, 291; social ideals
of unity 284–285; spontaneity 42–44;

Unhappy Consciousness 95–96, 265,
284
Heidegger, Martin 83–84, 246, 249
Heisenberg's uncertainty principle
100–101
Hendel, Charles 177, 199
Heraclitus 76, 92, 252
Hesse, Hermann 304–305
Hobbes, Thomas: "decaying sensations"
197, 237–238, 242; *De Corpore* 101,
198; *De Homine* 238, 254; egoism
46, 102, 258, 272; extensity 198;
freedom 103; *Leviathan* 46, 198, 258,
272; materialism 11, 101, 131, 153;
"mortalist heresy" 156; psychological
outlook 266–267; self-interest 254
Homer 26, 259
Hume, David: dualism 179, 249; feeling
171, 172, 254; influences 195–196,
199, 200; intimacy 191–192; loneliness
283; personal identity 178, 179,
180–191; science and ethics 173;
and Shaftesbury 171, 176, 177, 178;
skepticism 266; space and time 78,
195–205; *Treatise of Human Nature*
21, 78, 151, 172–173, 177, 178, 179,
180–182, 183–184, 185–186, 188, 189,
191, 195, 197, 199, 200, 202, 203–204,
205, 219, 239, 249, 254, 283
Husserl, Edmund: on Brentano 230;
Cartesian Meditations 117, 231, 246,
319–320; criticism of "psychologism"
68, 112; eidetic intuition 224, 225, 243,
319–320; empathy 319–320;
intentionality 225, 229, 231,
243, 244–245, 246; *Logical
Investigations* 246; phenomenological
methodology 68, 246; spontaneity
49–50; time-consciousness 227, 230;
transcendental ego 245–246
Hutcheson, Frances 171, 196

idealism 43, 66, 75, 80, 86, 178–179, 203,
230; conflict with materialism 174, 184,
194, 211–212, 248, 251–252; epistemic
92–93; objective 14, 36, 38, 81;
skeptical 194–195; speculative 77, 79;
subjective 13, 14, 34, 36, 38, 129, 146,
164–165, 173–174, 218, 231, 288–289
immortality of the soul 10, 18, 32, 61,
137–141, 153, 156–157, 184, 216,
232–233, 234

infancy 80, 94, 254, 256, 267–268, 270–271, 276–277, 288, 298

intentionality 118, 119, 241, 248, 307; Brentano 222, 223–229, 233–234, 243, 244, 246; Husserl 225, 229, 231, 243, 244–245, 246; moral 103; Sartre 246, 247; transcendent 1, 164–165, 187, 225, 227, 233–234, 257

intimacy: and empathy 19, 320; motivation towards 254, 256; as opposite of loneliness 257; as solution to solipsism 318–319, 320–321

introversion 254, 255

James, William 80, 214, 249, 250, 276

Japan 302

Jowett, Benjamin 26

Joyce, James 269

Jung, Carl 254, 255, 312–313, 314–315

Justinian 123

Kant, Immanuel: *Aesthetic* 39, 63–64, 65, 67, 77–78, 230; categorical imperative 320, 321; coherence theory 24; *Critique* 9, 11, 13–14, 17–18, 38–39, 41, 47, 61, 64, 68–70, 127, 197, 211–219, 226, 230, 250; ethical principle 173; freedom 103–104; principle of the Unconditioned 9, 126; Quantity and Quality 41–42, 75, 77–79, 127; reflexive self-consciousness 225, 227; on the simplicity premise 10–14, 15–16, 17–18; space and time 195, 197; spontaneity 38–40, 61–62, 71, 163–164, 217, 218, 226; subconscious 47, 48; synthetic *a priori* 38, 39, 40, 49–50, 53, 76, 104, 173, 216, 219, 225, 226, 257; time-consciousness 9; transcendental method 67, 68–70

Keeling, S. V. 132, 133, 134, 198

Kemp-Smith, Norman 69–70, 132, 177, 189–190, 212, 214, 216, 218

Kierkegaard, Søren 83, 114, 269, 276, 281, 309; existential values 320

Kowalkowski, Leszek 277–278

Laird, John 177, 199

language 25, 89, 115–116, 158, 256

Latta, Robert 34

Lawrence, D. H. 54–55, 278

Leibniz, Gottfried Wilhelm: and Aristotle 27, 35; Being 249; and Cambridge Platonists 155; debate with Clarke 199, 200–201; influence of 82; and Locke 165; Monads 12, 13, 14, 17, 34, 35, 37–38, 165–167; optimism 46; paradigm of the self 289; self-consciousness 164–167; simplicity premise 10, 11; space and time 201, 202, 204–205; spontaneity 34–35, 37–38, 291; subjective idealism 131, 202, 205; theistic theory 146–147

Leucippus 6, 9, 100, 102, 237

Lipps, Theodor 319

Locke, John: dualism 179; *Essay Concerning Human Understanding* 21, 152, 153, 157, 160, 161, 162, 165, 198, 238; extensity 198; on mind without thought 34; personal identity 152, 154, 155, 157–159; phenomenalism 195; reflection 152, 161–164; soul 153–154, 156; thinking matter 160–161

Loewenberg, Jacob 265

loneliness: in Christianity 264–265; in empiricism 283–284; in existentialism 267, 281–282; fear of 254, 255; as a feeling 255–256; global concern 279, 302; Hegel 95–96; intensity of 257, 274, 317; and intentionality 245; in literature 279–281, 301–312; and narcissism 19, 269–270, 271, 288–298, 317; and psychology 266–277; and psychosis 274, 307, 308, 317–318; relation to consciousness 120, 245, 257; requiring a substantial self 53; and sense of separation 258–259, 285, 317–318; and sexuality 26; and skepticism 265–266; and social ideals of unity 284, 285; in sociology 277–279; and violence 271, 272; in Western culture 259–264

Lonely Crowd, The 277

Lovejoy, A. J. 63–64, 74, 255

Lucretius 100, 237

Malebranche, Nicolas 17, 146

Marcel, Gabriel 273

Marx, Karl 83, 254, 266, 276, 284, 285, 310

Marxism 277–278

Masham, Damaris 154–155

Mendelssohn, Moses 17, 18

326 Index

Mersenne, Marin 137–138, 139, 144
metaphysical dualism 1, 21, 38; Aristotle
9, 36; Brentano 233; Descartes 54;
Hegel 92; Hume 179, 185–186, 249;
Locke 157; Plato 6; Shaftesbury
174–175
Mill, John Stuart 103
Mills, Jon 290, 291
Milton, John 153
Montaigne, Michel Eyquem de 124–125,
127, 181, 265–266, 279
Moore, G. E. 255
"mortalist heresy" 153, 156

narcissism: Freud 46, 71, 258, 292,
293–294, 295, 310; and intimacy 257;
and loneliness 19, 269–270, 271,
288–298, 317; and violence 271, 272;
see also egoism
nationalism 266, 274–275
Nazism 271–272
neuroscience: and determinism 102;
and personal identity 130, 188–189;
reductionism 6, 9, 49, 68, 131, 132,
248–249; rejection of Quality 75, 95,
240–241; space and time 102, 194,
205–206
Newton, Isaac 77, 102, 187, 195, 196,
200–201
Nietzsche, Friedrich 27, 45, 83, 260, 269,
282

Oedipus 96, 259, 260, 312
Overton, Richard 153, 156

Parmenides 85, 87, 88, 92, 252
Pascal, Blaise 250, 281–282
Paton, H. J. 63
personal identity 130, 151–167, 171–191,
220, 239, 241–242, 264, 265, 279, 301,
303–307, 315
phenomenalism 60, 151, 179–180,
194–196, 199, 223–224, 234, 241, 244,
294
phenomenology 49–50, 54, 68, 81, 127,
223, 224, 229, 244, 245–246, 305;
see also Brentano, Franz; Hegel,
G. W. F.; Husserl, Edmund
Philo of Judaea 89–90
philosophical counseling 321
Plato: Battle between the Giants and
the Gods 2, 16, 76, 95, 127, 167,

179; coherence theory 9, 24, 25, 105;
Divided Line passage 6, 24, 28, 76,
125–126, 128, 251–252; Good 89,
92, 126; *Ion* 26–27, 30; Knowledge
8, 9, 23, 24; loneliness 261; *Meno* 23,
53, 161; metaphysical dualism 6–8;
Parmenides 126; *Phaedo* 6, 8, 153;
Phaedrus 262; polis 263; psychology
254–255; and qualitative thought 6, 8,
9; Quantity and Quality 75, 130–131;
relexive model 248; *Republic* 9, 24,
89, 126, 153, 254–255, 262; *Sophist*
7, 129, 146, 179, 248; soul 6, 7, 8–9,
153, 262; spontaneity 26; *Symposium*
261; synthetic *a priori* 23–24, 53;
Theaetetus 7, 129, 146, 248; *Timaeus*
132–133
Plotinus 8, 10, 248
Popkin, Richard 124
Poulet, Georges 31, 32
predestinarianism 10
predictions 26, 78, 86, 102, 120
Pseudo-Dionysus the Aeropagite 90
psychoanalysis: and blame 309; as
coherence theory 9, 25; determinism 1,
25, 26; hedonism 106; limitations 26,
120, 276; and loneliness 267–268,
269–271, 288–289; *see also* Freud;
narcissism
psychology: behavioral 1, 4, 102, 112,
114, 238, 241, 242, 248, 276; history of
254–255, 262–263; and loneliness
266–277
psychosis 274, 307, 308, 317–318
Pyrrho of Elis 264

Quality: Bergson 109–111, 116–117;
Hegel 42–43, 75, 77, 80–81, 82, 85–86,
87, 94–95, 126–127, 251–252; Kant
12, 18, 41–42, 75, 77–79, 127; and
Quantity 24, 42, 75, 77, 78–79, 80, 87,
94, 109–111, 116, 126–127, 178–179,
251–252; *see also* values
quantum physics 100–101, 106

rationalism 77, 82, 151, 158, 171, 172,
214, 216, 241; criticism of 178, 181,
183–184
reflexive self-consciousness 1, 103,
132, 187, 229, 233–234, 239, 257,
260; Aristotle 9, 35; Cudworth 155;
Descartes 31, 130, 142, 161, 163–164;

Index 327

Hegel 37, 105; and intentionality 26, 187, 192, 223, 225, 227–228, 229, 233–234, 236, 245, 247, 248; Kant 18, 38, 161, 163–164, 216, 225, 227, 228, 245; Leibniz 12, 34, 37–38, 164–165; Plato 7; Shaftesbury 175–176

Ricoeur, Paul 231

Rousseau, Jean-Jacques 103

Royce, Josiah 39

Russell, Bertrand 284

Sartre, Jean-Paul: communism 310; freedom 117–120; intentionality 243–244, 246, 247; spontaneity 52–53, 247–248; "transcendence of the ego" 225–226, 247; view of psychoanalysis 309

Satir, Virginia 268

Schopenhauer, Arthur: on artistic genius 27; Being 249; denial of the self 315; freedom 108–109; influence of Kant 71; irrational Will 44–48, 61, 62, 71–72, 217, 294–295, 314–315; spontaneity 291; subconscious 288–289, 312, 313

Second World War 29, 60, 269, 279, 288

self-knowledge 44, 46, 65, 68, 71, 164, 260, 303, 311; limits of 312–313, 314, 315

Selkirk, Alexander 302

sensations 124–125, 130, 142, 146, 161

Sextus Empiricus 123–124, 265

sexual drives 26, 71, 254, 262, 294

Shaftesbury, Third Earl of *see* Cooper, Anthony Ashley, Third Earl of Shaftesbury

Sheeks, Wayne 48

Shikibu, Murasaki 301–302

simplicity premise: consequences of 199–200, 201; criticism of 178; employment of 41, 45, 107, 109, 112, 117, 119, 140, 152; history of 6, 10–11; *see also* Achilles argument

skepticism 82, 123–125, 175, 180, 187–188, 263–264, 265–266

Smith, Adam 189

Socinus, Faustus 10, 153, 156

Socrates 7, 23, 91, 261

solipsism 130, 231, 245–246, 279, 318–321

Sophocles 27, 260, 261

soul: immortality of 10, 18, 32, 61, 137–141, 153, 156–157, 184, 216, 232–233, 234; Plato's conception of 6, 7, 8–9, 153, 262

Spinoza, Baruch 80, 109, 129, 237, 254; *conatus* 45; "negation is determination" 40, 53, 86, 118, 295; pantheism 88, 94; "Problem of Divine Attributes in God" 114, 115

Spitz, Rene 288

spontaneity 22, 24, 25–30, 251, 270, 304, 305, 308, 318; Bergson 50–51, 112–114, 116; Descartes 30–33, 130, 142, 143, 146, 163–164; Fichte 40–41, 289–291, 295–296; Hegel 41–44, 80, 82, 92; Husserl 49–50, 163–164, 230; Kant 38–40, 61–62, 71, 163–164, 217, 218, 226; Lawrence 54–55; Leibniz 34–38, 167; Sartre 52–54, 117–120, 247–248; Schopenhauer 44–48, 62, 71, 108–109; transcendental 38–39, 62, 68

Stillingfleet, Edward 160

Stoicism 39, 89, 90, 104, 263

subjective idealism *see* idealism

suicide 113–114, 271, 272, 278

Sullivan, Harry Stack 273

synthetic *a priori* relations 9, 25, 26, 37, 54, 269, 276; Hegel 92, 107; Husserl 49–50, 245, 257; Kant 38, 39, 40, 49–50, 53, 76, 104, 173, 216, 219, 225, 226, 257; Plato 23, 24, 40, 53; Sartre 118

Taylor, A. E. 132–133

teleology 33, 87, 88, 103, 222, 241, 251, 256

Tertullian 10, 29

time-consciousness 50, 110–111, 114, 151, 177–178, 179, 230, 281; Kant 38, 62, 78, 190, 211, 212, 218, 230

transcendental ego 52, 231, 245, 246

values 7, 8, 30, 76, 178–179; ethical 76, 95, 129, 173, 250; and human consciousness 4–5, 74, 87, 88, 119–120, 222, 249, 276; and loneliness 245, 255, 256, 257, 274–275, 276, 279, 282, 308, 309–310, 318, 319, 320; and science 4, 5, 76, 106, 131, 173, 192, 246, 248, 250; *see also* Quality

Vienna Circle 100–101

violence 258, 271, 272

Virtue 23, 24, 27, 172, 222, 263

328 Index

Weber, Max 76, 173, 246, 250, 277, 310
Weiss, George 269
Whitehead, Alfred North 67–68
Wither, George 153, 156
Wittgenstein, Ludwig 242

Witty, John 155
Wolfe, Thomas 280–281
Wolff, Robert Paul 212–215, 216

Zeno's paradox 101
Zilboorg, Gregory 269–271, 291

Printed in the United States
by Baker & Taylor Publisher Services